THE ROUGH GUIDE TO

First-Time Europe

written and researched by

Doug Lansky

with additional contributions by

Henrik Harr

roughguides.com

Contents

Introduction to
First-Time Europe

Italians don't serve "deep pan" pizza. Swedes aren't all blondes. And the French probably won't French-kiss you when you first greet. But none of these little cultural realities is reason enough to put off your trip to Europe – the "Old World" offers more architecture, wine, music, fashion, theater and gastronomy per square kilometer than any other continent. Which means heading off the main routes will still land you waist-deep in cultural treasures. The continent (including Russia) boasts over seven hundred million people, in excess of 450 World Heritage Sites and more renowned paintings than you can point your camera at. And it's usually just a matter of a short bus or train ride to get from one place to the next – though even a bicycle will often suffice.

Europe stretches 3900km from the Greek island of Crete to Hammerfest, on the northeastern coast of Norway, and just as far from Lisbon to Moscow. But with the reunification of East and West at the end of the 1980s leading to widespread improvements in roads and rail, Europe became more accessible than ever. Despite the ongoing debt crisis, the existence of the eurozone has made spending easier across much of the continent, and means you're no longer giving away fistfuls of coins that the other countries won't accept when you try to change money. What you put this saving towards is quite limitless: climbing a Swiss Alp, tasting wine at a French château, renting a surfboard in Portugal, having tea and scones in England, chilling out in Sweden's *Ice Hotel* or sipping a local Karlovačko beer while soaking your toes in the Adriatic off the Croatian coast. For more clever budgeting tricks and strategies to help cut costs along the way, see "Costs and savings" (p.60).

Europe's riches are waiting; the decision to find them is yours. In other words, this book is not going to try to persuade you to travel, nor try to convince you that stomping around with a backpack will fulfill whatever may be missing from your life. Travel is an

RIGHT GUČA TRUMPET FESTIVAL, SERBIA

urge best cultivated from within. In fact, one of the biggest favors you can do for yourself is to travel when you want to, not when someone else thinks you should. The more eager you are to open yourself up to life on the road, the more willing you'll be to shrug off the prepacked experience and reap real rewards. In some ways it feels like there's never a good time to go – it can feel hard to disconnect from everyday life. On the other hand, there are some key junctures – before studying, after studying, before you have kids, after your kids have moved out – that lend themselves to extended travel.

Of course, that first trip overseas can be intimidating, and few people ever feel completely ready. You'll invariably make some mistakes along the way – we all have – but with this book you'll be able to sidestep the major pitfalls. The **big adventure** section will walk you through some of the more baffling bits of the planning process that tend to trip up many travelers, show you how to enrich parts of your travels that commonly get glossed over, and help you to make sure you have your gear and documents in order before leaving, as well as give you pointers on how to bring the entire overseas experience together well within your budget. You might start by opening the map (see pp.6–7) and letting your eyes wander over the possibilities. Then flip to Chapter 1 and learn how to start customizing your journey.

The country profiles in the **Where to go** section provide a glimpse into each country to assist with your preparation, highlighting landmarks and festivals, providing weather info and letting you know if there are any bus or train passes you should consider buying before your arrival. Of course, you'll want more specific information eventually, either from websites and apps listed in the **Directory** section at the end of the book or from your guidebook once you arrive, but at this point such facts and figures would bog down the planning process rather than help it along. Besides, there is such a thing as too much planning. One of the greatest thrills of travel is making your trip up as you go.

FACT FILE

- **Biggest countries**: Russia (17,075,200 sq km, over two-thirds of which lies in Asia), Ukraine (603,700 sq km), France (547,030 sq km), Spain (504,782 sq km) and Sweden (449,964 sq km)

- **Smallest countries**: Vatican City (0.44 sq km), Monaco (1.95 sq km), San Marino (61.2 sq km)

- **Highest point**: Mt Elbrus, Russia (5642m)

- **Lowest point**: Lemmefjord, Denmark, and Prins Alexander Polder, the Netherlands (both 7m below sea level)

- **Highest temperature**: Seville, Spain (50°C)

- **Lowest temperature**: Ust'Shchugor, Russia (-58.1°C)

- **Most sunshine**: Rhodes, Greece (3480hr per year)

- **Most rainfall**: Crkvica, Montenegro (4650mm per year)

- **Biggest economy**: Germany (GDP €3.5 trillion)

- **Highest per capita GDP**: Luxembourg (€82,075)

- **Highest life expectancy**: Andorra (83 years)

- **Biggest beer consumers**: Czech Republic (average 148.6 liters per year)

- **Biggest coffee consumers**: Finland (12kg per year – more than four cups per day)

- **Most paid vacation time**: Sweden (25 days a year, plus national holidays)

- **Most internet users**: Iceland (96.5 percent)

FAQ

Q: I've just got a month. Is that too short?

Well, it's too short to travel around all of Europe, but fine for hitting about 7–11 cities. You just need to figure out a manageable amount to conquer on your trip (see p.18).

Q: I've got $3000 saved up. Will that get me to Europe and around it for a month?

If you figure a tight budget of $50 per day, that's $1500, a rail pass will cost $400–$800 and a plane ticket from North America about $1000. You'll need some gear and an emergency stash in case things go wrong, so you might say three weeks to be safe. To figure out a daily budget that fits your comfort level, see "Costs and savings" (p.60).

Q: How do I use my smartphone while traveling without it costing me a small fortune?

You're going to have to make some adjustments to your mobile usage (see p.147). Exactly what depends on how long you're staying in one spot and what you're willing to spend for the convenience of constant connectivity. If you're spending a couple of weeks or more in one place, it can be worth your while to pick up a local SIM card. Otherwise, you'll probably want to shut off data roaming until you find a wi-fi hotspot.

Q: How do you know where to sleep each night, what to see during the day and how to get around?

Carry a guidebook – or a digital version of one. It will cover all the sights in each town, with a short review of the best affordable accommodation, often accompanied by a helpful map (although getting a bit lost now and then is a healthy way to travel). In peak season, you may want to book accommodation a day or two ahead of time, easily done on the internet, since just about every remote hostel can be booked online these days. If you want to think even less, just wander into the tourist office, often conveniently located in train and bus stations or in the center of town, tell them your budget, and they'll call around and make a booking for you, draw it on a free map, and tell you how to get there.

CLOCKWISE FROM TOP LEFT PRAIA DE VALE DE FIGUEIRA, PORTUGAL; RACLETTE, SWITZERLAND; ALHAMBRA, GRANADA, SPAIN

WHAT'S THE EUROPEAN UNION?

It's not a federal government, like the United States. Nor a continent. They like to call it "a family of democratic European countries, committed to working together for peace and prosperity." It started with a proposal by French foreign minister Robert Schuman in 1950 and originally consisted of six countries: Belgium, Germany, France, Italy, Luxembourg and the Netherlands. There are now 28 EU member states; Switzerland, Iceland and Norway are the most notable countries that opted not to join (but they, along with Liechtenstein, are members of the European Free Trade Association, which keeps them from economic seclusion). Not all EU members decided to adopt the **euro** – Sweden, Denmark, the United Kingdom and several Eastern European countries, still use their own currencies, while unofficial state members like Andorra, Monaco, San Marino and the Vatican City have taken on the euro. All in all, 338 million Europeans in nineteen of the European Union's 28 member states use the euro. The European Parliament, with 751 members, works from Brussels, Belgium, and Strasbourg, France. The Central Bank is run out of Frankfurt, Germany. And the Court of Justice is based in Luxembourg.

Little-known fact: even though Denmark is part of the EU, Greenland – which is part of the Kingdom of Denmark – isn't. The island became a reluctant member when Denmark joined in 1973, but left in 1985 after gaining home rule in 1979. It is the only region to ever leave the European Union without leaving its mother state.

Q: I can mispronounce about five words of French and fewer than that in Spanish. Can I manage traveling around Europe speaking English?

Better than your digestive tract will manage only eating at *McDonald's*. Learning the local language would enrich your experience and make it easier to understand your new environment, but even the least gifted linguist can pick up "please," "thank you," "excuse me," "how much?" and "no, that's my backpack you're smelling" in twenty minutes – about the time it takes to make the final descent before you touch down in the new country. If you must use English, lose the slang, keep your speech slow and basic; and don't take a puzzled look as a sign to speak louder. Besides, most Europeans speak English.

Q: Are there some basic precautions that can help me travel safer?

Quite a few. You can learn how to make yourself less of a target for pickpockets and muggers (see p.154), and learn how to avoid unsafe neighborhoods in each city (see p.155).

Q: I'm thinking of going with my best friend. Is that a good idea?

It's a tough decision. And if it doesn't seem like one, that's probably because you haven't fully considered what you're getting into. Learn what the potential pitfalls are and how to minimize them (see p.55).

Q: Will my credit cards work in Europe?

Yes, but they'll work far better if you take three basic steps: 1) alert your credit card provider roughly where you'll be and for how long so they don't block your card as a safety precaution; 2) make sure to learn your PIN code for the embedded chip; 3) select a credit card that doesn't charge you a conversion fee every time you use it (see p.120 for a selection of these cards) and combine it with a bank card that doesn't charge extra fees at ATMs (see p.121). These few actions will save you a huge headache and possibly a few hundred dollars as well.

Q: C'mon, do I really need travel insurance?

Only if you get really sick. Or injured. Or sued for some driving accident. In short, yes. But unless you get insurance that fits your travel plans, it won't do much good (see p.99).

RIGHT UMEÅ REGION, SWEDEN

Which means you shouldn't necessarily sign up for that convenient policy your travel agent pushes across the desk or the convenient "click here for insurance" button when you buy your ticket online. If you plan to ski in the Alps but your policy doesn't cover you for skiing (and you get injured), it's a policy payment down the drain and you've still got an enormous bill to cover. Oddly, insurance companies rarely cover the exact same things, so you have to read through the small print to find out.

Q: I want to make my journey alone, but I'm worried about several things… about feeling alone, about foreign diseases, about getting injured, about getting everything stolen.

There are hundreds of thousands of travelers out there right now making solo journeys and most of them had just as many concerns as you do. Loneliness can be a problem, particularly at the beginning of a trip and during some meals, but you'll find your stride and start meeting other travelers before long. For tips on coping with this, see our advice on "culture shock" (p.142). For advice on how to handle injuries, diseases and other survival issues, it's not a bad idea to pack a little emergency kit.

Q: I hear a lot about "attractions," "must-sees" and "wonders." Is it tourist-bureau hype or is there something to it?

A bit of both. When the hype lasts long enough, it seems to become legend, or even fact. Truth is there's no such thing as a "must-see" and you'll have a far more enriching trip if you personalize your journey (see p.31) and don't construct it around the major attractions.

Q: Is there one thing I'm likely going to forget?

Earplugs. Hostels and cheap hotels are often located next to busy streets and nightclubs. Some buses and trains have minimal ventilation and you'll need to keep the windows open, which lets in plenty of air but more decibels than you'd care for. And don't forget about the snoring roommate – there's typically one assigned to every dormitory room. There are a few more things you'll want to bring (see p.106).

16

ideas to enrich your journey

There are many lists telling you what to see before you die, but that's not a very immersive way to travel. Thinking in terms of "doing" rather than "seeing" will enhance that most vital and often elusive dimension to your travels: depth.

1 PARTICIPATE IN A FESTIVAL

Why just watch when you can get involved?

Oktoberfest, Munich, Germany

2 VIEW ATTRACTIONS EARLY, BEFORE THE CROWDS ARRIVE

Then catch up on your sleep with an afternoon siesta.

St Peter's Basilica, Rome, Italy

3 LEARN HOW TO MAKE A LOCAL DISH

This is one of the best "souvenirs" you can bring home.

Making pasta, Italy

4 TASTE SOME WINE AT A CHÂTEAU

It's hard to beat free samples.

Château de Monbazillac, France

5 RENT A BIKE AND EXPLORE

The best and quickest way to lose yourself in a new city.

Amsterdam, The Netherlands

7

8

9

6 TRY THE LOCAL FIREWATER

Think of it as travel experiences for your liver.
Riga, Latvia

7 WANDER THE BACKSTREETS

Get off the streets with English (tourist) menus.
Kotor Old Town, Montenegro

8 DISCOVER A PLACE THAT'S NOT IN THE GUIDEBOOK

The most unique and authentic experiences aren't found in guides.
Winterton-on-Sea, England

9 TRY THE STREET FOOD WHEREVER YOU GO

Don't forget to push your culinary boundaries – this is part of the adventure.
Jemaa el Fna, Marrakesh, Morocco

10 LET A EUROPEAN TRAVELER YOU'VE MET ALONG THE WAY SHOW YOU THEIR HOMETOWN

A great reason to stay in touch.
Gothenburg, Sweden

11 TRY A FAMILY STAY

Get an insider's glimpse into local living.
Loire Valley, France

12 TRAVEL BY FERRY

Remember, cruise-ship passengers pay big money for these views.
Cyclades, Greece

13 CHECK OUT A SPORTING EVENT

Watching on TV doesn't count – as long as you're there, see it live.
The Highland Games, Scotland

14 CLIMB A MOUNTAIN

Europe has numerous accessible and outstanding peaks to choose from.
Gesäuse National Park, Austria

15 VOLUNTEER TO DO SOMETHING YOU'RE PASSIONATE ABOUT

Travel doesn't have to be just about getting experiences; it can also be about giving.
Conservation work, Fuente de Piedra Lagoon, Spain

16 HUNT FOR BARGAINS AT THE LOCAL MARKET

Arrive early and learn the "real" price before you start bargaining.
Soviet army belts, Izmaylovo Market, Moscow, Russia

First-Time Europe

The big adventure

1

Planning your big trip

Deciding where to go, how to get there, what to do and how long to stay is a lot easier than it sounds. In this chapter, the planning process is chopped into smaller, easier-to-chew pieces that will get you under way, from figuring out what activities are available in each place to avoiding troublesome weather and catching the festivals you don't want to miss.

How much time do you need?

Here's a better question: how much time can you spare? You could easily spend a lifetime hopping around Europe and not experience all it has to offer. So, carve out whatever time you can and worry later about what you'll do with it. Besides, it's easier to come home early than try to push back deadlines once you're on the move.

The truth is, you won't know how long you'll want to go for until you get out there. You might meet someone who will invite you along on a camping trip, or you may stumble across a great course that lasts two months, or suddenly have a burning desire to sketch Italy's most famous frescoes. The trick at this point is to structure your trip so that those unforeseen experiences can happen. So, how do you do this?

If you already know how long you've got, you should be thinking about the pace of your trip. How many countries, cities and activities should you try to tackle in that amount of time? A good guideline is this: don't plan more than four multi-day activities per month in advance. (Sorry, visiting Spain doesn't count as a single activity; but things like a two-day cooking class, a short stay

In this guide, you'll find prices listed in euros (€) in nearly all cases. At the time of research, the **exchange rates** were approximately €1: $1.10 and £0.71 ($1: €0.90; £1: €1.40).

1

I DON'T HAVE MUCH MONEY – SHOULD I TRAVEL CHEAP OR WAIT UNTIL I'VE GOT THE FUNDS TO DO IT IN STYLE?

Independent budget travel in Europe isn't for everyone. Especially if you're not thrilled about eating most of your meals picnic-style on park benches or in youth hostel kitchens, or spending the night in a place that considers the urine stain on the mattress all the decoration the room needs. If this doesn't seem like it would faze you, you're in luck; the **cultural and social payoff** of budget travel is enormous, the experience invaluable. As nice as it may sound to travel in comfort, a thick wallet has a tendency to insulate you from the very culture you're trying to experience. That is, you don't want the only locals you meet to be the ones checking you into the hotel and serving you drinks. A tight budget will encourage you to seek out places you perhaps would normally overlook.

If you're not ready to travel on the cheap, you'll still find plenty of essential information and itinerary ideas from the ensuing pages, but you may have to limit your time on the road, or knock off a bank. Three months of air-conditioned tours, meals served on real tablecloths, comfortable hotel rooms and a plane ticket could set you back €30,000, whereas it can be done for €7000 or even less with a few tips (see p.61).

with a relative, a few days exploring a major city or a hiking trip do.) Fewer than four is even better. If you plan to see, say, Paris and Rome in June, that doesn't necessarily mean you're only going to see these two cities. It means you get to make up the rest of your plans on the move as you travel between the two. This approach allows for ample **flexibility**, plus any transport delays you may encounter (when it comes to transportation strikes, the French and Italians are in a league of their own).

If the length of your trip is largely dictated by budget, check out the "Costs and savings" chapter (see p.60) to help calculate your time on the road and maximize the funds you have. However, you don't need to let your initial funds shorten your trip. "Working, volunteering and studying" (see p.76) covers jobs and volunteer projects, so you can leave home with minimal money or stretch your trip for years.

Any amount of time is better than none, but less than a month doesn't give you much of a chance to get into the rhythm of travel. You may get accused by "hardcore" travelers of not getting a real taste of the road on a short trip, but don't be put off by their comments; if you concentrate your trip in one area and take a course in something or stay with locals, you'll get a more culturally enriching experience than those with a year of travel grime under their belts who merely look the part.

A year off has a nice ring to it, but that's not a realistic time frame for those with jobs to return to or student loans that need paying off. Two to six months is a reasonable target. It will give you a chance to do some exploring and even allow you to dig a little deeper with one or more cultures. The best option is to have a flexible ticket so you can return when you're ready.

WHY YOU NEED A PIT STOP AND WHEN YOU SHOULD TAKE IT

Travel can be **romantic** and **adventurous**, but finding your way around a city, coordinating train schedules, locating a place to stay, taking the stairs up every tall structure for a scenic overview, using perplexing toilets, sampling palate-numbing foods and testing each country's unique beers – the things that give independent travel its bite – combine to form an exhausting experience. Give yourself a **chance to relax**.

To some extent, taking a break is going to happen on its own. You might stumble upon a place you can't resist, get stuck waiting for a ferry that's not running due to inclement weather, find a fun person or group of travelers to hang out with or just hit the sensory-overload wall.

The last one will occur if the first four don't. This exhaustion – think of it as cultural burnout – typically occurs after two to four months of continuous, fairly fast-paced travel. There's one main symptom: you spend increasingly more time in cafés and hostel lounges and less time out exploring towns and museums. There's also one simple remedy for recharging your wanderlust: stay put. Give yourself a chance to absorb and process what you've seen. Write some long letters. Get to know a few locals. Volunteer. Earn some money. Fall in love. Whatever.

Give yourself the **flexibility** to stop when you need it, or plan ahead so you end up at your dream hangout, or take an interesting course. A decent formula is two weeks of "down time" for every three months on the road.

How much time do you need in each place?

Two days. That is, two days longer than you think. Maybe even two weeks. The faster you go and the more ground you cover, tempting though it may be, the less you'll see. According to the author Wendell Berry, "Our senses… were developed to function at foot speeds." The same way that slowing down improves your peripheral vision when driving, **reducing your speed** enables you to take more in while you travel. Or take the advice of travel author Peter Moore: "If you're having a good time – stay. If you've met someone you fancy and who fancies you – stay. If you're too buggered to move – stay. If the police are closing in on you – go." If you're not pressed to press on, you might forge a friendship with the traveler you met over breakfast or find out that your favorite musician is giving a concert in an ancient amphitheater nearby, or that the local cultural center is offering free palm-tree-climbing lessons. With enough time and curiosity, something interesting is bound to happen.

Where should you go? (Not where you might think)

Since no traveler can do it all, the tendency is to head for the "best" places. What are the best places? It feels like a natural question, but you're better off refraining from asking it as you gather information about your upcoming trip, because it isn't going to reveal much useful information. Ninety percent of your travel experience will be made up of the people you meet, the weather, spontaneous adventures and little cultural discoveries you make along the way. It goes the other way as well: a bad experience is colored with random mishaps ranging from bus breakdowns to bedbugs to boring travel companions.

Here's the good news: you can't miss. **There's no wrong place to go.** It's what you decide to do there that makes the real difference. Want to spend two weeks in France? Two weeks at a farmstay learning French, two weeks visiting the tourist attractions in Paris, and two weeks at an intensive cooking school are so different they can hardly be summed up as "spending a fortnight in France." Even on that same farm, at those same attractions and at that same cooking school, you'd have a hard time replicating the experience of someone else who did those things. There are simply too many variables. Forget about trying to find the "Top 10" this and the "best-of" that – you *can* find a magical experience, but if you don't push yourself off the tourist trail and do something that moves you, there will be very little "top" or "best" or "magical" of anything, unless you count "best staged photo in front of famous sculpture". And remember: what may seem awful at the time might, in retrospect, prove to be the most life-changing event of your journey.

To find the best places, the only person to consult is yourself. Grab a pencil, take a look at the five points below, and start jotting down places, sights and activities that sound appealing. You can figure out how to connect them later.

Go where you speak the language

No, not English. A second language (although an English-speaking country is a fine place to begin your travels). Even if you can just read a menu and a few street signs, you're off to a good start. Europe is a great place for the lingual novice; you can almost always find an English speaker when you need one. However, tapping into these ubiquitous translators should be your safety net, not your crutch. The idea is that once you start using a language, once you start looking around and trying to communicate where you need to go, the learning curve becomes nearly vertical and you're taking a big step into the culture you've come to experience.

WHAT IS ADVENTURE TRAVEL?

These days, with 70-year-olds waiting for hip replacements signing up for "adventure tours", it's hard to know exactly what the term means. An **adventure** used to involve exploring uncharted waters and lands with hidden dangers.

"**Adventure travel**" is typically applied to whitewater rafting, bungee jumping, trekking and getting spun about in jet boats, especially when these activities take place in foreign countries – that is, foreign from our own. The fact remains that they're completely packaged activities with a predictable outcome, rendering them closer to a fairground ride than what any explorer would dub an adventure. Does that mean you should avoid them? No. A little adrenaline is healthy and good fun. Does that mean there are no "real" adventures left? No. Just make sure you understand which kind you're signing up for. Come to think of it, if you need to sign up for an adventure, that's a pretty good indication of what kind it is.

1 Go where you have family or friends

Don't be afraid to look up that childhood pen pal in Estonia or your third cousin once removed in Portugal. To cover your bets, bring along some kind of document or a snapshot to help bridge any gaps. Despite any present-day politics, you'll find Europeans have a special place in their hearts for relatives and old friends who have been separated by oceans for years. With a little luck, you'll find you've got yourself a cultural guide. You'll almost certainly get a free place to stay and, if nothing else, an inside look at the way they live, from food and interior decor to bowling or strip clubs – whatever, in fact, your relatives happen to do for fun.

If you're still at university, take the opportunity to get involved with international groups. Students visiting your university from other countries for a year (or several years) are typically members of an international club, and tend to want to make friends with locals. Hanging out with club members is a nice way to start traveling while still at home and, better yet, you'll have some new friends to visit (and maybe free places to stay) during your trip.

Go somewhere you've longed to see

A little wanderlust goes a long way. If there's some place you've read about, heard people talk about for ages, or had some sort of childhood fascination with, then that's not a bad reason to go – at the very worst, it's a decent starting point. Let James Joyce's *Ulysses* be your tour guide through Dublin, or jump-start your wandering in Salzburg with sites from *The Sound of Music*. If it seems too trivial, keep in mind that many of the travelers who end up in Transylvania are there just because they like the sound of it.

Attractions of the world

When you start traveling, you hear a lot about "attractions" and "must-sees" and "wonders." Is it tourist-bureau hype or is there something to it? In reality, it's a bit of both. When the hype is old enough, it seems to become legend, or even fact. The classic is the "**Wonders of the World**", first referenced in the *History of Herodotus* in the fifth century BC. It proved to be such a public relations success that historians, writers and architects have been trying to create updated versions ever since. Not surprisingly, they can't quite reach consensus. Some assert, for instance, that the ancient list was flawed because the Greeks were unaware of such marvels as the Great Wall of China, and have filled in the gaps with a list of "Forgotten" Wonders. Today, numerous lists of geological anomalies and man-made structures have also emerged, each with its own merits. With so many attractions touting their particular wonder, this round-up may provide some perspective to the PR you're bound to encounter.

For the record, Europe had two of the original Seven Wonders of the Ancient World: the Statue of Zeus in Olympia and the Colossus of Rhodes, both in Greece. Unfortunately, they've both been destroyed. None of the twelve so-called "Natural" Wonders is located in Europe, and only five of the nineteen so-called "Forgotten" Wonders and just three "Modern" Wonders (see opposite). What's

ARE YOU A TOURIST OR A TRAVELER?

Why on earth should you go out of your way to try some sport or activity you've never heard of and will probably never do again? Why bother with any slower, less comfortable mode of transport? Why go anywhere near a squat toilet or, for that matter, a Parisian roundabout in a rented car? Because, if you're not doing something new, you're doing something you've done before. If you're not using the **local language** (or hand gestures and phrase books), you're often speaking with professional guides and concierges. If you're not eating **local food**, you're probably eating food you know from home. The creature comforts of Europe are likely to be similar to the ones where you come from, but finding the differences and trying them is up to you. If you don't, you'll be getting a Disneyfied view of the place you're trying to see. It's often the "strange" food and more uncomfortable elements that give travel its extra dimension, and separate the Eiffel Tower in Paris from the one at the Epcot Center, the gondola ride in Venice from the one in Las Vegas – and the tourists from the travelers.

left? Plenty – **Europe has 384 of UNESCO's 1007 World Heritage Sites**, more than any other two continents combined. These are the world's architectural and archeological treasures, as defined by this special United Nations body. There's a wide range of sites. Many, like the Cathedral of Notre-Dame in Paris or the archeological areas of Pompeii, you're familiar with. Others, like France's fortified city of Carcassonne or Italy's Botanical Garden in Padua, you may have never heard of. Are they less impressive than the more famous sights? Perhaps, but there are almost certainly fewer crowds. To find out where they are and their historical significance, visit ⓦwhc.unesco.org.

"Forgotten" Wonders

- The Colosseum, Rome, Italy
- The Leaning Tower of Pisa, Italy
- Mont-Saint-Michel, Normandy, France
- The Parthenon, Athens, Greece
- Stonehenge, Wiltshire, England

"Modern" Wonders

- The Eiffel Tower, Paris, France
- The Channel Tunnel, under the English Channel
- Big Ben (Elizabeth Tower), London, England

Follow your interests

This is perhaps the best tool to use to start picking your destinations. The concept is simple enough: instead of thinking about what you'd like to see, think about what you'd like to do. Approach the trip as a chance to collect **unique experiences**, not passport stamps, mementos and selfies in front of famous monuments. If you're a golfer, you might pursue the sport to its roots with a round at the Old Course in St Andrews in Scotland. Or try a twist, and stop for a game of ice golf in Finland, where you can play with a bright-orange

1

WANT TO TRY SOMETHING NEW?

Can't think of **something active** to do while traveling? Here are a few ideas. To find out where, simply enter the activity and the place you're heading into your favorite search engine.

Alpine skiing · Beer tasting · Bike touring · Birdwatching · Bungee jumping · Canal barging · Canoeing · Canyoning · Caving · Cross-country skiing · Deep-sea fishing · Fly-fishing · Golfing · Horseback riding · Ice diving · In-line skating · Kayaking · Kiteboarding · Learning meditation · Long-distance ice-skating · Mountaineering · Off-road driving · Painting · Paragliding · Rock climbing · Roller-coaster riding · Sampling haute cuisine · Scotch tasting · Scuba diving · Snowboarding · Studying martial arts · Studying photography · Surfing · Trekking · Visiting castles/palaces · Whitewater rafting · Windsurfing · Wine tasting · Yachting

---

ball, tee up on an ice cube, hack out of the fairway and putt on icy "whites." If you like to cook, you might take a crepe-making course in Brittany or try a day of pasta preparation at a villa in Tuscany. The more original your approach, the more unique your experience is likely to be.

Go somewhere you know nothing about

Consider Croatia. Maybe Latvia? How about Albania? Head off the beaten path and chances are that's where you'll find the highlights of your journey.

When to go

On a long trip, you can't be everywhere at just the ideal time. Don't knock yourself out trying. Usually, if it's too hot inland, you can head for the coast. And if it's too hot on the coast you can move to higher elevations, where temperatures are milder. Sweating it out in Rome? It's only 25km from the beaches of Fregene and Ostia in the coastal town of Fiumicino. Or take an overnight train into the Alps and hike around Lugano. It's pretty impossible to avoid a day or two of rain, but finding good weather typically requires just two things: keeping your eye on the **weather reports**, and a **flexible schedule**. What you need to investigate, therefore, is not the ideal time to be in each location, but if there are any dates you should absolutely avoid (see p.26).

Much of this depends on what you plan to do. Southern Italy in January may be chilly but it's fine for city exploring, especially if you plan to be inside museums and churches, whereas the weather in Chamonix in January may render mountain biking impossible. If you plan to hitch sections of your journey on boats, make sure you check out the seasonal schedule. Similarly, you'll want to know if there are any **dates not to miss**. If you're applying for a seasonal job, there's usually a tight window. And it's a pity unwittingly to arrive in Venice a day after Carnevale has ended; you're stuck with the crowds but have missed the event. See the individual country profiles in the "Where to go" section for more information on local weather and events.

Travel seasons

Traveling in the peak season is climatically favorable, but the advantages of touring Europe **out of season** are numerous: low-cost (sometimes over fifty percent less) and less-crowded flights, better chances of finding a room at the cheapest hostels, shorter lines at museums, less need for reservations and – best of all – fewer visitors to distract you from the culture you came to observe. However, you may be looking at a few hidden expenses. Some of the cheapest hotels shut down in the off-season, so you may be forced into more expensive digs. If it's cold enough to rattle your teeth loose at night, expect to pay extra for a room with heat. If you've arrived in the hot and sweaty season, be

---

MUSEUM HEAVYWEIGHTS

British Museum
Where: London, England
What: artifacts, architecture and other items uprooted (read: looted) by the British Empire
Most famous pieces: its mummy collection and the Rosetta Stone
ⓦ britishmuseum.org

Deutsches Museum
Where: Munich, Germany
What: natural sciences, technology and industry
Most famous piece: its aeroplane collection
ⓦ deutsches-museum.de

Hermitage Museum
Where: St Petersburg, Russia
What: classics, sculptures and artifacts
Most famous piece: possibly Cézanne's *Girl at the Piano*
ⓦ hermitagemuseum.org

Kremlin and Armoury
Where: Moscow, Russia
What: royal carriages, guns and tsars' clothing
Most famous pieces: Fabergé eggs, Orlov Diamond, Tsar Cannon and Bell
ⓦ kreml.ru/en

Kunsthistorisches Museum
Where: Vienna, Austria
What: classics
Most famous pieces: its Goya, Titian and Giorgione collections
ⓦ khm.at

Louvre
Where: Paris, France
What: classics, sculptures and artifacts
Most famous pieces: *Mona Lisa, Winged Victory* and *Venus de Milo*
ⓦ louvre.fr

Prado
Where: Madrid, Spain
What: classics
Most famous piece: *Las Meninas* by Velázquez (Picasso's *Guernica* is in Museo Reina Sofia)
ⓦ www.museodelprado.es

Tate Modern
Where: London, England
What: modern art
Most famous piece: whatever's in the Turbine Hall (exhibitions every six months)
ⓦ tate.org.uk

Uffizi
Where: Florence, Italy
What: frescoes and sculptures
Most famous piece: any number of masterpieces, from Botticelli's *Birth of Venus* to Da Vinci's *Adoration of the Magi*
ⓦ uffizi.firenze.it

Vatican Museums
Where: Rome, Italy
What: maps, frescoes and classics
Most famous piece: The Sistine Chapel
ⓦ mv.vatican.va

1

prepared to pay more for air conditioning. Sure, you can combat these with a good sleeping bag or a cold, wet sarong wrap, but you might not always be in the mood. As a general rule, the best times to visit are at the **beginning and end of the tourist cycles**, the so-called shoulder seasons (March–June and Sept–Nov for southern Europe; mid-April to June and Sept–Oct for northern Europe), when you get the good weather without the crowds. For skiers, the season slows down for a few weeks just after the Christmas/New Year rush and again at the end of March when the spring skiers head back to work. If there's any decent snow left on the slopes in April, it can be a great time to surf the slush.

When not to go

Rather than aiming for the perfect time to go, focus on **avoiding the wrong time**, bearing in mind that there are degrees of right and wrong to consider as well. For example, you might want to steer clear of Rome in August – all the Italians have left on vacation and the country is invaded by scores of tourists and endures sweltering temperatures. It's not a great time to be there, but it's hardly a catastrophe. However, if you plan on cycling across Scandinavia, you absolutely don't want to be doing it between November and March.

In general, winter (Nov–Feb) in northern Europe is cold and rainy, with snow at times in winter. Southern Europe can get chilly, but is typically quite mild. Summer (June–Aug) is pleasant in northern Europe (though the occasional rainy days can be difficult to avoid) and very hot in southern Europe.

Planning around local holidays and events

Your overnight train pulls into the station, you stagger over to the tourist information bureau and say you're looking for some budget accommodation for a night or two, and the person behind the counter is shaking their head like a paint mixer before you even finish your sentence. There's a Rotary Club convention and a national youth volleyball competition in town and they've taken up all the rooms. The best the tourist office can do is a double room at the *Ritz* for €295. Or you can stay an hour out of town at a little hostel situated next to a minimum-security psychiatric ward.

Occasionally, **scheduling conflicts occur**. A rock concert, business convention or sporting event unexpectedly disrupts your travel plans. So what do you do? First, try to avoid the situation by keeping an eye on your guidebook for national holidays or other events, such as festivals, that might cause a hotel-booking frenzy (see box, pp.28–29). Then, if you expect the

---

OFF-SEASON TRAVEL

It's not all gravy during the off-season. Some places just never quieten down. I was in Florence, Italy, one November and it felt as if I had taken a bus to Chicago, but for the old buildings and marble statues of pantless men. English, not Italian, was by far the dominant language on the streets, and the people walking around without a camera were in the minority. Florence (and Venice) aside, I found off-season travel to be hugely rewarding. I got into sites faster, my pictures weren't spoiled by people resting their behemoth bums on the 2000-year-old ruins and, above all, a surprising amount of local flavor surfaced, even in places like Paris.

Leif Pettersen

city's accommodation to fill up, email ahead for a reservation, or try booking rooms in advance via a site like ⓦhostelworld.com or ⓦhotels.com, or delay your arrival until a more auspicious day. If you're already there, the easiest thing to do is to simply move on to the next town. For this, the tourist office can be quite helpful. It's the perfect time to head somewhere not mentioned in a guidebook, but before you do, ask for the list of accommodation they represent. Often, there are several hotels, especially the cheaper digs, not on the list. Give those places a call first; they're the most likely to have a room. Or look for less conventional places to stay, such as university dormitories or campgrounds that rent tents. Better yet, try ⓦairbnb.com and other similar private rental solutions (ⓦtripping.com aggregates many). Or stay for free with a local via a service like ⓦcouchsurfing.com. Don't forget to ask about rooftop sleeping at hostels if the weather is favorable.

Researching special activities

The internet works a treat for trip planning. For specific activities, look at specialized magazines and their website. For a cooking course or fine dining, for example, you might look in *Gourmet Magazine* (ⓦgourmet.com); for photography trips, *Outdoor Photographer* (ⓦoutdoorphotographer.com). If you're looking for general ideas, major-city newspaper travel sections are invaluable.

For information directly from other travelers, you might try the straight-up reviews at TripAdvisor (ⓦtripadvisor.co.uk) or look for more broad and specific tips at **discussion boards** such as ⓦvirtualtourist.com, Rough Guides' Community (ⓦroughguides.com/community) and Lonely Planet's Thorn Tree (ⓦlonelyplanet.com/thorntree), where you can post and read messages on thousands of specific travel topics. Not to toot our own horn too loudly, but ⓦroughguides.com is packed with articles, features and practical information like sample itineraries taken from our guidebooks. **Travel blogs** and user-generated sites like ⓦwikitravel.org are other great sources of first-hand – and often recent – information.

Preparing your parents and employers

Not everyone may be as excited about your big trip as you are. Some parents might need a bit of convincing on the merits of such an endeavor, especially if you're making a large request for funding. Some employers will wonder what they'll gain by keeping your position available. So here's a little ammunition to help fight your corner.

Pre-talk

Start by softening them up with some early **hints**. Weeks, months or years before you reveal your plans, try to let it slip during conversation that

1

EUROPEAN FESTIVALS AND EVENTS

Cities and towns come alive during **festivals**. The locals are more upbeat and the experience is often more interactive. But if you miss a festival by a day or two, you'll arrive just in time to watch the streets get cleaned while you pay for the still-inflated hotel prices. Festival planning usually takes some advance legwork. Last-minute accommodation, if indeed there is any, gets snatched up several days before the event, but the extra effort it takes to attend a festival is almost always worthwhile. There are hundreds to choose from around Europe. In some you can participate, in others the spectators become part of the spectacle, but the exuberance is nearly always palpable.

Here are a few of the major events around the continent. To find some of the lesser-known festivals, turn to the country profiles at the back of the book.

- **Ascot Races** Berkshire, England. You can bet on the horses, but keep your eyes on the pomp on parade. Morning suits for men and formal dresses for women, not to mention hats of all sorts, from those with the shade coverage of a patio parasol to dainty little numbers not much bigger than a cinnamon roll. Third week in June, Tues–Sat; ⓦ ascot.co.uk.

- **Carnevale** Venice, Italy. A decadent Renaissance festival, pajama party and three-day rager against the backdrop of the world's most picturesque sinking city. The costumes are as elaborate as they are expensive. And guess what? They're for sale. Feb–March (the week prior to Ash Wednesday); ⓦ carnevale.venezia.it.

- **Cooper's Hill Cheese Rolling** Brockworth, England. People have been chasing a cheese down a sixty-degree slope here for over 200 years. Most tumble in a blur of legs, hands and dislocated shoulders all the way to the bottom. Don't worry, there are plenty of ambulances standing by. Last Mon in May; ⓦ cheese-rolling.co.uk.

- **Glastonbury Festival** Pilton, England. The biggest jam-fest in the UK, for which tickets sell out in hours, months in advance. Performers on the main Pyramid Stage have included Beyoncé, The Rolling Stones, Kanye West and a full cast of platinum-selling album holders. Elsewhere you'll find market stalls (thousands of them) offering everything from goat meat to henna tattoos. Not enough? Check out the freak show or help make a giant rhino out of mud. Late June; ⓦ glastonburyfestivals.co.uk.

- **Kirkpinar Oil Wrestling Tournament** Edirne, Turkey. Smear yourself with oil and wrestle for a camel and stack of cash? Believe it or not, it's been a winning formula for 600 years and it's still going. Over 1000 contestants sign up every year. July 5–11.

you've always wanted to travel to Europe, see a bit of the world. Or, if you have specific interests like learning a language or taking a cooking course, drop that in as well. Keep it casual and speculative. You don't want a conversation about it at this point; you just want to plant a few seeds.

Passion

Let your enthusiasm shine through. Few people like to get in the way of someone pursuing their dreams. Often, it's infectious, and you'll find parents and employers wishing they could take a journey of their own.

- **Oktoberfest** Munich, Germany. Just grab a seat and a frothy "mas" and start slidin' back the brew. The atmosphere (fourteen large tents with a combined capacity of almost 100,000 happy drinkers) makes the beer taste even better. But don't be fooled by the name; most of the event takes place in September. Sept–Oct; Ⓦ oktoberfest.de.
- **The Palio** Siena, Italy. With bribes, religion and dirty tricks, this horse race is straight out of the Middle Ages. To be precise, 1147. Riders representing Siena's different neighborhoods battle and race around the town square for three laps. Medical personnel are on alert for both riders and horses. The party starts days before each of the two big races. July 2 and Aug 16; Ⓦ ilpalio.org.
- **Paris Air Show** France. You don't need to be on the market for your own private F-15 to attend. The public, 350,000 of them, turn out to see new models unveiled and flown every other year on the spot Charles Lindbergh first landed. It's the biggest air show going. June (odd-numbered years only); Ⓦ paris-air-show.com.
- **Running of the Bulls** Pamplona, Spain. People have been testing out their insurance policies at this event for years. Eight days of drinking, reveling in the streets and, oh yes, attempting to avoid stampeding bulls on a narrow, winding, cobblestone street armed with nothing more than a pair of tennis shoes and a hangover. (Two days before, animal activists stage a "Running of the Nudes" in protest.) July; Ⓦ sanfermin.com.
- **St Patrick's Day** Dublin, Ireland. If you're not in green, you'd better have a good excuse. And a hangover that makes you feel green doesn't count. There's everything from a rowing regatta to a treasure hunt that has families scurrying around the city. The full week of *craic* culminates with half a million lining the streets for Ireland's biggest parade on March 17. Mid-March; Ⓦ stpatricksday.ie.
- **La Tomatina** Buñol, Spain. Ingredients: one small town that produces cement, one town plaza, 30,000 lunatics (mostly drunk) and 80,000 pounds of tomatoes. Mix aggressively for one hour or until town is sufficiently red, then rinse at a local watering hole. Aug; Ⓦ latomatina.org.
- **Whirling Dervish Festival** Konya, Turkey. The famed Whirling Dervishes spin their way closer to God only once a year, but the celebrations last a week. The dizzying ceremonial dance is accompanied with drums, flutes and tourist snaps. Dec; Ⓦ mevlana.net.

Educational value

Traveling through Europe will help instill many of the essentials you just don't get at university: self-reliance, confidence in navigating through new surroundings, a chance to view paintings and fine architecture and develop new language skills.

Use role models

The strongest examples you can find may be friends of your parents who have taken such trips, and still went on to successful careers. Do some research into some of your parents' favorite authors, cooks and TV personalities. Chances are

1

more than one of them has taken such a trip in their youth and has probably brought it up during an interview you'll be able to find archived on the internet.

Tie it to a university program

If you can find a study-abroad program that enables you to transfer credit, you may find you have a better argument for staying in Europe over the summer after the program ends or going a few months before it begins. For many parents, the university connection cements the educational value of the entire experience overseas.

Know what you're talking about

Read through this book and you'll have all the background info you'll need to answer your parents' questions about how you're going to get around, what you're going to do and how you can make it the safest possible experience. If you can demonstrate that you've done your homework, then they'll be able to see this is something you've put time and thought into, not just your heart.

Talking money

If asking parents for money, borrow a tactic from the politicians. First sell the concept, then worry about the funding. If they ask what it will cost, tell them you're not sure, still looking into it, but that you'll take all steps to keep it as cheap as possible. Even with generous parents, as a show of good faith, you may offer to put your own money into it to the extent that you can.

Prepare for your return

Some parents may worry that you won't come back for years. Or will become some sort of vagabond, drifting back overseas and never taking what they might consider a "real job" (for my parents, this turned out to be a legitimate concern). Put them at ease by talking about what you'll do when you return. Explain that the trip will help focus your plans for the future. Of course, this will require the daunting task of coming up with some plans. Remember: nothing is set in stone, so if there are some career buzzwords you know they like to hear (such as

---

DEAR MOM AND DAD,

I know you want what's best for me. I know you want me to be safe. And I know you want me to earn a living/attend university/stop moonlighting as an erotic dancer. We all want those things. But as I see it, life isn't about racing to the finish line. I'll get a job/ degree eventually, but I want to appreciate life first. Just now, I have a few things I need to work out, and there's no better place to get a taste of life's options than the world's biggest classroom. This is the perfect time in my life for free-spirited travel. I don't have kids. This may be the one chance in my life to do it on my own terms. And Europe is one of the world's safest destinations. Besides, plan B is to move back in with you.

DEAR BOSS,

I value my job and hope I'll be working here for years to come. But just now, I can feel I need an educational break. Some companies send employees to business school or to various workshops and courses. I'd like the education that comes from travel – an edification investment I plan to pay for myself on an upcoming extended trip to Europe. I will make sure all pressing projects are completed before departing and help train any transition personnel you'd care to bring in. However, if you would take me back upon my return, I believe the company will benefit from my experience. I know I can bring new value to the job: an international perspective, a familiarity with meeting people, more confidence and street smarts. And, with a long-time dream fulfilled, I think you'll find I'll have more focus and renewed energy for the tasks. On paper, it may not look as tidy as sending me to business school, but in real terms it will be more practical. And it will come at just a fraction of the cost with far less time away from the company.

"medical school"), this would be the time to toss them around. Point out that a gap in your CV (résumé) will not hurt. Employees often find journeys like these fascinating, especially if your passion for travel shines through.

How to customize your itinerary

OK, you've got a few places in mind, some weather you want to miss and a few dates you want to hit for festivals or seasonal activities. Before you start stringing it together, there are a few more things to consider.

If it's your first big trip, **start out gently**. If you're going to Turkey, Germany and England, for example, bear in mind that Turkey is the most challenging of the three and won't make the best starting point. Besides, after Turkey, Germany and England won't seem nearly as exciting. If you start in England, it'll still be exhilarating, but much easier. Once you get a feel of getting around on your own, move on to a more challenging country like Germany, where there's a solid infrastructure, but (perhaps) a language barrier. After that, navigating the bus stations and markets of Turkey will be significantly easier to handle.

Take a moment and **consider the balance of your trip**. You want a good mix of attractions, adventure, a course or two, a little wandering, a break, maybe a ferry or canal passage, a measure of hiking, and possibly even a dose of meditation. Chances are your trip may be thin in a few of these areas. Look back at the activity list (see box, p.24) for some ideas on how you might round out your experiences. Just remember to space them out. You don't want to feel like you're trapped in an adventure race, trying to tick a slew of attractions off your list before jumping on your flight back home.

A word of warning: it's not in your best interests to "do" Paris in two days, then "do" Rome in two days, then "do" Prague, and so on. The most you'll be "doing" with such an itinerary is getting a blurry view out of the train window and less cultural depth than can be found on a postcard.

To find out how to connect the dots with the best-suited transportation, see Chapter 2 (see p.35).

1

Register with the State Department/Foreign Office before you leave

Government state departments/foreign offices are all well plugged in with solid digital traveler assistance. Sign up for free and get the latest travel updates and – more importantly – travel alerts while you're on the move. If there's a natural disaster or terrorist act or riot surrounding an economic summit, those who are registered are more likely to get useful alerts about the help provided and direct assistance from the embassy. Depending on how you feel about it, it can be nice to have Big Brother know your whereabouts just in case. But remember to go online and update your travel plans if they change. (And this works well with short trips, too.)

Where to register

- **USA** Ⓦ step.state.gov/step
- **Australia** Ⓦ smartraveler.gov.au
- **New Zealand** Ⓦ safetravel.govt.nz
- **Canada** Ⓦ voyage.gc.ca/register

The UK used to have a similar program called Locate, but scrapped it in 2013, replacing it with updates on Ⓦ gov.uk/foreign-travel-advice, Ⓦ twitter.com/fcotravel and Ⓦ facebook.com/foreignoffice.

Why you need to book certain activities well in advance

Just because you find the ideal activity, that doesn't mean you have to book it there and then. In fact, you can often save more than fifty percent of the cost by foregoing the middlemen and making arrangements once you arrive. However, there are some courses and tours that fill up well in advance. You can't always tell which these are, but it's possible to make a

---

EASE OF TRAVEL

Easy (strong traveler infrastructure, many locals speak English):
Belgium, Denmark, Finland, Ireland, the Netherlands, Norway, Sweden, Switzerland, United Kingdom

Moderate (fair to good traveler infrastructure, some language barriers):
Austria, the Baltic States, Croatia, Czech Republic, France, Germany, Greece, Italy, Poland, Portugal, Slovakia, Slovenia, Spain

Tougher (mixed traveler infrastructure, considerable language barrier):
Albania, Bosnia-Herzegovina, Bulgaria, Hungary, Montenegro, Morocco, Romania, Russia, Serbia, Turkey

decent guess. You could reason, for example, that there's a steady stream of overnight hiking trips heading out in the Alps, so, if you're not too particular about which peak, you'll find a tour that fits your level, even last minute. If you're after something a bit more celebrated, and something specific, such as a short pastry course at Le Cordon Bleu cooking school (ⓦlcbparis.com), it's worth booking ahead. You can always call or email, say you're not sure about your arrival dates just yet and ask if they anticipate a problem booking a week or two ahead of time.

Sample itineraries

1. One month
Start in Dublin; bus to Limerick; bus to Doolin, ferry to Aran Islands; ferry to Galway, horseback riding tour; bus to Belfast; bus to Dublin.

2. One month
Start in Zürich; train to Interlaken, adventure activities; train to Montreux for the Jazz Festival; train to Zermatt, climbing course and hiking; back to Zürich.

3. Two months
Start in London; fly to Barcelona; train to Marseille; train to Florence, take cooking course; train to Venice; train to Italian Alps, mountain-biking tour; train to Vienna, visit relative; fly back to London.

4. Two months
Start in Amsterdam; train to Bruges; train to Paris, pantomime lessons; train to Bordeaux, wine tasting; train to Pamplona, Running of the Bulls; train to Barcelona; ferry to Ibiza, club hopping; fly to London; hitchhike to Edinburgh, single-malt Scotch tour; ferry to Amsterdam.

5. Four months
Start in Berlin; train and ferry to Copenhagen, rent bicycle, take train to Frederikshavn; ferry to Oslo; train to fjords, hiking and whitewater rafting; train to Stockholm, kayak in archipelago; ferry to Helsinki, train to St Petersburg; train to Vilnius; train to Kraków, visit Auschwitz; train to Prague, beer tasting; train to Berlin.

6. Four months
Start in Rome, study Italian; train to Brindisi, Greek island-hopping around the Aegean Sea; ferry to Athens, cooking class; train to Belgrade; train to Budapest; train to Vienna, take photography course; train to Salzburg, *Sound of Music* tour; train to Munich, Oktoberfest; train to Venice; train to Rome.

Hate to plan in advance? Consider this

Here's another way to go about it: get a passport, rustle up some cash and hop on the next plane to Europe and head in whichever direction cries out. The drawback to planning your trip, free spirits claim, is that, to a large extent, you decide in advance what you're looking for. So, while you'll

1

LESSONS LEARNED

This entire book is filled with lessons learned, but here are seven most noticeable things that have changed in the way I travel.

• I am no longer that interested in traveling someplace simply to see something, so going to a new city just to have a look around now holds much less appeal. These days, my motivation for travel is what I'm going to do when I get there: hike a specific trail, volunteer with an interesting project, try my hand at some new thing, or get to do one of my favorite things (such as kitesurfing) in a new spot.

• I'm more comfortable with a small pack. For some reason I thought I needed more stuff – you know – just in case. The more you travel, the more you realize you can find virtually anything you need on the road.

• I don't need to conquer as much territory. I used to think, for example, that a month in New Zealand was loads of time, and I'd start trying to figure out how much ground I could cover in that time. Now I'm happy (and realize I get more out of it) if I visit fewer places, stay longer in each one and try more of the local things in each spot.

• I plan longer pit stops, even look forward to them. If I travel quickly for a bit, I know I'll get sensory overload and appreciate the travel less. I count on this now and make some interesting plans to stay put a while.

• I take more pictures of the details along the way (road signs, toilets, meals, doorways) and fewer landscapes and posed shots.

• I always find out the approximate price for any taxi ride, then make sure I'm getting in the right type of taxi and that we've agreed on the price (or meter) before getting in. Even in the most developed nations (like Sweden), getting in the wrong taxi will cost you dearly.

• I'm less worried about the micro savings. I realized I don't sit around after a trip and think, oh, I should have walked an extra 3km for that slightly cheaper bakery that day I was hanging out in Rome. It's good to be frugal, but I'm better at not letting the tiny expenditures dictate my entire trip.

Doug Lansky

probably find "it", you'll likely miss many of the unpredictable things that are subtly trying to find you. The drawback to NOT planning is that you may miss things you would have liked to see because you were simply unaware of them, or because courses, volunteer projects or hotel rooms during festivals were already booked up.

2

Getting to Europe and traveling around

You can get a consolidated flight to Europe, buy a motorcycle in London, ride around Britain, sell it, take a ferry to Ireland and then buy a horse. Ride down the coast, sell it, take a ferry over to the European continent, zip along the Mediterranean with a one-month rail pass, then hitchhike to Paris and catch the Eurostar under the Channel to London for your return flight. The price, length of journey, reliability of arrival and comfort vary enormously with each. This chapter will help you compare the most popular choices so you can find the one that best fits your budget and itinerary (or lack thereof).

The trick to getting a cheap ticket to Europe

There's some truth to the famed airline axiom that savings come with restrictions, discomfort and stopovers. But only some truth. You can get **reduced prices** on tickets on major airlines with direct flights as well.

If you're not tied to one particular destination, you should check prices on flights to the cheapest gateways in Europe. Start with London, Amsterdam and Paris, then try Rome, Milan, Madrid and Frankfurt. Trying to begin your journey with a flight into, say, the Swiss Alps, isn't

USING ONE-WAY TICKETS

If I'm flying into Europe with a one-way ticket, I always get a flight to Amsterdam. You may want to buy a train, bus or plane ticket out of the country in advance, just in case the immigration officials ask. Don't fly into the UK (especially Heathrow or Gatwick airports) without a return ticket. If you are going to be working or studying in Europe (and therefore spending a year or longer) you'll probably want to get a one-way ticket and then take advantage of the cheap tickets out of London to come home.

Tim Uden, Editor, ⓦ bugeurope.com

going to do much more than make your travel agent light up with dollar signs.

If prices are relatively equal, book with a well-informed travel agent and get their email address and phone number. They can point out things you never thought of and provide access to consolidator fares. Besides, it's nice to have someone to contact in case you're in a jam.

But before you call an agent, do a little online checking on your own so you'll know a good price when you see one. Start looking on the major online booking engines (see p.334) and check out the lowest published fares for a particular flight. Here are a few tips that will help keep down the costs:

- Take a couple of hours researching combinations of dates into different major cities (Amsterdam, London, Madrid, Paris, Frankfurt and Milan are good hubs) at one or more of the online booking engines. Sometimes, just leaving a day later or flying into a different city can make a surprising price difference. In this sense, a little flexibility can translate into substantial savings.
  If you know where you want to go and when, sign up for online alerts so you can grab deals as soon as they become available.
- Once you find a good deal, go directly to that airline's site to see if they're offering any other special promotions to places nearby that are even cheaper, or any frequent-flier bonuses. Air India also offers cheap deals, and Icelandair has been offering cheap fares to Europe for backpackers since the 1960s. Now another Scandinavian carrier, Norwegian, is offering discounted trans-Atlantic flights as well.
- Keep in mind the cheapest fares are often indirect, less conveniently scheduled and may involve an airline you've never even heard of. If you have more time than money, this is a fine way to grab a deal.
- Don't let your frequent-flier plan get in the way of finding the best ticket. First, look for the best deal, then if two or three offer similar fares pick the one that fits with your mileage plan.
- Consider an open-jaw ticket – flying into one city and out of another. If you know your itinerary, you may be able to save by not backtracking.

Travel agents

The best reason to go through a travel agent is to have someone to ring who can help you out in a jam. This is more of an issue with complicated, multi-stop trips, but can offer some peace of mind whatever your route. Such a relationship is easiest to establish with someone local who you've met with face to face. They may be able to find you some deals, especially if it's a hotel package you're after, but if it's just a basic return trip, chances are you'll do fine booking it on your own. Don't assume, just because you're speaking with a "discounter" or "consolidator" (including those listed opposite), that you're getting the best deal. And don't assume all will spend a lot of time with your questions – many deal in bulk and are looking for a quick booking. Do a good deal of searching before you speak with an agent so you can ask better questions and act quickly (if there are limited seats left). Don't pay with cash or deal with a company that doesn't take credit cards.

- **Adventure World** Based in Sydney, Australia; ⓦadventureworld.com.au.
- **AirTreks** Multi-stop international low-price ticket seller based in the US; ⓦairtreks.com.
- **Flight Centre** Discount travel specialist with its origins in Australia. Now has offices in the US, Canada, the UK, South Africa and several other countries; ⓦflightcentre.com.
- **STA Travel** UK-based agent with hundreds of offices in the US (ⓞ1 800 781 4040) and coverage in all English- and German-speaking markets as well as France, Hungary, Scandinavia, Switzerland, Thailand, Singapore, China and Japan. Specializes in student and independent travel. Also sells ID cards, insurance and rail passes; ⓦstatravel.co.uk.
- **Student Universe** US-based. Also sells insurance and rail passes; ⓦstudentuniverse.com.
- **Trailfinders** UK-based all-round travel agent with offices in Australia; ⓦtrailfinders.co.uk.
- **Travel CUTS** Canada-based with offices in the US. Specializes in student and independent travel. Also sells ID cards, insurance and rail passes; ⓦtravelcuts.com.

2

Air travel within Europe

The "Costs and savings" chapter (see p.60) explains why augmenting your rail or bus pass with a cheap flight within Europe can be a great idea. This section will tell you how to get that cheap air flight. Zipping around by plane, no matter how cheap, is probably not the best way to see Europe (it's hard to make cultural inroads and experience the country at 30,000 feet), but it offers a great chance to connect two or three spots that might otherwise be out of range. For example, you might want to spend the bulk of your trip traveling in Spain and Portugal, but you can hop on a plane in Barcelona and get to Rome or Dublin for a long weekend without breaking your budget.

With cut-throat budget airlines battling it out in the skies, your biggest cost for a flight within Europe is likely to be getting yourself out to the airport. Really. It's not uncommon to find **flights for €10–30**, except for certain routes at certain times of the year, when demand is particularly high, though taxes can add to these prices significantly. Many "no-frills" carriers use minor airports located a little further from the city center, but if you've got more time than money, no worries. However, most of the airports are served by **regular transport** so getting to and from them is rarely complicated, just costly. When they say "no frills", they generally aren't kidding, but since the flights are usually less than three hours, it doesn't matter that it feels more like a bus. Pack a meal and fill up your water bottle once you've been through security and you'll be fine. No need to worry about safety. Whatever corners they need

2

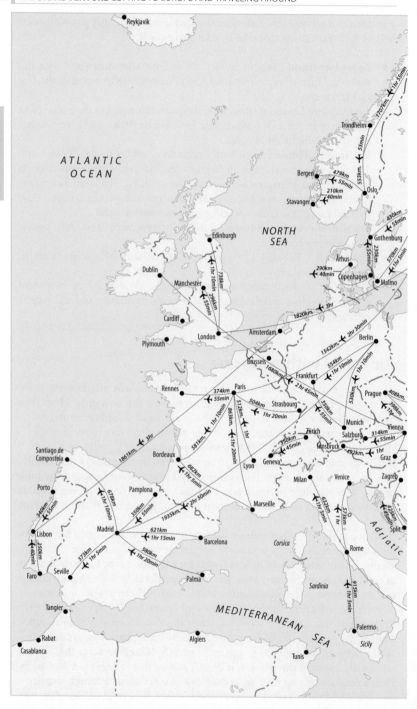

JOURNEY TIMES BY PLANE

to cut to streamline their company, there's no getting around the strict EU regulations that govern the flight industry.

Ryanair is the biggest player and London's Stansted Airport the budget epicenter. But if you're in Stockholm, Copenhagen, Birmingham, Venice, Rome, Milan, Stuttgart, Leeds, Cologne, Bonn, Bratislava, Vienna, Budapest, Dublin, Amsterdam, Rotterdam, Glasgow, Brussels, Barcelona, Frankfurt or elsewhere... you've got yourself a hub and a range of cheap destinations to choose from.

Budget airlines are not a big hit with travel agents, though. Many agents won't have anything to do with them (there's no commission). And perforce, there's not one agent or website with access to all the discounted fares offered (at least not at the moment), so to check rates you need to look online. For a list of airlines and search engines, see "Directory" (p.329).

Charter seats

Many Europeans take a holiday with the kids and fly charter. Which means you can catch a charter flight from any major city to the major resort destinations (the ones with overcrowded beaches and ski slopes). There are too many to list, though popular destinations include the Canary Islands, Ibiza, Mallorca, Cyprus, Greece and Egypt. Simply check the travel section of the local newspaper. You can find great deals on last-minute flights (you don't have to buy the entire hotel package – many offer leftover seats on the plane).

Air passes

- **Visit Europe** ⓦoneworld.com. Offers 220 destinations in 53 countries with member airlines of the One World Alliance; you have to fly into Europe with an Alliance carrier to qualify. Fares depend on the mileage you cover but often represent a fairly good saving on short routes. Buy the minimum two coupons before you leave for Europe; more can be purchased after you arrive. No upper limit.
- **Star Alliance Europe Airpass** ⓦstaralliance.com. Flights to 280 destinations in more than forty countries, with eleven Star Alliance airlines. Minimum three coupons, maximum ten, which have to be used within three months. Pricing is complicated, and taxes and surcharges are high – so keep a look out for this when you compare prices.
- **EuropebyAir FlightPass** ⓦeuropebyair.com. Flights on twenty-plus airlines to hundreds of cities in Europe from the US. Cheap prices are inflated by added charges for issuing and shipping paper tickets, which can be very high.

Traveling by train within Europe

If you don't set foot on a **train** at least once while you're in Europe, you're missing out on something. Besides the overpriced stale food they like to serve on board, Europe is train country. How else would you describe a rail network

SITTING ON A TRAIN

It's not quite as straightforward as it sounds. On most regular trains, you can just hop on board with your **rail pass**, grab a second-class seat (the train cars are marked as such on the outside, and the conductors are typically guarding the first-class entrances) and relax. But like a subway ticket, individual train tickets and rail passes don't guarantee a seat, just passage on the train. On some particularly popular journeys you may end up hopping from one free seat to the next at every stop, or get stuck standing in the aisles or in the noisy passageway between train carriages when the seats completely fill up. You can avoid that by paying to reserve a seat (about €10) or getting to the station early (or the day before) and asking at the ticket window how crowded the train will be.

All high-speed trains – crowded or not – require a **seat reservation**, which is going to cost €5–30 per ride, even if you have a rail pass. On high-end trains like the Eurostar from Paris to London, the mandatory reservation tops €90. You also have to pay extra for a **sleeper car or couchette** on overnight journeys. The sleeper is luxury train travel – at least, sometimes it is. Sleepers cover the range from a semi-soft bunk bed in a shared room to a real bed with a washstand and fresh sheets and towels. Prices for one night range from about €50 to €125, depending on the comfort level. The couchette is like a small cabin where the seats fold flat and you can sleep side by side with a few fellow passengers. Some turn into double-decker bunk beds with the sort of padding normally found in dentist's waiting-room furniture. A couchette costs about €20–40 a night. Some trains also have special reclining seats ("sleeperettes" or, more specifically, "lackofsleeperettes") like you might find in business class on a plane, which can also be reserved. You can find a place to sleep without a reservation, and many do, but you're taking your chances spending a night in an upright seat or getting bumped from your recliner in the middle of the night by someone who boards with a reservation. It could make the difference between a full day of sightseeing and spending your day passed out on a park bench for a four-hour nap.

2

totaling 240,000km? (By comparison, there's 45,000km of rail in the US and Canada, an area more than twice as big.) It's not necessarily the cheapest way to get around; it's simply the best way. And not because the rail routes are often more scenic: the facing seats provide an opportunity to meet locals or chat with friends, the aisles allow you to stretch your legs, some carriages allow full reclining at night and the train's chug-chug adds an authentic travel beat to any conversation. Plus, ethically, it beats flying.

Buying a train ticket is as simple as walking up to the ticket window, saying the name of the town you want to go to and handing over a credit card or cash. The biggest problem is that, in most European countries, this is a painfully expensive way to get around. Enter the rail pass (throughout this book: Eurail for North Americans and those Down Under; InterRail for Europeans). There are scores of options. You can buy a pass that allows either unlimited travel during a set period or a fixed number of days during a set period. Some allow travel in multiple countries, some limit travel to just one country.

There are several more passes available online at ⓦ raileurope.com and ⓦ interrail.eu. See "Costs and savings" (p.63) to take best advantage of your

JOURNEY TIMES BY TRAIN AND BUS

Tromsø

Rovaniemi

0 | 100
kilometers

2hr 5min
2hr 25min

Groningen

40min
1hr 15min

Amsterdam

Rotterdam

40min

Antwerp

2hr 45min

Bruges

1hr

Brussels

Maastricht

2hr 45min

Luxembourg City

Joensuu

9hr 30min
13hr 25min

4hr 25min
9hr 20min

3hr 40min
7hr

2hr
2hr

Turku

Stockholm

Helsinki

Tallinn

St Petersburg

4hr 15min

4hr 30min
11hr 15min

4hr 15min
8hr

14hr 20min
21hr 30min

11hr 30min

Moscow

4hr 30min

15hr 40min
15hr 45min

Riga

8hr 50min

BALTIC
SEA

4hr 20min
4hr 5min

Vilnius

Minsk

Gdańsk

3hr
5hr 10min

5hr 25min
8hr 25min

Warsaw

3hr 25min
5hr 20min

Kiev

Kraków

SEE INSET
ABOVE LEFT

HIGH-SPEED TRAIN TIMES
Rome–Naples 1hr 10min
Paris–London 2hr 20min
London–Brussels 2hr 5min
Paris–Bordeaux 3hr 20min
Paris–Brussels 1hr 25min
Brussels–Amsterdam 2hr 25min
Copenhagen–Stockholm 5hr 10min
Berlin–Hamburg 1hr 35min
Geneva–Zürich 45min
Milan–Zürich 4hr 5min
Madrid–Barcelona 2hr 35min
Madrid–Seville 2hr 30min
Madrid–Alicante 2hr 20min
Madrid–Marseille 7hr 45min
Barcelona–Paris 7hr 50min

Budapest

Suceava

5hr 15min
7hr 35min

7hr 30min
6hr

8hr 55min
11hr

2hr 15min
3hr

Timişoara

9hr 15min

8hr

Belgrade

Bucharest

Constanța

BLACK SEA

T'bilisi

Sarajevo

6hr

10min

7hr 40min
6hr

Varna

Yerevan

Dubrovnik

Sofia

6hr 35min
4hr 10min

Burgas

Podgorica

3hr
1hr 45min

Plovdiv

Tirana

Skopje

İstanbul

3hr 50min
6hr

Ankara

Thessaloníki

6hr 35min

Corfu

5hr 25min

5hr

AEGEAN
SEA

11hr 25min
9hr 15min

10hr 45min

İzmir

7hr 45min

Antalya

Athens

0 | 500
kilometers

pass. (Note that InterRail tickets are not valid in your European country of residence.) In general, a flexipass-type ticket will be the better option for most travelers as you don't want to be taking long train journeys every day (and short journeys will likely be cheaper to buy individually).

2 Traveling by bus within Europe

There are two bus passes worth looking into, and they both undercut the train fares: Eurolines (Ⓦeurolines.com) and Busabout (Ⓦbusabout.com). Eurolines is cheaper and functions as Europe's standard long-distance bus line, connecting 500 destinations across Europe, while Busabout is aimed specifically at budget travelers – taking you not just around Europe but right to a hostel (one they hope you'll stay at) – and provides onboard movies and a guide. That gives you less reason to look out of the window and less opportunity to meet locals, but it will save you the hassle of finding a hostel and will put you in touch with more travelers. They also tailor trips to big backpacker events like La Tomatina and Oktoberfest. For those just traveling in the UK, there's also Megabus (Ⓦmegabus.co.uk), which offers discount deals around the country for as little as £10 (€14), and have now expanded into other parts of western Europe.

Traveling by car within Europe

Driving offers the chance to take control of your itinerary, get to places you can't easily reach (or reach at all) with public transport and (with enough people) even save money. Whether you decide to buy or rent a car (both covered in this section), there are some basic tips that will make the experience more enjoyable:

- **Drive defensively** In Greece, Italy and several other countries it may seem like most drivers are making up new traffic laws as they go. Stay cool and follow the law, even if those around you aren't.
- **Know how to drive a stick-shift car** Automatics often cost more to rent.
- **Learn the metric system** FYI it's about four liters of gasoline to a gallon – yes, it is about as expensive as twelve-year-old Scotch. If you're in Germany, Italy or France and near the Austria or Luxembourg border, cross over to fill up and save up to €5 per gallon. Eastern Europe and especially Russia, Belarus and Ukraine are even cheaper.

> ### BORDER CROSSINGS
>
> There are **border crossings** in Europe, but chances are you won't notice them on a train or bus. Perhaps you'll spot names on road signs, or the train conductor may start speaking a different language. There won't be any sort of announcement or blinking lights. Few, if anyone, will actually ask to see your passport. And, unless you ask nicely, they won't put a stamp in it.

- **Don't use the car for city sightseeing** It's usually a lot cheaper and easier to find free parking well outside of the city, and use public transport to get into town. It's quicker, better and greener to get out and wander cities on foot, especially since most European cities have more curves than a bag of pretzels and half of them are one-way streets. There's a simple formula: tiny medieval roads plus stress equals scratches and extra rental fees.

- **Know where you're heading** You'll rarely see north, south, east and west signs to point you in the right direction: just directions to specific towns. Before you tuck the map away, take a good look at the next town's name and the next big city's name.

- **Stick to the back roads** Highways are fast but boring. Take advantage of your mobility and go places rail and bus travelers can't. Most back roads are in excellent shape and offer much more interesting food, and far more scenery (though they're not as well lit for night driving). Many of the major roads come with extra tolls and often they run parallel with the old road they replaced.

- **Be aware of hidden expenses** Super-freeways in France and Italy have tolls (about €5 per hour), and you may be spending up to €25 a day for parking in major cities. Since 2003, you have to pay a "congestion charge" to drive in central London (£11.50/$18 a day; ⓦcclondon.com). Oslo also has one, as do Stockholm, Gothenburg, Milan, Rīiga, Valletta (Malta) and Durham, England. And driving in Norway and Sweden in winter without proper winter tires is fineable. Several European countries require drivers to get a sticker called a vignette to use their national motorways. Getting caught driving without one can land you with a fine of €40–800. And tax on your rental is typically 18–25 percent (zero in Switzerland, but its rates are higher).

- **Know the signs** Thanks to EU regulations, road signs have been standardized. There are only a few you really need to know, so take five minutes to learn them. To get to the center of town, you can typically find signs pointing you to *Centre-ville*, *Zentrum* or *Stadtmitte*, while the tourist office is designated by "i", "VVV" or *turismo*. The signs can be found online at ⓦideamerge.com/motoeuropa/roadsigns.

- **Don't speed** Many European countries take speeding seriously: Germany, because you can go as fast as you like (at least on some of the Autobahns), and other countries because they seem to be financing their government with the fines. A €100 ticket is not uncommon. Some places have speed cameras mounted on the side of the road. If one flashes when you go by, just smile. You'll pay the fine later when the rental company tacks it on to your credit card account.

- **Prepare for emergencies** European law now dictates that you must carry the following items in your car: first-aid kit, reflective jacket for each person in the car, hazard triangle, fire extinguisher, spare bulb for every exterior light. Also, UK drivers need to adjust UK cars' headlamps with beam adjusters when driving in mainland Europe, and France requires a breathalyzer to be carried.

2

Renting a car

This is probably the most hassle-free way to drive. But then, you're paying for that convenience. If you can put together a group of travelers, however, you may not be paying so much. It depends on how much you drive. With two people in a rented compact car with unlimited kilometers driving five hours every other day, a month is going to cost about €1000 per person. Driving five hours every fourth day will set you back about €600 each, or roughly the same as a rail pass. With four people driving a slightly larger car five hours every third day, this will bring the costs down to just under €500 per person.

Weekly rentals with unlimited kilometers are the most economical short-term solutions and can be booked over the web, via a travel agent or directly with the company. It's usually cheaper to book from home. Having said that, it's worth taking a look at the pricing of some rental consolidators (ⓦautoeurope.com and ⓦkemwel.com). As with flights, these agents buy in bulk and pass on the savings. If you're traveling for more than three weeks, a lease (sometimes called a "buy-back") is going to be the best option. You get a new car and unlimited kilometers, plus breakdown cover and zero-deductible (zero excess) insurance for a great rate. In addition to the sites above, try ⓦeuropebycar.com and ⓦrenaultusa.com.

DRIVING IN ITALY

"OK," Renato explained, as I adjusted the rear-view mirror of my red Ford Fiesta, "driving in Napoli is like a video game. You just have to relax, stop thinking, and feel it in your stomach."

I fastened my seat belt.

"What are you doing?!" he reprimanded. "No one in Napoli wears seat belts. You want to look like a tourist?"

I unbuckled. Renato told me that about a decade ago when the mandatory seat-belt law was passed and briefly enforced, people started wearing T-shirts with a black stripe painted across the chest.

We came to the first traffic light, but cars were only stopping if there was faster traffic coming from the other direction. It seems red, yellow and green lights are, in the eyes of Napolitano drivers, just colors, and should be obeyed no more than Christmas decorations.

I asked Renato why the drivers ignored them. "If they followed rules," he explained, "they'd be stuck in traffic for hours."

"But they are stuck in traffic for hours," I pointed out.

"Well, yes," he admitted, "that's true."

My lesson also had an acoustic component. In Napoli, the horn is not just a warning device, but a musical instrument, and Renato played it beautifully. When we passed a voluptuous woman walking on the sidewalk, he reached over and hit the side of the horn, delivering three short, cute squeaks. No one looked over at us except the woman he was honking at, as if everyone knew only she was the object of the honk. Later, five machine-gun-style honks got the attention of his friend on the other side of the street. One quick blast warned a driver not to cut us off. When we were in a crowd of people, Renato reached over and honked with a short double-tap to the center of the horn, and people moved. A few were slow to get out of our way, and a two-second blast was required. This longer honk was quite effective, but protocol dictated that they shoot us a nasty look as they stepped aside.

Watching some Napolitano drivers squeeze past me on the right, drive up on the curb, and triple-park, I wondered aloud how they ever passed their driver's tests. "They probably didn't," Renato answered. "Up until a few years ago, anyone could buy a black market license for around €500."

Now that I was getting the hang of it, it was time for a little sightseeing. Renato gave me the three-second tour: "University there, church there, blonde there!" (honk).

Doug Lansky

An RV (Recreational Vehicle) is another option, especially for families, as it makes the more affordable campsites accessible – some are little cities unto themselves with large swimming pools and waterslides. However, the gas-guzzling motors make it less than ideal for covering long distances. Figure on about €100 per day for rental, not including gas or campsites.

What you'll need

2

Remember, when you rent a car, you're liable for the whole shebang. There's a Collision Damage Waiver (CDW) supplement, which covers the car (usually with a deductible fee of a few hundred euros – roof, tires and windshield aren't usually covered) and costs €15–25 a day, depending on the country, the car and the rental company. There are two ways to do it cheaper. The first is to call your credit-card company and ask if they offer coverage for free with your card if you use it to pay for the rental. Some do, some don't, but always ask them to spell out exactly what happens in case of an accident. Plan B is to buy the CDW elsewhere: Travel Guard (Ⓦtravelguard.com), for example, sells it for $9 a day, though check validity for Italy and Ireland, as they may not allow it.

Most rental companies won't hand over the keys if you're under 21 or don't have a credit card. Many want you to be 25, or will stick you with under-age insurance fees. If you're considered too young, leasing may be a better option, as the leasing companies are more relaxed with age limitations. STA Travel (Ⓦstatravel.com) may also be able to help with rentals for the under-25 set.

A valid **driver's license** is all you need in most European countries to rent a car. In Austria, Bosnia-Hezegovina, Bulgaria, the Czech Republic, Greece, Hungary, Italy, Poland, Portugal, Romania, Russia, Spain and Ukraine, you'll need an international driving permit (IDP), which is simply a translation of your license. It feels better to hand to a police officer if you get pulled over, but it just makes it easier for him to write out the ticket. It's simple enough to get from your national auto association (see p.335).

Airport or town

The surest way of saving money with your rental car is to make sure you **don't pick it up at the airport when you land**, if you plan to start your trip by exploring a city for a few days. Paying €30–50 a day for the car plus another €20 to park it safely is a quick way to flush around €250 down the drain. Instead, pick up your car after your initial city sightseeing and plan to return it before sightseeing at the end of the trip. And if you're not picking up the car at the airport when you arrive, you won't need to bother to go back there to drop it off again. Pick it up in town (away from the train station, as well), and you may skip an ugly tax (possibly as much as seventeen percent) on the total rental fee.

If you can get a good deal, try renting a car with a built-in GPS system. These incredible inventions may never serve you better than they can in Europe, even if they're not as much fun as looking at an old-fashioned map.

Buying a secondhand car

The UK seems like a good place to buy a used car because there's a great market for vehicles aimed at travelers; everything is in English, so contracts aren't so intimidating; it's a common point of entry; and if you're going to buy a car, doing it at the beginning of your trip makes the most sense. The problem is driving in Europe can be tricky enough without having to worry about being on the left-hand side of the road. Taking the vehicle over to the Continent (and back if you plan to sell it) gets expensive as well; and you don't really want a right-hand drive there where they drive on the right. Naturally, if you plan to do your driving exclusively in the UK, buy your car there. If not, you might consider picking it up on the Continent. If you have a friend or relative who is willing to help you register the vehicle, let them help. Frankfurt, Amsterdam and Paris are particularly good car-buying cities for travelers. Look on the web (the Netherlands ⓦzoekertjes.net; France ⓦjannonce.com; Germany ⓦzweitehand.de), in classified papers and on notice boards at hostels. You should be able to find a car for under €900 that will get you around. Even if you sell it for €450 after two months, it'll still be cheaper than a rental.

But **if you buy a car you need to insure it**. And this is the tricky bit. Talk to the sellers and see what they did and if they'll help you sort through the paperwork and provide any tips. Otherwise, consider buying the car in a place where you have friends or relatives who can help with translation and bypassing complex bureaucracy.

Another option is to try the eBay site for the particular country you're visiting.

How to hitch safely and quickly

In many countries around Europe, **hitchhiking is an accepted way of getting around** and drivers are sympathetic to your roadside plight (as many have done some hitching themselves). In others, such as parts of Scandinavia, you're something of a pariah, although it's still eminently possible to thumb your way around. Bear in mind, though, that there are dangers inherent to hitchhiking beyond the normal traffic risks. The driver who seemed nice enough to stop for you may not in fact be very nice at all. And, once you're in the car with such a person, you're at a serious disadvantage. Female travelers in particular are at a higher risk; it's advisable for women never to hitch alone. Rough Guides doesn't recommend hitching as a safe means of getting around, but if you do choose to hitch, be aware of the risks and check out the security section (see p.153) for tips on making hitchhiking as safe as possible.

How to get a driver's attention

- Start by dressing well. You've only got a few seconds to make an impression. This is the time (in case it's been a while) to wash your clothes and tuck in your shirt. A jacket and tie is out of place – you should look like a budget traveler; just a clean and trustworthy one. Leave the black and camo colors in your pack.

- Remove the hat and sunglasses. They need to be able to see your face clearly, see that you're not hiding anything.
- Don't smoke while waiting for a ride.
- Minimize the luggage. The four-piece custom luggage set with a windsurfer isn't going to get you far. One bag – a midsize backpack – is ideal.
- If you're standing on the side of the road, place your pack neatly in front of you to show that you're a backpacker traveling their country on a budget. Some (not Americans, typically) like to put a flag patch of their home country on their pack to highlight the foreign-traveler angle.
- Hold up a sign. Not a necessity, but it can help. Carry a permanent marker and then just look for an old pizza box or chunk of cardboard. Try to pick a place that's not more than two hours away so you've got an excuse to get out if nine hours with this driver seems intolerable. Similarly, they may be intimidated about spending a full day giving you a ride. If it goes well, you can explain that you're actually going a bit further. Some people use a sign with a giant smile on it. Or "Student traveler". Or "I don't smell funny". If you're standing at or near a stoplight, you might try something humorous on the back, so you can flip it over if you've got someone's eye for a few seconds.
- Hitching is easiest for people traveling on their own, a man and a woman or two women. Three of anybody is too many – it's hard to find anyone with enough room – and intimidating. Two guys can be intimidating to many drivers as well. Although not advisable, if you do decide to hitch as a single woman, see the "Security" section (p.153).
- The typical age range is 18–30. If you're over 30 and look young, you can pull it off, but drivers tend to shy away from people who aren't in this group.

Where to stand makes all the difference

- Usually the best place to hitch is at a gas station near the motorway. This means getting directions from the tourist office or a website (⊕ hitchwiki .org has all the best places in Europe to hitch) and taking a bus or subway there. Simply ask people who are at the pump (a captive audience). Say you're a student trying to see their country cheaply and you'd appreciate a ride. Offer to chip in for some fuel as well. Or buy a coffee/Coke for the journey. With this method, it should take between, say, five and thirty minutes to get a ride. Besides, you'll have plenty to eat and someplace to stay warm/cool while you wait.
- If you need to stand on the side of the road, make sure there's plenty of room for the driver to stop; that they're going slowly and don't need to concentrate on merging or accelerating; and that you can be seen from a distance.

Hitching security

- Safety starts with your appearance. You're going to likely get safer rides if you look the part. Kind drivers (and owners of nice cars) are far less likely

2

to pick up travelers who look like street urchins or seem even remotely like they might be a threat to their safety.

- If you're hitching on the side of the road and a car pulls over, don't just run after it and jump in. Take a moment to go to the passenger side window (open the door if the driver doesn't put down the electric window) and ask where he/she is going. Use those precious few seconds to see if the driver looks dangerous in any way; if there are other potentially dangerous people in the car; or if there's any smell of alcohol or open bottles.
- Women are not advised to hitch alone. If you do choose to do it, you should only consider hitching at gas stations. If anyone looks mildly suspicious, don't even ask them for a ride. In fact, try to restrict your hitching requests to families with young kids and single women drivers who look presentable. Also, non-hitch hitching can be an option (see below).

Hitching tips and strategy

- If you're going further down the highway and the driver needs to let you off, ask him to stop at a well-positioned gas station before the city he's heading to. If he takes you into the city, you can't hitch there, so you'll need to take a bus back out to a gas station on the other side of town.
- If there's a chance it might rain, buy a cheap umbrella. No one wants a soaking-wet person in the car.
- Bring enough food and drink to last you for several hours.
- As a rule of thumb, give a place two hours before you give up. You'll normally find a ride well before that.
- Learn the local protocol. It's not always a question of putting your thumb out. That's just the standard. In Latvia, you use an open hand instead; in other parts of eastern Europe you flap your arm like a bird with a dislocated wing.

Be a good hitcher

- You represent the hitchhiking community when you accept a ride. If the driver has a good experience, they may stop for more hitchers later, so be a good ambassador.
- Don't smoke unless you get permission first.
- If they picked you up because they wanted some company on a long ride and feel like talking, talk back. If you must sit silently and don't feel like making conversation, come up with a good excuse or stop hitching.
- If you arrive at a spot where there are already one or more hitchers, the etiquette is that you head down traffic (the direction cars are headed) and stay 20–100m away. Sometimes drivers zip past the first person, then get a bad conscience and see you and stop (or slow down for the first person but don't like the look of him), so it's not the worst place to be.

Non-hitch hitching

- Put up a notice in your hostel saying that you're looking for a ride and you don't mind sharing fuel expenses. Put up notices in other hostels as well. Often groups of travelers will have rented or bought a car and will be looking for some help with the costs.

- Contact a rideshare or lift center. Some organizations are paid a small fee both for membership and per kilometer driven, while others request a donation. In Switzerland, for example, many cities offer a ride service called Mitfahrzentrale. See ⓦhitchhikers.org for more info.

Traveling by ferry around Europe

Obviously, you can't realistically travel the whole of Europe by **ferry**, but the services on offer do provide interesting alternatives and handy little shortcuts here and there. For a list of ferry operators see "Directory" (p.329). A few routes, including their journey times, are:

- Brindisi, Italy–Kefalonia, Greece (12hr)
- Copenhagen, Denmark–Oslo, Norway (16hr)
- Gdańsk, Poland–Nynäshamn, Sweden (19hr)
- Helsingør, Denmark–Helsingborg, Sweden (20min)
- Helsinki, Finland–Stockholm, Sweden (15hr)
- Helsinki, Finland–Tallinn, Estonia (3hr 30min)
- Newhaven, England–Dieppe, France (1hr 15min)

Traveling by bicycle within Europe

This is a continent that deserves to be seen from a bike. The hamlets that tour buses and cars roll past regularly are some of the greatest treasures. With the great road races (Giro d'Italia, Vuelta de Espana, the Tour de France) ripping by at one point or another, you find a great respect for cyclists (though not always much actual room on the road). In fact, taking a bike around Norway or Sweden and camping for free among the fjords or on the coast is quite possibly the single cheapest way to see these countries. You just pay for your plane ticket (plus some of Norway's and Sweden's overpriced food). Denmark offers some of the **best biking**, with 12,000km of bike trails packed into a country that's not more than 300km wide and 500km long. The Netherlands also has excellent flat bike trails.

Europe's larger cities all have daily and weekly rentals – as well as, increasingly, good bike-sharing schemes – plus you can rent privately using a service like Spinlister (see p.337). Or you can buy a local bike when you arrive. You'll find everything from €40 rusty wrecks that work to the very same top-of-the-line Treks, Cannondales, Giants, Bianchis and the like you can find at home.

And just because your bike holds four **saddlebags**, that doesn't mean you should bring all four. You'll probably need them all if you're camping. But if you're planning to stay at hostels or pensions (and there are plenty along the way to keep you from camping if you'd rather have a comfortable bed

2

WHY TRAVEL BY BIKE?

Modern transportation, especially in Europe, is reliable. That's the problem. It's so easy, and rather tempting, to book your way as you go. Biking doesn't quite let you get away with that. Bad weather, fatigue and punctures force flexibility into your trip and make you stop where you never thought you would. OK, you look a bit silly interacting with the locals while wearing black spandex shorts with a built-in sweaty maxi-pad. But if you take that next step and shave your legs, it somehow looks more natural. Some countries, like France, have great respect for this type of travel. There's a historical precedent for it – the concept was sold to them long ago as the horse that needs no hay. Trucks make room for you on narrow roads, and the locals cheer you along. Even if, like me, you don't feel that sporty when you start, you'll be in incredible condition by the time it's over. And at the end of a 100-mile day, when you pull into a pub or café and see the people who've just been sitting around, there's a tremendous feeling of accomplishment, and a touch of arrogance. You almost want to sit down next to someone and ask, "So, what did you do today?"

Tim Moore
Author, *French Revolutions: Cycling the Tour de France* and *Travels with My Donkey: One Man and His Ass on the Pilgrimage Way to Santiago*

after a long ride), two saddlebags should be sufficient. The reduced weight is a godsend going up hills. But, more importantly, it makes security less of an issue. If you want to head into a market or restaurant, or up a flight of stairs to check the availability of a hostel (something you'll be doing daily), it's easy to lock up the bike and carry your two bags along. With four bags (or five, including a front bag), that's not much of an option, so someone will get stuck guarding the gear – or you'll need one impressive security system.

Bringing your bike on a plane can be an issue. That is, a cost issue. Some carriers will provide you with a bike box, some won't. You'll need to find out in advance. The easiest thing to do is to get a bike box for free at your local cycle shop and then buy a pedal wrench to remove the pedals yourself (even if they do it for you, you'll still need the wrench to put the pedals back on when you arrive). Take off the handlebars and tape them to the frame of the bike, lower or move the seat as well. And don't forget to let some air out of the tires. Then make sure the whole thing is well padded. Another option, if it's OK with your airline, is to simply put it on board without a box. Just leave it as is, with a huge "Fragile" note on it. Chances are, handlers will be gentler with it if they can see what it is.

When biking around Europe, you can put up a tent in a campground or open field (if legal) more easily than if traveling by train or bus, since you'll be passing through the rural areas anyway. You can also easily make hotel reservations by carrying a cell phone and a guidebook; just call ahead to a hostel or B&B once you get a sense of how far you'll get that day. A phone is also particularly handy to have along in case of any falls in fairly remote areas.

Traveling with a tour

If you'd rather follow a leader than a map, guidebook or your nose, then taking a tour will certainly provide some peace of mind and remove any worry of planning. Or maybe you think you'd like to go it alone but want a **bit of**

2

handholding to start out your trip and boost your confidence. Tours are also a good idea if you want to visit a few places you otherwise couldn't. There are plenty of operators happy to take your money. The tough part is just deciding which tour you want to do.

Regional tours

These include everything from four-star luxury tours to local packages that can be arranged in almost any midsize city. There are thousands of tour companies to choose from at any number of levels, and it certainly helps to get a personal recommendation or find some favorable reviews before you sign up to one. In many areas, hostels team up with local tour operators (or allow them to leave posters around, for which the hostel may get a commission); the operators typically offer off-road budget trips to scenic spots in the area that are hard to access by local transport. Often, these tours are good fun, but try to get a sense of what the guide is like beforehand and trust your instincts.

Bicycle tours

A support vehicle and leader provide a good deal of assistance on a week-long bike trip. However, this turns one of the cheapest ways of seeing Europe into a rather expensive one.

- **BackRoads** Classic upscale tours; ⓦbackroads.com.
- **Bicycle Beano Tours** Vegetarian bike tours in Wales and the west of England; ⓦbicycle-beano.co.uk.
- **Butterfield and Robinson** Luxury tours; ⓦbutterfield.com.

GUIDED EXCURSIONS

Despite the general reluctance of **independent travelers** to sign up for just about anything, for small portions of a longer trip jumping on a tour can be an excellent way to get some **professional supervision** for something you haven't done before. There are glacier treks in the Alps, kayak trips in Norway's fjords – the list goes on. Some of these activities are difficult to arrange on your own and they can, oddly, be cheaper if done with a tour. You can usually get good, impartial information from your guidebook and from other travelers while you're in the region. A few questions to ask when inquiring about an activity are:

- How easy is it to book on the spot, without a reservation?
- Are there any possible (likely) weather-related conflicts with the intended activities? If so, are there any discounts (if they're not available when you arrive)?
- Does the price include taxes and tips? If not, what's the total cost?
- What are the living conditions like? Private room? Private bathroom? Washing facilities?
- What meals are included?
- For walking and cycling tours, are baggage transfers or porters included?
- What's the cancellation policy, and what kind of insurance is included?

- **Euro-Bike Tours** Midrange tour company with over thirty years of experience; Ⓦeurobike.com.
- **Pack and Pedal Europe** Among the cheaper tours; Ⓦtripsite.com.

Europe-wide tours

2

You can get everything from fourteen cities in six days on a bus ("on your right, the blur of lights out of the window is Paris") to a specialty tour that visits the best restaurants in one tiny region for over a week. However, think twice before signing up for anything more than a day or two – there's a decent chance the guide or one of your fellow passengers may rub you up the wrong way and you may regret having to spend so much time with them.

The three main bus tour companies shuttling travelers (often at breakneck speed) around Europe are Contiki (Ⓦcontiki.com), Trafalgar (Ⓦtrafalgar.com) and Cosmos (Ⓦcosmos.com). All three typically start and end in London. One of the main differences is the age of passengers (Trafalgar's and Cosmos's are older). However, Trafalgar has a special "break-away" tour aimed at 21- to 38-year-olds. Contiki caters to 18- to 35-year-olds, and has a slightly more party atmosphere. All companies run more than a dozen tours within Europe, but here's a snapshot of the routes they can provide, with costs ranging from €2100 to €3100 for twelve days:

- **Sample Contiki tour:** Belgium–Netherlands–Germany–Ausria–Italy–Vatican City–Switzerland–France.
- **Sample Trafalgar tour:** London–Brussels–Rhine Valley–Heidelberg–Lucerne–Venice–Rome–Florence–Pisa–Monaco–Nice–Paris.
- **Sample Cosmos tour:** London–Amsterdam–Rhineland–Lake Lucerne–Paris–London.

3

Traveling alone or with others

For many, this is one of the most difficult decisions of the trip. And understandably so. There are several factors to consider before making this choice, with sizeable pros and cons for each. All things being equal, you'll probably want to travel solo, at least for some portion of your trip. Even if all things aren't equal and there's someone you'd really like to travel with, read through this chapter so you know the risks you'll be taking and how to minimize them. Getting around requires a bit of thinking, but not all that much. Europe has an ingrained culture of travel. They're used to foreigners wandering around, and nearly all Europeans have done it themselves to some degree. Everything is set up to make travel easy.

Why you should at least consider traveling alone

Obviously, this is the more intimidating path. But it's also the most potentially rewarding. And it's not nearly as frightening as it may sound.

1. Traveling solo does not necessarily mean you'll be traveling alone for the bulk of your trip. Quite the opposite, in fact. Most solo travelers just end up traveling with different people for different legs of their journey. Everywhere you go, from museums to hostels to cafés, you'll run into other solo travelers who'll be delighted to travel with someone and, because there are often significant price breaks on rooms for pairs, there's a good chance you'll be sharing accommodation. Even the shyest travelers find the dialogue easy to start: you already have your travel destination and independent spirit in common, not to mention doubtless shared frustrating experiences. At times, it can almost be more difficult to find periods to be on your own. For those who are still uncertain about their ability to meet travel partners on the trail, you can, virtually everywhere, sign up for a group tour along the way and surround yourself with an entire platoon of companions.

2. You learn about yourself. You'll find out what your likes and dislikes are, and be able to act on them. Often travelers spur each other on to check off a "to do" list (with no one looking, maybe you'll give that famous museum a miss and rent a bike and head for the countryside instead). You'll spend more time writing your journal, taking photos, reading, studying the culture – absorbing more of the country you're traveling in.

3. You'll be less distracted by a friend and more likely to notice the small things happening around you. As a single traveler it can be easier to blend in, and you're less likely to be attracting attention by speaking English with your partner. Single travelers attract single travelers.

4. You'll be approached by more locals. They're often anxious to meet foreigners but can be intimidated by couples, feeling reluctant to interrupt a conversation or intrude. Which means solo travelers are much more likely to return home with an address book filled with great contacts from around the world.

Is it safe for women to go alone?

Women can and do travel solo throughout Europe. Some countries, such as Norway, Sweden, Denmark, Finland and the Netherlands, make this quite easy and thus provide a better starting point. In southern Europe, you'll rarely feel threatened – for safety tips, see "Security" (p.153) – but you may be perceived as something of an oddity, so expect numerous inquiries. It is helpful to have a story for the men (you're meeting up with your husband in the next town, for example), but many questions will come from women, which is a great conversation starter and can often offer interesting insights.

The possibility of rape and robbery **should be taken seriously**, but can be minimized (see p.157). Most likely, the harassment you get will be a mild irritant: an admirer on a long train ride who thinks he can charm you with a six-hour story, or a whistle on the street. But it can be more offensive as well: an anonymous hand brushing your breasts or ass in a crowded market. The trick is being able to distinguish between a tactless man and a dangerous one. Always trust your instinct. If any man makes you feel at risk, simply move to a train compartment where there are safer-looking people (preferably women or

---

TOURISTS VS LOCALS

I first went to Europe just after I graduated from college. I bought a Volkswagen right from the factory in Germany and drove around the continent – drank wine in Pamplona during San Fermín and downed beers in Munich's *Hofbräu Haus*. But the stronger memories are meeting up with friends from college and doing things I could have done at home. I wasn't in a tour group, but might as well have been.

I learned that you learn far more during your travels if you go alone. Or as a couple. Or with children. When I travel with a film crew, for example, there are typically two campfires: one with me and the film crew and one with the locals. When you're alone, there's just one campfire. You sit with the locals and find out what's important to them. It's moments like that that provide the reason for travel.

Tim Cahill, author of *Lost in My Own Backyard*, *Hold the Enlightenment* and *Jaguars Ripped My Flesh*

other travelers), head to a more crowded street, pop into a busy store or stop a police officer.

If you're heading overland into a country or region that you're a little unsure of, you can almost always find a trustworthy travel companion to accompany you for at least a few days, if not longer, provided you're going in the same direction. It may take a day or three to find the right person, but in places where the hassle factor is high, such as crossing into Morocco or heading to Turkey, a male companion can make things much easier (especially if you tell people you're married).

3

The benefits of bringing a companion

Traveling with a friend isn't all bad. In fact, there are some nice benefits: minimized culture shock; medical security (they can help get you to a doctor if you get sick or carry you back to the hostel after you've passed out in a bar); money saved when staying in double rooms and taking taxis. For many, though, a travel partner's most important role is offering **moral support** for the never-ending onslaught of new situations to face. And helping avoid the fairly frequent party-of-one meals or having your ear bent by some garrulous locals.

How it can risk your friendship

Twenty-four hours a day of reassurance and sharing for months on end can put a serious strain on any relationship. Having to make decisions constantly, often in uncomfortable conditions, can strain the tightest bonds. Remember: **compromise** means that on this "trip of a lifetime" you probably won't get to see everything you want, and certainly not at your own pace. Just because you're the best of friends, or even partners, there is no guarantee you'll travel well together. Something else for friends traveling together to keep in mind: if you think it would be nice to stumble upon some romance on the road, you better pray you meet twins going in the same direction, because your friend isn't going to want to hang around while you fall in love.

How to keep the travel friendship from unraveling

If you do decide to go with another person, give yourselves the option of **separating for a while**. Even just a morning or afternoon apart every few days can be enough breathing room to sustain a travel relationship. A better bet,

3

SNOWBALLING INTO LARGE GROUPS

When I arrived at the train station in Madrid, I sat down at a bench beside two Australians. We started talking and decided we'd buy some beer while we waited for our train to Lisbon. One of the Aussies did the buying, so we still had plenty left over when we got on the train and were joined in the couchette by a Dutch couple and two Danish women. The night train turned into something of a night party and by the time our train pulled into Lisbon there was some sort of unwritten rule that we weren't going to split up.

First, we waited for the Aussies to find a bank machine, then the Dutch wanted to buy some stamps and send off a few postcards, while one of the Danes went in search of water. We waited. The Danes had already picked out a hotel they liked from the guidebook, but no one else thought it sounded that appealing, especially since it was on the other side of town and getting there would be a minor logistical hassle, short of chartering our own bus. So, we kept walking and making suggestions and the only ones we could agree on didn't have room for all seven of us. Meanwhile, it felt like I was part of some kind of tourist platoon walking down the street in V-formation with large backpacks. We'd been in Lisbon for well over two hours and at this rate it didn't seem like we'd ever be able to shed our packs, much less find a place to stay without renting an entire floor at the Hilton. I half-heartedly suggested we abandon the group lodging idea, find our own hostels and meet up for drinks later. The quick consensus had us all in rooms within twenty minutes.

Doug Lansky

however, is to build some solo time into the trip. Perhaps a week or two apart every other month: sign up for different courses or adventure activities in the same region or tackle a city separately.

What to look for in a travel partner

First, you want **someone with the same budget**. If you don't see eye to eye (or wallet to wallet), it's going to be a straining trip. If one person is going down the comfort route while the other is on a tight budget, you won't be staying at the same places, eating at the same restaurants or doing as many activities together. Or, more likely, you will, but neither of you will be having a good time doing it. The one on a tight budget will feel like a Scrooge, always getting their budget pushed too far, having to eat plain rice at a nice restaurant or sit outside while the other goes to a string of expensive museums. The one on the bigger budget will be roughing it more than they'd like, yet feel they're shamelessly indulging in front of their companion the entire time.

Does it make sense to find a travel partner before leaving?

Not really. Many people find the prospect of traveling alone so daunting they try to line up a travel partner before leaving. They place personal ads on websites and in travel magazines. These arranged partnerships may work out, but all too often they don't: heading out on the road together is like getting married after one blind date. There's no need to do this, especially without taking at least one short local trip together first. You'll meet **so many travelers** during your trip, it's much more natural and sensible to make friends first, travel for a while without commitment and only continue together as long as it's working out. This is extremely common and no one gets insulted if and when you part ways.

Traveling with a crowd

With more than two people you're going to find yourself taking votes, which is a fine way to run a democracy but a maddening way to set an itinerary. Whether you leave with a group or simply snowball into an international party on the move, beware: you're going to be about **as subtle as a G-20 protest rally**. Another potential problem is getting anything done. Before you can all head out to explore a famous museum together, a few people will have to use the bathroom, someone will have to fix a button that's about to fall off, someone else will need to mail a postcard, two others will have to stop at a bank and one will have to bargain for a souvenir on the way. What's more, you're going to have **a difficult time finding hostels, buses and restaurants** that can accommodate all of you. It's nice to find a social group. But instead of corralling yourself into a tour group, a better idea is to pick a bar or restaurant in the next town and a time and say you'll meet there. Then everyone breaks up and goes their own way.

3

Friendships on a long organized tour

This locks you in with a group for the duration of the tour, for good and bad. Such trips tend to bring out the best in some and the worst in others. Lifelong friendships are common, but so are group conflicts, and you won't be likely to see much about the latter in the brochure. So make sure you ask about how much time is available away from the group, then take advantage of it when you get the chance.

4

Costs and savings

How much does it cost to travel around Europe? Seems like a reasonable question, but it's a bit like asking how much a car costs. It depends very much on the type of car. Or in this case, the type of trip. A personalized, independent journey doesn't come with a standard price tag, so you're going to have to make some fundamental calculations based on your level of travel comfort, the activities you want to do, where you want to go and the length of your trip – and this chapter will show you how.

Without narrowing down these factors, you'll have a hard time getting within €2000 of an accurate figure on a three-month-long trip. Why? Take a typical European budget of €50 per day, plus €700 for a plane ticket (if you're flying from the US or Canada in the summer), €1037 for a three-month youth Eurail ticket, €300 for insurance and €400-worth of gear, and you get a total of around €7000. If you stop and work at, say, an ecological farm for two weeks, you're down to €6000, plus whatever you manage to earn. If you stay with relatives/pen pals for a week and spend a week in a cheap hangout collecting your thoughts (and a tan), you're down to €5600. If you confine your travels exclusively to cheaper countries and use other budgeting tricks to bring your daily rate down by €10, and you use a two-month Flexi Rail pass coupled with additional local transport that you pay for along the way, that

---

STARTING COSTS

Backpack: €140–220/£100–155/$155–240
Travel gear, toiletries, medical kit, emergency kit (depending on what you have already): €140–450/£100–320/$155–495
Insurance for twelve months: €380–900/£270–640/$420–1000
Vaccinations: Not required, though you'll probably want protection from Hepatitis A if heading to less-developed areas like rural parts of Turkey.
Two-month Youth Flexi Pass with ten days of travel: €446/£316/$491
Return plane ticket to Europe: €700/£500/$750
Approximate total: €2250/£1600/$2500

will cut your costs down to €4600. Conversely, if you decide to have two nice meals a week, stay in two decent hotels a week and take two courses during your trip, you might be looking at a daily budget of €100, which would bump that original trip plan from €7000 to €11,500.

Daily costs on the road

Even with a rail or bus pass and plane ticket paid for, it's still possible to spend anywhere between €2500 and €25,000 on a three-month trip. It all depends on how you want to live while you're there (see box, pp.64–65). So, you can either make do with what you have or gather more funds before you depart.

How do you travel cheaper?

Without a number of budget tricks, you may end up traveling on a high-end budget while only getting midrange value. The key to saving money on the road is not to concentrate exclusively on the big expenditures, but to find **small savings** along every step of the way. Beyond picking countries where your funds will last longer, savvy saving is about using a combination of tricks and making a deliberate lifestyle adjustment that rations out the creature comforts, or drops them altogether. People love to spend countless hours surfing the web and calling around to find the cheapest ticket to Europe. Of course, you don't want to end up paying more than the guy sitting next to you on the plane, but don't knock yourself out in a massive effort that will not likely save you more than €50–200. Why? That's not where the real savings are found. With some self-discipline and a few budget tips, you can reduce your daily budget by as much as €30. Over a three-month-long trip, that's a saving of €2700. Even on a one-month trip, that's €900 you can leave in the bank.

4

Discount cards

There's no magic wand to wave and guarantee savings everywhere you go, but for €4–23 (depending on the country of issue) the widely accepted International Student Identity Card (ISIC) comes close (ⓦisic.org). There are also youth cards (for under-26s) and teacher cards issued by the same organization that offer similar discounts. These provide significant deals for museums, local transport passes, plane tickets and more. You may very well make up the cost of the card on the flight over. The trick is remembering to ask for the discount. It won't help you much in restaurants, but nearly anywhere a ticket is required be sure to ask. Also, use it as a backup ID card you can leave behind when renting bikes and so on.

Another popular card is the Hostelling International Card (€3.50 per night – six nights will earn you membership – or €18 for immediate membership; ⓦhihostels.com). See "When you arrive" (p.129) to find out if you like the sound of hosteling. If you want to get this card, you'll need to do so in your home country before leaving. With it, you get discounts on about 2000 affiliated hostels around Europe, plus reductions on transport, including discounted car rental, bus and train travel. The card will pay for itself within four nights. The downside is that you can get many of the same transport discounts with an ISIC or youth card, and these official hostels don't pack the party atmosphere of the private hostels and are often not centrally located. But if you're hoping to get some peaceful sleep, they can be ideal.

Once on the road, you may find you're staying at a number of VIP-affiliated private hostels (there are over four hundred across Europe). If so, you might as well pick up a VIP Backpackers membership card (ⓦvipbackpackers.com) and start getting roughly five percent discounts per night – that is, if you think you'll use it more than forty nights, which is what it takes to earn back the card's value.

Flights

The "Getting to Europe and traveling around" chapter (see p.35) has more details on how to get the cheapest flight, but a good basic guideline to follow before booking any flights is to do a little checking on your own so you'll know a good price when you see one. Start looking around on the web (see p.334), and check out the lowest published fares for a particular flight. Then, all things being relatively equal, book with a well-informed travel agent and get their email address and phone number. The advantages of using an experienced travel agent are twofold: they are aware of the finer points that most travelers overlook, such as ease of airport connections, and they are able to access considerably cheaper fares.

4

TOP TEN THINGS YOU CAN DO TO SAVE MONEY

1. **Couchsurf.** Use this network of people willing to let you stay for free each night (see p.68).
2. **Spend more time in countries/cities where your money will last you longer.** It's cheaper in rural Portugal than central Paris.
3. **Eat in.** Dine on supermarket food and cook in hostels or with the people you Couchsurf with.
4. **Work along the way.** Take small jobs to earn a bit of cash as you go.
5. **Hitchhike.** Rough Guides can't officially endorse hitching, but there are safe and quick ways to do it.
6. **Fly into hub cities rather than smaller places at the start and end of your trip.** For example, think Rome, not Florence; London, not Edinburgh.
7. **Check the web on the cheap.** Most hostels and many cafés offer free wi-fi, but if you want a comfortable and free place to surf with a keyboard, the local library often offers desktops.
8. **Limit your cell phone charges.** Use voice mail, text messages and free (or cheap) internet calling services like Skype.
9. **Use discount cards.** Some, like the International Student ID card, can earn back the investment in a few days if you remember to ask for the discounts.
10. **Minimize cash withdrawals.** Those ATM fees add up, so figure out what you think you'll need before you tap a nice round number.

WHERE YOU CAN STRETCH YOUR MONEY

Some countries are more expensive than others. Here's how they stack up based on a statistical ranking of consumable prices.

COST INDEX

Top 10 most expensive countries

Switzerland 154
Norway 148
Denmark 138
Sweden 125
Finland 123
United Kingdom 122
Luxembourg 120
Ireland 121
Iceland 117

Midrange countries

The Netherlands 111
Belgium 109
France 108
Austria 107
Italy 102
Germany 102
Spain 93
Cyprus 89
Greece 86
Slovenia 83
Malta 82
Portugal 81
Estonia 79

Cheapest countries

Latvia 72
Slovakia 69
Croatia 67
Czech Republic 64
Lithuania 64
Turkey 61
Hungary 57
Montenegro 57
Poland 56
Romania 54
Bosnia-Herzegovina 53
Serbia 53
Albania 50
Bulgaria 48

EU28 average = 100
Source: Eurostat, 2014

Typical hostel dorm-room bed
€15 cheap countries – €25 expensive countries

4

A FEW THINGS TO CONSIDER:

Sweden and Norway have free camping rights. France and Italy have more museums you're likely to pay for. And, in the summer, you'll likely be buying more drinks and ice cream in southern Europe's sweltering heat. Just as you might even be more likely to splash out for an air-conditioned room. Also, in the Scandinavian countries, alcohol is very expensive (helping push up the consumables index) so if you don't drink, or don't drink much, they're more affordable. Since there's not a huge difference in the range of the cheapest supermarket food, these things can make a significant difference.

Rail passes

Most Europe **rail passes** can only be purchased in your home country, but if you buy online this isn't such a problem. If you're already in Europe, or on your way there, you can order a pass online (check out ⓦ raileurope.com, ⓦ railpass.com and ⓦ interrail.com), have it sent to your parents or friends and then get them to forward it to you. The more difficult task is selecting the right one. You can't bargain your way to a cheaper rail pass, but there are several ways to get more for your money:

CALCULATING YOUR DAILY BUDGET

Select your level of comfort from the list below, then figure out how many weeks or months you plan to travel and which countries you plan to spend the most time in, then add up the costs. For example, using the information below for a three-month trip, if you plan to spend one month in Norway on a low-end budget (€1300), one month in Spain on a medium budget (€1700) and one month in Romania on an upper budget (€2000), it will tally up to a total of €5000 for three months.

Wherever you go, your daily budget will reduce significantly if you Couchsurf.

LOW-END BUDGET

Accommodation: sleeping in hostel dormitory rooms, sharing rooms in the very cheapest hotels (no matter how bad the guidebook description), camping or renting a tent at campgrounds, sleeping on trains and buses.

Transport: your rail or bus pass can be supplemented with some hitchhiking or very short local bus rides, plus a flight or two under €30.

Food: eating cheap food purchased at supermarkets, and the lowest-priced side dishes at budget restaurants or at street stalls.

Lifestyle: no clubbing and nothing more than the occasional beer. Limited museum visits and no leisurely drinks at nice cafés. Consequently more time could be spent at journal writing, sketching and digital photography.

Low-end budget expenses:
Expensive country: daily €42; monthly €1300
Midrange country: daily €36; monthly €1100
Cheap country: daily €28; monthly €850

MIDDLE BUDGET

Accommodation: cheapest digs, occasionally sharing a two-person room and sleeping on a train or bus without reserved bed.

Transport: bus or rail pass can be supplemented by occasional hitching, but more often side-trips just under one hour by train or bus, plus one or two flights under €55.

Food: eating cheap food purchased at supermarkets and at budget restaurants.

Lifestyle: a few coffees a week at nice cafés. Museums are not limited but adventure activities are. The occasional night on the town, but not more than one reasonably priced drink per day.

- If you plan to stay in one spot for a while, try to time it at the beginning or end of your journey so your active pass isn't sitting idle more than it need be.
- Consider a Flexi Pass (certain number of travel days allowed within a fixed time period) instead of an unlimited travel pass. You don't want to spend every day on the train anyway.
- Supplement a Flexi Pass with cheap, shorter trips. If you calculate the per-day value of a Flexi Pass, it's around €35–40. If you're only traveling, say, the 97km from Florence to Siena in Italy, it's going to be cheaper to buy a second-class ticket at the window and save travel days on your pass. Typically, this is true if the journey lasts less than an hour and you're not on a high-speed train.
- Check for weekend deals before using your Flexi Pass. In Germany, for example, you can land bargains with Deutsche Bahn's "Schönes-

Middle budget expenses:
Expensive country: daily €72; monthly €2200
Midrange country: daily €60; monthly €1800
Cheap country: daily €50; monthly €1500

UPPER BUDGET

Accommodation: occasional splurge on decent budget hotel; otherwise, private rooms in hostels.

Transport: rail or bus pass can be supplemented by a few additional days of travel. Train beds on overnight journeys.

Food: one decent restaurant meal per day.

Lifestyle: unlimited coffee, liberal drinking, two nights out per week and several adventure activities during the trip.

Upper budget expenses:
Expensive country: daily €110; monthly €3300
Midrange country: daily €95; monthly €2850
Cheap country: daily €75; monthly €2250

HIGH-END BUDGET

Accommodation: quaint hotels and B&Bs.

Transport: comfortable sleepers on night trains; high-speed trains with mandatory reservation supplements; some taxis in cities; plane travel for short trips to other parts of Europe.

Food: eating out two meals a day at moderately priced restaurants; inexpensive wine with dinner and occasional beer or wine with lunch.

Lifestyle: concerts and clubbing three nights a week, accompanied by moderate drinking; almost daily stops in cafés for coffee and snacks; no limit on museums and occasional adventure activities.

High-end budget expenses:
Expensive country: daily €220; monthly €6600
Midrange country: daily €190; monthly €5700
Cheap country: daily €135; monthly €4050

4

Wochenende" ("Happy Weekend") ticket.

- Don't be afraid to use flights just because you have a rail ticket. You need to balance this, of course, with your environmental philosophy. But you'd spend a few days of your trip on the train (and use up a few days of your rail pass, plus some not-so-ecological packaged food and drinks) to get, for example, from London to Portugal or Greece. With budget airlines practically giving tickets away, chances are you can find a one-way flight for less than €55, possibly even less than €35. That will save you time and roughly €70-worth of travel on your flexi rail pass; not needing to pay overnight and reserved-seating supplements will push the total saving to over €110.

- As a rule of thumb, the less flexible the rail pass, the cheaper it is. In other words, if you know more or less where you plan to go (and you don't feel obligated to hit every single region or country), you can get a much better deal. However, sometimes it's not much of a bargain. For example, a youth traveler can get ten travel days in two months in five adjoining countries for €398 with the Select Pass. To access all seventeen countries with the same number of travel days, it's just €452. €54 seems like good value for the extra flexibility.

- If you only want to travel in one country and can't decide which, know that some single-country passes cost more than others. In Portugal or Greece, you get three travel days within one month for €122 (first class); Hungary, eight days within one month for €260 (first class); and Sweden, three days within one month for €215 (second class).

Buses

Buses are going to be **cheaper than trains** almost every time. In England (home of Europe's most expensive trains), they'll be roughly one third of the cost. So, it's a good way to save some money. However, you can't get up and stretch your legs the same way. And, if you're using Busabout, you won't be rubbing elbows with the locals. If you're looking for travel or party partners, however, that can be a good thing. For bus passes, follow the same basic strategy as for rail passes.

4

HOW TO BENEFIT FROM THE SHARING ECONOMY

A range of new travel-related services is grabbing the limelight. And for good reason. They are typically cheaper, more convenient, more educational, more authentic and simply more fun than the traditional travel industry. A good sign that they're doing something clever is the crunching sound of toes being stepped on. Two of the companies grabbing the most headlines in the **shared-economy movement** – Uber and Airbnb – have faced repeated legal opposition to their industry-rattling business models.

The sharing economy is particularly well suited for travelers. Being able to tap excess capacity has long been a fantasy of pragmatic types. ("I know every house on this street has a washing machine, and I need to wash my clothes. Why can't we work something out?") The only way to get something like that together before was to knock on doors or put up a note at the local supermarket, and then hope for the best. Neither of which produced stellar results. Now, smartphones and apps make the connection possible, and more and more people are getting in on the action.

In the case of the pioneers at **Uber** (🛒 uber.com), the service is transportation. When you want to go someplace, you open the app on your smartphone and Uber will let you know which driver is closest to you and send him (or her) your way with a single tap on your phone. On the hospitality side, **Couchsurfing** (see p.68) shook things up well over a decade ago by matching travelers with people who didn't mind letting travelers spend the night. Millions of backpackers have taken advantage of this, but there are understandably many who want a bit more privacy, and don't mind paying for it. Enter **Airbnb** (🛒 airbnb.com), which does exactly that. For a fairly reasonable price, it opens doors (literally) to thousands of unique homes you never would have access to otherwise. And there is nothing to stop you from renting out parts of your own home, if your living situation allows it.

Accommodation – the biggest potential savings

Europe is equipped with some of the world's best hotels, and you could blow a month's budget (and then some) on a single night in any one of them. (One Swiss hotel has a suite that goes for over €31,000.)

Your guidebook and online research will steer you to the type of place you're after, but at this planning stage one of the best things you can do to save money on the road is prepare yourself for sleeping in no-star accommodation. (If you're traveling for over two months, accommodation will be your single largest expense, thus the first place to look for savings.) That means sleeping in dorm rooms when available, trying to share a room with another traveler if there are doubles with low rates, and not letting yourself be put off by places described in your guidebook as basic, or even grungy. If you're armed with earplugs and a good sleep-sheet, you'll be fine. Or opt for Couchsurfing.

Free accommodation

In 2001, a 24-year-old Dutch traveler named Ramon Stoppelenburg hitchhiked his way around the world for two years "without any money" by setting up a website called ⓦletmestayforaday.com, through which he found sponsors and took up the 3577 invitations to stay which came in from 77

4

As with all infancy businesses, there is a certain amount of fuzziness concerning exactly what the sharing economy is and isn't. Some say that as long as you're charging for a service, you're not really sharing anything. It's still a monetary transaction and nothing like the "gift economy" it was supposed to be. But most often as a traveler, money is all you have to offer. Other times, you can put your **skills** to good use, for example mowing somebody's lawn in return for getting to do your laundry. Or tutor someone's kids in English so you can borrow their car over the weekend.

Apart from lower prices (although that is not always the case) and convenience, many curious travelers enjoy the interaction with "real" people, as opposed to tourism professionals. There are benefits both in authenticity and in the satisfaction of sidestepping The Man. Because for all the talk of consumer choice, the tourist economy has not been very interested in increasing the freedom for travelers that has come out of the sharing economy.

Having said this, the size of the sharing economy is still minuscule compared to the global tourism behemoth, causing some to accuse the industry of "Uber-reacting" when they sue and lobby for legal protection. Airbnb, for example, is said to have only one percent share of New York City's tourist accommodation market. And most business travelers will probably continue to prefer the non-adventurous reliability of a chain hotel. For the rest of us, it's as if an online swap shop for services has just opened up – one that's worth looking into both for savings and for more **authentic experiences** than the traditional tourist industry can provide.

The sharing economy as a whole (travel-related and not) has spawned a wider community of enthusiastic supporters. Many of them cluster on sites such as **Shareable** (ⓦshareable.net), where you can find news and insights, and make connections. New sharing economy sites are popping up all the time, but you can find some of the most useful ones in the Directory at the back of this book (see p.329).

countries. Seems like a cool idea? Well, these days, it's available for everyone. You may have heard of it; it's called **Couchsurfing**, and as well as being a great way to meet locals, it's probably the single most effective thing you can do to save money during your trip.

At the original site ⓦcouchsurfing.com and the similar sites that have since sprung up (see the Directory at the back of this book for more), you'll find a network of people willing to host travelers for free, and a network of travelers happy to get a free place to crash. It has proven overwhelmingly popular with younger travelers, and now has over ten million members around the world. It works like this: you register your "couch" for free and agree to let travelers stay for free when it's convenient for you; in return, you get access to everyone else's sofas or guest rooms.

If you don't mind staying in one place a bit longer, you might consider a house-sit via ⓦcaretaker.org. For an annual membership fee you get access to a list of homeowners looking for someone to water their plants, turn the lights on and off, feed the family pet or help keep an eye on grandma. Some will even pay you for your house-sitting skills.

Flat rentals

Another route is to rent someone's flat or even just a room in it. Airbnb (ⓦairbnb.com; see box, pp.66–67) jumpstarted an entire industry and turned almost everyone into a potential B&B owner. It's a great way for hosts to augment their income and visitors to find a reasonably priced, authentic local place to crash.

Backyard rentals

Yes, you read that correctly. Thanks to the new website ⓦcampinmygarden.com, people are now renting space in their backyards for travelers who bring their own tents and just need a place to use the toilet and perhaps get access to wi-fi (all depends on what the owners specify they are willing to provide).

Other money-saving ideas for bottom-end digs

- Stay in small towns and rural areas – hostels and pensions in large cities pay the most rent, and pass the cost on to travelers.
- Make a point of getting addresses of travelers you meet (or just befriend them on Facebook) then stay with them if you're heading to their home town or city. Try to give a few days' or weeks' notice. Taking a photo of yourself with them is a good idea in this respect – it's nice to attach a picture of you together when you request a place to stay. They might have offered their address to dozens of travelers or had a bit too much to drink and have trouble remembering your name when you make contact.
- Cram the rooms full. Go for a quad and find three other travelers to take up the extra beds so you all get a better deal than sleeping in a single or double room.
- Head to campgrounds just out of town and rent their walk-in tents (with real beds).
- Check out housing at universities over the summer. Empty dorm rooms are often rented out at cut-rate prices.

- In eastern European countries, you can find deals at train stations; often, old ladies wait around to try to rent out their spare rooms (typically those no longer occupied by their adult children) to travelers.
- If staying in private rooms, accepting one without a private WC and shower can save you €20–30 per night.
- Hang out around the students' union and look for a friendly group. Introduce yourself and ask if you can crash on someone's floor or sofa in exchange for a beer or two, plus free accommodation at your parents' home if they ever get there. Women can do this safely as well (and will likely have an easier time of it) by approaching a group of women.
- Stay with relatives (no matter how distant) and friends of friends.

Museums

With the abundance of world-class museums Europe has to offer, chances are you're going to be visiting several. Look into multi-museum passes if you know you'll be visiting a few in the same town. The Paris Museum Pass (ⓦen .parismuseumpass.com), for example, pays for itself in just a few visits and lets you stroll by the snaking lines. Even a single pass to the Louvre is worth picking up in advance, if only to avoid the long lines during peak season. Check **online** before visiting any major museum.

4

BUDGETITIS SYNDROME

When you first start traveling, **spending comes naturally**. Almost too naturally. A beer here, a T-shirt there, a few museum passes, a nice meal. Maybe you're too caught up in the excitement of arriving or spending to cushion your landing into a new culture. Whatever the case, after a few days or weeks, many realize they're over budget and begin to feel the stress of a money belt getting thinner. The natural response to this relentless stream of expenditure is an attempt to stem the outflow. And when travelers meet and compare notes, boasting rights go to the one surviving on the lowest funds. When it gets competitive, that's when **budgetitis** really sets in. Symptoms include: walking an extra twenty minutes to find a bread shop whose loaves are three cents cheaper; full-blown arguments with taxi drivers over the equivalent of 25 cents; and skipping a meal because the local supermarket prices seem a little high. In extreme cases, travelers might party all night (without drinking… well, not much), then sleep in a park during the day. They'll only travel by hitchhiking and show up at soup kitchens for food, paying with the minimum donation. This is one of the most common budget travel afflictions (followed closely by exaggerated storytelling), and at some point during a long trip you'll likely suffer from it yourself.

When you sit back and think about your trip in a year or two, you won't be rejoicing over the extra three euros you have in your pocket: with budgetitis, many rationalize spending hundreds to get there, plus lodging and food, then not coughing up the last few euros for the thing they had come to see.

If you can sense this happening, you have to take a step back and remember why you're traveling. It's fine to save money while you're on the road, but you need to balance this with the fact that you're not traveling in order to save money. Better to come home a week or two early and suffer a little less.

Food

Cozy restaurants and old-world cafés are tempting places to relax, socialize with other travelers and people-watch. They're also nice places to run down your budget: those double café lattes add up in a hurry. And fleeing to *McDonald's* isn't always going to help. Switzerland has, on average, the world's most expensive *McDonald's* – over €6 for a Big Mac. Minimizing these little luxuries is the first unpleasant step. Here are a few others:

- Stick to restaurants that don't take credit cards or have English menus. Places smart enough to do this are usually savvy enough to jack up their prices as well. Another approach is to choose places where you don't see other foreigners.
- Look for restaurants near universities. Students worldwide have little money for eating, and there's almost always a cottage industry set up to serve them.
- Sample the street food, find a few favorites, and make meals out of them. Two full days of street- or vendor-bought meals costs the equivalent of one decent restaurant meal.
- Cook in hostels. Search out hostels with kitchen access. It's always cheaper to cook as a group, so don't be afraid to stick your head into the lounge and ask if anyone wants to pitch in and make a communal dinner.
- Supermarket-dining works. You'll soon learn how to survive on fruit, yogurt, sandwiches and potato chips.
- Try the samples. During weekends and busy shopping times in large supermarkets in developed countries, you can often find a tremendous range of free samples available. With a little luck, you can get an entire meal, as long as you don't mind getting it in fifteen small servings.
- Walk for ten minutes away from major tourist areas and watch the prices drop by the block.
- To increase your options in markets, keep a kit of salt, pepper, olive oil, knife and spoon in a small container, and use it to prepare salads and the like.
- Think pizza. In Italy and elsewhere, pizzas come in just one size, which more than covers a typical plate. These single servings provide some of the best deals in Europe and can typically be had for €5–8. If you've got a small appetite, they're enough for two.
- If you want a recommendation, ask a construction worker. They're often on a limited budget and know where to find a filling meal nearby.
- Bring food onto trains. Trains throughout the world are united by one common theme: bad food at ridiculous prices. Bring more than you think you'll need, plus water.
- Hit the buffets and salad bars: look for a cheap salad bar or buffet and then stack your plate about a meter high. This may require some advanced engineering skills.
- Pizza gathering – not officially recommended, but it works. Travelers have been known to hang out in franchise pizza joints, order a small salad, then grab the untouched slices from other tables when groups get up to leave.

- Order economically. A restaurant is a great place to rest your feet and socialize, but to keep the bill down consider ordering one appetizer and complementing it with a few filling side dishes instead of a main meal.
- Eat seasonal. Fruits and veggies getting shipped in out of season aren't as fresh, taste worse and cost more.
- Gallery openings typically serve free wine and hors d'oeuvres, but you'll need to make yourself presentable enough to enter.

> **THE PRICE OF SAVINGS**
>
> I was in Crete in a picturesque little fishing port. I had my watch-every-penny mindset going, so when a festive outdoor taverna wanted to charge me $2 for a cold beer, I passed on the apparent rip-off and bought a warm one at a liquor store for 70 cents and sat on the curb and drank it – a savvy budget victory. Now, thirteen years later, I've got an extra $1.30 in my bank account… and my memories from that evening are immeasurably poorer.
>
> John Flinn, Travel editor,
> San Francisco Chronicle

Saving on restrooms

There are savings to be had here, and not just from trying to hold on to it. It's not often you'll encounter a squatter, or hole in the floor where the toilet is supposed to be, but you'll run into restroom attendants everywhere who'll charge for use of their facilities, or automatic WCs that require coin activation.

At some point you'll need to use one, so carry change. Tipping the attendant is often optional, but if you can splash a few small coins in the cup it at least sounds generous. Some have specific fees for things like toilet paper or hand towels and some have outrageous admission rates, as much as €1, no matter what you plan to do.

It's best to find free toilets, though they're not always easy to come by. *McDonald's*, traditionally one of the most popular free bathroom options, have more recently set up security measures – typically, keypad locks with codes only available to paying customers. If you're reasonably presentable and not toting a large backpack that denotes you as a budget traveler, you might be able to pop into a nice hotel. If questioned by the doorman, you can say that you're scouting the place for your parents or checking out the restaurant's menu as a possible dining option that evening. One of the best options, especially while waiting in train stations where you almost always have to pay for toilet services, is to spot a train that isn't due to depart for a while, then hop aboard, use the restroom and hop back off.

What's the deal with tipping?

If you can figure out a formula that works for tipping across Europe, you should probably be working at NASA or cracking codes for MI6. Tipping in Europe is a confusing affair. In some upscale environments, you might be giving a waiter ten to fifteen percent, while in that same country it would be perfectly fine to leave nothing at a lower-end café.

4

To generalize, tipping in Europe at the lower levels of service is more about **rounding up** and token tips than straight percentages. For instance, if your lunch tab comes to €5.60, you might leave an even €6. With a tab of €9.80, round up to €10 for service you could have just as easily done without. In some places, it's just as appropriate to leave a fifty cent or €1 coin, even if that works out to be a two percent tip. The same basic concept applies for taxi rides. If the ride comes to exactly €5, you're fine without a tip (unless carrying bags or some other service was provided). If it's €5.70, you should probably just pay €6 and tell the driver to keep the change. In a crunch, you can always ask a fellow diner (especially if you're treating yourself to a meal in a swanky restaurant, where the tip will more likely be ten to twelve percent) or your hotel concierge for some guidance. But the final decision is up to you. Give what you feel is appropriate and leave the restaurant or cab with confidence.

Changing money

Aside from using an ATM, changing money isn't as straightforward as money changers would like you to believe. In fact, in many cases it's a mathematical mind-twister and, like in Vegas, the house has you by the short and curlies. There are a few tips that will help keep more money in your pocket after the transaction is over:

- Avoid changing money at hotels, hostels and bureaux de change. They're well situated, have great opening hours and charge you a fortune for all that convenience.
- Always compare before changing money. The rates can differ even on the same street. Check banks or the post office.
- When you shop around, **don't be fooled by nice rates**. Money changers specialize in fee juggling. They use a few mechanisms to make sure they get your money. They either use a flat fee (as a minimum) or a percentage of the total amount changed. Which one you use often depends on the amount you're changing. Typically, if you're exchanging a lot of money (say €500), the minimum fee will be irrelevant so you should look at rates and commissions. If it's a small amount, you'll want to pay closer attention to the minimum fee and rate.
- Look for the buy rate and sell rate. The difference (exchanger's profit) is probably around five percent. If it's more or they don't show it, something may be fishy.
- **Minimize transactions**. Take a moment to calculate what you'll need, because every time you change cash or withdraw money from a bank machine, you're probably paying for the transaction (see p.121).
- If you're comfortable with high-tech solutions, try out a "social currency" site like **WeSwap** (ⓦweswap.com), which matches travelers crossing currency boundaries and gets them to change directly with each other. Their app can handle up to sixteen currencies, all bouncing onto and off your WeSwap MasterCard as you trade.

WATCH FOR CONS AND EXTRA FEES

At restaurants, waiters may play more tricks than just serving warm soft drinks and seeming to squeeze in a round of golf before getting the food to your table. They may also incorrectly add up the bill, conveniently in their favor. Always **double-check** it.

One popular gambit in tourist areas is to place a bread roll on your table right when you sit down, then charge a whopping fee for it if you so much as breathe on it. If you're not interested, have them take it away. It may be as tasty as a stone, but it's difficult to stare at when hungry.

If you're trying to have an **inexpensive meal**, make sure you don't pick a place with a cover charge – a fee for just sitting down at the table. Feel free to ask if there is such a fee (sometimes called a "service fee"). If there isn't, make sure it doesn't magically appear on the bill.

If the menu says that tax is included in the prices, they shouldn't be adding the tax fee on top of the total price.

How to bargain like a pro

You can't walk into a European shopping center and start bargaining for food. But there are a number of excellent handicraft and knick-knack markets across the continent where you can barter, and these offer some of the best shopping you'll find. You can also negotiate your hostel/hotel room rate down during off-season and negotiate book swaps – the basic bargaining concept is the same for all of these.

The golden rule of bargaining is to keep a smile on your face. It's OK to be firm with your offer, even walk away at an impasse, but if you think of it as a game and keep the atmosphere light and friendly, it's hard to go wrong. The other rule is not to start bargaining unless you're truly interested – it's not fair to waste the seller's time.

Getting an excellent price on an item, however, is another story. The sellers are the experts, but you hold the cash, so you're in control. The first thing to do is find out from a local or fellow traveler who's familiar with the market what the **real going rate** is for the products you like. In Europe, there typically isn't a special price for locals, so you have one less barrier to hurdle. Now you've got a goal. More importantly, this little bit of research will help you recognize any serious price gouging. That is, sometimes vendors, just for sport, like to see how much they can get for an item and may throw out a completely outlandish price and see if you'll take the bait.

The next step is to **take a look at** what you're wearing. It's hard to haggle a price down with a ring on every other finger or Apple Watch on your wrist. Leave the tablet, jewelry and the €200 Gore-Tex jacket in the hotel room (or in your daypack) if you know you're heading to a market to do some bargaining. Then **go early**. Many vendors share the belief that a sale early in the day will bring them good fortune, so they may be more likely to lower their prices than they would otherwise. This also increases your chances

4

that you'll be alone with the vendor, which works to your advantage. With other potential customers browsing within earshot, the vendor may feel pressure to keep prices high.

The next step may be the most difficult: **hide the true extent of your interest**. That is, you don't want to hold something up to show your travel partner and say: "Look at this. It's perfect!" The vendors may not be fluent in English, but this exchange won't escape them. You might start out by lifting the item you're interested in for a moment and casually asking how much it costs. They'll either respond with an inflated price, a decent price or this question: "How much will you give me for it?" If you've done your research, you're in good shape for any of these. If you get an inflated price, make an offer that's equally below your target price. The vendor will immediately dismiss it as unfair, and you – here's where that smile really comes in handy – can say: "Maybe we could start the bargaining over again, but this time at a more realistic level." Your next offer should be 5–10 percent under your target price. On the other hand, if the vendor starts the bargaining at a very reasonable level, don't expect it to go down much. Pick a price just under your target and be prepared to raise it fairly quickly. Finally, if you're asked to start the bidding, you might say: "Actually, I spoke to a few people who bought these as gifts, and they told me I shouldn't pay more than €X." The vendor will immediately know that you've been doing your homework, but may not be ready to give it up to you at that price. If that's the sense you get, you can say: "Perhaps that's the local price I heard about. As a visitor to your country, I'd be willing to give you a little more." Then offer a price that's one or two percent higher.

Other bargaining tools

Another trick is to point out the **small, obvious flaws** in the item – cracked glazing, discoloring, etc. This can quickly put vendors on the defensive, so a cleverer way to introduce it is (assuming there are several identical items) simply to pick up another one you'd be happy with that has essentially the same minor flaws and say, "How about if I take this one instead, which has some cracks. Surely it's worth less than the other one?" Few vendors will take up the argument that the first one you had was just as flawed. But if they do,

---

BASIC EXCHANGE MATH YOU NEED TO LEARN

Let's say you want to change $100 to euros. Bank #1 is offering €0.70 to the dollar with a two percent **commission** and a €1 **minimum fee**. Bank #2 is offering €0.74 to the dollar with a 1.5 percent commission and a €3 minimum fee. And bank #3 is offering €0.76 to the dollar with a six percent commission and no minimum fee. At bank #1, you'll get €68. At bank #2, you'll get €71. And at bank #3 (the one with the misleading best exchange rate) you'll get €70. Earning €3 for a minute of elementary-level math may sound OK on paper, but it seems like cruel and unusual punishment when you're there. Of course, you can bypass all of this with a cash machine or a social currency site (see p.72).

you've got a small advantage. "Since you yourself agree that this product is flawed, perhaps you'd be willing to part with it at a fairer rate?"

A more businesslike approach is to introduce yourself to the vendor and tell them that you're considering doing all of your shopping in their boutique and try to get a **bulk discount**. After some small talk, the vendor will probably let you steer the conversation to prices. If you're still not close by the second round, let them know that you're sorry it doesn't sound like it's working out and thank them for their time. They've already put some time into the deal and won't want to lose a fairly substantial customer, so chances are they probably won't let you go that easily.

In the end, it should be a win-win experience. And if you keep the negotiation friendly, **keep your cool** and only buy at a price you feel good about, it will be. Despite any dramatic claims of losing money, a vendor will never sell you merchandise at a loss, so you shouldn't leave feeling guilty that you obtained an unjustly low price.

4

5

Working, volunteering and studying

If you're European, your passport is a ticket to landing jobs around the continent. If you don't have an EU passport, you might find yourself in this typical scenario: you've finished a semester of studies in Europe, you've got two months to bounce around before you need to return home, and you've got some kind of rail or bus pass burning a hole in your pocket with sixteen major cities, twelve beaches and fourteen museums on your wish list. Here are two reasonable questions to ask: is there really time to find a job, volunteer or pick up a new skill? And why should I bother?

You should at least consider making the time. Especially if you want a truly unique, enriching travel experience. Because, no matter how many museums and handicraft markets you hit, no matter how many kilometers you log on buses, trains and ferries, no matter how little you pay for your night's accommodation, you're not likely to get under the skin of a place until you stop and engage yourself. Whether you're working, volunteering or studying, all it takes is some ongoing interaction with locals to develop a connection and make some friends. If you've studied, consider the relationship you've had with your closer classmates compared to the one you've had with people you've shared a bus ride with. It's a different level entirely. Some jobs, volunteer projects and courses immerse you in the culture more than others, and it's not always easy to tell in advance which will and which won't, but at least you'll still be earning money, helping others or learning a skill – not a bad way to pass your time in Europe.

Note to EU passport holders: you may wish to skip ahead to the section on choosing and finding a job.

Working

For years travelers have been running out of money before they've exhausted their wanderlust. Every day, people hit the road with just a few months' or weeks' worth of cash in their pockets. Depending on your age, nationality and professional skills, there are countless options available to keep yourself financially afloat.

Bad news first: the European Union doesn't really want non-EU passport holders to waltz over and land a job. Especially Americans. For New Zealanders, Canadians and Aussies, there are special visas called "working holiday visas" that make things quite convenient (see p.78). Without such agreements, even a very short-term job can come with Himalayan hurdles. Now the good news: you can still get a job almost anywhere.

For a **legal job**, the most important thing to remember is that you need to enter the European country you'll be working in with the proper stamps and papers to be eligible for work. If you don't, and find a job after arriving, you'll still have to return home, fix the paperwork, and then re-enter the country with all your documents in order. Some organizations can help you with the application forms, especially if you're a student or recent graduate.

Work placements for students and recent grads

Several agencies have popped up to help students and recent graduates (those who received a degree within the last four months) get special visas. These agencies apply mostly to Americans, but they can help just about anyone if the country you want to work in doesn't have some sort of holiday work-visa arrangement with your country. In which case, they provide the easiest way of taking care of the paperwork. You still have to pound the pavement and find your own job (one where the employer doesn't mind taking you on for just a few months), but at least you can show you've got a work permit. The drawback is that this handy red-tape-cutting service doesn't come free. In fact, it may run you about a month's wages: €500. Typically, the short-term jobs you'll be able to find aren't going to come with meaty paychecks or bonuses. And you've still got to pay for accommodation and food. In other words, you'll be paying to wait tables full-time in Paris for two months, even if you speak fluent French. Other common jobs include au pair work and teaching English. If the paycheck isn't as important, some of these organizations offer help arranging interesting internships. You should probably think twice about handing over funds for this. You can call up the companies directly, say you're a student and that you want to work for free to get some first-hand experience, and no paperwork should be necessary.

- **American Scandinavian Foundation** ⓦamscan.org. Does exchange programs for Americans in research, study or practical training, as well as fellowships and cultural programs.
- **Bunac Working Adventures Worldwide** ⓦbunac.org/usa. Exactly what the name says. European programs are centered on Britain and Ireland,

5

but occasionally other countries are offered as well.

- **Council Exchanges** ⓦciee.org. Offers teach-abroad programs in Spain.
- **Cultural Vistas** ⓦculturalvistas.org. Programs in Germany, Russia, Switzerland and Spain aimed at young professionals seeking international experience.
- **InterExchange Work Abroad Programs** ⓦinterexchange.org. Programs for Americans and Canadians aged 18 and older in France, Germany, the Netherlands, Italy and Spain.
- **International Cooperative Education Program** ⓦicemenlo.com. Eight- to twelve-week paid internships in Belgium, Finland, France, Ireland, Germany, Poland, Spain, Switzerland and the UK for those with foreign language skills.

The "working holiday"

If you're between 18 and 30 years old and not American, you are eligible to seek employment while "on holiday" in the UK and several other countries. In the UK, the Youth Mobility Visa (£225) allows visitors aged 18–30 from Australia, New Zealand, Canada, Japan, Monaco, Hong Kong, Taiwan or South Korea to work for two years. You will have to prove that you have £1890 to qualify for the so-called "Tier 5 Visa", and you have to apply for it before you get to the UK. You also have to leave immediately when your two years is up (and the clock starts ticking the moment your visa is issued); and you can't have dependent children under the age of 18. You can always go back home and apply for a Tier 1 Visa (for highly skilled workers) or Tier 2 (for sponsored skilled workers), but these are much more expensive and involve more paperwork and waiting time.

"Working holidays" for Australians

For a UK visa, contact the UK embassy in Australia (ⓦukinaustralia.fco.gov .uk). In the rest of the EU, you have "working holiday" arrangements with: Belgium, Cyprus, Denmark, Estonia, Finland, France, Germany, Ireland, Italy, Malta, the Netherlands, Norway, Sweden and Turkey. Check their embassy websites in your country for application information.

"Working holidays" for New Zealanders

For a UK visa, contact the UK embassy in New Zealand (ⓦukinnewzealand .fco.gov.uk). In the rest of the EU, you have "working holiday" arrangements with: Belgium, Czech Republic, Denmark, Estonia, Finland, France, Germany, Ireland, Italy, Latvia, Malta, the Netherlands, Norway, Poland, Slovakia, Slovenia, Spain and Sweden. Check out their embassy websites in your country for application info.

"Working holidays" for Canadians

For a UK visa, contact the UK embassy in Canada (ⓦukincanada.fco.gov .uk). In the rest of the EU, you have working holiday arrangements with: Austria, Belgium, Czech Republic, Denmark, Estonia, France, Germany,

Ireland, Italy, Latvia, Lithuania, the Netherlands, Norway, Poland, Slovakia, Sweden and Switzerland. Go to their embassy websites in your country for application info.

Britain's ancestry clause

If you're a Commonwealth citizen and you want to work in Britain and have a grandparent who was born in Britain or Northern Ireland (and you can prove it), you can apply for a special UK Ancestry Visa that enables you to live and work in Britain for an initial period of five years. Visit the website of your nearest British embassy for details.

Starting your job search online

It's not just au pair gigs and private English lessons. You can find IT jobs, translation positions, adventure-guiding jobs, fruit-picking work, wine jobs (grape picking and hauling grapes), ski resort posts and more. Your best starting point on the web is probably ⓦanyworkanywhere.com. Even though landing most holiday jobs involves sidewalk-pounding upon arrival, the web can still be of some help. Once you learn the basics below, you'll be able to fine-tune your web searching. See our tips on landing work (p.86) for more.

Direct employment

The hardest jobs to get are the ones that you set up on your own by applying directly to European companies before you leave. To get a job offer without an interview takes some serious legwork, luck or great connections – typically, all three, plus a low-budget miracle. That may mean starting with a bulk mailing of your CV (résumé) and cover letter followed by hours of overseas follow-up calls. Let's say you get a job offer. In order for the company to arrange a work visa for you, they need to be able to show the government that someone from their country or elsewhere in the EU couldn't do the job. Once you understand this position, you can better focus your job search to fit your unique skills. Say, for example, you've got web-programmer skills and have been doing campus promotions at your university. You'd have a good shot landing a job with a European company trying to target English-speaking university-age customers with a new website. And they'd have a good chance of getting you a work visa. Some creative thinking is in order to figure out what marketable skills (in addition to your English speaking and writing) will make you an appealing candidate and also make you an easy sell to the immigration bureau. At any rate, all such permissions must be arranged long before your arrival, so this is one of the first things you'll want to do when planning your trip.

Illegal work

If you do illegal work, you could very well – depending on the laws of that country, which are certainly worth looking into – find yourself slapped with a fine, thrown out of the country (guess who gets to pay for the ticket home?) or landed behind bars (picking up free language lessons from your cellmates!). With that little disclaimer out of the way, there are scores of employers who don't mind hiring unregistered foreign help and, from experience, know that the authorities will turn a blind eye. In fact, you may go to great lengths to secure a **work permit** only to be paid under the table. They often just like knowing you have a permit in case the police show up requesting documents.

Seasonal work

One of your best chances of turning up and landing a decent-paying job with no previous skills (or a work permit) is going to be taking advantage of the seasonal openings. It's largely a matter of being in the right place at the right time, and if you know what you're looking for it's easy to coordinate.

Ski jobs

Working in the Alps or Pyrenees can be a fantastic experience, especially if you find a job that allows you to put your skis on daily. Unfortunately, those precious jobs aren't as easy to land as you'd think. For a job, either apply in writing for work with a tour company in your country six to eight months in advance or arrive at your desired resort around mid-November and start walking the streets (the ski season runs from the beginning of December to May in most places, depending on snowfall for that year). Be especially careful about hiring yourself out as a freelance ski instructor – most resorts keep a keen eye out for unofficial lessons on the slopes and prosecute. Possible jobs include: ski tuning, rental-shop fittings, ski guiding, lift operator, bartender, dishwasher, table waiter, restaurant cook, chalet cook/housekeeping, childcare, singer/guitar player at bars, reception staff, maintenance staff, sales clerk, supply driver, bouncer and DJ. Countries with ski resorts include: Andorra, Austria, Bulgaria, France, Germany, Italy, Norway, Poland, Scotland, Slovakia, Slovenia, Spain, Sweden and Switzerland. If you want to find out a bit more on the web first, try ⓦnatives.co.uk or ⓦski-jobs.co.uk; or look up the resort you want to go to and send out your CV to shops around town. The largest ski resorts include:

- Chamonix ⓦchamonix.net
- Les Trois Vallées (Courchevel, Méribel, Val Thorens, all interconnected) ⓦles3vallees.com
- Val d'Isère ⓦvaldisere.com

For other ski areas, try ⓦresortsonline.com.

Summer resort work

For **summer resorts**, you may want to turn up a month or two before the season begins (March–May) to beat the rush for jobs, then go traveling regionally and return when the job starts. On the hotel/bar/restaurant side, women tend to have an easier time finding work. Common jobs include: camp counsellor for kids, bartender, waiter, hotel receptionist, hotel housekeeper, cook, baker, sales clerk, supply driver, singer/guitar player at bars, DJ, rental-shop clerk, cleaner, bouncer, guide, sports instructor, lifeguard, scuba instructor and campground maintainer.

Harvest season work

If you can eat it, you can probably find work picking it if you turn up at the **right place in the right season** – from strawberries to dates to apples. Most harvesting jobs are in the autumn (fall), but they can be found all summer long. The best place for pre-trip research is the internet: try ⓦfruitfuljobs.com and ⓦgrapepicking.co.uk. Pay is often based on the amount you pick, and it may take a few days to get up to speed. No one is going to remind you when to drink water or that you should protect yourself from the sun, so take care of that yourself. Bring a good hat, sun cream, and drink throughout the day. And remember to ask for adequate protection when pesticides and other noxious chemicals are sprayed.

Manual labor

Construction jobs tend to be underpaid and overworked. There's often a spot or two in cities where laborers show up each morning and get selected by employers. If no such place exists, or the competition is too fierce, look for large construction sites and ask for work directly from the foreman. There's also plenty of factory work; the nastier tasks usually come with a higher wage. If they don't, don't do them. Possible jobs include: house renovation, road building, landscaping, shrimp peeling and fish packing.

Working independently

Money-making opportunities for the creative entrepreneur are almost endless. You could discreetly sell cool drinks on a hot beach or cheap umbrellas on a busy street when it rains. And if you have a trade that allows you to work independently, even better. But unless you have a work permit, do find out about the penalties, **assess the risk** and keep a low profile. If you're looking for a street to perform on, think about good acoustics, an original act and a place where the police are kind (northern Europe tends to be popular in this regard). Often, small towns, with many pedestrian streets and few buskers (street performers), bring good fortune. Also, keep an eye out for festivals, which attract crowds with ample pocket change and time to stick around until the end of your act, when the hat gets passed. A clever performance with showmanship and a dose of humor will out-earn a talented musician nine out of ten days. Other possible jobs include: masseur/masseuse, private cook, private music instructor, street juggler, house cleaner, window washer, gardener, language tutor, jewelry street-seller, T-shirt designer and peddler, and promotional pamphlet distributor (to other travelers for local bars/hostels).

5 Teaching English

If English is your mother tongue, you have a university degree of some kind, can dress smartly and carry yourself with confidence, you have a decent shot at landing a job without a TEFL or similar certificate. You can certainly hire yourself out as a private tutor. But there's a lot more to **teaching a language** than just being able to speak it, and any amount of instruction will be helpful. The problem is, the instruction isn't that cheap (€1050–1950) or quick (roughly 100hr of coursework), and not all programs are created equal. In Europe, the British-based CELTA (Certificate in English Language Teaching to Adults) is probably the most recognized brand of TEFL/TESOL certificates, and you can take them just about anywhere. (Quick decoder: TEFL is "Teaching English as a Foreign Language" and TESOL is "Teaching English for Speakers of Other Languages" – basically the same thing.) If you decide you want to go after a TEFL certificate, you have a few options:

- **Get it near where you live** – search ⓦtefl.com for the closest location.
- **Get a certificate online** – a bit shady and probably not as useful in terms of practice and feedback.
- **Take a CELTA or other reliable course in the city or country you want to work in** – you can find out the reputable courses by asking local employers or checking out a TEFL forum like the one at Dave's ESL Café (ⓦeslcafe.com), a good source for general job searching and classroom-teaching tips and lessons. This is probably the best option because it means spending more time in the country, and the local language schools have the best job-placement connections. In addition to CELTA, Trinity College London programs (ⓦtrinitycollege.com) are also well known.
- **Go where it's a bit cheaper to get a TEFL degree** – in places such as Thailand or Egypt, you may get accommodation thrown in for free. (If you're paying €20 a night for six weeks in Europe, that's €840. And you can probably buy a return ticket from London to Bangkok for less than that. Try ⓦteflinternational.com.)

In Europe, most of the jobs these days can be found in eastern and central Europe, where the TEFL isn't quite as critical. If you do have a TEFL certificate, though, you'll probably land a better job or beat unqualified competition, and find it easier in the classroom than if you were winging it. Is it worth the money and time to make that "livable wage"? That's your call. But you probably needn't bother with the expensive weekend introductory course; those who require a real certificate won't be impressed. Most of the best jobs require a six- to twelve-month contract to prevent you from skipping out and leaving their students with verbs unconjugated and participles dangling.

Teaching diving

Europe may not be anyone's top pick for an exciting dive, but Europeans still want to get certified, and often before they go on holiday. With a Divemaster certification (⍟padi.com), you may be able to find some work, especially at swimming pools in large cities, provided you speak the language. Unlike resorts, schools prefer people for longer stretches, so that may make things a bit more challenging on a traveler's schedule. Greece, Cyprus, Croatia, Malta and the Canary Islands offer the best diving. You might start by searching "PADI" and whatever city you're heading to. In terms of landing a job, most certified instructors have success making personal contact with schools or dive shops and get paid under the table for their work. Or they return later, once the proper work visa has been processed back home.

Telecommute

Depending on the nature of your job, you may be able to **reduce your workload** to part time and get the work done while you're on the road. Skills like translating, accounting and copy editing don't necessarily require a fixed address. Pack along a laptop if need be and back up your data on an external drive or the cloud (or both). Have a look at the book and blog *The 4-Hour Workweek* (⍟fourhourworkweek.com) by Timothy Ferriss for additional insights on making this work.

Journalism and photography

Travel writing and travel photography are very competitive fields, and in both cases, your chances of supplementing your income or supporting yourself while traveling will be greatly enhanced with well-honed skills from a course or formal education. No matter, however, how much skill you may possess, selling your material without an established track record is extremely tough.

But that's only if you go the traditional route. If you have a Facebook or Twitter account or are keeping a travel blog, you're already a travel writer. Several writers have launched themselves this way, or built up a following, then monetized their site with links, sponsored content and adverts (have a look at ⍟nomadicmatt.com, ⍟everything-everywhere.com and ⍟johnnyjet .com for examples). The competition is tough, so standing out from the crowd will take a good deal of effort (and possibly some decent programming, video and photography skills), but it can be done.

If you're serious about going the more traditional route, writing your way around the world, you'll want to give yourself a **head start** by making inroads in the industry before you go: get some articles or photos published (no matter what the subject), build a relationship with one or more editors and start putting your portfolio together.

Another popular approach, especially for photographers, is to document your trip and try to sell the images upon your return. This can certainly bring in some money, but generally very little, and you're not likely to get it until

5

long after you return. **Cold-calling an editor** just before you leave and asking if you can, despite your complete lack of experience, report your way around the globe, is a textbook example of how not to go about it.

Multinational jobs

If you happen to live near the headquarters of an international company, surf their website and find out where their overseas offices are located and what they do. If you've got some language skills or other marketable training that may interest them, try to arrange for an interview. If you don't live near the headquarters, that doesn't mean you need to give up just yet. Not all require you to interview at their central command center.

Wine jobs

There's everything from tasting to sales to grape picking to estate management to biology work. Try ⓦwinecountryjobs.org, or go to ⓦwineweb.com/mapeuro .html, get the contact info for European wineries and contact them directly.

IT jobs

There are hundreds of IT recruitment firms in just about every European country. If you want to go down that route, you might do an internet search with the name of the country you want to work in plus "IT jobs" or "IT recruitment" or "computer jobs." Otherwise, take a look at ⓦdice.com and ⓦeurosearch.net.

Au pair jobs

Assisting with children can, depending on the family, be a good arrangement. Live-in au pairs typically earn less in Europe than in the US, but rates are often adjusted if you have a college degree, childcare education, special language skills and great letters of recommendation. And, of course, if you work more hours or care for more children (for more than three children, wages should go up roughly ten percent for each child). Wages may also be slightly higher in major cities, where there's more competition. The workload varies from one family to the next, but for €70 a week you might expect about five hours of work per day for five days, with two or three babysitting evenings – more for live-out au pairs. Keep in mind that by staying with the family you'll be saving €5000–15,000 in annual accommodation costs. Typically, you get your own room, about €300 a month, and perhaps use of a car and a chance to accompany the family on vacations. So much depends on the family, so ask lots of questions before taking the job. Start your research with these websites:

- ⓦaupair-agency.com
- ⓦaupair.com
- ⓦaupair-world.net
- ⓦgreataupair.com

CAN YOU SPOT A BAD TRAVEL JOB?

So many travelers who head abroad end up in the **worst travel jobs**. The reason isn't so surprising. They can't tell a great travel job from a lemon. A great job, they think, is any one they can get. So, they take the first one that comes along without ever checking if it fits with the travel experience they're after.

Let's take a typical job search. Say you want to work in a **ski resort**. You go to the French Alps, search frantically for a job and land one washing dishes, realizing you were lucky to get anything with your dodgy language skills. You're thrilled to have work, but the minimum wage doesn't get you very far in a pricey resort. After working eight-hour days six days a week (fairly standard), you notice you've only put your skis on a few times and, as the lone washer, you've been kept too busy to meet anyone at the restaurant. Eventually, you'll wonder what the point is. It took me about three weeks.

The fact is, very few jobs in ski resorts pay well (considering the high cost of living) and many don't allow you much time to ski. Savvy ski bums now prefer to work overtime at a better-paying job elsewhere, then head to a ski resort, find some cheap accommodation and ski their asses off for a month.

Contrast this with picking grapes in France. Even if you can't arrange to get paid, you can probably get your room and board covered. Let's say you work a week at a small château, meet loads of people, drink as much wine as your liver will permit and leave with a memorable experience that didn't bankrupt you.

Still not sure what a bad job is? If you can't answer "yes" to at least one of the following questions, you'd do well to look for a different job. Factoring in living costs, does the job bring in enough money to cover future travel? Does it make for an interesting experience or provide you with a valued skill? Is it a relatively easy workload and/or does it offer a lenient schedule that allows you to partake in local activities you enjoy?

Government and NGO jobs

Landing work for a government isn't as intimidating as it might sound. In fact, governments may even offer more opportunities for people to start their careers overseas than any company, and you don't necessarily have to carry a gun, classified microfilm or a pen that doubles as a rocket launcher to get your paycheck. The US government alone has 50,000 employees working overseas. Non-Governmental Organizations (NGOs) are typically major charities, environmental groups or human rights organizations, and they need willing overseas workers – some are volunteers, but most offer paid positions. For a solid listing of NGOs, check out NGO Watch, at ⓦglobalgovernancewatch.org.

Australian government jobs

- Department of Foreign Affairs and Trade ⓦdfat.gov.au/careers/Pages/careers.aspx

Canadian government jobs

- Foreign Affairs, Trade and Development Canada ⓦinternational.gc.ca/development-developpement/index.aspx

5

New Zealand government jobs

- New Zealand's International Aid and Development Agency ⓦnzaid .govt.nz
- Overseas diplomatic posts ⓦbit.ly/NZdiplomaticposts

UK government jobs

- Department for International Development ⓦdfid.gov.uk
- Foreign and Commonwealth Office ⓦfco.gov.uk

US government jobs

- Central Intelligence Agency ⓦcia.gov
- Department of State ⓦstate.gov
- Peace Corps ⓦpeacecorps.gov
- US Agency for International Development ⓦusaid.gov
- International Information Programs ⓦstate.gov/r/iip

United Nations Development Program

- Eight to ten weeks of on-the-job training for enrolled graduate students fluent in two of the United Nations' official languages (see ⓦundp.org).

United Nations Junior Professional programs

- Junior professional posts are given for short assignments. UNICEF has one (requires master's degree, age 32 years or under and fluent French), as do UNESCO and UNDP. See ⓦun.org/staffdevelopment for more information.

Landing a job while in the country

OK, let's say you've splashed out for a work permit organized by a student work-permit agency, or taken advantage of a "working holiday" visa (see p.78). You still have to find a job... yourself.

Wake up early, check the classified ads, check notice boards, put up your own messages, dress smartly, don't wear sunglasses, take off the hat, lose the body piercings, cover any tattoos that may frighten small children, dye your hair back to a color that could at least pass for real hair, leave your shorts in the hostel as well as the loose-fitting jeans that expose your designer underwear, double-check your emails for typos and return calls promptly – easier with a local SIM card for your cell phone or a local Skype Call-In number (see p.146). In short, don't give them a reason to dismiss you.

No potential employer wants to read over a sampling of your term papers. Let's face it, you probably don't want to look at them again, either. Nor are they going to read through a stack of recommendation letters. What you should bring is some appropriate clothing, or enough money to pick some up when you arrive. If you think a suit is appropriate for the job, you may wish to cart one along. A current CV (résumé) will come in handy. As will a few official copies of your diploma.

If you are rejected, take it with a smile, thank them for their consideration and always take the opportunity to ask them where you might find work. If you've made a good impression, most people won't mind providing a few leads. Furthermore, don't cross off a potential employer just because they said no a few days or a week earlier. Things change. One of their employees may quit or get sacked. Or perhaps someone they were expecting never showed up. They might even realize that they needed more help than they thought. And as long as your approach is polite, your perseverance will be respected.

If you're going after a more corporate-type job, the best thing you can do once you've arrived is arrange for an interview. Buy yourself a phone card or a local SIM card for your phone and start making calls. If you know you really want to work in a certain field, try to arrange a quick meeting even if you've heard they don't have any openings. You might start by saying something like "I expected there weren't any openings at the moment, but as part of my foreign study experience I need to at least do a short interview to get an insider perspective. If you could spare, say, ten minutes in the next day or three I'd be grateful." Or figure out your own way in. Then, when you get the meeting, ask a few questions, see if a free internship might be possible. Before you accept an offer for free work, though, say you just need to explore a few other leads. If you like the place, at least you'll have a fall-back opportunity. Or ask if this person knows anyone else in the industry worth contacting. Who knows: if you make a good impression, you might at least get a good referral.

If you're going after a restaurant/bar/resort job, just show up and ask for the manager or owner. They'll want to take a look at you, check that your brain can handle the tasks required and test out your language skills.

If nothing comes along, you'll need some imagination. And funds – a good month's worth or longer if you're prepared to accept a position that doesn't pay. You could also consider entrepreneurial jobs (see p.81).

For more info on landing a job, try *Work Your Way Around the World* by Susan Griffith or the following websites:

- ⓦjobmonkey.com
- ⓦmonster.com
- ⓦtransitionsabroad.com

You got the job

Once you get a job offer you plan to accept, ask for a few days to fix housing arrangements. Look into family stays, university-room rentals, and inquire at various hostels to see if they'll offer you a long-term deal.

If you work abroad and declare your earnings there, knowing that the amount is too small to be taxed in that country, bear in mind that you might be **taxed** for the amount in your home country, depending upon reciprocal agreements and any other income sources.

5

Volunteering

It may not seem like Europe needs saving. There's certainly not the level of poverty and disease you'd find in Africa, or other developing countries, but there are people, parks and political groups in need of help and absolutely no shortage of organizations that would like you to come and volunteer for them.

Donating your time can be a tremendously fulfilling experience, but picking a good program is not as straightforward as you'd imagine. If you don't select carefully, your time contributed may feel like time wasted. Or it may be fulfilling for you, but little benefit – if any – to the community. The fact is that some organizations' definitions of efficiency and utility will differ substantially from your own, or the flashy review quotes dotted about their website.

And many of the volunteer ventures are almost identical to English-teaching and labor-intensive work projects that you could be getting paid for. You might be moving boxes, doing dishes or shoveling cow dung, which is fine, provided you know what you're getting into. So, before you sign up, make sure you get an **exact description** of what you'll be doing and what they expect you to accomplish during your visit. You'll want some local orientation before you're dropped off at your project, and a reliable local contact for emergency support, supplies and advice. You can ask for these things because you're not just going to be working there for free; you're almost certainly helping finance it. And perhaps the most surprising thing about volunteering is that it isn't as cheap as it sounds. First, there's the air fare or rail/bus transport. Then you often need to pay a fee that covers your lodging, food, insurance and the entire screening and orientation process. It's not uncommon to be shelling out more than €400 a month. As a guideline, the more exotic the project (such as studying dolphins in Europe's aquariums), the more you pay to assist.

Most projects have specific dates for training and transporting new volunteers. Plus, the organizations prefer to screen applicants, so showing up to lend a hand, though well intentioned, can actually backfire. Your best bet is to make arrangements long before you leave. If you're already on the road, your time will be well spent making contact by email – you may be able to take care of all the details before you arrive.

More and more families are taking volunteering trips as well. These tend to be short term, more expensive and better coordinated (see ⓦmetowe.com

---

VOLUNTEER PROJECTS

Projects change all the time, but here are a few ideas:

Build a school or clinic • help staff an "eco-house" • renovate hiking paths in parks and nature reserves • track animals • assist at a camp for children with learning disabilities • develop ecotourism • promote health care • work with a women's cooperative • practice sustainable agriculture • teach English • join an archeological dig • help renovate a castle or monastery • develop a small business enterprise or support human rights efforts.

and ⓦglobeaware.org). For those who do decide to bring their kids, it can be traumatic, but you are the best judge of what your kids can handle. Dr Harold S. Koplewicz, president of the Child Mind Institute in New York, commented on this in *The New York Times* (Aug 14, 2012): "Generally, I think during the teen years, a time when most kids are very self-absorbed, it is not a bad thing to take them out of their comfort zone."

Rewards of volunteering

- Feel that you're helping to leave the world in a better condition than when you arrived.
- Live and work in a community where it's easy to make friends.
- Learn customs and language skills.
- Get to know volunteers from around the world.
- Get hands-on practical experience.
- Put your professional skills to use to make a tangible difference in people's lives.

Types of volunteer projects

Some organizations want strong backs, others strong minds. All want good attitudes and your financial support. As you begin your search, you'll find some of the projects are seasonal, some go year-round and some are unique ones that pop up when a university professor has received a major research grant. If possible, try to take advantage of the time of year you'll be volunteering (ie you don't want to be volunteering indoors in Portugal in springtime when the weather is great). Here are a few volunteer sites to get you started:

- **Idealist** ⓦidealist.org
- **Taking It Global** ⓦtakingitglobal.org
- **Go Abroad** ⓦgoabroad.com
- **Volunteer International** ⓦvolunteerinternational.org
- **Archelon** (the Sea Turtle Protection Society of Greece) ⓦarchelon.gr
- **WWF** ⓦpanda.org/how_you_can_help/volunteer

Learning new skills

If you don't have time to work or get involved with a volunteer project during your trip, it's always possible to find time for a course; some take just half a day. **Taking a course** is one of the most enriching things you can do on your trip: it's a chance to learn a new skill that will remain with you long after you've returned home. Education aside, many offer a nice break from the travel scene and provide a chance for you to meet up with some locals or other foreigners with similar interests.

Many courses can be arranged at the last minute, but most often the better programs require some advance booking. Look into this well before you arrive;

5

in some cases, well before you arrange any flights. Unless you're absolutely sure about the soundness of a course, don't pay the entire fee in advance. And pay with a credit card to help protect yourself. The courses listed below are by no means a definitive list; they are meant to provide a sample of some of the activities out there, and are only intended as a starting point.

Learning to cook

Want a great souvenir? Learn how to make one amazing local dish. You'll be impressing friends and family with it for ages, provided you don't keep serving it to the same people. France, Italy and Spain are the most popular destinations for the gastronomically inclined, but cooking schools can be found almost anywhere. If you find you're really enjoying a local cuisine, talk to the local tourist office about courses available. Most last from a half-day to a month, with widely varying prices. As well as the listings below, try Ⓦcookforfun.shawguides.com.

- **APICIUS Cooking School** Florence, Italy Ⓦapicius.it. Taught in Italian (recipes can be translated, individual courses can be held in English). One-day wine class (in group); three-hour private cooking course; one-week summer workshops. Email for current prices.
- **Ballymaloe Cooking School** Cork, Ireland Ⓦcookingisfun.ie. Full-day course in the art of spit-roasting or cooking warm winter stews start at €195.
- **Diane Kochilas Greek Food for Life** Ikaria, Greece Ⓦdianekochilas.com. Indoor/outdoor kitchen, with classes that can vary in size from five to forty.
- **Le Cordon Bleu French Cooking** Paris, France Ⓦcordonbleu.com. The Grande Dame of cooking schools. You can take a single-day introductory course on nearly any subject, a four-day elective course or a one-month intensive certificate-level course, among others.

Learning a language

Learning a language isn't as difficult as you might think, even if you've taken a language in school for years, hated it, learned next to nothing and vowed you'd never bother with it again – as I did.

Taking that step back towards language learning can be a humbling experience. And if you get a headache for the first couple of weeks, it just means your brain is working overtime – a sign that you'll have things figured out soon.

One thing you can say about intensive language schools is that they work. The combination of small groups or even one-on-one tutoring plus a family stay, or simply living in the country, is a sort of magic formula, and you walk away with a better grasp of the language than you might get in years of regular schooling – and often without the brain-crushing boredom you associate with learning the past imperfect subjunctive gerund form of exceptions to masculine nouns. Again, that doesn't mean it's easy and that you'll be able to

5

CREDIT CRISIS

OK, you've found the perfect foreign language school and plan to study for about three weeks, all the while enjoying horseback riding and beach parties with your newfound classroom friends. For North Americans, the only thing stopping you now is transferring the classes so your university knows it's actually an educational experience and not just a pseudo-academic vacation.

Attaining credit for studying in a language school takes persistence, though. Make the effort to find the school that's right for you with professional courses and a certified staff, referrals and contacts – basically, anyone that can sell the point that this language school is not one big fiesta, and that you learn more words than just "pintxos" and "cerveza".

These programs can have significant value, even if you don't get academic credit for them. Consider the economics: the average US student spends an average of two years studying another language at university. At the University of California, for example, it takes three consecutive courses for two years to fulfil this requirement. These classes are an hour a day, four days a week. Two years of this instruction will cost over $3000 in the public system (well over $6000 at a private college), and often students (like myself) still feel unskilled in the language. Look at it that way and the intensive programs start to look like a bargain. You can actually become proficient in the language and the average cost for two months (about 120hr) of classroom instruction, room, board and travel excursions runs to about $1500. After one of these intensive courses, it's not unusual for students to test out of language requirements with less time, less money and more fun.

Eric Tiettmeyer,
ⓦ studenttraveler.com

down beers at the local pub while you suck up linguistic nuances (unless you count pronouncing the beverages correctly). That bit comes later, after you've picked up the basics.

"Hello", "please" and "thank you" won't take more than five minutes to learn, no matter what the language. If you want to move beyond a few words, a regular language course is a great way to start your travels in a new country. Aside from tools that will help you unlock the cultural codes of the country, you'll meet more locals, be able to get assistance when needed, keep your gray matter active and make your travels far more meaningful. You'll need at least three weeks to make real progress, no matter how intensive the course is. Two months should provide good conversational skills, depending on your study habits.

Many of the better-known language courses take place in towns packed with English-speaking students – great for your social life, but lousy for language discipline. It's better (and cheaper) to select a smaller or less popular town where you'll get an experience far more intensive than the more expensive "intensive" courses offered in major language-learning centers.

If you're set on a specific course, you may need to sign up in advance. Otherwise, you can walk in off the street and usually start the same day. And, naturally, you can find inexpensive private tutors to teach you in nearly any city. Put up a notice near a university and you'll have a few offers within hours.

Studying photography

Even if you're just taking a pocket camera, or even just a smartphone, learning how to **compose your photographs** is going to get you a lot further than an overpriced lens. You may not learn anything more valuable than basic tips, but you'll need to practice them and develop an eye for what works and what

5

doesn't. That means taking oodles of photos and having them critiqued. You can find community photography workshops for less than €100, but the upper-end instruction doesn't come cheap. It does, however, often include a trip to Europe, which may be how you'd like to begin your journey, getting comfortable with a group before venturing out on your own. For more advice, pick up a copy of *The Rough Guide to Digital Photography* by Sophie Goldsworthy. Yes, you've spotted some cross promotion here, but it's a good book and ideal for travelers, with listings of travel-specific photography websites and technical tips.

- **Close Up Expeditions** ⓦcuephoto.com. Workshops in over forty countries concentrating on nature, landscape and traditional cultures.
- **National Geographic Expeditions Photo expeditions and workshops** ⓦnationalgeographicexpeditions.com/triptypes/photography. European destinations include Provence, Turkey, Scotland and the Greek islands. Several prominent National Geographic photographers and photo editors come along to hand-deliver personal tips and tricks to budding photographers.

Wilderness survival and alpine courses

You hardly need one of these to get by in Europe, but you never know when survival skills will suddenly come in handy. Most survival schools are run by – here's a real shocker – Americans, but many of the programs take place outside the US (and you might feel more confident by taking a course before you leave). Some, such as NOLS and Outward Bound, place more emphasis on the group experience, while others are more technically oriented. If you already speak French, German or Italian, you might feel comfortable jumping right into a European course in the Alps. Make sure you ask plenty of questions before making your decision.

- **NOLS** ⓦnols.edu. US organizer branching out with a thirty-day sea kayaking and backpacking course in northern Norway. Also one-month or two-week courses in the US. Transferable educational credit is possible with some universities.
- **Outward Bound** ⓦoutwardbound.org. Courses of one to eleven weeks. Focuses on wilderness training and team building.
- **Objective Team** ⓦobjectiveteam.com. Put your parents at ease by starting your trip with a one-day travel-security course (they specialize not just in backpackers, but corporate training for hostile environments) in London.
- **Adventure Lifesigns** ⓦlifesignsgroup.co.uk. British expedition training, remote medical training and independent travelers' courses for 1–2 days.

Before leaving home:

- **Colorado Mountain School** ⓦcoloradomountainschool.com. Avalanche courses and backcountry skiing safety in the Rocky Mountains. Plenty of one-day courses.

5

- **LTR (Learn To Return) Training Systems, Inc.** ⓦsurvivaltraining.com. Alaska-based emergency survival training in arctic, mountain and sea environments, as well as for natural disasters, industrial accidents and terrorist attacks. Over 25 specialized courses that range from 2 to 70 hours.
- **Karamat Wilderness Ways** ⓦkaramat.com. Canadian wilderness survival specializing in the northern boreal forests. Week-long courses with summer or winter theme.
- **Aboriginal Living Skills School** ⓦalssadventures.com. Living off the land in Arizona. Learn desert survival, winter camping and primitive camp-craft skills with one-day to week-long courses.

If you're more interested in staying alive in the mountains and ticking off summits in the process, check out the list of **international mountaineering courses** at ⓦdmoz.org/Recreation/Climbing/Guides_and_Schools, or the two listed below:

- **Bob Culp Climbing School** ⓦbobculp.com. Rock- and ice-climbing trips in Chamonix and the Italian Dolomites; five days or more.
- **Swiss Association of Mountaineering Schools** ⓦbergsportschulen.ch. Select schools by specialty (ice-climbing, high-altitude skiing, etc) or region, and the links will put you in touch with professional Swiss guides.

Meditation

If the fast pace of life on the road starts taking its toll on your nerves, the regular pub visits aren't helping and your Valium prescription has run out, consider taking a personal time-out. That might mean a couple of yoga classes or a week in silent seclusion. Getting back in touch with your mind and body, however you decide to go about it, can be an invigorating pit stop – just what you need to continue on your physical and inner journeys. Many courses are offered in English and the ones that aren't are easy enough to follow by looking at the instructor's movements. Just keep an eye out for local yoga, qi gong and meditation centers as you go. Here are a few links to a variety of yoga schools in Europe to get you started:

- **Ashtanga** ⓦashtanga.com/html/Europe.html
- **Blue Mountain Center Meditation Centres** (UK and the Netherlands) ⓦeaswaran.org
- **Iyengar** ⓦiyengar-yoga.com/Yoga_Centers/Europe
- **Shambhala** ⓦshambhala.org/centers
- **Sivananda** ⓦsivananda.org

6

Documents and insurance

Getting your documents in order for a big trip to Europe isn't nearly as much of a hassle as it sounds – just a case of sorting out your passport, any necessary visas and some travel insurance. Hardly any European countries require visas (or they make it easy for you to pick them up upon arrival). See which apply to your nationality (p.95) and be sure to check out the all-important departure countdown (pp.104–105).

Passports

Without a passport you're looking at a short trip. Probably to the airport and back.

Two or more passports

The important thing for dual or triple passport holders is that, while it can be good to carry two passports, you **pick one passport to use during your entire trip** – the one that grants you the most visa-free access or work privileges – and only use the other for emergencies (leave the third one at home with your document copies so it can be mailed to you if a crisis should arise). It may be tempting to swap when you can save a little money on a visa, or – if you're an EU passport holder – so you can negotiate the lines at immigration a little more quickly, but if you get questioned by a customs official you need to be able to demonstrate a clear travel history. Any gaps will raise suspicions. To keep the customs process at borders moving smoothly, don't bring up your multiple citizenship unless asked.

GETTING A PASSPORT

AUSTRALIA

Normally issues visas within ten working days; can be done online or at post office, but you must be interviewed. Additional fee to process in two working days. Detailed guidelines on website.

Valid for: ten years

ⓦ passports.gov.au/Web/newppt/index.aspx

CANADA

Can take up to four weeks (not including mailing time), ten days if you show up in person. No renewal available – new passport must be purchased. Photocopies of identity documents (eg driver's license) must be signed by a guarantor. Express handling: two to nine days for an additional fee. Urgent: same day or next day (only available on case-by-case emergency basis).

Valid for: five or ten years

ⓦ cic.gc.ca/english/passport/index.asp

NEW ZEALAND

Ten or three working days, depending on how much you want to pay. Or call-out service, when urgent delivery falls out of working hours.

Valid for: ten years

ⓦ passports.govt.nz

SOUTH AFRICA

Four to six weeks, so apply well ahead of time. Form DHA-73 can be picked up at any Home Affairs Office, which also accepts your completed application.

Valid for: ten years

ⓦ home-affairs.gov.za

UK

Three-week service at post offices, two weeks if applying at certain Post Office branches. One-week service at passport offices (not possible with first-time passports).

Valid for: five years

ⓦ ips.gov.uk

USA

All first-timers must apply in person. Handling takes four to six weeks. Two to three weeks expedited processing can be requested, with an additional fee. Or make an appointment to visit one of the fifteen regional passport agencies near you. If you're lucky, they will expedite in eight days.

Valid for: ten years

ⓦ travel.state.gov/content/passports/english.html

Visas

Visas are essentially stamps (but sometimes stickers or entire documents) inserted into your passport by immigration officials or embassies or consulates acting on their behalf, and grant you permission to enter their country for a specified period of time. There are other conditions that can be included as well – such as the right to work, the right to re-enter the country multiple times and the right to extend your visa – which may require special approval. Much of this depends on which passport you hold. Each country has its own set of agreements with other countries, with fees yo-yoing (with diplomacy) in the region of €20–160.

In Europe, **visas** are not an issue for most passport holders, and once you're on the continent you'll rarely have to show your passport when crossing

6

THE NOTORIOUS THIRTY-DAY RUSSIAN TOURIST VISA

Russian tourist visas are valid for a period of up to 30 days, and obtaining one entails suspending all notions of rational thought. This is the old-school method of tourism – make visitors jump through daunting hoops of red tape.

You need a **passport** that's valid for six months after your intended *departure* from Russia. Easy. A photo or two. Or even more just to be on the safe side. Easy. In the worst-case version, you will need a **podtverzdeniye** (standard tourist invitation) from an authorized hosting Russian travel agency, registered with the Russian Ministry of Foreign Affairs (MID RF). Huh?! A **tour voucher** or its copy, attested by said authorized Russian travel agency. Yuck. And a cover letter from your travel agency at home containing dates and points of arrival and departure to and from Russia; means of transport; itinerary in Russia; confirmation of hotel bookings; the name of the hosting Russian agency and its reference number. Double yuck. In the best-case scenario, you will just need your original passport, a photo, a tourist invitation from a travel company and an application form from the Russian consulate.

Since 2014, individual travelers from a select group of 38 countries can visit for 30–90 days without a visa. This group includes former states of the Soviet Union, most of Latin America and an assorted sprinkling of other non-English-speaking countries. Cruise ship passengers who promise not to explore on their own are allowed 72 visa-free hours on shore.

The rest of us need visas, and they aren't cheap: around €43 for most EU citizens (but £50 for UK), plus a £38.40 service charge for a basic one that's ready in five business days and good for single entry, escalating all the way up to £288 for Americans who want a double-entry visa processed the same day. Has the Mafia got into the visa office?

What the tourist bureau wants is for you to book everything in advance – preferably an **expensive tour**. The traditional way around this is to get an invitation from a hotel or hostel (who can offer invitations for any length of time, provided you spend one night with them) – typically, a youth hostel in St Petersburg (Ⓦryh .ru). When contacting any hotel or agency in Russia regarding visas, ask about their recent experience with the particular consulate to which you intend to apply. Also – watch out for this – when contacting the consulates, some like to charge you extra for replying with information by email. For additional general info on obtaining a Russian visa, see Ⓦrussianvisa.org, Ⓦwaytorussia.net or Ⓦexpresstorussia.com.

AMERICANS

The processing of Russian visas in the USA has been outsourced to Invisa Logistics Services (Ⓦils-usa.com), who add a hefty US$33 for their "services" if you show up in person. And US$103 if you prefer mail.

Costs range from US$160 for a single-entry visa that takes ten calendar days to process, to US$450 for the three-business-day processing of a three-year multiple-entry visa.

borders. Many countries don't require any visas for some passport holders, or simply hand them out at the airport or border crossing for free or a small fee. Otherwise, they can take anywhere between a day and a few weeks to process, but they can usually be taken care of within a few days if you opt to pay an additional fee to expedite the application.

Austria, Belgium, Czech Republic, Denmark, Estonia, Finland, France, Germany, Greece, Hungary, Iceland, Italy, Latvia, Liechtenstein, Lithuania,

6

AUSTRALIANS

All applications for Russian visas have to be submitted using the Electronic Visa Application form at ⓦ visa.kdmid.ru. The basic fee is Aus$120 and processing takes ten working days. A single-entry visa issued within two days costs Aus$240 (Aus$402 for double-entry).
Sydney: ⓦ sydneyrussianconsulate.com

CANADIANS

As of 2014, you can only apply for visas through Invisa Logistics Services, at Visa Application Centres in Ottawa, Toronto or Montréal (ⓦ canada-ils.com). The Russian embassy also has info at ⓦ rusembassy.ca. Costs range from Can$100 for a single-entry visa that takes ten working days (eighteen in Montréal) to process to Can$175 for the three-day processing (five in Montréal). For all visas, there is an additional Can$45 processing fee.
Toronto: ⓦ toronto.mid.ru; Montréal: ⓦ montreal.mid.ru

BRITISH CITIZENS

The Russian Embassy in London outsources its visa application processing to a private company, VF Services (ⓦ ru.vfsglobal.co.uk). You need to print out your application and fill it out beforehand. And you need to apply in person at the Russian Visa Application Centre in either London or Edinburgh. Like in the US, VFS add a service fee on top of the cost of your visa – £50 for five working days, £100 for next-day service. As of January 2015, UK citizens are required to leave fingerprint scans in connection with their visa applications.

NEW ZEALANDERS

The Russian Embassy in Wellington (c/o Karori Post Shop) processes visas in ten working days for NZ$70, in three days for NZ$140. Visa applications must be filled in online ⓦ visa.kdmid.ru, printed out and signed. They can be either presented in person or mailed in.

SOUTH AFRICANS

You need to have medical insurance for the entire visa period, plus a copy of a return air ticket. Applications need to be handed in at least three days before the trip. Standard processing time is 4–20 days and costs R880. Urgent three-day handling raises the fee to R1430. Cash only. See ⓦ russianembassy.org.za.

THE FINNISH OPTION

St Petersburg is just a three-and-a-half-hour train ride from Helsinki. Book a short, on-the-spot tour (try Finnsov Travel at ⓦ finnsov.fi), skip the whole application process and away you go. The drawback is that you only have a 72-hour window to see the city.

Luxembourg, Malta, the Netherlands, Norway, Poland, Portugal, Slovakia, Slovenia, Spain, Sweden and Switzerland have joint visas that allow you to spend three months in total in the entire group of countries, known as the Schengen Area. Notably, the UK and Ireland are not members.

Americans, Canadians, Australians, New Zealanders, Irish and UK citizens do not need a visa to enter Europe or Morocco for less than ninety days. There are, however, a few exceptions: Americans, Canadians, Australians, South Africans and UK citizens require visas for Russia and Turkey in advance (at the time of writing, visas on arrival were still issued for Turkey but were due to be phased out); New Zealanders require visas for Russia (in advance) but not for Turkey. And holders of South African passports do need visas.

If you plan to stay **more than ninety days** in any one country, check the website of its embassy in your country (⊕embassypages.com lists all embassies). New Zealanders, for example, have a special deal: the right to spend three months separately (not just three months in total) in each of the following countries: Austria, Belgium, Czech Republic, Denmark, Estonia, Finland, France, Germany, Greece, Hungary, Iceland, Italy, Latvia, Lithuania, Luxembourg, the Netherlands, Norway, Portugal, Spain, Sweden and Switzerland.

Getting visas at home

If you're planning to work legally in a country, apply for that visa first, since it must be arranged from your home country. For more details on working abroad, see Chapter 5. Also, if you're planning to stay more than three months, you'll need a visa before you arrive. For instance, Australians heading to France must pay Aus\$142 for a visa allowing them a stay of more than three months without a work permit. Getting such a visa requires a certificate of Police Record, proof of medical coverage while in France, proof that you can support yourself financially, and a signed declaration that you will not take up employment during your stay.

Entry for students on study programs

If you're arriving in Europe to study for a semester or more, you should have all your **study abroad documentation** (eg an official paper stating where and when you'll be studying and living) with you to present to the customs officer. Your study abroad program will tell you if you require a special visa and how to obtain it if you do, but it will be your responsibility to make sure it's processed and ready in time.

OTHER CONSIDERATIONS

Be aware of **local holidays**, as visa-issuing offices at home are likely to be closed on these days. Don't list your **occupation** if it may give them reason to be suspicious, such as journalist or security analyst. Be vague: writer, editor or data processor gives them less reason to question you.

Insurance

Here's the most important thing you need to know about travel insurance for an extended trip: **get some**. To find out why, what makes a good policy and what it costs, read on.

Why get insurance?

6

Just as experienced drivers still need to get car insurance, experienced travelers know that travel insurance is a necessity. All it takes is one mishap – a drowsy bus driver, a patch of sand when you try to brake your rented scooter, a knee twist during a mountain hike – and your family might be stuck selling their home to cover your rescue by helicopter, air-ambulance ride home, surgery, plus ongoing treatment (which may not be covered by your home insurance policy). Any of these things could happen to you in your own country, but at home you're probably covered. Overseas, where your coverage is unlikely to apply, this could easily top €100,000, not including any long-term medical expenses. A comprehensive health-insurance plan may cover some of your medical expenses, even those incurred overseas, but it's unlikely to pick up some of the major rescue and repatriation costs. Even among countries that have reciprocal health agreements (such as those with European passports traveling within the EU, who need to carry an EHIC card), you will not be fully covered, and certainly not for repatriation.

If, at the last moment before your trip, you get terribly sick, called up for jury duty, robbed or whatever, you don't want to get stuck with cancellation fees on top of it. A good policy will cover this, but for this service to kick in you need to get insurance about the time you buy your ticket (not the day you get called up for jury duty). Also, if your trip is disrupted for an emergency, your insurance company should assist with arrangements to continue your trip once you're ready.

No one plans on legally defending themselves while abroad. But if it happens, it's unlikely to be cheap. Say you hit a local cyclist while driving a rented car on a difficult-to-navigate road. Or scuff a new Mercedes with the rusty pedal of your rented bicycle. Travel insurance is about the only way to prepare for such unfortunate events.

Finding an insurance policy

First, you need to find out what you're insured for already so you can pick out a policy that covers the gaps. Without this knowledge, you'll likely be wasting your money on double coverage. Unfortunately, this means sifting through the fine print. You might start with your **homeowner's insurance policy** to see if it covers lost luggage (even your parents' policy, if their home is still your official residence, may have you covered).

Second, check to see what kind of travel insurance your **credit card company** offers for free, and whether it is solely for tickets or goods purchased using the card. Some credit cards offer flight insurance in the event of a plane crash or other transportation accidents. Then take a **look at your medical**

6

ROUGH GUIDES TRAVEL INSURANCE

Rough Guides has teamed up with **WorldNomads.com** to offer great **travel insurance** deals. Policies are available to residents of over 150 countries, with cover for a wide range of adventure sports, 24hr emergency assistance, high levels of medical and evacuation cover and a stream of travel safety information. Roughguides.com users can take advantage of their policies online 24/7, from anywhere in the world – even if you're already traveling. And since plans often change when you're on the road, you can extend your policy and even claim online. If you buy travel insurance with WorldNomads.com you can also leave a positive footprint and donate to a community development project. For more information go to ⓦ roughguides.com/travel-insurance.

policy. Will it cover you for illnesses or accidents incurred overseas? If so, keep a list of activities it will cover you for. Finally, check out your life insurance policy. Will it still pay out if you die bungee jumping in France or mountain climbing in Switzerland? You want to make sure you're covered for these things. Plus many others. You may work up more courage than you think once you start traveling.

For lost luggage, it's worth noting that airlines will reimburse international travelers for up to 1131 SDR (Special Drawing Rights, a pseudo-currency created by the IMF and based on the yen, the euro, the US dollar and the British pound), which equals about €1730 per passenger, but the process is time-consuming and potentially exasperating.

In terms of dedicated travel insurance, not all policies are created equal. The best don't tend to be cheap, but that doesn't mean the most expensive policies are the best. One sign of a **good insurer** is a featured list of what they will and won't cover – most prefer to bury this information, knowing you'd rather hack off your arm with an old butter knife than dig through the fine print of their policy. Especially since it can be rather gruesome at times – with payouts listed for things like dismemberment or loss of an eye. But it's important to know exactly what you're getting.

No two lists of activities seem to be the same. Some policies will require a supplement for an activity that other policies include in the most basic package. And some won't cover you if you get hurt or injured in countries that appear on your foreign office's travel-warning list. Some give you extra money if you're taken hostage on a plane and some won't cough up a cent. Some provide excellent emergency assistance, but little medical coverage. And many pad their list of benefits with things like "money transfer referrals" and "embassy referrals" – which is nothing more than a referral that you could find in half the time with a search on the internet, or in this book.

It's best to scan through a few brochures or websites and **compare** (start with ⓦ insuremytrip.com or ⓦ worldtravelcenter.com). If you're checking the web, be aware that some policies only apply to certain nationalities. STA Travel's insurance, for example, has a nice package for UK citizens, but its policies for Americans and Australians are rather feeble and more expensive by comparison. Find out who the underwriter of the insurance is (it's almost never the travel agency issuing it), and try to contact that company direct to see if they're offering a deal. Again, check what you're covered for already.

Many policies provide 24-hour emergency assistance – a collect-call phone number you can ring from anywhere and get access to an English-speaking operator, who will keep you on the line while you sort out your troubles. With standard, inexpensive travel gear, you needn't bother with protection against theft unless it's either already included in the policy you want or you're carrying something expensive (a laptop, swanky camera, watch, etc). But such items may be covered in your homeowner's insurance. Besides, in the event of a theft, replacing your backpack, some clothes, toiletries and a pair of sandals with items available locally is going to be quite cheap and a lot less hassle than trying to get reimbursed for every little well-worn item. (If you do have theft insurance, take a photo of all your gear, save the receipts and store them in a safe place at home.) Find out if your insurance provider will pay your expenses directly or reimburse you. In either case (but especially the latter), ask for and hang on to receipts for everything.

Another common insurance perk is cancellation and trip interruption coverage. However, when they say that you have coverage for this, it doesn't mean you get your money back if you suddenly decide not to go. Such expenses are only covered if the reason for cancelling or interrupting your trip is stated in your insurance policy. Typically, it applies if you or your travel partner gets sick or injured, or if there's a death in your immediate family. There are other reasons as well, but you need to read the fine print to discover what they are.

In addition to the comparison sites above, other providers worth investigating are: Rough Guides' travel insurance with World Nomads (see box opposite), ⓦinternationalsos.com and ⓦtravelguard.com.

Insurance for specific activities

It's hard to anticipate what opportunities may come your way while you're traveling. Even timid travelers work up considerable nerve to try new things after a few months on the road. Remember to check the fine print for the activities you hope to do, but also try to give yourself as much leeway as possible, in terms of your policy, to try new things. In fact, a quick way to find the relevant section of your policy is to scan through the fine print until you see a list of activities grouped together. There's a good chance you'll have to call and inquire about some specific activities they've left out.

6

7

Before you leave home

Assuming you can't squeeze everything into your backpack, you'll need a place to store the possessions you don't take with you to Europe; preferably, somewhere they'll remain until you return. Keeping your plants green and pets alive is another trick. This chapter will help with the arrangements you'll need to make before you can head out. (To get your finances squared away for the big trip, see Chapter 4.)

Renting out your property

The two best ways to go are renting to a trusted friend, who can take care of things for you while you're away and handle any problems that may arise; or to a corporate company, which will probably be willing to pay more, and provide a guarantee of payments and the safekeeping of your property (of course, not everyone has an apartment that would appeal to an executive).

To avoid the hassles of dealing with tenants (or Airbnb guests), you may wish to work out an arrangement with an estate agent or property manager, who will not only lease your place, but also collect the rent and handle any problems that may arise. This service isn't cheap, but if you're less worried about turning a profit than having to deal with day-to-day problems, this could be the way to go.

Otherwise, you can take out an ad. Ask around before ringing a local newspaper. Often there are much cheaper alternative publications that attract a much better targeted group.

If you do rent your flat to previously unknown tenants, it's worth taking the following precautions:

- While you are with your tenants, video yourself as you walk around the property, recording everything with running commentary. ("There's a little hole in the wall I made while practicing my approach shot with an 8-iron. There are eight wine glasses in the cupboard.") This will help protect them against minor damage you may forget about during your trip, and keep you protected against anything new that appears. Plus, it's a nice reminder that you've got the evidence and they should be on good behavior. If you're going with an estate agent, you may wish to do this before you leave anyway, so you can prove any damage upon returning.
- Agree on anything that requires maintenance, such as plant watering or garden care.
- Show the tenants that things are in working order (refrigerator, washing machine and so on), and make sure as many of these points as possible are listed in the contract.
- Remove and store personal treasures and anything that would cause the slightest emotional stir were it to break or grow legs and walk off.
- Have some family member or friend keep an eye on the tenants and deal with any emergency situations that may arise. And let your tenants know that someone will be watching them.
- For minor issues, let them know you should be emailed. Bring the number and email address of a trusted electrician and plumber with you, so you can take care of things that pop up with minimal effort.
- Arrange for your mail to be held for you by the post office or forwarded to parents or friends, who can sort out the junk and send on what you need at your next port of call.

7

Leaving an empty flat

If you're leaving your flat empty, unplug appliances, cancel your subscriptions, cancel the cable TV, have your phone turned off, clean out the fridge and make sure someone is coming by every so often to check on the property. If you do leave your phone on, change the message on your answering machine, but keep your whereabouts discreet for security purposes. "Hi, I'm in Europe for the rest of the month. Leave a message and I'll return your call when I get back in August" is only advised for those who want to test the limits of their homeowners' insurance.

Plants

Don't just hand over your plants to a friend, unless you happen to know their horticultural survival record. It's more important to pick someone who's good with plants than pick a good friend. Just about anyone with a green thumb

DEPARTURE COUNTDOWN

You could theoretically get everything together in less than a week. You might pick up an ulcer in the process, but you could do it. You'd also pay more and miss out on valuable pre-trip research. Better to start **two to four months in advance**.

MISCELLANEOUS

- Suspend your gym membership.
- See if your phone and internet provider will allow you to suspend or cancel your service without penalty.
- Leave a key with a trusted friend.

THREE TO FOUR MONTHS BEFORE DEPARTURE

- Get a passport (see box, p.95). If you have a passport, make sure it has several blank pages left.
- Figure out what sort of jobs, volunteer programs or courses you'd like to do (see p.76). Gather applications and apply to those that require advance submissions.
- Consider your budget (see p.60). If you don't have the funds for the trip you want, perhaps you should think about picking up some extra work before you leave.
- Start checking the web for plane tickets (see p.35 & p.334).
- Start looking around for the right insurance policy (see p.99). If you're going to try to reach Europe by yacht or cargo ship, check ideal times and places to start your trip (see p.99).

TWO TO THREE MONTHS BEFORE DEPARTURE

- If you're flying, book a plane ticket and try to get insurance at the same time to cover you in the event of cancellation.
- Start thinking about the things you'd like to do and see.
- Arrange visas (see p.95) for any extended stays due to work, volunteering or study, plus the first country of entry (if necessary) and any countries with complex visa requirements.
- Make arrangements for your room or flat rental (see p.102).

7

will be happy to find some space for your flora, and possibly take better care of them than you would.

Pets

It's not always easy to find someone who will love your pet as much as you do. Your best bet is going to be leaving your canine, feline or fish with a friend or family member, which may involve some carefully chosen endearment opportunities (long-term kenneling is both unkind to your pet and expensive). However, there can be a lot of effort involved in finding a pet-sitter, so think of your pet's most attractive qualities and try to coordinate those with visits from prospective pet guardians. If you have a dog that can catch a Frisbee, play catch with the friend who would find that most appealing. If the pet is cute and friendly and successfully helps you line up dates, let your desperate

ONE TO TWO MONTHS BEFORE DEPARTURE

- Get a medical and dental checkup if you haven't had one for a while.
- Get credit cards and bank cards (see p.119), and meet with your banker to set up your finances so they can be handled while you're away, either with help from your parents or via internet banking. Try to set up a line of credit.
- Get any discount cards (ISIC, teacher card, youth card, HI card) you need (see p.61).

TWO TO FOUR WEEKS BEFORE DEPARTURE

- Buy your travel gear. If you're bringing or sending ahead new hiking boots, start breaking them in.
- Arrange for a global SIM if you plan to use one, and a cell phone, if you plan to take one (see p.147).
- If you need to get more rugged glasses, order additional contact lenses or determine your prescription, visit an optician.

ONE TO TWO WEEKS BEFORE DEPARTURE

- Leave parents or friends an envelope with copies of your documents (credit cards, passport, etc) that can be sent to you in case of an emergency. Take a photo of your travel gear to leave behind.
- Take care of any veterinary needs your pet may have before dropping it off with the pet-sitter.
- Arrange for your mail to be forwarded/held if your parents or roommate aren't willing to handle it.
- Check the CDC website (Ⓦcdc.gov) for any medical outbreaks you should be aware of.
- Check the websites of one or two state departments for updated security issues.

TWO TO THREE DAYS BEFORE DEPARTURE

- Pack.
- Test your pack (see box, p.108).
- Reconfirm flight.

DAY OF DEPARTURE

- Run over checklist one last time.

7

friend see this in action. If it cuddles up on your bed and keeps you warm, ring your pals with poor heating. If it's sweet, but looks menacing, perhaps some security-minded woman living alone might find this useful. A creative solution may be in order; think outside the litter box.

8

Packing

Ask a dozen "packing experts" for a list of what to take and you'll get a dozen different lists. Packing is neither an art nor a science; it's a combination of practicality and personal preference. And the only list that really matters is yours. The problem is it will take you a good six months on the road in various conditions to get a solid grasp of what you actually use and what you can do without. Until then, it's better to bring less and pick up any additional items you need along the way. This may sound like twisted logic, but throwing things away is actually far more difficult – at least, nobody seems willing to do it. In this chapter, you'll get the lowdown on selecting a backpack, which things you can leave at home, what to do with souvenirs and how to put together your own medical kit.

Why take less

For starters, it's going to be a lot cheaper. And that's not just the cost of the gear itself. With airlines now **charging crazy fees for excess baggage** (as much as €45 per kilo) while at the same time lowering the standard baggage weight allowance, you would do well to check online for the airline's baggage requirements and weigh your bag before heading to the airport. (British Airways' limit, for example, is now only 23kg.) The pros of a large pack may seem tempting: you have more stuff you might need, more clothes for the right occasion, plenty of toothpaste, and a few creature comforts from home. The cons are perhaps less obvious, but very much worth noting:

- A bigger risk of getting robbed – you're easier to spot, have more stuff to steal, and it's harder to run away.
- Bigger locker fees – it's harder to walk around with a large pack so you're more desperate to find a place to leave all your stuff, and you'll need a bigger, more expensive locker each time.

WHAT TRAVELERS ARE CARRYING

In the middle of the summer, I spent a few days walking around Stockholm's central train station with a notepad and a scale to see what (and how much) backpackers take with them. I spoke to every traveler I managed to stop, and weighed their packs. The average weight was just over 20kg. Some of the heaviest packs (over 25kg) belonged to women who weighed less than 55kg. It looked like they were going to be crushed at any second, Wile E. Coyote-like, under their packs. Everyone I asked had something they wished they hadn't brought. I asked several of them to open up their packs so I could peek inside. If you're wondering what people with huge packs are carrying around, here's what's taking up about seventy percent of their load: shoes, a sleeping bag, souvenirs and a full load of dirty laundry. Least used items: formal shoes for going out, textbooks and extra novels.

Most used items: sandals and rain jacket.

Doug Lansky

- Big sweat stains – the more odor you emit, the more often you have to wash. Spend five minutes walking in summer weather with an 8kg pack on your back and five minutes with a 20kg pack and you can see for yourself.
- Transport problems – it's more difficult to run for a train or bus (and you will have to run at some point), and it's harder to lift the pack over your head into a luggage rack without disturbing the people around you.
- More gear to lose or forget to pack, and more time spent packing things up each day.

8

Picking a pack

A standard suitcase or duffel bag won't serve you well for a journey with this much carrying involved, unless you're up for the challenge or don't mind having your arms lengthened to the point that your knuckles drag on the ground. A **rolling suitcase** is a popular option for many, but those little wheels weren't built to contend with European cobblestones. You can, of course, roll them in some places, but there are just as many where you can't. And in most airports (where they work best) you can find free trolleys. There are now a number of packs that have both wheels and backpacking straps. For urban travel, these can work extremely well. If you're planning on doing a good deal of hiking, however, the extra weight of the wheels coupled with a less flexible plastic suspension isn't worth it. At the risk of sounding like a drill sergeant, if you can't carry it, you don't need it.

Newton's law for **backpacks** would have read something like this: no matter what size pack you bring along, you'll always manage to fill it. No one travels with a half-empty pack. At least, I've never seen a traveler with a partially empty pack. Therefore, the single best thing you can do is start by buying a small rucksack: 40–55 liters – slightly bigger than your average day-bag. Once you do this, it's pretty hard to go wrong. The stuff you don't need simply won't fit in. I managed for nine years with that size just fine, and thousands of others have as well.

But be forewarned: that's not likely to be the advice you'll get from the travel shop assistants. Just remember where they're coming from: the bigger the pack, the more it costs and the more stuff they can sell you to put in it.

THE BACKPACK TEST

- You should be able to pack it in five minutes.
- You should be able easily to lift it over your head and you should be able to wear it for two hours without suffering minor back spasms.
- Someone (maybe even you) is going to sit on your pack, step on it or drop it at some point, so toss it across the room and then step on it – you may as well get it over and done with now.
- Don't pack breakables – or make sure you pack them well.
- Even if the odds are that your pack won't get stolen, prepare as if it will – leave your mother's pearls, your snakeskin cowboy boots and your collector's-edition silver-plated backgammon set at home.

A pack is not the place to try to save money. Take an internal-frame model for support. Couple that with a major brand name (you don't want it coming apart at the seams) and you're looking at prices in the range of €75–165. There are a few bells and whistles that are nice to have, but be selective. If you're going to forego the wheeled pack, your best bet is likely to be the rucksacks used by climbers. They keep the gear closer to your torso for a fuller range of motion and better balance.

8

- You'd do well to skip the zip-off daypack; they don't make the best bags and, when attached, tend to unbalance the main pack and keep your valuables furthest from your body.
- Packs that extend wide with side pockets make it extremely difficult when you're getting on and off trains and buses.
- Packs that extend straight back (such as those with attached packs) force you to lean forward to counter the weight.
- There should be some kind of alternative opening that allows you quick access to the inside or bottom of the pack for things like a rain jacket or first-aid kit.
- Make sure there are compression straps on the outside (usually, the sides) to keep the stuff inside from jiggling about while you walk and to make the pack smaller.
- Look for a top compartment that's completely detachable, because if you can raise and lower that, you can stuff things under it more easily, like a rain jacket during a hike or a damp towel on the way back from the beach. If you need to carry a bag of souvenirs to the post office, for example, the pack can "grow" to accommodate the extra gear temporarily. Also, you could detach it completely, clip on a camera strap, and you've got a shoulder bag that makes an ideal daypack.

The most important feature is that it fits comfortably. This is not something you should buy over the internet, unless you've tried it on first. The waist strap should not dig into your hips and the straps should be easily adjustable when you're on the move. Sometimes, there's one strap that's meant to be sized to the wearer, and it's not that simple to find or adjust. Have the salesperson do it for you. Every pack feels great when there's nothing in it. Drop something heavy in before you try it out. (Good shops have weighted inserts for this very purpose.) There are now a number of special packs for women that are worth checking out, especially if you have a more curvy or petite body type. These packs feature narrower shoulder straps, a shorter frame, more cant on the waist strap and a pack mounted lower on the frame.

Organizing your pack

To facilitate the almost daily packing ritual, make things easier to find and minimize the damage of a sudden rain shower or a broken shampoo bottle on the rest of your gear, keep things in separate bags, one for each of the following: clothes, toiletries, first aid, miscellaneous items, plus an extra plastic bag for wet clothes.

All of your clothes, minus what you need to wear, should fit nicely into a compression sack; one that holds a midweight sleeping bag will do nicely. With a few yanks on the cords, your clothes will be compressed to the size of a rugby ball. Crumpling is unavoidable unless the clothes are wrinkleproof, and even then they won't look perfect. To minimize creases, try rolling your clothes first.

8

Clothes

If you've gone on a short family vacation to a resort with white beaches or ski slopes, you're familiar with the luggage situation: bring as much as you feel like. Two suitcases the size of Japanese import cars aren't an issue. They only have to be dragged into and out of the airport – and there are people around to help with even this. The problem, you're thinking, is that it was difficult enough to figure out how to get a week's worth of stuff into just two enormous suitcases. How on earth are you going to get several weeks' or months' worth into a single tiny backpack?

To customize your packing list, there's **one important question** you need to ask. What clothes do I need to survive a day (not just any day, though: a day in which you go from swimming in the ocean to tanning on the beach to

---

JUST ONE OUTFIT?

There are **two basic approaches** to dressing: stay in the same town and change clothes every day, or wear the same clothes and just change towns. When you travel, you just have to accept that your general standard of cleanliness is going to be lower than you're used to. Also, you're going to have to wash your clothes daily, or tri-weekly – if you try doing it monthly, you're in for some strange looks, not to mention rashes.

Once you get the hang of this, you'll see you don't need more than one set of clothes. If you wash the clothes before you go to bed, hanging them on a clothes line outside, they'll be dry by morning. If you wash the clothes before taking a siesta in the afternoon and hang them in the sun, they'll be dry in about forty minutes.

a cool evening walk in the rain to a moderately nice dinner at a place where there's casual dancing), and be able to wash it all in the sink afterwards, and let it dry without ironing?

Once you've got the clothes for such a day, consider if there is anything you could replace with a similar item which would better serve multiple functions.

Let's start with the swimsuit. For guys (and possibly ladies), make sure it's quick-drying and has pockets you trust enough to put car keys in while you swim – probably some kind of zipper–Velcro combination that'll foil pickpockets as well. The shorts should cover your legs modestly so they can also be used for city exploring – they're the only shorts you have along. For women, it doesn't matter if it's a bikini or a one-piece. You'll also want a beach towel. It should be fairly thin, but long enough to stretch out on comfortably and wrap yourself in modestly (there are special travel towels that work a treat). Later in the day, you'll want a hat and T-shirt to help ward off additional sunburn after your stint on the beach, and to cover yourself when you run over to a café for a snack.

For a cool evening walk, you can get by with sandals. You've got long, comfortable walking trousers. They should have deep front pockets that will deter thieves and not spill your valuables if you need to make a pit stop in the woods (front pockets, like the type found on jeans, tend to work the best). On top you've got a long-sleeved polypropylene shirt that wicks away sweat, a micro-

8

CLOTHES PACK LIST

- 1 T-shirt – if it's a little longer, women can double it as a nightshirt.
- 1 long-sleeve polypro shirt.
- 1 micro-fleece – keep it smart and it can be worn as a pullover in a nice restaurant.
- 1 rain jacket – even expensive Gore-Tex and similar high-tech rainwear won't help much when it pours for hours, and cheaper versions are less likely to get stolen.
- 1 plastic poncho – this covers your pack as well.
- 1 thin beach towel or sarong – an XL special travel towel is ideal.
- 1 swimsuit – doubles as walking shorts for men.
- 1 pair of trousers – not black (because dirt shows), but a good, dark, dirt-hiding color is ideal. Also, make sure they're lightweight, wrinkle-free, comfortable, fairly stylish and easily washable, with good deep pockets.
- 1 wrinkle-free travel shirt – either short- or long-sleeve is fine.
- 1 pair of socks – for cool overnight bus rides and cold hostel floors.
- 2–4 sets of underwear – special travel underwear dries quicker and lasts longer.
- 1 pair of sports sandals. You don't want to skimp on these. They should be reasonably stylish (smart enough for a decent restaurant), have good support on off-road terrain, stay on during a swim, not rot when they get out of the water and allow you to run for a train. You can even use them in the hostel shower.
- 1 collapsible hat.
- 1 bandanna – soak it with water to keep you cool on warm nights. Cover your mouth with it to protect your lungs from dust. Use it to dry off in the shower when you don't have time to let your towel dry.
- 1 wrinkle-free travel skirt or dress, mid-calf in length (women).
- 1 pair of shorts (women).

fleece pullover (not cotton) and a nylon rain jacket and a cap or bandanna. You're carrying your plastic poncho in your small daypack in case it really starts to pour.

For dinner, you can still get by in sandals, especially if they're black or solid earthy colors. You've got a smart, short-sleeved or long-sleeved lightweight, wrinkle-free shirt/blouse. If it's still a little chilly inside, the micro-fleece should be stylish enough to wear. For men, walking trousers will suffice, provided they're not the "adventure travel" type with more zippered pockets and removable bits than a 1980s breakdancer. They should be dark enough to hide any dirt you might have picked up on your walk. Women might also elect to go with a long wrinkle-free mid-calf-length skirt. For day two, wash and repeat.

If you're heading to Europe in the winter, you'll want, of course, warm shoes, wool socks (or "smart wool"), a good jacket, hat and gloves. If you find you need long underwear, you can pick that up once you arrive.

Sleeping items

Brace yourself: for summer travel in Europe, you don't need to take a sleeping bag. Yes, many people take them and find occasion to use them, but not necessarily because they need to. Nearly every hostel can produce a blanket for you as long as you have a **sleepsheet** (which you do need). And in budget digs where air conditioning is typically not included, you'll rarely need more than a sheet. Beyond that, if you layer on all your clothes for a chilly night on a train or bus, you should be fine. In a worst-case scenario, if the weather does get a bit cold and there is no blanket available, you can always pick up a cheap secondhand one or move on to a hostel that does offer blankets.

8

The previously mentioned sleepsheet is – well, just that – a sheet in the form of a sleeping bag. You can sew one yourself from a queen-size flat sheet or buy a premade model. The nicest are silk, which cost a fortune, but can be worth it, as they keep the occasional bedbug out better than the others.

Leave your **pillow** at home. Instead, use the ones provided at the hostels, hotels and pensions. You can bring a pillowcase, but it's a better use of space to simply use your T-shirt or micro-fleece as a pillowcase. If no pillow is available, stuff your towel and micro-fleece and a few other items into your T-shirt and use that. On train rides, if you put your towel in your micro-fleece and gently tie it around your neck, you'll get the same effect as one of those inflatable neck pillows, which can also be left at home.

Toiletries

Start out by buying a toiletry bag with a built-in mirror and hanger, since you can't count on much counter space in the bathroom or having an unfogged mirror surface. Many travelers find that a short haircut makes both the grooming and reduced need for hair products more convenient for travel. There are two odor-related steps: 1) transfer your perfume/cologne from the heavy, breakable, chic bottle to a small sturdy glass one with a tight, screw-on lid (or get a tester vial instead); 2) bring a foot file to help shed dead skin common with extended sandal-wearing so people don't smell you before they see you.

Major-brand contact lens fluid can be found at supermarkets, opticians and pharmacists, so there's no need to bring enough to last an entire journey. Bring a pair of glasses along just in case, plus your prescription in case something happens to your glasses. Pity to travel the world, then have to check your photos back home to see what it looked like in focus.

Again, only buy the miniature travel containers and restock as you go. Local toothpaste is especially interesting to sample and – there's at least one traveler doing this – collect.

For women, tampons and pads are no harder to find in Europe than they are at home. In remote locales they may be slightly more difficult to come by, so make sure you have what you need, especially if you'll be out in the countryside/ forests/mountains. Another alternative (for those with a higher yuck tolerance) is the Mooncup, a reusable diaphragm-like device made from soft silicon.

Miscellaneous gear

8

There are a few tiny items that, when you need them, you need them immediately. And they're not always easy to find. Pick your requirements from this list and keep in a separate bag:

- Earplugs – don't leave home without them. Hostels have a nasty habit of occupying the space above nightclubs and next to busy streets. Plus, every dormitory seems to come with at least one snoring champion.
- Media storage device – mini hard disk, USB keychain, or iPod to back up photos, video or audio.
- Portable battery charger. If you're carrying electronics, you'll want a little backup juice.
- Permanent marker – for making hitchhiking signs and other notices.
- Superglue – this fixes just about everything (keep it in its own plastic bag).
- Duct tape – this fixes nearly everything the superglue doesn't (wrap it around the marker to save space).

TOILETRY PACKING LIST

(Mini-sizes only)

- Toothpaste
- Toothbrush
- Dental floss
- Cologne/perfume
- Foot file
- Contact lens fluid (if needed)
- Lip balm
- Comb/brush
- Face and body lotion
- Razor (not electric)
- Sunscreen
- Mosquito repellent with DEET
- Mirror
- All-purpose soap/shampoo
- Conditioner (if needed)
- Deodorant
- Condoms

- Guitar string/wire – fixes whatever's left.
- Sewing kit – OK, that's a lie. *This* fixes whatever's left.
- Padlock – many hostels have lockers.
- Lighter – you don't need a €70 lighter that works on top of Mount Everest, just something to light candles, camping stoves and certain Dutch coffeehouse products.
- Power adapters (if needed) – the Brits have one bulky kind, the rest of Europe uses another. You can pick up a double adapter at major airports when you land, or before leaving (see ⓦ voltagevalet.com for country requirements).
- Pocket knife – you can leave the Rambo survival blade at home, but make sure yours has a can opener and corkscrew to assist with budget picnics. (You might want to wait until you get to Europe to pick up your knife, as you're unlikely to be able to take one on board your flight. On the way back, you'll likely be checking in a bag with souvenirs, anyway.)
- Spoon – it comes in handy for supermarket-food dining.
- Clothes line – you'll need about 10m of nylon cord. The slightly more expensive version found beside the climbing rope at outdoor shops tangles less.
- Water bottle – for the cheapest version just reuse a water bottle you buy while traveling. Tap water is fine for drinking even if it doesn't always taste great.
- Sink plug – make your own with a piece of duct tape stuck over the drain or chop the top third off a racquetball and you've got one.
- Plastic bag – for wet clothes.

Optional extras

Here are a few extras that you might want to bring along.

- Small travel games: backgammon, chess, Uno and cards are the most popular. They can keep you sane on an overnight train ride, and can be a nice way to meet locals.
- Instrument: OK, it's a cliché, but a guitar can be worth the effort, especially if you're good and plan to earn money playing it on the street or in bars. A harmonica is better suited for transport and not as likely to make people cringe when you take it out.
- Frisbee: doubles as a plate and soup bowl.

First aid

Most prepackaged first-aid kits sold in outdoor stores are borderline worthless. And those nylon sacks don't keep your bandages and pills from getting wet or crushed. Make your own. Start out with a Tupperware container large enough to hold about four muffins. You should be able to resupply all you need (see box, p.114) on the road.

A lot of travelers like to take antibiotics along. And if you're whacking your way through a rainforest for weeks, it's probably not a bad idea. But in Europe you're never that far from a **local doctor or hospital**. If you get sick enough to require antibiotics, you should visit a doctor who can prescribe the best ones for your condition. Plus, many antibiotics don't travel well. If you do take antibiotics, take the full course, even if your symptoms abate after just one or two days. Otherwise, the few microbes that don't get killed off tend to mutate and come back stronger.

MEDICAL PACK-LIST

European **pharmacists** have the authority to prescribe many medications that require a doctor's note in North America, and you'll find any **medication** you might need in western Europe. Since you usually won't be more than a short hop from a pharmacy (most have a neon-green cross above the door), few items are really that essential. It's nice to have a small kit, though, just in case. You don't need much medicine for a few weeks or months of travel. A few pills of each will usually do the trick. Make sure you bring the directions for consumption, and label the pills if you don't bring the entire packet.

- Elastic wrap bandage – if you or a fellow traveler has a major accident, this is the most important thing to have within arm's reach. Vital for twists and big cuts.
- Anti-diarrhea medicine – few forget to bring these.
- Laxatives – few remember to bring these; especially useful for those who don't like dirty bathrooms.
- Antihistamines – you never know what will spark an allergic reaction.
- Hydrocortisone cream – cures most rashes and skin irritations.
- Aspirin/paracetamol – for minor aches and major hangovers.
- Compeed – modern science has created the wonder blister cure.
- Band-aids – put them into a clear plastic sleeve that holds photos or credit cards.
- Iodine – for sterilizing cuts and, for those doing extensive hiking and camping, purifying particularly spooky-looking water (5 drops per liter clear water, 10 drops for cloudy water, then let stand for 30 minutes). If you can't deal with the taste, then water purification tablets or drink mixes are a good idea.
- Rehydration packet – one is enough to get you started (in a crisis, make your own mix: 1 liter water, 1 teaspoon of salt, 8 tablespoons sugar, dash of juice if available).
- Melatonin/arnica – helps with jet lag.
- Motion sickness pills – curvy roads and stale air on bus rides make a lethal combo, not to mention stormy ferry rides.

MEDICAL EXTRAS

If these don't fit in your first-aid container, toss them in the gear bag:
- Tweezers – find a good pair with a sharp point for removing splinters.
- Vaseline – prevents chafing and blisters during long hikes.
- Sports tape – it's mostly for blister prevention, but helps hold band-aids on.
- Antiseptic wet wipes – a great refresher for when you're stuck in a hot bus seat for hours, trying to clean up before a meal, or helping dab a wound.
- Tiger balm – the all-purpose sports cream that also clears up clogged sinuses and soothes headaches.

8

Daypacks

Even a relatively small, internal-frame pack is not a joy to lug around the entire day while you explore ruins, museums and cities. A daypack is a more sensible way to carry the few necessities you'll need.

Most travelers opt for small backpacks, such as the detachable ones that come with packs. To avoid quick-handed thieves and (for women) groping hands in crowds, wearing the daypack on your front is an excellent idea. While it's on your back, though, it can be hard to protect. Some prefer the comfort of a waist pack, but this, too, is something of a thief magnet and looks awfully odd when worn in front. A better idea is a **shoulder bag**. It's easy to tuck under your arm to protect from pickpockets, can be accessed more quickly while you're on the move and doesn't peg you as a tourist, especially in bars and nightclubs. If the top compartment of your backpack detaches, a camera or guitar strap can turn it into a decent shoulder bag. If not, a collapsible one with zipper/Velcro closure is fine.

What to keep in your daypack

- Guidebook – lighten the load by ripping out unneeded sections, or load it on to your tablet or e-reader as an e-book (Ⓦroughguides.com/shop/ebooks).
- Sunglasses – shades without UV protection allow your pupils to widen and expose your eyes to more damaging rays. You'll want a hard case to keep them in one piece.
- Journal/address book and pen – a necessity.
- Something to read – see "Guidebooks and other reading" (p.126).
- Pocket knife (but not on flights) – you don't need the Swiss Army knife with all fifty functions.
- Flashlight – the little LCD key-chain ones work well, and the LCD headlamp with retractable band is even better for cooking in badly lit areas.
- Pocket camera – you can get a good one for under €80. See "Documenting your trip" (p.180) for advice on which type of camera to bring.
- Cell phone and charger (optional) – a tri-band phone works almost everywhere these days and, even if you keep it off, it can be worth it in the one emergency when you need it.

Camping gear

If you already have camping equipment, using it can save you money, but will more than double the size and weight of your rucksack, so **think twice** before carting it along. It's really only sensible for those planning to camp the entire time. If you're not sure, leave the gear at home. Even if you only thought about camping a little, you'll be happier with less stuff and a few extra nights in a hostel. Yes, it is legal to "free-camp" in Sweden, and it is possible to pitch a tent after dark on the edge of small towns elsewhere – if you're sneaky about it – but in most decent campgrounds near popular cities, it's not all that cheap and you'll be spending more time and money on local transport getting in and out of town. And you may worry about your belongings when your tent is unattended. If you do decide not to bring camping gear but change your mind later, you can always buy excellent stuff in Europe, and will likely pick up good secondhand gear from other travelers selling theirs on hostel notice boards.

Checklist

- Light, rainproof tent
- Cooking stove
- Pot with lid
- Cooking utensils
- Sleeping bag
- Sleeping pad
- Headlamp (when you need a light, you usually need your hands as well)
- Tarpaulin to lay under tent
- Water-purifying tablets (iodine works) or small water-purifier pump (don't forget drink mix to add to chemically treated water to improve taste)

8

What you don't need and why

- Shoes – this may come as a shocker, but if you're traveling between May and September in Europe with a decent pair of sandals, you can get by without shoes. And, more importantly, the pairs of nasty socks that stink up your pack. If you find you're going out clubbing regularly, need shoes for work or if it's just getting too cold, buy a cheap pair and ditch them when you're done. This is personal preference, but it's a great way to save space in your pack.
- MP3 player/iPod – this is a great way to tune out and relax. However, you're also cutting yourself off from the sounds of the country which, though often annoying, are part of the experience. More importantly, it discourages locals from making contact with you. Besides, it's something else that can break or get stolen. Unless you need it for digital photo storage, either leave at home or use sparingly. Read a book instead.
- Electronic language translator – just try to have a conversation with one of these! I have yet to see someone pull it off. The most common words and phrases can be looked up in nearly all guidebooks. Better still, take twenty minutes and learn a few words and phrases before you arrive.
- Currency converter – your primary school math skills or smartphone calculator should get you by nicely.
- Pro-camera setup – if you're a serious amateur or professional photographer, bring what you need. If not, this is probably not the time

to start. Forget the SLR, lenses and tripod. Stick with a pocket camera or iPhone and you'll get more use out of it.

- GPS – if you're charting new territory, fine. If not, leave it at home.
- Jeans – resist the temptation to pack your favorite pair, no matter how good you may look in them. They're too warm in hot weather, too difficult to wash by hand and take too long to dry.
- Sweatshirt – the comfort is alluring, but it will take up far too much room, offer no warmth when wet, and require about two days to dry on its own. A micro-fleece (or some petrochemical equivalent) is the way to go. Besides, they're more culturally sensitive than sweatshirts sporting giant university or fraternity logos.
- Water filter – the water in Europe isn't going to kill you. It's easier and more affordable to drink from the tap; just buy bottled water in extreme situations.
- Compass – the sun rises in the east and sets in the west. That knowledge should get you by. At least, if you're not in Scandinavia, where the summer sun never seems to set. If you feel better having a compass along, take a tiny key-chain model. If you set off without a compass, and regret it, you can always buy it along the way.
- Mosquito net – there are mosquitoes in Europe, but such measures aren't typically necessary.
- Mini "travel towel" – the beach-towel-size ones are great. The mini ones preferred by Olympic divers and car washers aren't as practical for the traveler.
- Hair dryer – if you find you must have one, buy a tiny one in Europe so no adapter is needed.
- Full makeup kit.

8

OUR SOUVENIR HABIT

Consider the alchemy: the exuberance of travel mixed with the excitement of shopping. It shouldn't come as any surprise that people have a hard time restraining themselves. It's common to want to bring home little pieces of your journey – no problem there – but why buy things that have nothing to do with your trip other than that they were the items available at some kiosk along the way? Either that, or I must have missed the hotel that requires guests to don Dutch clogs and orange windmill hats.

For some reason setting foot in a country (or continent) seems to give a few people carte blanche either to decorate their living rooms with traditional trinkets which others would consider bad taste, or wear an Oxford sweatshirt when the only affiliation they have with the university is having a beer once at Oxford train station. Perhaps, like overzealous cell phone use, we simply haven't got around to establishing the social etiquette for souvenirs.

Having said that, I must confess, I've got two travel items around the house. One is an automated Japanese toilet seat with a remote control, the other is a Thai bicycle rickshaw I use to pedal my kids to daycare. Admittedly, both items are a little over the top and the rickshaw certainly looks out of its element, but I use them daily, they're experiential, and they provide me with that little taste of travel at home. The mementos that mean the most are the ones I gathered for free – a label from a beer bottle I stuck in my journal, a photo of the travelers I met while on an overnight train journey to Madrid. The rest of the things I bought along the way are all sitting in a box in the basement. They looked so irresistibly cool in the shops I found them in, and the bargaining processes and subsequent mailing experience at the post office were memorable, but I just couldn't find a way to display them that didn't feel forced. When I see that box, it just reminds me I should have spent more time and money traveling and less time shopping.

Doug Lansky

Resupply on the road

There may not be toilet paper in every stall or ice in the drinks, but you can get sweaters, T-shirts, socks, toothpaste, soap, band-aids, contact lens fluid, superglue, all kinds of film, sport sandals, trendy clothes, hats – nearly everything – almost everywhere you go. If 740 million Europeans can survive with the supplies they have, there's a good chance you'll find what you need to get by for a couple of months. Just start out with the smallest tubes and bottles, plan on buying supplements, and special-order something on the internet to your next destination if you simply can't find it. If you're taking medication, bring what you need or bring along your prescription for a refill.

Sending gear ahead

If you're going to be trekking in the Alps or Pyrenees, or hiking national parks every other week of your trip, bring your favorite **hiking boots**. If not, they're going to take up thirty percent of your pack and make the other seventy percent smell. Tying them to the outside of your pack may be even worse: the dangling-ornament look makes it tricky to run for departing transport, knocks people in the head as you enter and leave trains, and creates a stench that circles you like the moons of Saturn. Better to use the postal service to get your boots to the place you'll need them (and send them back when finished). Or simply rent boots when you get there. All major trekking centers have boot rental and cheap secondhand ones for sale, but make sure you give yourself a day or two to wear them in before taking off on a serious hike. For easy hiking in good weather, you can also get lighter weight walking/outdoor shoes which are much less bulky than hiking boots and are both comfortable for walking around cities and useful when it rains.

Sending souvenirs home

Many souvenirs get bought, but far fewer make it home in one piece. The best way to make sure your purchases survive the journey home is to **send them back** as you buy them. With almost daily packing and unpacking, plus the normal wear and tear of the road, your souvenirs have a far better chance of getting lost, broken or stolen in your backpack. Check the local postal regulations before you start boxing up your items. Sometimes there's a certain weight or container size that's extremely cheap, and you can divide your purchases into separate parcels accordingly and save a mint. Overland shipping takes a few months but it usually gets there. If you'd rather not take the chance, try registered mail. (Simply request it at the post office and pay the supplemental fee.) Or, if it's of considerable value, look into FedEx, DHL or another reputable courier. If you can wait until your last stop before stocking up on trinkets, simply buy a cheap duffle bag for €10–15 and courier home the items yourself.

9

Carrying valuables

With a steady stream of Europeans walking the streets in designer suits and custom-made leather shoes, you may not feel like much of a target for theft in Europe. However, with half a glance thieves can see that you're a foreigner and, as such, are probably carrying a bundle of cash, credit cards and a camera. And, with a backpack on, you may not notice their quick hands or be able to give chase if you do. Therefore, you need to handle your valuables with care.

There are several options these days. Passport pouches, also known as money belts, come in a variety of styles. Some go around the waist (just under the trousers), some hang around the neck and others fasten to your leg. Choosing which one to wear is a combination of personal preference, how it works with your clothing and how easy it is for thieves to spot (see p.154). Try a few on before you make a purchase, since this is something you'll be wearing round the clock.

Before you leave, remember to photocopy the cards in your money belt, leave a copy with your family or trusted friends and take a copy with you and store it separately from your money belt or with your travel partner. To save space, try to get all the vital information onto the front and back of one piece of paper.

Scan it as well and email it to yourself or upload it to a trusted online backup vault. There are many to choose from, including: ⓦmyvaultstorage .com, ⓦsafedatastorage.co.uk and even file-sending services like ⓦhightail.com and ⓦwetransfer.com.

Credit cards

A credit card is a fine way to handle (and track) your purchases. In fact, take two. Visa and MasterCard are the most widely accepted. EMV (those little chips embedded in the card) have finally rolled out across North America. Just be sure to know your PIN associated with it, as European merchants require it. Important: you should call your card issuer to activate your credit card for international use when traveling overseas so they don't freeze your account when these charges from numerous countries start rolling in.

9 The benefits

- You can access emergency funds and cover many daily expenses without carrying a thick bundle of cash.
- You can track your finances easily with an online account.
- Parents, relatives and friends can send funds to your account, which you can quickly and easily withdraw.
- Cards can be quite easily replaced if stolen or lost.
- You're entitled to additional insurance when you use the card to make purchases or rent cars.

The drawbacks

- Most credit card companies charge a flat fee (usually a few euros) for foreign ATM use, as well as a clearing-house surcharge. They've also tacked on "conversion fees" (up to five percent) for cash withdrawals and credit card purchases. Having said that, the EU Single Euro Payments Area, SEPA, is trying to harmonize fees across the continent, making things clearer – if not always cheaper; check with your card provider for an update. Sticking to euros wherever possible will minimize fees.
- You'll have to pay interest (around seventeen percent) on the withdrawn cash until your next bill is paid.
- Hold on; it gets worse. If you buy something with your credit card, find it doesn't work, give it back and get the purchase removed from your credit card bill, it gets reconverted back through the whole process, with the credit card company getting a commission and conversion fee again.
- Merchants who accept credit cards pay a small percentage fee to the credit card company for the right to accept their card. Although they're not supposed to do this, many smaller companies make no secret about passing that percentage on to you (though paying it is still often cheaper than withdrawing money from a cash machine, especially for one purchase).

Choosing a credit card

Some credit cards are better than others. It depends on the bank or financial institution behind them and what deals they're offering. When deciding on a credit card, make sure you ask about the surcharges for foreign purchases and cash machine withdrawals. More and more cards are adding a three percent conversion fee (in the UK, for example, Halifax Clarity may be the only remaining card that doesn't do this). Try to find one that doesn't. If you do, cancel your current card and tell them why. These credit cards currently waive the three-percent conversion fee, and many include other perks like mileage credit.

- Barclaycard Arrivals Plus
- Capital One No Hassle Card

- Chase Sapphire Preferred Card
- United MileagePlus
- World Elite MasterCard
- Some Discover cards

Ideally, you will get a credit card that avoids a conversion fee and a bank card that helps you avoid or minimize ATM fees (see below). Together, this amounts to a huge saving.

- Try to boost your spending limit before leaving. Simply call the credit card company and ask if you can get your limit raised. You may have to put more expenses on the card (or cards) than you're used to, and with an emergency purchase, such as a plane ticket or hospital bill, you might be quickly out of funds.
- Many credit cards or bank accounts can be set up for "Auto-pay" ("direct debit"). Each month, your credit card bill (or a minimum payment) will be automatically paid from your check or savings account. That way you don't have to worry about missing any payments and getting hit with the high interest rates credit-card companies thrive on. Of course, what you may have to worry about is having enough money in your bank account. To be safe, meet with your bank manager before you leave and set up a line of credit (€1000–5000) to cover you in a pinch. All this can be easily monitored with an online bank account.

Bank cards and debit cards

Try to take along a card that taps directly into your check or savings account. Some of these bank-issued cards can be used for purchases ("debit cards"), some can't ("cash cards"). Both types can be used to withdraw cash, though. You may still be slapped with a withdrawal fee and perhaps a conversion fee, but you won't have to pay interest on the money withdrawn, which makes them better than credit cards for this purpose. For those who don't trust themselves with the spending limit granted on a credit card, this can be a good alternative, but the drawbacks are clear cut: there's no credit, which is no good when you're faced with unexpected, urgent expenses. "Offline" debit cards are generally less secure (they don't require a PIN and it's a few days before the money is taken from your account). "Online" debit cards ("Chip and PIN" cards in the UK) require a PIN but have instantaneous processing; if they land in the wrong hands, your money could be as good as gone, especially if the loss is not reported immediately. Check the written policy of the card: some limit the stolen amount to €50, others €500, depending on how long it takes you to report the theft. If you can't arrange a credit card, or want to use this as a second credit card, you'll need to ring or meet with your bank. To ease transactions, reduce withdrawal fees and quickly remedy any theft problems, it's a good idea to select an international bank with branches across Europe, such as Citibank or HSBC.

9 | Cash machines

Holes in the wall, or **ATMs**, are everywhere, but they're not infallible: they sometimes run out of cash, break down and may even occasionally swallow your card for no good reason. When that happens at home, it's a hassle. Abroad, it can make for a very unpleasant day. With all the fees involved, it can cost as much as €4 to take out as little as €20, so the fewer the withdrawals, the better (though bear in mind that some banks don't charge a fee for international withdrawals, so you may want to shop around). See "Directory" for ATM locator websites (p.332). Stick to ATMs in banks. The ones in gas stations, hotels, 7-Elevens etc, often offer worse rates or extra fees.

Many merchants now offer a service to let you pay in US dollars. Always choose to pay in the local currency instead. Why? Because that US dollar-rate they can display with the push of a button typically includes a lousy exchange rate.

Avoiding ATM charges

Here's an important development: the formation of the **Global ATM Network**, a number of large banks which have come together to waive fees on cash withdrawn from their ATMs (yes, free ATM withdrawals). Just be sure to check that the ATM is part of the Global Network, as those outside the network have among the highest fees. In North America, the banks in this network are Bank of America (ⓦbankofamerica.com) and Scotiabank (ⓦscotiabank.com). If you pick up one of their bank cards, when you get to Europe you can get fee-free use at ATMs from Barclays (UK, Spain, Portugal), Deutsche Bank (Germany, Poland, Czech Republic, Spain, Portugal, Italy), and Banca Nazionale del Lavoro (Italy). It will likely require some extra walking to find one of these ATMs, but these large banks should have branches in most major cities. (Now the bad news: Bank of America charges a 3 percent conversion fee on those withdrawals.)

Here's another option. Use a mega-universal bank card like HSBC and pay a reduced fee of $2.50 per withdrawal. For US residents, Charles Schwab currently has the best deal with their high-yield checking account, with no fees at ATM machines – they get reimbursed at the end of each month – no minimum amount and no monthly service fee.

Travelers' checks

Travelers' checks were once a great idea. Now technology has caught up and the conventional wisdom is that travelers' checks are defunct – certainly they're hard to cash across much of the world – having been replaced by convenient ATMs. So while it's a good idea to have more than one form of payment (cash, credit card, bank card), travelers' checks don't need to be part of this equation.

Cash

Of course, you'll want to **carry cash** as well. The question is how much. For starters, you should try to keep a €250–500 emergency stash on you at all times because… well, you never know – a bank's computer system is down, you get fined by a conductor for failing to make a reservation on an overnight train, the guy selling the last ticket to a Madonna concert in a stone amphitheater in Greece will only take cash, and so on. I've had to dip into my emergency fund more times than I care to count. Consider keeping €50–100 of your emergency stash separate from your passport pouch. Perhaps taped to the inside of your backpack – just enough to spend a night in the hostel, get some food or take transport to the nearest embassy.

If you're using credit cards and bank cards, it's a better idea to use them for as many purchases as possible. That way, you've got records of your expenses and you can limit the amount of cash you need to carry. You'll still need some pocket change, though, as it's not possible to put every beer, postcard or subway ticket on a card. Minimizing cash withdrawals (ie the cash withdrawal fees) is a huge saving. Finding the balance between curtailing cash withdrawals and not carrying too much money is largely dependent on your comfort level and how much you're spending. Some find €50 is fine for pocket change. Others prefer €250. It may take a week or two to find an amount that works best for you.

Other items for your money belt

Passport

The money belt is, in fact, where you want to keep your passport. To find out how to get a passport, see "Documents and insurance" (p.94).

Train/bus pass

For a long trip, you may want to protect these with a bit of plastic wrap or a zip-lock bag as well.

Driver's license

It's helpful to have an official photo ID besides your passport, especially since there's a chance you'll end up driving a car at some point. There's little need to get an International Driving Permit (which essentially makes it easier for the police to write you a ticket), but it is "recommended" in Albania, Belarus, Bosnia-Herzegovina, Bulgaria, Croatia, Hungary, Iceland, Italy, Macedonia, Montenegro, Portugal, Romania, Russia, Serbia, Spain, Turkey and Ukraine – to find out exactly where it's required, see the updated list at ⓦ theaa.com. They are easy to get – see the "Directory" chapter, for a list of automobile associations (p.335). Should you decide to pick one up, be warned: the document won't easily fit in your money belt.

9

THE DECOY WALLET

Most thieves want nothing more from you than your **money**. They're not interested in your novel or sandals or designer toiletry bag. They don't want to hurt you, either. You should always be cooperative, just in case. Nothing in your pocket is worth your life. But before you hand over everything you've got (or let a clever pickpocket nick it), consider carrying a fake wallet. That is, a cheap wallet with an old library card, some used airline ticket stubs, an expired credit card, and about €10 in change. This gives you something to hand over (or a more obvious target for pickpockets) to thieves who may not study the contents until they've made their getaway.

Student ID card/under-26 youth card/teacher card

If you qualify for one of these (see p.61), probably best to keep it close by. It's not as valuable as the other items in your money belt, but its size makes it easy to lose.

Hostel cards

If you plan to get a Hostelling International card or VIP Backpackers card (see p.61), remember they need to be purchased before you leave home.

A few extra passport photos

If you decide to make a side trip from Europe because you found a cheap flight and some friends to join, know that visas and such often need three photos just for one application. Local transport cards sometimes require them as well. Better to take a few extra than have to wander off looking for a place to get a snapshot in a hurry. If this is expensive to arrange at home, pick them up once in Europe. Photo booths can be found in virtually every major train station.

Insurance card

If you've got insurance (see p.99), carry the card. If you're just issued a large piece of paper, make your own card with your account number and emergency telephone number and laminate it.

Phone card

These cards list the local access numbers you'll need (available online if you misplace the card), so you have them handy in case of an emergency. You can get them free from the phone service you plan to use.

Other licenses

If you're a trained scuba diver or pilot, or hold other such licenses that easily fit into a money belt, bring them along. You never know when you might need them.

One anti-diarrhea pill

It's hard to predict when dysentery is going to strike. Inevitably, it'll happen while you're out wandering around town or on a long bus ride with your medical kit stored in the luggage hold below. Best to keep one pill handy for such emergencies.

A small pen

Always comes in handy. Pico-pad (ⓦpicopad.com) makes a pen and pad of paper that is the size of a credit card.

10

Guidebooks and other reading

This is precisely where you might expect to find a few sentences of Rough Guide propaganda. Happily, you won't. Not much, anyway. Naturally, the editors and writers at Rough Guides are proud of the guidebooks they produce, but they also understand it comes down to individual taste, trust, and how you like your information gathered and presented.

Besides Rough Guides, guidebook publishers aimed at the independent traveler include Footprint, Let's Go, Lonely Planet, Time Out city guides and (for French speakers) Le Guide du Routard. For more mainstream travel, there's also Frommer's, Fodor's, the design-intense DK Eyewitness guides and Rick Steves' self-guided tours.

You'll want to bring some pure pleasure reading as well. This chapter will explain how many books you'll need to cart along – or download – on your trip, no matter how many weeks or months you'll be spending on the road.

How to pick a guidebook

The best thing is to **"test-drive"** a few different guides in your home town or on your next short trip and see which one suits you. At the very least, you should go to a bookstore and pick up a few guides on the same country and compare a few paragraphs on the same topic. Start with a city or town you're particularly interested in. Is the layout and writing easy to follow? Are the maps clear? Also take a look at the author bio – you'll want someone (or several people) who has spent considerable time in the country they're writing about. It's always helpful if they speak the language and have been able to get information by conversing with the locals.

How to use your guidebook

If this trip to Europe will be your first time using a guidebook, you'll be amazed. Guidebooks have everything you need to know to get around: where to stay, where to eat and what to do while you're there. However, this does more than just provide incredible help; it removes some of the adventure. Moreover, it sends everyone to the same places; not just the same towns, but the same cafés, hostels, bars and scenic overlooks. Ask nearly any guidebook author and they'll tell you their book is best used as a reference, not a bible or substitute tour guide. The little maps are great for helping you navigate your way from the train station to a hostel at 3am, or finding a vegetarian restaurant in Scandinavia, but your best guide is still your own nose. Seek out for yourself those undiscovered restaurants and lodgings, and you'll likely have a much more memorable experience.

10

Here's another common misuse. The temptation is to sit on the bus or train approaching the city and scrutinize the hostel descriptions. Then, you compare your favorites over and over until you get them into your head, and before you know it you've got the experience largely mapped out before you've even done it. Save yourself the effort; it's not worth it. There's not that much difference between four recommended hostels (the first few on the list are usually the most popular). And if you don't like it you can move out the next day once you've had a chance to look around, or just crash there at night and spend your waking hours elsewhere in town (or lounging in the lobby of a four-star hotel, if you prefer).

You'll eventually find a system that works for you, but mine is something like this: if I'm tired out or staying somewhere a bit longer, I'll pick a place further from the center. If I'm just staying a day or two and feeling fresh, I'll go for the best-rated of the fleapits in the center. If I'm not feeling well, I'll go for the cheapest room with an attached bathroom. If there are a few decent choices in any of these categories, I'll typically go for the ones that are the easiest to get to and within walking distance from the center. But, whatever the case, I won't spend more than five or ten minutes deciding.

How many guidebooks to bring

Here's some good news. Just because you're planning to hit twenty countries on your trip doesn't mean you need to pack twenty guidebooks – or download that many on your phone (Kindle or tablet). Just take the one for the country or region you're heading to first and buy, download or trade for the rest as you go. Relevant guidebooks (those for that country or city, plus surrounding ones) can be found in hostels, hotels, bookstores and airports – virtually everywhere (sometimes cheaper, sometimes more expensive). Someone in the hostel is sure to have a more detailed book you can borrow for an hour or two. Ideally, you'll be able to locate someone who's heading in the direction you just came from and make a straight swap. If you're trading with a hostel or secondhand bookstore, you may have to throw in some money or a novel to complete the deal.

Digital guides vs print

Print guides: Nicer to hold, easier to flip, maps are far easier to read and navigate, not reliant on battery and easier to see in the sunlight.
Phone/tablet guides: Cheaper, take up less space, can be used in poor lighting and you don't look like a tourist when you use your phone in public. One word of advice: it's not worth uploading your guidebook to your Kindle as the maps will be barely legible. Far better to use a tablet or smartphone.

What to read along the way

One of the very best ways to add richness to your trip and bring the locales to life is to read up on them. This entails putting aside the iPhone, getting beyond the brief guidebook descriptions and finding stories that explore cultural nuances and history easily missed while searching for your hostel or a better exchange rate. The **Travelers Tales** series of diverse and well-crafted anthologies on popular destinations do just this (ⓦtravelerstales.com). If you can find room for (or manage to lift) James Michener's *Iberia* or *Poland* tomes, you're in for a treat, with folklore and fiction woven into the countries or regions named in the title. But it would be a pity to miss out on some of the **classics**, especially in the regions where they are set. Reading books like *Ulysses* in Ireland, *Crime and Punishment* in Russia or *Death in the Afternoon* in Spain is not just one of the great joys of travel, it's a snap. The classics are among the most popular titles read along the appropriate routes and can be bought or traded quite easily. Even the popular modern travel books, such as Bill Bryson's *Neither Here Nor There: Travels in Europe* or Adam Gopnik's charming bestseller *Paris to the Moon*, are easy to find. So, when you're starting out, one paperback will do. Start with something you like and let your continuous swaps serve as a literary adventure that runs parallel to your trip.

Tips for using your tablet abroad

Another way to go is the tablet route. As long as you remember to keep it charged (and from getting broken or stolen), this can be a great way to access any book you like. The Kindle's battery (two months on a single charge), daylight reading screen, lower cost, and smaller/lighter body make it better suited to travel reading than an iPad. But here's an important setting to consider: though there are no longer international charges for Kindle downloads over wi-fi, you can get hit with $4.99 per week charges for using 3G (or faster). This can change at any time and by country (and there may be fees for magazines, but not books), so check their website for the latest updates.

For iPad users, consider investing in a good case... something both solid (like the defender case from ⓦotterbox.com) and that doesn't draw too much attention, like the BookBook case (ⓦtwelvesouth.com) and a portable battery charger like the Power Monkey (ⓦpowertraveler.com).

11

When you arrive

Take one step off the plane into the cultural mystery of Europe and – bam! – everything is still in English. Most of the major European gateways provide soft landings in this respect. There are free luggage carts and easy-to-use automated ticket machines (with English directions) that accept credit cards. High-speed rail links whisk you to the city center. Tourist information booths provide enough brochures to fill a small library, and the person behind the desk will answer any question you can think of, probably in no fewer than three languages.

11

Some people like to book a room for a few nights in advance. That's fine. You can let your travel agent do it or you can find a hotel/hostel or Airbnb place on the web. Others prefer to begin honing their room-finding skills right off the bat. That's not a bad idea, either. After consulting your guidebook, you might book a room from the airport through a tourist office. Or take a train or bus into the center of the city and book via a tourist office there. Alternatively, you might buy a local phone card in the airport and make a few calls to see who has space. Or simply use public transport to get to an area with several hostels and walk from one to the next to check them out on your own.

OK, you've found a place to stay and put your pack down. Now it's time to see some of Europe's sights, right? Sure, but don't forget that you're already traveling. The subway ride to the hostel, asking directions, finding a bite to eat en route… that's all part of the experience. Traveling is just as much about getting there as arriving, or maybe even more so.

One of the best ways to take advantage of your time on the road is to vary the way you travel down it. How you get around, whether it be on water, in the air, on wheels or on the back of an animal, will shape the memories you bring home. And that doesn't just apply to transport. You can be adventurous or timid in your choice of accommodation, what you eat, even the bathrooms you decide to use. It's always going to be easier to travel in the style you are accustomed to at home, but making the choice (often several times a day)

POINTS OF CONFUSION

- Cities aren't always spelt the same way in their native language. For example, Cologne is Köln, Copenhagen is København, Florence is Firenze, Geneva is Genève, Munich is München, Prague is Praha, Venice is Venezia and Vienna is Wien.
- Nor are countries: Austria is Österreich, Croatia is Republika Hrvatska, Finland is Suomi, Germany is Deutschland, Hungary is Magyar Köztársaság, Italy is Italia, Norway is Norge, Spain is España, Sweden is Sverige, Switzerland is Schweiz or Suisse, and Turkey is Türkyie.
- Often the countries have abbreviations, commonly seen on vehicle license plates or as a sticker. Some are less than obvious. For instance, BiH is Bosnia-Herzegovina, CH is Switzerland, D is Germany, E is Spain, FL is Liechtenstein and GB is the United Kingdom.
- A comma is used instead of a period or full stop in prices. €3.50 is often written €3,50. The UK, however, uses the same system as the US.
- The date is typically written day/month/year.
- Time is posted military style when written – 09:00 is 9am, 14:00 is 2pm, 23:00 is 11pm. Again, the UK and US use the same non-military system. Verbally, the am/pm system (ie "meet you for dinner at seven") is used.
- A road sign of a town's silhouette with a slash through it means you're leaving the town and can resume the speed limit at which you were driving before you had to slow down to pass through the town.
- European banks often close at 3pm, and at noon on a Saturday, if they're open during the weekend at all.
- Many stores in rural areas close for lunch.

11

to try the local alternatives will ultimately enrich your trip. This chapter will provide you with a little taste of what lies ahead.

Transport

Take as diverse a range of transport as you can. Hail a black cab in London, jump on a tram in Vienna, ride a bike in Amsterdam, and hop on every subway you come across. If you have the chance, skip the air-conditioned bus and try... well, anything. Here's a guide to getting yourself around. To find the transport that best fits your schedule and budget, see Chapter 2 (p.35).

Bicycle

Bikes can be rented nearly everywhere. And where they can't be rented you can pick up a low-tech, used model for €40–70. Take advantage of this. It's an ideal way to get to know an area, particularly those set up to accommodate bicycles: you can stop whenever you get the urge, yet you're more inclined to venture further off the main tourist routes, which will afford you some of the most interesting views. Most major cities, like London and Paris, have free (or very cheap) bike schemes, though the bikes aren't quite as nice as rental cycles.

Bicycle rickshaws

Some cities offer a sporadic bicycle rickshaw service, including battery-assisted aerodynamic models. But they are essentially for tourists and, as such, overpriced, especially compared to India, Thailand or wherever the concept was imported from. There's no meter, so always fix the price before you depart.

Buses

Long-distance buses are convenient and well air-conditioned. Try to get a window seat near the front to help avoid nausea on curvy roads. Sit on the side that's not getting direct sunlight (take a moment to figure this out before you step onto the bus – heading south in the afternoon, you'll want to be on the east side, the side to the right when entering; that way, you can keep the window shade open and get a nice view). For safety, keep a few rows between

11

HOW TO TRAVEL RESPONSIBLY

No matter what your position is on climate change – man-made or not – there's no denying that traveling impacts the environment. In fact, the very best thing you can do to combat global warming is to never leave home at all unless you're doing it on foot or on a bike. But back in the real world, we enjoy traveling and are not willing to give it up. What to do? Here are a few things you can do to minimize your impact and travel responsibly:

- **Stay longer.** By far the filthiest part of your trip is going to be your flights, so repeatedly flying back and forth across the Atlantic is releasing more CO_2 than you want to know about. Save up for a longer trip instead.
- **Take the train.** Even if the electricity powering the train was produced by burning coal or oil, your contribution to global warming will always be less than if you took the plane.
- **Bike.** City councils all over Europe have been pouring millions into making their towns bike-friendly. Make use of that and get some exercise and a better look at the town while you're at it. The only downside is the rain, but chances are there is a café nearby that you can linger in while it passes.
- **Plant trees.** They suck pollution right out of the air, so if you plan to work with a forest conservation group or similar during your trip you can ease at least a few minutes of that eight-hour flight.
- **Carbon offset.** Especially if you can't do the above, you should think about carbon offsetting your trip. Do your research, though – some carbon offsetting schemes are much more effective than others, and you may prefer one which invests in clean technology to one which plants trees. Some only calculate flight offsetting, while others also cover trains, cars, buses etc.
- **Recycle.** Europeans are generally really good at this. Take some time to figure out what goes where in public trash cans.
- **Clean up dive sites.** Okay, this one won't reduce global warming, but it's a nice way to give back to the local diving community and help make sure the reefs are still alive for your next visit. Many dive shops will give you a free dive if you come along to help.

you and the front to cushion any collision. For Busabout and Eurolines information, see Chapter 2 (p.35).

Canoe

Paddle your way around parts of Iceland, Scotland or France. You can find places to canoe just about everywhere, as well as places that will rent you canoes. Pick up a good map, some local tips and a few trash bags to waterproof your backpack, and you're ready to go.

Car

See Chapter 2 (p.35) for general information on transport, and buying, selling and renting cars as you travel.

11

Cruise ship

This doesn't fit the traditional traveler image. The cabins aren't conducive to drying hand-washed laundry, the staff don't appreciate people walking down the corridors in just a towel, and body art and piercing may frighten some of the other passengers. But this can be a way to connect certain legs of your trip at a decent price. Especially if you hop aboard an EasyCruise (ⓦeasycruise.com), which is relatively inexpensive and full of young, independent travelers.

Ferry

Many of these are nearly as luxurious as their cruise-ship cousins, with hot tubs, saunas, movie theaters and discos, and are more expensive if you try to bring along a car.

Horse

Equestrian travel can be incredibly romantic and exciting. You can take a horseback tour on the coasts of Ireland or Spain or in the forests of Germany. But in the words of Ian Fleming, "A horse is dangerous at both ends and uncomfortable in the middle." Make certain, therefore, that you get a little practice before you head out on a longer journey, and spend some time getting to know your steed's signals before you need to interpret them in an emergency.

Motorcycles

There are probably two hundred safer ways to navigate your way around Europe, but few that offer the opportunity to do so in leather. Helmets and protective clothing are a must, as road conditions change around every mountain curve, and European drivers can be… well, capricious.

Planes

No need to confirm your flights, but it's a good idea to make sure there haven't been any cancelations. If you check in before heading to the airport – a good idea with many budget airlines to avoid extra charges at the airport – getting there an hour in advance at a small airport and ninety minutes in advance at a larger airport is typically enough, unless they've advised you otherwise.

If you're nervous about flying with budget companies, that's normal, but remind yourself that they have a strong safety record and it's statistically safer than other modes of transport, including walking. Flying during daylight may help with some of your worries.

River-kayak

11

These are short and rugged, and they tip over easier than a toddler on Rollerblades, so it's best to take a course when getting started. Because handling is so sensitive, most serious kayakers prefer their own boats (and helmets). However, on a long trip, you'll probably just have to make do with what's available. If you stick to the main rafting centers (Austria, Germany, Slovenia, Czech Republic, Switzerland), you'll find there's good equipment on hand and, depending on your skill level, you may be able to catch free rides on rafting trips, working as a safety kayaker.

Sea-kayak

Both the hard-shell and the collapsible variety have their merits, depending largely on how you're able to transport them. They're increasingly available for rent, so inquire before you drag yours halfway around the globe. You'll also need to check with airlines to see what additional fees are involved for taking them on board.

Subway

No matter how little there is to see out of the window, a subway is an integral part of any big city's character. Some offer incredibly high-speed and efficient transport, some are overdue for repair and some are simply underground marvels. The lines in Moscow, St Petersburg and London, and some of the stations in Stockholm, are particularly worth a look.

Taxis

At home, you might order a taxi or flag one down for a short ride. You can do that on the road as well. From a financial viewpoint, make sure you know what you're getting into. A ten-minute ride in a Swiss taxi might cost you as much as €40. Also know that, possibly as a result of high fuel prices, many taxis wait at designated spots around the city instead of driving around. So it may be far quicker to ask directions to the nearest taxi stand than wait for one to pass by.

Trains

Important: remember to check that the train carriage you are boarding has the name of the city you are going to posted on the side, or at least a city beyond the one you're heading to. If the individual carriage says "Hamburg" on it, that's where it's going. But that doesn't mean the entire train is going to Hamburg. In fact, there's a good chance it isn't. Trains drop off some carriages and pick up others along the route, so you can easily end up someplace you hadn't counted on – and many people do.

It's tempting, especially with rail passes, to save money by spending a few nights on the train. Overnight trains aren't the safest form of accommodation or quite the bargain they might seem, so learn about supplementing your pass with other cost-effective travel (see p.63).

11

High-speed trains have become more common around Europe with France's TGV, Germany's Inter-City Express (ICE), Spain's Alta Velocidad España (AVE), Italy's Pendolino and Thalys in Belgium and Netherlands. There are even high-speed lines in the UK. With high-speed comes high prices, so it's almost always cheaper to get some type of rail pass. (It may even be cheaper to fly.)

There's a monopoly on the food, so plastic-wrapped sandwiches are priced like Michelin-star entrées; fortunately, though, the rides don't last that long, so a few pack-along snacks should see you through.

Water taxis/buses

Water taxis are found in several cities, from Venice to Stockholm, and are usually priced for vacationing millionaires, so make sure it's a special occasion before you flag one down. Water buses, or *vaporetti* and *traghetti* as they're known in Venice, are quite reasonable and good for getting around. *Vaporetti* travel on fixed routes and *traghetti* are flagged down, but cost just 70 cents to take you to the other side of the Canal Grande. It's the gondolas that require a wallet the size of a life jacket.

Accommodation

Barcelona is a little too far to travel to stay at the *Hilton*. And your budget is likely to suffer from even one night's plush rest. It may take some time to get used to staying in budget digs, but it's more rewarding than it might initially seem. There's a sense of camaraderie that you simply won't find at the *Ritz*. You can swap tales at breakfast, make dinner together, play backgammon – it's a nomadic commune of sorts. The atmosphere changes from place to place, even from day to day if enough new travelers pull in. You can also seek more interesting places from time to time: a hostel in a cave, a bed in a backyard tree house, an ice hotel. Even if these unconventional digs cost a little more, it's usually worth the experience.

Camping

Traveler camping falls into two categories: free camping, which is usually illegal but pretty easy to do outside of big cities; and paid camping, at designated campgrounds with bathrooms and other amenities. If you plan to go down the free-camp route, you'll probably need to give big cities a miss. Many of the city parks are too dangerous to sleep in, or too likely to be patrolled by police. In smaller towns, you can usually find a field, perhaps even a remote part of a park, if you're discreet. Some designated campgrounds are quite extravagant, with a restaurant, supermarket and pool, but even the smaller ones can be surprisingly expensive. For just a little more, you can often rent a walk-in tent with a "real" bed. Sweden and Norway allow you to put up tents legally, even on private property (if 100–150m from the nearest residence and you don't stay more than two nights; as a matter of etiquette, ask the permission of the owner if possible), which makes these ordinarily expensive destinations a good deal cheaper.

11

Farmstays

The name conveys the gist. You stay on a working **farm** where the family has made a few rooms available to those who are willing to pay for the experience. It's a bit like a B&B with animals. There's a significant range in comfort and price, but many of them dip well into the budget range (€30, including breakfast). Some offer courses in riding or gardening, many provide family-style meals, and you can sample everything from grape growing to feeding pigs to making cheese to horseback riding. For lists of farmstays all over Europe, visit ⓦagritourismworld.com/directory/international/europe.

Free accommodation around the world

Yes, this has appeared in other sections of this book because it affects so many things – budget, cultural immersion, etc – but the emergence of Couchsurfing may be the single biggest advancement in budget travel since the guidebook came along (see p.68).

Guesthouses, pensions & B&Bs

These are typically private homes or apartments with a few spare rooms or bungalows. They're often run by older people whose children have moved out, and who are looking to earn a little extra money by letting travelers into their private living space. This means showing a little more respect and courtesy than you might at a hostel. Even if these places are rather lacking in services, keep in mind you're living in someone's home.

With the success of ⓦAirbnb.com, everyone seems to be opening a pension in their house/flat or renting their places out while they're away to earn a little extra money (see box, pp.66–67 & p.68).

Independent hostels

Independent hostels come in as many different shapes and sizes as rocks, which, coincidentally, is what some of them seem to stuff their mattresses with. You'll find some setups extremely professional, and others lacking. Some have great bar scenes with cheap food and people dancing on the tables in the evenings; others feel like giant, anesthetized dormitory-type buildings with concierges who could easily double for nurses in *One Flew Over the Cuckoo's Nest*. Others are blissfully charming and serene with hammocks and sofas. Some are even housed in converted boats moored to the pier or in disused trains permanently parked near the train station. They can be both centrally located and fiendishly remote, with little commonality other than being the cheapest digs in town.

For general **hostel bookings** around Europe, try ⓦhostels.com, ⓦhostelworld.com or ⓦeurotrip.com. Also, ⓦhostelz.com offers reviews. For other travelers' opinions go to ⓦtripadvisor.com.

International youth hostels

You don't have to be a certain age to stay at a youth hostel. Being young at heart is enough. With all the senior travelers around, some hostels even seem more like retirement communities. Official Hostelling International (HI) hostels are part of an organization, which means there are certain standards, although it doesn't mean the standards are terribly high. Nearly all of these are well cleaned, some practically sterile, with dormitory-style rooms and separate quarters for men and women, self-service kitchens, common rooms, lockers and a cost of €10–30 per night if you're avoiding any of their "luxury" rooms. Some are equipped with pools, hot tubs and barbecues, while others are about as basic as their tree-and-hut logo. Although there are many notable and award-winning exceptions (with new updates occurring all the time), official HI hostels aren't known to score high in the architecture or roaring-social-life departments. Most are located a little way out of the center of town and a few come with a curfew or kick you out during the day for cleaning. There are almost always budget alternatives, but if this sounds like your cup of discounted tea, pick up the membership card. Without the card, you're still welcome, but you will pay slightly more. Try to book in advance if you know when you're arriving, especially in high season. There are several other discount cards worth considering (see p.61).

- **Hostelling International** ⓦhihostels.com. A not-for-profit association (and brand name) of hostels (over 4000) around the world, with discounts for members.
- **European Alliance of YMCAs** ⓦymcaeurope.com. Similar in atmosphere to the HI hostels, the YMCA also offers health-club facilities and fairly inexpensive accommodation for members.

Hotels

These are still often judged on a "star" ranking system, and it's often hard to know who's doing the officiating. But typically, one star denotes low budget, sometimes without maid service. Two stars usually has daily maid service. Three stars is supposed to be a moderately priced (for the region) middle-class operation, sometimes with a pool. Four stars is an expensive, top-tier hotel with luxury services. And five stars is the ultimate in luxury – just park your private jet at the front and the staff will offload your polo ponies for you.

Sleeping rough

Ah, the last resort of the traveler, the safety net that leaves your back out of alignment, the experience that will help you overcome whatever was annoying you about hostels. At some point, it's possible you'll be spending the night on a park bench or in a train station or airport lounge. There are obviously risks associated with sleeping rough. In particular, it's not a good idea for single women travelers, especially in (or just outside) a train station – in fact, train stations are best avoided by all, really. And a secluded park bench at night is even riskier.

11

But if you do find yourself having to sleep rough, bear in mind the following tips. Firstly, you probably won't be the only one doing it, so when it looks inevitable start trying to secure a good spot. What's a good spot? You'll know it when you see it (if there is one). Not too hidden, not where people have to step over you, not right under bright lights. Corners are usually quite nice, and frequently coveted. You may be inadvertently borrowing the resting place of a "regular" – so be forewarned that they may not take too kindly to this. Look for newspaper or cardboard to place under you; a cold marble floor will drain your body heat and make it difficult to rest. If you've got a travel partner, take turns staying awake. If not, make sure you're bear-hugging your backpack while you sleep. Alternatively, look for an all-night snack shop or bar and sip tea or coffee until the sun creeps up, then find a more comfortable place to sleep at a park or beach.

Eating

No matter what level of comfort you choose to travel in, you don't want to circle the globe without sampling the local cuisine. Check out the produce, meat and fish markets, or follow your nose into a tiny restaurant and discover hand-rolled pastas in Sicily or fresh tapas in Seville. There's no need to be paranoid about what passes your lips. If it looks truly vile (like greenish drinking water, for example), you might want to give it a miss. Otherwise, eat, drink, be merry, and invest in some lightning-fast cures for diarrhea (see p.167).

Hostels

They know the budget of their customers better than anyone. They also take advantage of traveler physics: a traveler not yet packed tends to stay that way

---

MCDONALD'S

On the one hand, there's simply too much wonderful food out there to justify a trip to the **Golden Arches**. On the other, *McDonald's* has some rather interesting (albeit processed and chemically enhanced) dishes in addition to the old classics. Italy (some argue you should be shot for entering a *McDonald's* while in Italy) has a Caprese salad with mozzarella and tomatoes; Germany has a shrimp lemon burger and beer to wash it down; Greece has a Chicken Mythic burger with Monterey Jack cheese; Spain has gazpacho; and Turkey has the Köfte Burger, a spiced patty inside a bun enriched with yogurt mix. Poland even tried a McKielbasa that flopped. The point is, if you absolutely must get your McFix while you're on the road (and these places are packed with travelers), you can at least give yourself a push by trying something you haven't seen before or can't pronounce.

11

for a while. Once in "hangout" mode, it's tempting to stick around the hostel. Many hostels offer extremely cheap stews, sandwiches and plates of pasta. The ones that don't may offer cooking facilities. Team up with another traveler, or an entire group, head to the supermarket and make a meal together.

Restaurants

Eating at restaurants can run up your expenses quickly so choose where you eat with care. As comforting as it may be to dine with other travelers, you'll often get a better deal ditching the guidebook, heading to the poorer parts of town and checking out the places (normally packed with locals) that don't take credit cards.

Street vendors

Don't believe the intestine-quivering rumors. Not every **street snack** leads to a week in bathroom solitude. In fact, buying food from street vendors is a wonderful way to supplement your diet: some travelers manage to exist entirely on these budget snacks. As a tip, when possible pick the vendors who prepare the food right in front of you.

Personal hygiene

Staying clean on the road is a challenge at times. It becomes particularly rough during the back-to-back long-transit stretches (an overnight train ride followed by a day walking around a hot city followed by another overnight train ride). If you encounter some intimidating toilets, that can be a problem as well. Either way, relief can be found.

Airports and buses

Many airports now have showers available for a few euros. Some have a sauna and gym as well. You may have to hunt around a little, as they're not as well situated as the duty-free items and postcards. Even if you have to put your yet-unwashed clothes back on, a refreshing shower can be an enormous boost. And you'll probably have some spare coins to get rid of anyway. If you don't take the opportunity during a long haul, the smell is only going to get worse. The budget route, of course, is simply to wash up in the restroom, perhaps with a damp paper-towel "shower", and swing by the duty-free and take a squirt of perfume before the next leg of your journey.

On nicer bus rides, particularly around eastern Europe and Turkey, don't be surprised if an attendant comes by and offers you a splash of unisex perfume or some fragranced towelettes. They're not as pleasant as the warm washcloths distributed by many airlines, particularly considering they have the olfactory properties of toilet-bowl cleaner, but it's still better than being trapped beside someone with nuclear BO. The individually wrapped moist tissues function better, since they also remove the dirt and odor rather than simply masking it. Bring some of your own just in case.

Turkish baths

You'll find some classics in Turkey but also in other cities around Europe, like Paris, Stockholm and London. Look for the word "hammam." They're a perfect remedy for travel grime – the accumulated film that covers your body after weeks of low-pressure showers. These medieval bathhouses are mild steamrooms with washbasins, and most offer, for an additional fee, a joint-cracking, back-popping, skin-blasting "massage" that will leave you feeling like a boneless chicken. Upon exiting, you can cool down wrapped in towels with a refreshing yogurt drink.

HOT HAMMAMS

Galatasaray Hammam, İstanbul, Turkey
Built by Sultan Beyazit in 1481, now an upscale classic more popular with visitors than locals. The full treatment includes massage and abrasive sponge scrub-down Ⓦ galatasarayhamami.com.

Gellert Baths and Spa, Budapest, Hungary
Budapest has some of the planet's top Turkish baths, some complete with Ottoman architecture Ⓦ gellertbath.com.

Harrogate Turkish Baths, England
England's most famous Turkish baths Ⓦ turkishbathsharrogate.co.uk.

Les Bains du Marais, Paris, France
Elegant upscale hammam and sauna, with a restaurant and hair salon as well Ⓦ lesbainsdumarais.fr.

Portobello Swim Centre, Edinburgh, Scotland
An old restored bathhouse at a good price Ⓦ edinburghleisure.co.uk.

Sturebadet, Stockholm, Sweden
Upscale, luxury bathhouse in the city center Ⓦ sturebadet.se.

TURKISH BATHS FOR WOMEN

Traditional Turkish bathing rituals are a little complex, but I kept reminding myself: how many mistakes can you make when you are naked? Well, after visiting numerous hammams across Turkey, I came up with my eight rules for women:

1. Wear nylon panties. (Just because it's a bathhouse doesn't mean they're really prepared to see you naked.)
2. Carry travel-sized soap and shampoo.
3. If you want to bring a razor, put it with the soap and shampoo in a small plastic bag.
4. Never put anything in the washing basins, but your dipping bowl. No soap, razor, washcloth or anything. The basin needs to stay perfectly clean. Never use another person's basin unless invited.
5. Do not take a single step without your bath slippers on. (You're provided with a pair when you enter.)
6. Always have a massage (personal rule).
7. Bring a bottle of water to drink.
8. Put €2.50–5 in the bathhouse jar if you enjoyed your bath.

Justine Merrill, travel writer

11 Toilets

Find out how to sidestep pay toilets (see p.71), and how to keep from having to visit too often (see p.167). Meanwhile, here's a look at what you may end up facing.

There aren't too many squatters left in Europe, but you may stumble across one. The trick is not to stumble while you use it. Place your feet on the small foot-size platforms provided and align your bottom with the hole in the floor, which usually means facing the way you came in as you would on a Western toilet. There's rarely anything to hold on to, or anything you'd *want* to hold on to, so beyond the obvious danger of tipping over, the position causes your trouser pockets to become somewhat inverted, so your valuables may go sliding irretrievably down the hole. And if this doesn't sound challenging enough, remember you may have to hold a flashlight in your mouth, since these lavatories often don't have any lighting. How to flush the hole is not entirely apparent. There's no little handle to push. No knob to turn. You have to fill up the plastic bowl a few times, dump the water into the hole and let water displacement take care of the rest.

More commonly, you'll happen upon toilets that look like Western models, but which were installed by someone who may not have fully understood the directions that came with the assembly kit. Or who lacked the necessary tools. If so, notice the seat has usually been secured by something with the equivalent strength of chewing gum, so if you don't sit down exactly straight, the seat detaches and you slide right off the porcelain rim, which – take it from me – can be pretty painful. Sometimes, the plastic seat is missing altogether. This means that you're squatting again; only now it's more difficult than a standard squatter, because you have to do a "standing squat" to clear the rim of the toilet. This usually entails bracing yourself with one hand on the wall behind you, which is highly exhausting for your arm and leg muscles and often makes them cramp painfully.

When using a toilet on a train, remember that some of the older trains will empty directly onto the tracks, so try to refrain from going while at a station.

A few of these bathrooms do come equipped with paper, but it's rarely the cottonsoft kind. So, while you're sitting there (or semi-squatting), use your time wisely by crumpling and uncrumpling a piece of paper (from an unused section of your guidebook if necessary) until it's almost tolerable. This takes about five minutes (twenty with the glossy stuff), so you may want to start working on it before you actually get to the toilet. Important: if there's a little waste bin beside the toilet, put your used paper there. Don't even think of throwing it into the toilet. Though they may look vaguely like the ones you have at home, they can have a violent reaction to toilet paper: just one square of paper can clog it beyond repair.

In other words, whatever the road sends your way, don't shy away from it. It's all part of the travel experience.

11

12

Culture shock

It may sound like what happens when Justin Bieber visits the opera, but culture shock is simply a dramatic way of saying that things aren't quite the way they are at home. When you change everything you eat, say, do, smell and hear at the same time, the effect can be jolting, especially if amplified by sadness or apprehension about leaving home, fatigue from the journey or illness. The natural tendency is to return home immediately. But if you give yourself time, the bout of anxiety or despair will almost certainly pass.

FOUR STAGES OF CULTURE SHOCK

Anthropologist Kalfery Oberg first introduced the term in 1960 and defined it as a state precipitated by the anxiety that results from losing all our familiar signs and symbols of social intercourse. Everyone has slightly different reactions, the speed of the process varies and many people go through different phases more than once, so this may not provide a complete blueprint for your adaptation.

1 Honeymoon
Cultural differences are intriguing and new sights fascinating. You are still comforted by the close memory of your home culture.

2 Crisis
After some time abroad, differences begin to affect you. Differences in language, concepts and values begin to create feelings of confusion and anxiety. This is normal – it's a sign you're reconnecting with your own cultural values.

3 Recovery
You begin to accept the differences and feel comfortable in new situations. Often the crisis dissipates as lingual skills improve.

4 Adjustment
Despite occasional bouts of strain, you're enjoying the new culture and able to make choices based on preferences and values.

FINDING THE REAL EUROPE

Everything seems so new and exciting when you first arrive that it's possible to overlook the **tourist infrastructure** that surrounds you. But as with bad toupees, once you notice, you'll wonder how it ever eluded you. A well-decorated Greek restaurant in Paris with an overpriced menu (in six languages) on a touristy street may seem exotic, but it couldn't be less authentic, even with Greek waiters and a Greek owner and food imported from Greece. You may be used to these things in your own country (a Texas steakhouse in Vancouver with waiters wearing cowboy hats, for example), but in Europe, where you've come to see the culture of the places you're visiting, it seems somehow painfully false. There may be an excellent Greek restaurant tucked away in an immigrant area, but that's a different story. As a rule of thumb, if you're the only traveler in the place, you've stumbled into somewhere authentic.

Naturally, in your hostel, you'll be surrounded by other travelers, as you will be at all the major attractions, on popular beaches and along the most famous shopping streets. You're not likely to escape this **bubble** by traveling longer or further or faster. Instead, go deeper. Hang out in places where the tourists don't go. Learn a language, communicate with the locals, spend time with them (a lot of time), and form your own first-hand perspective.

One of the best ways to do this is to work for them or alongside them. **Volunteering** is another excellent path (see p.88). Joining a local sports club or choir will also create inroads. Since there's no membrane on this bubble, it's impossible to say when you've burst it. But there are a few signs. Can you describe the character of the local people to someone back home? Do you have the phone numbers and addresses of local friends you've made? Have you been invited over for dinner? Have you invited others to visit you back home? These are certainly more worthy things to strive for on your trip than passport stamps.

12

Combating culture shock

Researchers in the 1970s and 1980s developed an idea that the individual traveler didn't need to embrace all or even most aspects of the society, just some key features to be able to operate within the culture. By simply **being aware** of this phenomenon, you're already a step ahead. Here are several practical things you can do to minimize culture shock:

- Recognize it for what it is: a reaction to sensory overload and unfamiliar surroundings ("Oh, that's just a bout of culture shock – I'll be fine soon"). Look at the upside of what it represents: you're having new experiences, new insights and a new perspective. How bad is that?
- Start your journey in countries similar to your own. The UK is ideal in this respect.
- Read up on the place before you arrive. You're going there to experience what that country has to offer, but a little knowledge can decrease the number of cultural surprises. It can be enough for some just to buy the guidebook a day before departure and start reading background information, but reading a novel set in that country will do far more to get you in the mood.

- Jet lag gets your trip off to a poor start (see p.168), so get some sleep on the plane.
- If you're making a large cultural jump early in your trip, you can do a number of things to ease into your new location. Start by staying in a Western-style hotel for a day or two, and looking for cheaper, local digs after you've had a chance to acclimatize. Or simply spend some time just relaxing in a nice hotel lobby free of charge and don't return to your hostel until you're ready to examine the back of your eyelids.
- Speak to other travelers and compare observations.
- Keep a journal.
- Allow yourself to get excited about your trip. It's natural to be a little nervous about what's ahead, but focus on converting that into positive energy.

Your travel philosophy

What you take with you on your trip will, to a large extent, determine the experience you take away from it. And in this case, I'm not referring to the dual-current hairdryer that you should probably leave at home. I'm talking about your **travel philosophy**: your approach to dealing with the cultures you encounter.

12

You'll face this the moment you begin your journey. The locals you meet in more out-of-the-way places will tend to be more genuine, as they haven't been hardened by years of loud tour groups and tough-bargaining backpackers. Likewise, the travelers you run into off the main routes are likely to be a bit more interesting and into their trips. If you're passing through small towns not plagued with tourists, you're in a more culturally fragile environment and should thus move about and interact with care.

Here are a few concepts to keep in mind:

- You are a guest in a foreign country. Be gracious. Travel with an open mind and a desire to learn.

TOURISM IMPACT

With good reason, travel publications have long asserted that **mass tourism** destroys the very things – quaintness, genuine hospitality, serenity, unique culture – that attracted visitors in the first place. There are still thousands of small, picturesque towns and villages around Europe that haven't found their way into guidebooks and are yours to discover. But it doesn't take long before they've got parking lots to handle dozens of tour buses; view-blocking, shadow-casting luxury hotels right on the beach; colorful costumes for evening cultural dance programs; light shows with multilingual recorded voiceovers; and air-conditioned restaurants serving food the locals would never touch. Truth be known, we independent budget travelers contribute to this as well, probably more than we'd care to admit. Simply by being aware of your impact, though, you'll probably make more thoughtful decisions about where you spend your money and how you interact with people.

GETTING AWAY FROM IT ALL

But why are we so seduced by the idea of getting away from it all? Maybe it's a reaction to the travel industry telling us where to go (tour operators lure us into "escaping" but then stick us in living conditions with a higher population density than the urban slums of Bangladesh). Some of us simply want the opposite.

The last time I tried to seek out solitude was during a two-week layover. My wife and I were hoping for some cultural decompression before heading home after a long trip, a chance to scrape off six months of accumulated travel grime, and find a little spinal realignment after countless overnight bus rides. We ended up at a backpacker-style beach compound on a beach that seemed well suited for our needs. After a few days of delightfully brainless hammock testing, we began to wonder where the other travelers were going during the day. Most, we learned, were heading to a remote beach several kilometers away: there was a beach right in front of our little cottage, but that was evidently not remote enough. The one on the other side was obviously whiter, the water clearer, and had trees that jutted out like the horticultural equivalent of dislocated shoulders.

So we dutifully trudged off to find this isolated nirvana. After an hour's hike, we arrived at a postcard-perfect beach. The shin-deep water made it too shallow for swimming, but it felt like Mother Nature might cast down a few lightning bolts if such critiques were muttered aloud. Upon closer inspection, we could see there were many other travelers hanging out here as well. There we all were, trying to get away from everything... together – trapped on the backpacker equivalent of a cruise ship.

The thing is, even if you do succeed in getting away from it all, as I've done on a few occasions, you may come to the conclusion that there's no one there for a good reason. Sure a dose of serenity can be wonderful, but it's hard to summon mutative thoughts while being blasted with horizontal freezing rain on the west coast of Ireland. I guess it just never feels quite as glamorous as it's portrayed on the postcards or in the advertisements.

Besides, as Benjamin Franklin pointed out, "The trouble with doing nothing is not knowing when you're finished".

Doug Lansky

12

- Familiarize yourself with local customs and make an effort to learn at least a few words of the local language. Your efforts will make an impression on those you meet. (How would you react to someone who came to your country and asked you for directions in another language, then spoke louder and slower when you didn't understand?)
- Be a sensitive photographer. Be discreet or ask permission before you take someone's picture. And consider the long-term implications before paying someone in cash or confectionery to take their photograph.
- Resolve conflicts with a smile.
- Look beyond the tourist streets and resorts. Here's a worthy goal: meet and spend time with at least one local who is not trying to sell you any goods or services.
- Pay attention to what the locals are wearing. Shorts, vest tops and other revealing items often aren't appropriate. Better to choose styles and colors that help you blend in rather than display the latest fashions from your own country.
- Try to refrain from beginning sentences with "back home..."
- Do not litter.
- Get used to secondhand smoke. In parts of Europe – particularly the east – smokers are not treated like crack dealers.

13

13

Staying in touch

Not so long ago, staying in touch was a reasonably straight-forward affair. Unreliable mail services, expensive telegrams and uncooperative pay phones that ate coins by the fistful were your only options. Now, perhaps the most difficult aspect of staying in touch is choosing how you want to do it. On a bare-bones budget you can get by with just about all international communication for free (or the cost of wi-fi).

The best way to keep your friends and family informed on a budget

With time zones and long-distance charges, email, Facebook, Twitter and a travel blog are going to be your best allies for almost-immediate contact. The bigger trick is getting used to not being quite as connected as you are back home – or paying more for that service. Naturally it depends on the destination. Most hostels/hotels/restaurants/libraries offer free wi-fi, though some don't.

Unless you're writing a novel or editing a movie along the way, the cons of bringing a laptop may outweigh the pros. You can get internet access virtually anywhere. And by anywhere, I really mean anywhere. And, in case you haven't brought your own device, nearly all hostels are now equipped with a connection, often with their own computers to which you can plug in USBs and SD cards to send photos and backup files.

VoIP: The cheapest way to phone home

The technical name is VoIP… you may know it better as **Skype** or one of the other services listed below. Set up a free account with one, set your friends and family up with free accounts and then test it with them, so everyone is comfortable using it.

For those travelers who don't have their own smartphones or tablets, connected computers are widely available, many of them with headphones you can use. But it's not a bad idea to carry a little wire headset/mic (like the type that come with most smartphones) that you can plug in.

A free Skype account (you only pay for calls made to phones) should get you by just fine and will connect you with most. If not, Google Hangouts (also free) is a solid bet. There are a few others to check out as well:

- **Vbuzzer** Like Skype, but with cheaper rates if you plan to call to phones.
- **Viber** Much like the others, but a bit easier to use on your smartphone. With the free app, you get free smartphone-to-smartphone calls over 4G, 3G and wi-fi connections.
- **ooVoo** Free multi-user when you have a group video conference call.
- **FaceTime** Apple's own video chat app comes preinstalled and can be found on iPhones and iPads. The video quality is high but may take more bandwidth.

How to manage your cell phone so it doesn't cost you a fortune

Warning: if you get email on your cell phone or are used to surfing or updating social media, and you don't turn off the data-roaming function while abroad, you can get slapped with high international fees worth hundreds or even thousands of dollars. But you can avoid this with some smart shopping. For US residents, the current best deal is T-Mobile, but they may change their plan or other carriers may offer a better one at any point, so check online for the latest deals. For about $70 a month, you should get free data and texting internationally (at the fastest speeds of the local carriers that T-Mobile partners with), plus pay 20 cents a minute for roaming. Note that some deals will run out after a few months, so always check the small print.

Benefits of changing your mobile habits

The easiest and cheapest workaround to traveling internationally with your mobile device is changing your habits. First, turn off data roaming. Or keep it in flight mode, where you can still use downloaded digital guidebooks and other useful apps that don't require an internet connection, plus save your battery. If you're keeping the same phone number you've had before and don't want a bunch of expensive "I'm on the road" explanations for friends who forgot you were away, just leave a voice recording that you're traveling and that people should text, email you or use social media instead of leaving a message.

Keep the phone's data off during the day, then use wi-fi when you get to a hostel or free wi-fi hotspot and download/upload what you need there. Then don't forget to turn it off again. You can find several free wi-fi-hotspot finder apps for iPhone and Android phones in their respective app stores.

13 Benefits of a local SIM

If you have an unlocked phone (or can get your provider to unlock it for you), you can take advantage of local SIM cards. If you're in one country for a few days or more and want to do some on-the-move surfing/calling, you can buy a local SIM card (you can fill it up as needed) – these local cards are always cheaper than a global SIM. If you want to keep your main cell number for emergencies, you might just pick up a cheap extra phone for these local calls/ surfing. Some SIM cards offer special deals for calling internationally and some have better surfing – just check with a local mobile shop for a deal that best suits your needs.

MAKING DIRECT CALLS

To make a **direct-dial** call from Europe (that is, one from a private phone, hotel phone, or phone booth with coins or a locally purchased calling card), dial the international access code (usually ☎0 or ☎00) plus the country code and number. So, to dial Australia, ring ☎0061 plus the number; for Canada and the US, it's ☎001 plus the number; for South Africa, it's ☎09 plus the number; and for New Zealand, it's ☎0064 plus the number. See below for how to dial the UK.

CALLING EUROPE

Calling Europe is just as easy. To call from Australia, Canada or the US, dial ☎011, then the country code and number. To call from New Zealand, dial ☎00 then the country code and number. If the European number you're calling starts with a zero or has it wrapped in parentheses like this "(0)" after the country number, you typically don't dial it when calling from overseas. So, if calling England from the US, and the number is written "☎+44 (0)70 222 2222", you would dial ☎011 44 70 222 2222.

In case you want to make some pre-trip plans, here's a list of country codes:

Albania	355	Luxembourg	352
Austria	43	Montenegro	382
Belgium	32	Morocco	212
Bosnia-Herzegovina	387	The Netherlands	31
Bulgaria	359	Norway	47
Croatia	385	Poland	48
Czech Republic	420	Portugal	352
Denmark	45	Romania	40
Estonia	372	Russia	7
Finland	358	Serbia	381
France	33	Slovakia	421
Germany	49	Slovenia	386
Greece	30	Spain	34
Hungary	36	Sweden	46
Ireland (Republic)	353	Switzerland	41
Italy	39	Turkey	90
Latvia	371	UK	44
Lithuania	370		

TIME ZONES

Britain, Ireland, Morocco and Portugal
Five hours ahead of New York, eight hours ahead of Vancouver, eleven hours behind Sydney.
Albania, Austria, Belgium, Bosnia-Herzegovina, Croatia, Czech Republic, Denmark, France, Germany, Hungary, Italy, Luxembourg, Montenegro, the Netherlands, Norway, Poland, Serbia, Slovakia, Slovenia, Spain, Sweden, Switzerland and Turkey
Six hours ahead of New York, nine hours ahead of Vancouver, ten hours behind Sydney.
Bulgaria, Estonia, Finland, Greece, Latvia, Lithuania and Romania
Seven hours ahead of New York, ten hours ahead of Vancouver, nine hours behind Sydney.

Benefits of a MiFi device

If your phone is locked in with a specific provider or you'd just rather keep your main phone number for emergencies, this could be a solid alternative to the SIM card. You even have the choice to rent or buy a MiFi device that will give you a hotspot for up to five devices. Some of these can be rented or bought before leaving, but will likely cost you more (€15 and up per day) and are therefore only realistic options for much shorter trips. With MiFi, you can use VoIP for your regular calls and then use your phone for basic online communication.

Benefits of a global SIM

The global prepaid SIM card option isn't all that cheap, but it may be better than using your current plan while traveling (depending on your carrier or what offers are available in your country). It provides bigger savings in certain countries and is aimed more at sending/receiving SMS and receiving phone calls. Data roaming can still be crazy expensive. Here are a few options to compare online for up-to-the-minute rates.

- **WorldSim** (ⓦworldsim.com) Free incoming calls in 90-plus countries; data roaming can be off-the-charts expensive.
- **Sim Card Global** (ⓦsimcardglobal.com) Free incoming SMS globally and free incoming calls in 65 countries. Surfing/email is possible.
- **One Sim Card** (ⓦonesimcard.com) Cheapest outgoing calls but uses callback service except for the Europe & More card. You dial a number, get a call back, then dial. Free incoming SMS globally, free incoming calls in 162 countries – unless they are using one of the local numbers you set up, which adds a small fee. Seems to work best on jailbroken iPhones.

More tips to minimize mobile costs

- **Use SMS-to-Email** One such service is ⓦipipi.com. With pre-loaded funds, you can send texts to your friends' email addresses for 10 cents apiece. For your friends to email-to-SMS you back, they have to fill in their message on the ⓦipipi.com site.

- **Use offline maps and other apps** iPhone users can try Skobbler's ForeverMap app. Android users can pre-download Google maps within a 10-mile radius (enable the "Download map area" feature via the Labs tab in the Google Maps app). In fact, we have a list of other great apps (see p.330), many of which work offline, that you may want to have with you.
- **Compress your data** Onavo (ⓦonavo.com) offers this service as an app. It will at least help minimize the data you are sending.

Are those special international cell phone service budget plans a good option?

There is a crop of companies that offer "amazing deals" for international calling. They may be cheaper than your current service plan, but they aren't nearly as cheap as just using VoIP when you have wi-fi or at least a cheap internet connection. Check the websites of the major providers in your area to see what special deals they may have around the time of your departure.

Speak with your service provider about any **global data-roaming deals** they may have. Often these are prepaid arrangements, but you may be able to top them up online as you go.

How to stay connected when you're off the grid

If you're planning to be in the middle of nowhere on your own for a while and want to be able to call in the cavalry, or if you're on a guided trip and you want to be able to update your social media continually, you'll probably want one of the following palm-sized gadgets:

- **Spot Satellite GPS Messenger** You can send out an SOS to local emergency services, or send "HELP" or "I'M OK" to a preset list of contacts. You can also make a custom message that goes out to your contact list as well. All messages include your current coordinates. Rugged, good for check-ins and emergencies.
- **Delorme inReach** This two-way GPS communicator pairs with your Android or iPhone via its Earthmate app and allows you to send SOS beacons and text messages, lets people follow your every move on a map and even posts messages on Facebook/Twitter. Better for sending personal messages, social media.

Try the lost art of snail mail

Sadly, letter writing has dried up. There's still nothing quite as nice as receiving an actual letter from abroad: the stamps, the smell and knowing it had to travel around the planet to get to you. The proliferation of email simply makes the occasional postcard or letter all the more special. It's easy to forget this while you're on the road, but it's worth the effort and is likely to strengthen friendships and ensure you'll be getting mail from your traveling friends in years to come.

The trick to sending packages as cheaply as possible

Depending on the place, sending a package can take anywhere from two minutes to two hours. There are a few tricks you can use to simplify the process, but they all revolve around the same concept: scout out the sending requirements before you try to mail (or buy) something. In some countries, there are special postal boxes you can buy that will speed up the shipping process. More often there are package weight limits in various price categories. (It's a drag to show up with your carefully wrapped package, only to learn you're 20 grams over a price cut-off, which will cost you an additional €10 to send.) Sometimes you can get good bargains within a lower weight range, so if you divide up a larger package into two or three smaller ones you can actually save money.

Before you start wrapping (or shopping), swing by the post office and find out about the rates and any wrapping requirements.

Surface mail – the slowest, cheapest way to send packages

Surface mail is fairly reliable, cheap and slower than a snail with a hangover. It's perfect for sending home items you realize you no longer need (or never did): inexpensive souvenirs, worn-out clothing you simply couldn't part with and so on. Just about the time you've forgotten you sent it, it'll arrive, prodded and shaken by countless customs officers, like a gift from the heavens.

Registered mail and major couriers

If you're sending anything of value, such as jewelry you purchased or a filled diary, it's worth spending the extra money for registered mail to make sure it arrives. If the local mail service has an especially shoddy track record, go straight for a private delivery company such as DHL or FedEx.

How to pick up mailed packages

If you're organized enough to plan an itinerary, it's a good idea to send yourself bulky gear you'll need later in your trip (like hiking boots). The old-school method was to address it "Poste Restante, Central Post Office" or send it to an American Express office. With shoddy Poste Restante service and few AmEx offices, a better route is to figure out when you'll be passing through a town, book a night in a hotel and write them to say you'll have a package arriving just before you get there and if they would please take care of it before you arrive you would compensate them for the service. If you're using a private delivery firm (DHL, FedEx etc., you can let them know when you want the package delivered.)

13 How to get your mail forwarded

You may just want to switch as many bills as possible to online payments and then ignore your mail. If there are mailings you don't want to miss, check with your national mail carrier to see if your post can be forwarded for free or for an additional charge:

Australia ⓦauspost.com.au
Canada ⓦcanadapost.ca
New Zealand ⓦnzpost.co.nz
UK ⓦroyalmail.com
US ⓦusps.com

Best, of course, is if you can have a friend or relative filter out the junk mail and send stuff on.

14

Security

Europe is, for the most part, no more dangerous than your local health-food store. However, though violent crime is rare, Europe is hardly devoid of thieves. Your rental car and pockets are at risk virtually everywhere if you're not on your toes. For off-the-beaten-path security, consider taking a survival course (see p.92) and packing a tiny survival guide.

How to figure out if the destination is safe to visit

Start by getting the official position of state departments. But keep in mind, a country can be very safe but for a single, remote border dispute. The UK Foreign Office website (ⓦfco.gov.uk) is more likely than the others to specify the volatile area when they place an entire country on warning; crosscheck with Canada's Consular Affairs department (ⓦvoyage.gc.ca), Australia's Department of Foreign Affairs and Trade (ⓦsmarttraveller.gov.au) or the US State Department (ⓦtravel.state.gov).

If you're still uncertain, check online for tourist bureaus. You can almost always find an email address of a specific office within that country. The people who staff the counters meet travelers all day and generally have a good feel for travel conditions. Tell them your nationality, when you're planning to travel and roughly where you hope to go. Ask if there are any security issues you should be concerned about. Lastly, check with other travelers. Visit internet forums so you can hear directly from travelers who've been there in recent weeks, or are still in the country: try Rough Guides' Community (ⓦroughguides.com/community) or Lonely Planet's Thorn Tree (ⓦthorntree.lonelyplanet.com).

What to do if the political climate changes

If the political conditions take a turn for the worse, you probably won't want to stick around to check out the mass riots, no matter how exciting it may seem.

And if you're American, you probably don't want to go to the US embassy either (often a prime target, so they shut their doors when the going gets rough). The Australian, Canadian, New Zealand, UK and other embassies should be fine – even for American citizens. The other option is to **get out of town** immediately (it's rarely a country-wide riot). If you hadn't picked up some discreet local clothes yet, this would be the right time. Keep an eye on the local news, and check online to find English updates.

14

How to avoid being robbed

The basic trick here is to **blend in**, keep out of areas where you're likely to become a target, stay alert, carry your gear discreetly and provide yourself with a quick exit when you need one.

Start by removing all jewelry (if necessary covering a wedding or engagement ring with a band-aid or tape). Wear a cheap digital watch or no watch at all. Keep your camera concealed (not in a case that says "Nikon"). Then you'll want to wear clothing that blends in, the more discreet (think earth tones) the better. A little tip: safari pants with zip-off legs and a photojournalist vest are generally not what the locals are wearing.

It's a bit like outrunning a bear… you don't have to be faster than the bear, just faster than the other people around you. Show that you don't have much to steal – or that you have less than other potential targets. With just a backpack and no carry-on bag, you have both your hands free and can remain mobile for a quick getaway, so robbing you looks like more of a challenge. The small padlocks and wire mesh pack-covers will do little to protect your pack, but they will draw attention to the value of its contents. Plastic rice bags are easy to find, dirt cheap, decrease the perceived value of the pack's contents, and make great rain covers. It takes five or ten seconds more to access your pack's interior, but it can make you less of a target. Cut two slits for your shoulder straps, then sew or use duct tape to fasten the rice bag around your pack.

If you're traveling with a partner, make sure one person isn't carrying all the cash and valuables. And at ATMs, have one stand back a bit to guard against someone who might grab and dash.

And remember: put nothing (you can't afford to lose) in the overhead compartment on overnight trains. Your pack is your pillow (or at least spoon with it).

Packing to prevent theft

Don't keep your money and passport in a handbag or daypack, or even in a wallet. Use a **secure travel pouch**. A waist pouch kept under the waistline of your trousers is quite effective, and similar pouches that hang around your neck (under the shirt) or fasten to your ankle are also available. Just make sure you don't access it in busy areas like train stations and markets. Walk over to a more discreet spot and, if you have a travel companion, you can make a privacy shield if you stand between them and a wall so that your actions are hidden.

To protect your slightly-less-valuables, wear your **backpack** on your front in crowded places and don't use a backpack for a day-bag. Because it's inconvenient to wear a day backpack on your front all day for city exploration, use a **shoulder bag** and keep it tucked tighter under your arm in crowded places. Try to find a model with Velcro flaps, which are difficult to open without you noticing, or a double-entry system (eg a zip plus a clasp). "Bum bags" (waist packs) are thief magnets and as such are best avoided – at least avoid keeping your valuables there. If you must use a backpack as a daypack, make sure it's packed carefully (valuables at the bottom, away from the zippers).

14

And finally, don't keep all your **money** in one place. Stash some emergency funds in the secret compartment of a belt, or tape some (in a small plastic bag) to the inside of your backpack.

Another trick is to keep a **decoy wallet** in your pocket. Empty your wallet except for €5–20, a non-essential ID and a few random photos or business cards.

Avoiding dangerous urban areas

Often a hundred meters can be the difference between a completely safe street and a dangerous one. And these boundaries may change after dark. Ask your hotel clerk or tourist-office staff to mark the dangerous areas on your map (both day and night). No matter where you are, get in the habit of checking over your shoulder and across the street every now and then. Even in crowded markets, you can see if you're getting followed after a few turns. But be particularly aware after dark. Muggers can easily hide in doorways, so the closer you are to the street, the less chance they have to surprise you. If you spot one or more suspicious characters in a doorway up ahead, cross the street. Or hop in **a taxi** if you've got a bad feeling about the area. Trust your gut feeling and always keep enough change ready to pay for a short cab ride. For less than €3, you can quickly get yourself back to a safer area. When you're in an area you're not sure of, resist the temptation to pull out a map or your phone on a street corner. Walk purposefully, even if lost, and duck inside a coffee shop or store to check the map or ask directions.

Take a few extra precautions in bus and train terminals, where many pickpockets lurk. If you need to pretend you're a secret agent to stay alert and pull this off, so be it. One simple method is to walk around the perimeter of the station instead of crossing it so you can keep a wall on one side and your eyes on anyone approaching.

Also, get in the habit of avoiding the tables near doors or bordering sidewalks in cafés. A quick thief can grab your gear and run. Keep your bag under your table while you eat, with the strap around your leg. If you need to use the toilet, take your bag along. You can't expect someone else to guard your bag as closely as you do.

Accommodation safety

It's not just local thieves – travelers steal as well. Sad, but true. There's not much threat to your dirty laundry, but your valuables still need to be guarded.

At night, cameras and suchlike are better left at the reception desk in a safe, in a hostel locker if provided, or behind the counter if there's someone keeping an eye on it. Some places also offer the reception safe to travelers who need a place to keep their passport pouch while at the beach – which is better than taking it along. Otherwise, **treat your passport pouch like your spleen**: sleep with it (or put it in your pillow case) and take it along when you shower – you can hang the pouch on the hook, just under your towel inside the shower stall.

Some hotels require your passport for a few hours to gather information. They should not require it any longer than that. Ask for it back as soon as they're done.

What to do if you have everything stolen

Fortunately, this is not as much of a hassle as it used to be. You could very well have everything you need – credit cards, passport and cash – in one to ten days. But act immediately to get the process started. Your first job is to **file a police report**. Go to the nearest police station (nearest to where the robbery occurred), report the robbery and ask for a numbered copy of the police report. Presenting this at your embassy will speed up the issuing of a new passport. You will be waiting a while at the police station for the forms to be processed, so use this time to make phone calls. Have someone look online for you to find reverse-charge numbers. Start with a call to your **travel insurance company** (assuming you have one). Most good insurers accept charges and keep you on the line while they cancel your credit cards and have new ones issued. Otherwise, you'll have to cancel them yourself by phone or email. If your insurance or credit-card provider doesn't supply emergency cash, Western Union (UK ☎0800 833 833; US ☎1800 325 6000) can assist, if you have someone at the other end to put money in. They can also provide this service online (🌐westernunion.com). Expect to pay a fee of 4–8 percent, depending on location. If you don't have ID, you can make arrangements to pick up the money with a code word.

Put a stop on your cell phone if you've had it stolen. Then call your embassy, tell them what happened and that you'll be on your way over as soon as you get the report. Ask for an appointment or a specific name you can request at the gate. Make sure you have a few passport photos before you show up at the embassy. If you don't have copies of your documents or haven't emailed them to yourself, left a backup disk with a trusted friend or relative, or uploaded

---

STAY ALERT

I've never had anything stolen in a war zone, but my track record isn't nearly as impressive in developed countries. You're on vacation, your guard is down, and you're thinking, "Hey, I'm a tourist, there's a cop, nothing to worry about." That's when I always get nailed. Heading for a tour of the Vatican, I parked and locked all my possessions in the trunk of my rental car. When I returned, everything was gone except a few rolls of film on the trunk floor.

You have to remember that, just like everyone else in civilized countries, Europe's criminals go to work every day. They feast off the herds of roaming tourists, showing up in droves at the same place and same time every year. The crooks get away with it because they use kids for the theft, and keep it mostly non-violent – so as far as the police are concerned, it's a catch-and-release sport.

Robert Young Pelton, author, *The World's Most Dangerous Places* 🌐 comebackalive.com

them to an online vault, and you don't have any ID, find a fellow citizen who has their passport and ask them to come with you to the embassy and vouch for you. The embassy can help make arrangements for your friends and family to email photos to help confirm your identity.

How to avoid sexual harassment

Harassment is (of course) never your fault, but there are a few things you can do to minimize it, and doing so means you'll likely have a much more enjoyable trip.

Most harassers get information direct to their libidos via their eyeballs, so let's start with appearance. Look at how the local women dress, and try to approximate that (or a slightly more conservative version). Unfortunately, even if your clothes aren't racy by your own standards, shorts, short skirts and tight-fitting clothes can be more likely to denote you as promiscuous than they do at home.

Sometimes more important than how you're dressed is how you act – if you appear comfortable, confident and at ease you don't seem like so easy a target. You may also want to come up with a story about your husband coming to meet you soon, and perhaps even buy a cheap, simple ring to back up your story.

That should take care of much of the harassment, but count on some rude remarks, catcalls and pinches anyway. Do your best to ignore them and keep walking. Or, alternatively, react with clarity and confidence and tell them you don't like it. If you get followed, head into a nearby busy shop and tell the owner.

If you're alone and see a crowded or well-lit area in sight, consider running. If the harasser chases or grabs you, **scream for help**. This is, in fact, how most women escape rape: pleading and stalling are not very effective. Kick in the knees or privates and don't think twice about jabbing him in the eyes. Feel free to use any objects nearby to aid your fight: pen, car antenna, rock or camera.

How to avoid scams

The best trick, really, is just to learn some of the most **common scams**. Con artists are hatching new plans all the time, but they tend to be slightly mutated versions of the ones you'll read about here. Keep your guard up, but not too high. Few locals will be out to scam you. Many of their gestures, although odd, are genuine acts of hospitality that you wouldn't likely experience at home. You'll have to learn to trust your instincts.

Repair scam

You rent a car/scooter/motorbike. It's almost guaranteed to break down. The rental agency helps you get it to a garage where they can hit you with hyper-inflated repair fees. Or they suddenly notice small damages that weren't there before and want you to cover them.

How to beat it: Take several photos of the vehicle before you leave, making sure to get close-ups of any scratches… and do this together with the person who is renting you the vehicle.

Cardboard scam

14

You're walking from one ancient architectural treasure to the next in Rome when a group of kids approaches you, one carrying a big piece of cardboard. The seemingly innocent kids in torn clothes swarm around you while one holds the piece of cardboard to your chest much like you might hold a map (it might even be a map they're showing you). While you're trying to give them a few coins, explain you don't understand, or even back away, the other kids have picked your pockets under the cover of the cardboard. Some aren't even subtle about it, but what are you going to do: push or kick a small child?

How to beat it: When you see them coming, keep a firm hand on your belongings and head quickly in another direction. Throw in a firm "Go away!" if they start to follow.

Local "assistance"

Having trouble with a subway ticket machine, train station locker or ATM? If someone starts offering help before you've had any problems, beware. They get a free look into your wallet or chance to guide you to a locker that they have rigged.

How to beat it: Thank them, but refuse help. Look around for someone to ask; chances are you'll find a good Samaritan happy to help within a few seconds.

Pay-it-later scam

Your taxi driver tells you not to worry about the price, or the meter, that you'll work it out later. Then, upon reaching your destination, he stings you for many times the actual fare.

How to beat it: Always agree on a price before getting in the taxi, or make sure the meter is on. If it's too late, do your best to bargain, try to attract the attention of a nearby police officer and take down the driver's ID number and name so you can report him or her. Tour guides have been known to practice this technique as well.

Cab dash scam

You've paid your cab and the driver leaves before you can get your bag out of the boot.

How to beat it: Leave your door open or don't pay up until you've got your bag.

Football moves scam

A friendly guy on the street offers to show you a cool football move. It results in you being knocked over and mugged.

How to beat it: Decline any offers for demonstrations of contact sports and walk away immediately.

Drug-buy scam

Especially common for those heading over to Morocco for a quick visit: you buy a small amount of hashish from a local dealer, then he tips off his buddy, the police officer, who comes knocking at your door to demand a fee for not taking you to prison.

How to beat it: It's a dangerous game of chicken. You can pay the fine, try to bargain a little, or call their bluff and tell them you have no money, you were set up and that you're happy to go to police headquarters and explain it. Best just to avoid buying the drugs in the first place. If you absolutely must, make sure other travelers have bought from the person previously.

Fake travel agent scam

You buy a ticket from a travel agency you found on the web in your own country or even in Europe (most likely in London). The ticket never arrives and when you try to call, you find the place has gone out of business.

How to beat it: Make sure you're signing up with an accredited agency. In Australia, check with the Australian Federation of Travel Agents (ⓦafta.com .au); in Canada, the Association of Canadian Travel Agencies (ⓦacta.ca); in the UK, the Travel Association (ⓦabta.com); and in the US, the American Society of Travel Agents (ⓦasta.org). And pay with a credit card so you can stop payment if necessary.

Help from your embassy or consulate

If you think of your government's embassies, consulates and high commissions as a **safety net**, you're liable to slip through one of the holes. They can't do much if you've been arrested for violating local laws, and they won't help send you home or give you a place to sleep if you run out of money. They can, however, help you in the event of a lost or stolen passport. They can also provide contact information during emergencies; give you the latest travel advice; allow you to register your travel plans if you're heading into areas for risky adventures (don't forget to check back in); and assist with overseas marriage and birth documents. And most of them make excellent cocktails, should you manage to attend one of their functions – consider swinging by if you're in the neighborhood during a national holiday.

14

15

Health

Europe is hardly a petri dish of virulent microkillers waiting to pounce on unsuspecting travelers. In fact, many of the vaccinations and precautions suggested below are also recommended to European travelers heading to your country. The things you should concern yourself with are actually quite basic: get your pre-trip health details in order before you leave (including any necessary immunizations); take some fundamental precautions; keep an eye out for specific symptoms, and get yourself to a doctor if you encounter any of them. Despite the tales you may have heard, many of the common illnesses are avoidable or easily curable with some of the basic information you'll find in this chapter.

Health warnings for Europe

According to the Centers for Disease Control and Prevention (CDC), **diarrhea is the top illness** among travelers in Europe and motor vehicle crashes the leading cause of injury. There's risk of salmonella, hepatitis, *E. coli*-associated diarrhea, tick-borne encephalitis (certain areas) and Lyme disease (certain areas). Read on to see which vaccinations you need. Apart from these, there are periodic outbreaks of rare but serious diseases such as bird flu and Ebola. Some areas with large influxes of non-European refugees have also had a rise in the number of diphtheria cases.

Pre-departure checkup

Far too many travelers neglect basic pre-trip medical arrangements and suffer needlessly as a consequence. Your first order of business is a checkup. Don't make the common mistake of putting this off till the last minute. A month or two before departure is a more sensible time to schedule an appointment (though some vaccinations require more time before they start working). If the doctor finds something during the checkup and wants you to come back for a second consultation, your next-day flight is buggered. Besides, you'll want to get your checkup before you start getting your vaccinations. Some vaccinations should not be given if you have so much as a cold, or if you're taking other medications. Make sure to ask for a copy of your clean bill of health to take along so you don't have to pay for one again if you end up working or volunteering for an organization that requires such a document.

Schedule a visit to the dentist as well. It would be a serious setback to get a gnawing tooth problem while you're in a country like Romania or Turkey, which are not exactly world-renowned epicenters of dentistry. Needless to say, getting this taken care of beforehand is a lot cheaper than flying home to do it.

If you wear glasses or contacts, you'll want to swing by the optician. Make sure you have enough contacts and fluid to keep you going (you can always send some lenses ahead as well). Glasses are important backups, even if you never wear them at home – you may find yourself in dusty environments where contacts don't function well. If you're trying to decide between two frames for your glasses, take the most durable, even if they're not the most flattering. Make sure you bring along a copy of your prescription and your optician's contact details in case you need emergency replacements on the road or ordered from home.

15

Vaccinations

Generally speaking, you shouldn't really need any for a basic trip to Europe. But once you decide the jabs you want (visit the CDC's website, ⓦcdc.gov, or its European equivalent at ⓦecdc.europa.eu, for updated info), call around to make sure you get a good price.

Confirm the information you get from the CDC with the doctor or clinic administering the shots, and be sure to inform them of any medical conditions (even allergies) and medications (including the contraceptive pill) you're taking. Also, explain where you'll be staying and how long you'll be there.

Some vaccinations, such as hepatitis B, require a course of shots over six months to take effect, so don't leave it until the last minute, or even the last month. If you're getting several jabs, bear in mind that you may not be able to get them all on the same day. They may conflict with one another, require more than one injection or take time to become effective. However, if you're not entirely sure where you're headed, you don't need to get every needle in the cabinet. Vaccinations are all available on the road. Just make sure the clinic looks clean and professionally run, and that it uses sterile needles. If you have the option, try to get this taken care of in more developed countries.

Where medications are listed, you'll only find the generic medical name. These are known by various commercial names in different countries. Simply check the label or consult your pharmacist or doctor.

Get a vaccination record card and keep it with your passport while traveling. It's nice to have it to hand. With all these mega-syllabic names, it's hard to remember what you got, what you didn't want to get but got anyway, and what you were going to get but decided not to at the last moment.

Update your basic vaccinations

Start by dusting off your medical records to see which boosters you're going to need.

Diphtheria

You'll definitely want to make sure you're vaccinated against this bacterial illness. It's passed person to person quicker than a dancing cat video on Facebook, and typical unpleasantness includes fever, chills and a sore throat. Eventually, it can cause heart failure and paralysis. Be aware that if someone you know has it, they're highly infectious for ten days. Seek medical help if you suspect it; a quick throat swab can determine if you've got it or not.

Tetanus

You've probably been vaccinated against this already. However, you may be due for your ten-year update. Check your records to be sure the booster is taken care of. With tetanus, spores enter the body through open wounds as small as a pinprick, and can be picked up through contact with dirt, manure and – the classic – rusty nails. You won't get the symptoms for five to twenty days, but the one that should get your attention (and any doctor's) is spasms of the jaw muscle. Those will spread across your face and into your torso, and that's when things get really nasty. It is potentially fatal, so if you recognize these symptoms yourself, get thee to a hospital immediately.

Other possible vaccinations

Hepatitis A

This is a shot I'd get. It'll come in handy if you're planning on eating seafood (particularly shellfish) in southern Europe, where high temperatures and dodgy refrigeration can provide ideal breeding grounds for the disease. Contaminated water and people (who don't wash their hands well) also pass this bowel blaster along. Good news: there's a vaccination. One jab of a Havrix vaccine will last a year. Follow it up with a second injection six to twelve months later and you're good to go for a decade. The downside is it takes nearly a month after the first dose to take effect. The more traditional gamma globulin shot works right away, and provides protection for three to six months. There is also a Hep A and Hep B combination called Twinrix, which will also give you ten years of immunity. It normally takes six months to get all three shots taken care of, but you can ask for an accelerated schedule that will do the job in 21 days. If you opt for this, you'll need a booster shot after a year. Or ask your doctor about Hepatyrix, fifteen-year protection against Hep A and typhoid in one stab.

15

TRAVELING WITH IMMUNODEFICIENCY

If you have special health considerations that render you **immuno-compromised**, keep in mind that the bacteria and bugs that affect all travelers may have a more profound effect on you. Less developed countries in particular pose significant risks for exposure to opportunistic pathogens. Your consulate or the International Association of Medical Assistance to Travelers (ⓦ iamat.org) can provide trained English-speaking physicians in Europe.

VACCINATIONS

The CDC currently recommends that "killed vaccines" such as diphtheria, tetanus and hepatitis A are OK for "healthy" HIV-infected travelers. However, the degree of immunity after a vaccination may vary with the degree of immunodeficiency caused by the HIV. For more information, visit ⓦ cdc.gov.

MEDICATIONS

Discussing an emergency plan with your doctor prior to departure is an excellent idea. The CDC advises all immune-compromised travelers to talk to their doctors about getting a shot of immunoglobulin for diarrhea before heading out, although alternatives (such as TMP-SMX) should be discussed with a doctor. If the diarrhea does not respond to this treatment, there is blood in the stools, fever and shaking chills, or dehydration, get to a doctor.

GOING THROUGH CUSTOMS

If you are carrying a full array of HIV drugs, or just the virus, be aware that some European countries have vague restrictions preventing those with "communicable diseases" from entering. So, faced with an inquisitive customs officer holding your medications, you might offer other half-truths about the things you're suffering from first (such as liver/heart/kidney problems), and delay mentioning HIV. If you're staying for an extended period to work or study, you may face a serological screen in many countries.

15

Hepatitis B

This vaccine is recommended for healthcare professionals, but it's transmitted through sexual contact and needles, so if you're planning on some heavy romance or heavy knitting (in the vicinity of drug users), it's probably worth the extra jab. Even if you're just considering a tattoo, it's not a bad idea. The vaccination is a bit of a drag – three jabs over seven months – but well worth it for a long trip. For those who put it off to the last minute, it's possible to get three jabs in three weeks with an additional booster, but this is slightly less effective. As previously noted, there's also the Hep A and Hep B combination jab Twinrix to consider, which will give you fifteen years of immunity.

Rabies

The CDC recommends this one, but a lot of people survive in Europe without it. If you steer clear of packs of wild dogs in Istanbul and strays in rural areas, you'll probably be fine. Always inquire about a dog's biting habits before petting – it's cheaper than getting the vaccine (three shots over a month, plus another two if bitten, scratched or even licked by a rabid animal), but possibly not as effective. Without the vaccine, you're looking at nearly twice as many shots – although no longer the nasty ones in the stomach. If you have an encounter with an animal that puts you at risk, get tested immediately.

15

VACCINATION ROUNDUP

HEPATITIS A

Full course Single dose
Booster After 6–12 months
Comments Gives good protection for at least twelve months; booster protection lasts more than ten years
Time before effective immunity One month

HEPATITIS A (IMMUNOGLOBIN TYPE)

Full course Single dose
Booster Only gives protection for 2–6 months, depending on dose
Comments Needs to be given close to departure
Time before effective immunity Immediately

HEPATITIS B (OPTIONAL)

Full course Two doses one month apart, plus a third dose six months later
Booster Provides protection for at least ten years; booster dose is not recommended for adults with intact immune system
Comments More rapid three-week courses are available if you're close to departure, but this gives lower immunity and requires a booster after twelve months
Time before effective immunity One month after final dose

RABIES (OPTIONAL)

Full course Three doses over one month
Booster After 2–3 years
Comments Pre-exposure immunization gives greater protection but does not eliminate the need for prompt treatment if bitten by a rabid animal
Time before effective immunity Two weeks after completed course

TETANUS

Full course Three doses: leave 4–8 weeks between first and second doses; third dose 6–12 months after second. Usually given with diphtheria
Booster Every ten years
Comments Full course usually given in childhood. If pressed for time before departure, only first and second dose can be given
Time before effective immunity A few days after third – or second, if only two can be given – dose

TICK-BORNE ENCEPHALITIS

Full course Two doses over a month
Booster After 1–3 years
Comments Fever a common side effect after first dose. Not needed for children under 7. Get in Europe once you arrive, if necessary
Time before effective immunity Ten days after final dose

Tick-borne encephalitis

This viral infection of the central nervous system comes from tick bites and is untreatable. The CDC says it exists in central and western Europe, but that doesn't mean it's everywhere. For example, if you're going to Stockholm, you're not at risk. But if you're planning a kayaking trip down the east coast of Sweden, where you'll be camping in the forest, you are. Some Stockholmers who live in these tick-infested areas in the woods get the vaccination. Others chance it. Removing the tick doesn't work – if you find one, you may be too late. But just one tick bite is very unlikely to bring on the virus, and only one in 250 who get infected develop the symptoms. For those who do, it starts out like flu, and then causes dizziness, tremors and paralysis. The risk is seasonal, occurring when ticks are out and about: May to September.

15

What you can't get vaccinated against

These are the ones you'll have to watch out for, and may just get anyway. Some maladies are more common than others and some more severe, so read through the descriptions to get acquainted with the symptoms and dangers you may face.

Allergies

If you experience allergies at home, you'll probably encounter them on the road. Watery eyes, a runny nose, sneezing… you know how it goes. Pack an antihistamine (chlorpheniramine or loratadine) to relieve the symptoms. If these don't help, or your experience more serious symptoms such as hives, difficulty breathing or swelling of the throat, visit a doctor ASAP.

Altitude sickness

This is more dangerous than most people believe, especially when those who don't have it are egging you on to keep going up. "High altitude" is considered 2438–3658m; "very high altitude" is 3658–5487m. If your head feels like it's about to implode or you're dizzier than a wino trapped on a Ferris wheel, then head down the mountain. It doesn't mean making a beeline for the bottom (unless it has reached a critical stage), but descent of some kind is vital. Usually, the symptoms will abate after just a small drop in altitude, and you may even be able to continue once your body has adjusted at its own pace.

Fitness is only one factor: you could be a champion triathlete or an Olympian on performance-enhancing drugs and still get a case of altitude sickness worse than the couch potato with a liver condition hiking beside you. Follow a careful acclimatization plan and, most importantly, listen to your body. Diamox (acetazolamide) is most useful as a high-altitude sickness preventative, but will require a doctor's prescription. Take 125mg (half a

15

GASTRO-INTESTINALLY CHALLENGED

You can travel the world and never get a single bout of dysentery. For that matter, you can also find a customer service representative who actually cares about your two-hour flight delay.

When I started traveling, there weren't many more fearful eaters than me. I followed the conventional wisdom of "cook it, boil it, peel it or forget it." And when that wasn't possible, I sought refuge under the wrapper of a Big Mac or – as a last resort – in an all-beer diet.

My first gastro-intestinal challenge (still not sure what caused it) lasted about a week and made me even more meticulous about what passed my lips: no ice in my bottled drinks, only reputable restaurants, no street food. Like many other travelers, I was far more willing to bungee jump, mountain climb and whitewater raft than eat a fried grasshopper.

After a few months, another traveler set me straight, "Whatever you do, don't try to ride it out. Get tested. Immediately." It may be the best travel advice I've ever received, acting as a sort of insurance for gastronomic experimentation.

Armed with this knowledge, the only reason you should be spending a week in an uncomfortable squatting position is if you decide to circumnavigate Europe on budget airlines.

The most noticeable side effects of this were huge savings (less bottled water, much more cheap street food) and an enriching culinary journey that ran parallel to my trip. In every town, I began to make an effort to seek out the local dishes and snacks. What I had dismissed as foolish risk-taking was now one of the highlights of my travels.

Doug Lansky

---

tablet) twice a day for two days at sea level a few weeks before the trip. If your body accepts the drug without side effects, take the same dose for three days just before heading to 3500m and continue taking it for two or three days until you feel acclimatized. Do not take it for more than five days.

Bedbugs

These aren't merely bedtime-story myths. They're out there, typically in the cheapest hotels, and they do bite. The bites aren't serious, but they seriously itch. And you'd have a better chance spotting Elvis than some of these critters (they hide during daylight, though you might be able to spot small black or brown spots of dried insect excrement). Your best defense is a good sleep sheet: make sure it's big enough to cover the pillow as well. A tight weave should keep most of them out. Failing that, they hate light so you could always sleep with the light on if that's an option. The bites look like two or three little red dots in a row. Treat with hydrocortisone or antihistamine cream and – easier said than done – refrain from scratching. Also, wash all your clothes and sleep sheet in hot water (60°C) if you suspect you may have been exposed.

Cold sores

Don't kiss people with lip sores or blisters. Don't share water bottles with them either. There's really nothing cold about these sores, which are actually herpes picked up by oral contact (fellatio and cunnilingus included). If you get one, you've got a recurring menace for life, often triggered by too much direct sunlight. To keep the sores at bay, keep your lips well glossed while exposed to the sun and apply aciclovir cream (may require prescription) as soon as you feel the tingling sensation coming on (apply five times a day for five days). Once the sore breaks open, the medicine won't help.

Constipation

Travelers get all worked up over diarrhea, but forget about an opposite ailment that is nearly as uncomfortable and troublesome. Travelers who are new to the trail and spending time in eastern and southeastern Europe are especially susceptible. They take one look at a squat toilet (or even an unsanitary Western version) and suddenly they don't need to go any more. A few days later, the mental block has become an intestinal one. This can often be solved by trying some natural laxatives (coffee, prune juice, psyllium seed). Better yet, make yourself go when you have the urge, no matter what the loo looks like. And a little diet altering won't hurt: more fruit, bran and fluids.

Dehydration

15

The trick here is to **drink before you get thirsty**. For a full day of walking in, say, Rome, during summer, you should be drinking about four liters of water. In the Alps you'll need even more, as the wind masks the amount you're sweating away. Once you're dehydrated, you'll experience a dry mouth, dark urine, headache and, in extreme cases, fainting. Find some shade, take it easy and mix your water with a rehydration solution so you get your salt balance back, and if fluid can't be taken orally, get to a hospital for an IV.

Diarrhea

The good news is that it's most often treatable and the troublesome symptoms can be cured in less than a day. The following advice may save you a week of traumatic toilet dashes – in which case this book will have paid for itself a few times over. You'll meet numerous travelers suffering from diarrhea for days or weeks. The typical reason is that they're **trying to "ride it out."** You want to do exactly the opposite.

The moment you start to "go liquid," drink a bottle of water mixed with a packet of rehydration mix that you should be carrying in your first-aid kit. And keep drinking. The biggest danger with diarrhea is dehydration. The next biggest risk is that you sit by the toilet for days waiting for the diarrhea to abate. As soon as possible, bring a little plastic film canister (or something similar) and put a stool sample in it. Either take the sample to a nearby clinic yourself or have a trusted fellow traveler do it for you if you can't risk leaving a toilet for that long. With a quick look under the microscope, a doctor will most often be able to identify the cause. If so, they'll write a prescription on the spot, which will likely include the pharmaceutical equivalent of a cork. Less than a day after you start taking the medicine, you may feel back to normal, or at least better. While recovering, stick to simple, unspiced foods like rice for a day or two just in case. Little tip: carry an anti-diarrhea pill (such as Loperamide) in your money belt. If you're on a long bus ride with your pack in the baggage bin underneath or you're walking around town, it will come in handy more than you can imagine. Women travelers should be aware that diarrhea can reduce the effectiveness of the contraceptive pill.

E. coli diarrhea (aka food poisoning)

You may hear this name tossed about. It also goes by its given name of *Escherichia coli*, and it is about the most common type of diarrhea, though it comes in several different strains. It's about as nice to contract as it is to spell. Often picked up from eating undercooked, contaminated ground beef, it can also be passed from person to person. Drinking raw milk and swimming in or drinking sewage-contaminated water may also do the trick. The infection makes itself known with bloody diarrhea. Hang out with people who wash their hands carefully.

Hepatitis C

Less common than Hep A and Hep B (but with no vaccination) this one requires contact with contaminated blood – so stay alert where any needles are concerned. It can be spread by sexual activity, but this is rare. Symptoms include dark urine, nausea, jaundice, abdominal pain and loss of appetite.

15

Hiking blisters

The face of Mont Blanc is not the ideal place to try out a new pair of hiking boots. If you buy or rent some, give yourself at least a day or two for your feet to adjust (especially with new boots). For serious treks, make sure you bring a skin-like blister cover (such as Compeed), sport tape, petroleum jelly or a silicon spray, and scissors (with antiseptic to sterilize) to cut the dead skin from blisters. Professionals recommend cutting away all the dead skin so the tender skin underneath gets exposed to the air and hardens and heals quicker. Tape should be applied in advance to trouble spots, then sprayed with silicon. Two pairs of socks are advisable, neither of them cotton. Polypropylene or silk (next to the skin) and wool make an excellent combination.

HIV/AIDS

You've probably heard an earful about this already, but it can be caught in Europe as well – something to consider before you have unprotected sex or share a needle.

Infected cuts and scrapes

In humid coastal environments, cuts don't tend to heal that fast. They're easily infected and can actually grow in size. So if you pick up some scooter road rash around the Med, head up to the Alps where it can more easily dry and heal. Visit a doctor if you're unable to stop the growth of the wound on your own.

Jet lag

It's a fancy way of saying you spent your flight over watching a B-movie or glued to a book instead of getting much-needed sleep. An alarming number of travelers don't take simple steps to combat jet lag, and are then plagued by fatigue for days (typically, one day per time zone crossed), starting off their trip on the wrong foot. If you can sleep on the plane and get a good night's sleep the first night in the new time zone, you're not going to experience much, if any, jet lag. Sleeping on the plane, if you're not naturally gifted at the art, can be achieved with an over-the-counter or prescribed sleeping pill.

According to studies, drinking **alcohol** is exactly the wrong approach. The next worst thing you can do is stay up late. There's no reason to eat dinner at 11pm, then watch a movie at midnight simply because you're at 30,000ft. Eat a meal in the airport, pop the sleeping pill when the plane leaves the ground and drink plenty of water when you wake up. Once you've arrived, refrain from naps (this is a great chance to try some of that strong European coffee) until bedtime (when the locals sleep), and take another sleeping pill if you wake up during that first night, or pop a Melatonin tablet (available by prescription only in the UK and NZ) before bed to ensure you sleep a little longer. Arnica tablets are also reputed to alleviate jet lag.

15

Lyme disease

Ticks carrying the disease are found in the forest, long grass and trees, waiting for a host animal (typically deer, but humans will suffice) to pass by. The ticks need around 24 hours attached to your body to transfer the disease, so, if you give yourself a good check a few times daily, you'll spot them in time. You'll have to check in hard-to-view places, though, including the hair on your head as well. If you miss it at the time then you'll notice a few days or weeks later, when the classic "bull's eye" appears at the bite site. It can affect the nervous system, joints and heart, and can become very serious if not treated (with amoxycillin or doxycycline).

Motion sickness

It's not serious, but it's bad enough to ruin a day or two of your trip. On a winding bus ride, try to sit near the front and next to a window or air vent (motion sickness is also related to breathing exhaust fumes). Make sure you get out to stretch your legs whenever the bus stops. On a boat, stay above deck and try looking at the horizon. Take deep, relaxing breaths or simply try to stay busy. And, in any event, have a motion sickness pill or a skin patch (such as Hyoscine or Scopolamin) ready just in case. It takes at least an hour before the effects of these pills are noticeable, so you may need to take them in advance of boarding.

Rashes

You'll be encountering plants, fruits and bugs that your skin has never been exposed to before. It's common for travelers to experience a host of new body art. Try applying topical antihistamine, calamine lotion or steroid creams (hydrocortisone) to the area. If it persists, visit a local doctor.

Salmonella

This is the one most commonly associated with eating undercooked chicken. Or when the cooks forget to wash their hands after a trip to the toilet. The food gets contaminated from animal (or human) feces. And here's the scary part: you won't be able to smell or taste infected food. Most of those who get salmonella develop diarrhea, fever and abdominal cramps 12 to 72 hours after infection. That's the bad news. The upside is that most people recover without treatment (4–7 days). However, if the person becomes severely dehydrated (see p.167) or the infection spreads from the intestine, it should be treated promptly with antibiotics (such as ampicillin or gentamicin).

15

STDs

Just because you're choosy about whom you have sex with doesn't mean *they* were. And once is all it takes to wake up with syphilis (which is resurging), gonorrhea, chlamydia, chancroid, trichomoniasis or herpes. Symptoms include: a rash on the palms, unusual vaginal or penile discharge, pain when passing urine, itching, abnormal vaginal bleeding and genital ulceration. There's only one thing to do if you get any of these: go to a doctor. With chlamydia, it's a little trickier. Most women don't know they have it. Some never find out. Some only learn of it at an infertility clinic while trying to find out why they can't get pregnant. The best way to avoid getting an STD is to use a barrier method of protection for any sexual contact (condom, femedom, dental dam etc), and if you're sexually active while you travel make sure you get checked regularly, even if you don't have any symptoms.

Sunburn

Sunscreen keeps you from burning, but it also keeps people out in the sun longer with more UV exposure, and the long-term effects of this are yet to be determined. Still, burning is bad. So get in the habit of using **sun block** (minimum SPF 25) and reapplying it frequently. Note that some medications reduce your skin's ability to fend off the sun's powerful rays: ciprofloxacin, tetracycline-group antibiotics, sulphonylurea (for diabetes) and thiazide (for high blood pressure).

Vaginal thrush

Warm climates, tight nylon underwear and increased sexual activity are among the factors that lead to a higher incidence of yeast infections on the travel circuit. Men who carry the fungus rarely show any signs of it. For women, soreness, discomfort during sex, pain while urinating, and passing a white or yellowish discharge are among the symptoms. It's easily treated by an antifungal preparation that should be straightforward to find in most countries, but you may want to carry one just in case. In a jam, try applying regular plain yogurt and altering your diet briefly: no sugars, breads, beer, wine, mushrooms, Vegemite or other yeast-containing or yeast-encouraging foods.

If you do get sick

Here's the basic approach: with a high fever, loose stools or vomiting – anything very painful or unusual – get to a doctor and have blood and/or stool tests conducted. It's generally quick and cheap and far better than trying to weather it. With a quick diagnosis and the right medicine, you could be feeling fine within a day or so.

This is also a great time to check into a decent hotel with a private toilet and phone. You owe it to yourself and your fellow travelers. Hostel dormitories are not meant as recovery wards (beyond temporary alcohol-related afflictions). When you check in, tell the desk clerk that you're not feeling well and see if they have a doctor who can pay you a visit. You can always ring for an ambulance or cab if things take a turn for the worse.

If things seem serious, **don't take chances**. Get yourself to a hospital and contact your family and travel insurance company. If you're in a remote area, get to a major city immediately.

15

16

Travelers with special considerations

For many, just navigating your way around Europe – or even just one large city – with transport strikes, spaceship-like pay toilets and incomprehensible menus is challenge enough. But there are some groups who must also cope with a number of issues, from a medical condition to sexual-preference discrimination. This chapter focuses on the concerns these travelers face and offers a few tips that will hopefully smooth out their journeys.

Discounts for seniors

There's enough material to write an entire book on senior discounts. In fact, several people have. One of the things that seems to get better with age is the amount of rebates available. Seniors might get anything up to fifty percent off museums and other sites, and local transport. Look for notices at ticket windows, check your guidebook and – most importantly – **get into the habit of asking**.

Budget flights

On airlines, the magic discount age is usually 60 or 62. Rates vary, but you can typically get ten percent off "the lowest published fare." And that's exactly how you should phrase it when you ring a travel agent. Not only that, but you're often allowed to bring someone of any age along at the same rate. Several struggling airlines have cut back senior discounts lately, but it never hurts to ask, since they are still available, if only for select destinations or times.

Budget accommodation for seniors

There's nothing that says you have to be a youth to stay in a youth hostel. In fact, in many of the calmer hostels, senior travelers far outnumber the youths. International Youth Hostel cards (ⓦhihostels.com) in the US cost just $18 if you've turned 55. There are also special organizations, such as the non-profit-making Road Scholar (ⓦroadscholar.org), which run trips around the world for those aged 55 and older. For roughly €140 a day, you get a room, food, educational classes on a variety of subjects and the chance to meet plenty of like-minded, interesting people. Seniors may also be offered ten to fifty percent off normal rates at major hotels (and some minor ones) across Europe. Always inquire when you book.

Travel agents

- **CARP** ⓦcarp.ca. Not the most inviting acronym, the Canadian Association of Retired Persons is a travel agency for Canadians over 50.
- **Senior Women's Travel** ⓦposhnosh.com. They ditch the "old lady" image, with adventures for the 50-plus set with a thirst for active travel.
- **Wired Seniors** ⓦwiredseniors.com. Under "Travel guide", they have lists of "senior friendly" travel agents and hotels.

16

Senior gear and gadgets

There are a number of specialty items available these days, from lightweight canes that can be collapsed and stored in hand luggage to inflatable back-support rests, that can make a mild trip comfortable and rough ride tolerable. Browse senior-travel websites such as ⓦseniorsuperstores.com for ideas.

Considerations for travelers with special health conditions

When planning your itinerary, think about the medical facilities of the country you're visiting. The Netherlands, for example, will have a more modern healthcare system than Romania. But that doesn't mean you can't find decent healthcare in Romania; guidebooks list such facilities where reputable care is available. You can also find information online before leaving home at ⓦhospitals.webometrics.info.

Consider also the **temperature** of the places you're headed. Even if you've experienced sweltering heat before, it can be another thing entirely if you're out walking in it or staying in places without air conditioning.

If you're concerned about pre-existing ailments, discuss them with your doctor before leaving and keep an eye out for symptoms. Depending on your case, it may not be a bad idea to bring a copy of your medical file along, or at least the relevant pages. Check your medical insurance for travel coverage and supplement it with any special travel insurance you may need (see p.99).

How to bring your meds

Bring your prescriptions if you want to get refills, but ask your doctor to include the generic name since some brand-name prescriptions are not available abroad. Keep medicines in their **original labelled container** to avoid problems at customs, and have the prescriptions handy. (The label on the plastic bottle is not always enough, especially if you're transporting stronger pain medications which may require a special permit obtained at the pharmacy.) If you need medication refilled in an emergency, a good travel insurance plan will assist. And keep the phone number of your doctor and pharmacist with you for backup.

Travelers with disabilities

16 Don't let anybody tell you that you're not physically able to get around Europe. There's going to be more planning than an able-bodied person may face, more hassles, and you may have to give up more independence than you'd prefer at times, but if you're prepared to accept this, the rewards are immeasurable.

Some parts of Europe will be better suited to deal with your disability than others. But no matter how much planning you manage, you'll still need to prepare yourself for the unexpected: unstable or missing handrails, faulty ramps, narrow passages, and assigned assistants with little training and even less enthusiasm. Greet them with good humor and look for ways to solve the problems on the spot.

What you can do to prepare

Much depends on your type and degree of disability, and no one has a better grasp of that than you. Stay in control of your options. An activity that may not be a possibility for someone else could be fine for you. But if a travel agent or tour operator hears that you're disabled first, they may decide which things are suitable and present you with an inappropriately limited selection. In other words, look into things you'd like to do, then find out what can be done to accommodate you. Don't simply look for "activities for the disabled."

Before you begin your trip, whether you're joining a tour or doing it alone, think about ways to enhance the experience of travel and **remove potential obstacles**. For example, a deaf person may wish to purchase a rail pass in advance to avoid the hassle of buying individual tickets at a station counter, and a sight-impaired traveler might pick up souvenir replicas of the famous monuments once they arrive to help get a better feel of the structures they're standing in front of. Consider activities that can be done on an equal level. For those in a wheelchair, a cultural show, botanical gardens and recommended restaurant should take minimal preparation beyond confirming that they can accommodate you where stairs and doorways are concerned.

What you'll face

In most European countries, **accessibility** will range from excellent to completely nonexistent. However, there should be a fundamental infrastructure in place and your requests for assistance will often find an experienced ear. In less developed countries, expect to find little infrastructure, if any at all. What you may experience, however, is a refreshing abundance of helpers with an enlightened indifference toward disability. On the other hand, you may feel like a novelty act at times. If so, keep in mind that you may be one of the first independent disabled people that locals have seen. And even if it doesn't seem appreciated at the time, the inspiring tale of seeing you will likely find its way to those locals with disabilities who need to hear it most.

Most of Europe's great attractions are accessible to all. A few aren't or are at least extremely difficult for maneuvering, like the tower of Notre-Dame. At such times, you'll either have to content yourself with a view from afar, have a traveling companion record it for you and replay it on the spot, or seek alternative activities. Though accessible toilets are widely available, it won't be possible to find them everywhere you go.

These websites should also prove useful:

- **Mobility International USA** ⓦ miusa.org. Sponsors international exchange programs for people with disabilities, and sells books and even a DVD (*All Abroad*) to help those with disabilities cope on the road.
- **The Society for Accessible Travel and Hospitality** ⓦ sath.org. A nonprofit organization with membership and a magazine and special deals for seniors and students.
- **Disability Rights UK** ⓦ disabilityrightsuk.org. Publishes a guide for disabled people in Britain and Ireland, with hundreds of places to stay while traveling.

Getting around

Around Europe, **trains** may just be the best of your options. The *European Rail Timetable* (ⓦ europeanrailtimetable.eu) or individual country rail websites (see the "Where to go" section for these) detail which trains are specially equipped to handle wheelchairs.

Next in this somewhat sorry selection is **air travel**. The toilets may be impossibly narrow and the seats painfully uncomfortable, but at least it's generally the quickest option. Always call the airline well in advance if you need any special assistance. If you have a wheelchair, let them know which kind and be prepared for a transfer to a special aisle-sized chair. At Disabled World (ⓦ disabled-world.com), there's a list of flying tips for those with disabilities. Click "Disability" and choose "Disability Travel" from the menu.

16

Cabs are usually the most convenient and most comfortable option for getting around a city, but also the most expensive. In some enlightened cities (Stockholm, for example), there are elevators that take wheelchairs down to the subway at every station (though most subway transit systems are ill-equipped) and buses that dip down and provide space to roll on.

With assistance, the transport possibilities are as limitless as your imagination. If it still seems a bit overwhelming, or you'd like some help just getting started, there are a number of organizations set up for this very purpose:

- **Accessible Europe** ⓦaccessibleurope.com. Has a collection of agents and tour operators who specialize in disabled travel.
- **Flying Wheels Travel** ⓦflyingwheelstravel.com. Specializes in escorted and disabled tours.
- **Travel Eyes** ⓦtraveleyes-international.com. Pairs sighted travelers (who get a discount) with blind travelers.
- **Can Be Done Travel Agency** ⓦcanbedone.co.uk.
- **Accessible Journeys** ⓦdisabilitytravel.com.
- **The Society for Accessible Travel and Hospitality** ⓦsath.org.
- **Trips Inc. Special Adventures** ⓦtripsinc.com.

Where to stay

Not all hotels and hostels have special facilities, but many do. Often, the local tourist bureau is well versed with this information.

Access-Able (ⓦaccess-able.com) has a database of hotels that accommodate those with disabilities, plus listings of places where you can rent special medical equipment and get it repaired; Accomable (ⓦaccomable.com), meanwhile, puts travelers in touch with hosts of apartments and holiday homes. Hostelling International (ⓦhiusa.org) has a listing on its website of the hostels that can accommodate disabled guests.

Traveling with kids

Just as it's possible to travel with a disability, it's possible to travel with kids. It's just different. Often very different. First of all, face the fact that your own needs are no longer the priority. Clubbing in Ibiza is not going to happen. Your pace will be slower, your adventures more juvenile and your backpack heavier. Unless they're over 10, your children will likely have a sizeable part of their travel gear in *your* backpack. Oh, and your budget will go out the window.

On the other hand, if your children are old enough (at least 6–7 years old), an extended trip to foreign lands will create memories that last a lifetime. A few things to keep in mind, though, to make those memories pleasant: just like at home, your primary concern is safety. Roughing it will have to come in moderation, so sleeping in parks and hitchhiking are out. Make a plan about what to do if your kids get separated from you, and make sure they

16

understand it. Write your cell phone number on their arms, put the business card from the hotel/hostel you're staying at in their inner pocket and coach them about staying calm and what steps to take.

If you are the only parent traveling with your children, prepare an "Affidavit of Parental Consent" form signed by the non-traveling parent. This permission to take the children out of the country will avoid trouble with immigration officers.

For everyday health, make sure you bring a solid kit of everything you need to combat allergies, fevers, headaches etc. If you need stronger stuff, ask your GP for a list of alternative product names for the children's meds in the countries you are planning to visit. And check with the airline that you will be allowed to bring everything onboard.

See ⓦroughguides.com/activity/family-friendly for advice and ideas on where to go with kids. If you're traveling with a toddler, check out ⓦholidaywithbaby.com, while for older children, ⓦtravelforkids.com has suggestions on where to stay, what to see and do, and localized reading suggestions. The websites ⓦknok.com (a home-swapping site for families) and ⓦmetowe.com (which can arrange family volunteering trips) may also be of use. The two European mega-magnets for kids are Legoland (ⓦlegoland.com) – the original in Billund, Denmark, plus sister sites in Günzburg, Germany, and Windsor, England – and Disneyland Paris (ⓦdisneylandparis.fr).

16

THE RELUCTANT FAMILY TRAVELER

There are a few things I never thought I'd do, and buying a charter trip for my family was one of them. I'd spent nearly a decade regarding tour groups with the sort of suspicion normally reserved for unsolicited email from Nigerian bankers. But as I repeated the mantra, "I'm an independent traveler", my fingers – the same ones that had once crumpled torn pages from guidebooks into emergency loo paper – clicked the online purchase button for a week-long trip.

This was no doubt an overreaction to my previous attempts not to let a child change my ways. When our daughter first arrived, we kept packing her along for transatlantic journeys without much of a thought. As she got older and more fidgety, it became more of a challenge, but we were determined to remain backpackers. When she was older – old enough to carry her own mini-rucksack – her bladder wasn't quite prepared to go four hours on a rustic Dominican Republic bus. And, on several occasions, we crammed her into budget accommodation so tight we had to fold ourselves into a family lotus position to squeeze onto the single bed. Nothing that required professional counseling, mind you, but if this continued, how would I avoid a lifetime of resentment from the very person I was trying to "educate" with real experiences?

Maybe the charter trip would lighten things up.

I knew I had crossed over to the Dark Side when the plane touched down in Gran Canaria and I saw a woman with our hotel's logo embroidered on her shirt pocket standing there with a little clipboard, directing people onto numbered buses. I was no longer finding my way through the maze of public transport to some obscure dwelling; I had simply become human luggage. There would be no encounters with actual local people on this trip. Sure, there was plenty for kids to do and it was child-proof, plus there was enough space at the complex for a cargo plane to airdrop all the kiddy gear we'd hauled along (note to self: actually airdrop it next time), but I had strayed too far into the cultural void.

The trick, I now realize, is to find the middle ground between fleabag hostels and generic hotel complexes.

The antidote, if there is such a thing, is going to vary from family to family, but there are at least two key ingredients for a successful journey. 1: Other kids. Consider a family-stay or farmstay where the host family has kids of roughly the same age so you know the place is kid-proof: the children will likely get an instant "cultural" connection and the adults will have something in common. 2: It doesn't have to be exclusively kid-oriented. You shouldn't have to "put up with" your own travels. Remember: happy parents, happy kids. Or perhaps that's what Prozac is for.

One thing you should not do is plan for your kids to have some sort of cultural awakening during the trip. If you try to force the Louvre on them just because it means something to you, you may end up creating more conflict than positive memories. Just keep in mind that your children aren't trying to disappoint you; they just may be interested in other stuff. Relax your grip and the travel bug just might bite them.

LGBT travelers

It's certainly much easier now for LGBT travelers than it was twenty years ago, with scores of websites, books and travel publications devoted to gay travel; for example, Spartacus Gay Guides (spartacusworld.com/en), OutTraveler (outtraveler.com) and gaytravel.com. And Europe offers numerous social scenes, depending on what you're looking for.

Europe is about as enlightened as a continent gets, but that doesn't mean that **public affection** is welcomed in all settings. The International Lesbian and Gay Association (ilga.org) has some useful resources on this. Holding hands won't land you in jail, but it can do more than turn a few heads, even in socially liberal cities like Amsterdam. Just make sure you look around and inquire about any potential risks before you make an active protest against an intolerant rural community. If you're not sure, simply avoid public affection, which is often frowned upon no matter who's doing it.

Equally, trans travelers are by no means guaranteed a harassment-free trip, though you'll be legally protected in most countries, and awareness is growing. The TSA's screening process guidelines are available online (tsa.gov/traveler-information/transgender-travelers).

Vegetarian travelers

It's one thing to organize your diet at home, and quite another to maintain your eating habits in a new setting every day. But it can be done. And it doesn't even have to be stressful. Naturally, your chosen destinations are a major factor. Knowing where to look is another. A number of supermarkets, restaurants, resorts and B&Bs around Europe cater specifically to **vegetarians**. Produce markets offer an incredible variety of fresh fruit and vegetables.

Bear in mind that, even now, in some parts of Europe chefs may have a different idea of what vegetarian means. You can repeat "no meat" eight times, but your dinner will come drenched in beef-stock soup or topped with bacon. Many seem to think it only applies to the main ingredient, so you need to be specific in this regard when inquiring.

Scandinavia doesn't offer much of a vegetarian selection outside of major metropolitan areas, but delicious non-meat Italian pastas and pizzas can be easily found, not just in Italy but all across Europe. Salad bars are becoming more and more common; large supermarkets are increasingly well stocked with vegetarian food; and the produce in southern Europe is outstanding

16

(Italian tomatoes alone might convert thousands of meat-eaters).

There are a few excellent online resources that will lead you to a vegetarian restaurant anywhere in Europe: Ⓦvegetarianguides.co.uk, Ⓦhappycow.net, Ⓦvegguide.org and Ⓦvegdining.com. The International Vegetarian Union (Ⓦivu.org) also lists foreign phrases to help you explain or at least state your dietary requirements. Most good guidebooks suggest vegetarian alternatives where available.

Eating veggie as you travel

Start your trip by booking a vegetarian meal when you arrange your flight, then confirm it when you check your luggage. It's that easy. If you forgot, you can usually request the meal up to 48 hours before departure. Some veggie meals receive better reviews than their carnivore counterparts, while others are dire.

Trains, ferries and buses have captive audiences. Your best shot at feeding yourself a decent vegetarian meal during the trip is if you buy one at a supermarket before boarding. Doing this is also a great money-saver, so you're helping your wallet as much as your digestive tract.

16

17

Documenting your trip

Just because you're traveling with your best friend, or an entire overland group, doesn't mean you're going to collectively remember everything. When you're going solo, it's even harder. A journal, camera, video camera, color pencils, paints and watercolors (or a tablet with a sketching app) are the most common tools for recording your journey and its impact on you. Taking along all these is overkill, but keeping some record of your trip is an excellent idea.

Why you should keep a journal

Many travelers say this is the single best thing they brought on their trip. Or **buy it when you arrive**: hand-pressed paper from France or elsewhere gets you off to a good start. If you've kept a journal before, you'll be bringing one anyway. If not, this is the perfect time to start. It's not easy to process, or even remember all the places and people and stories. And simply putting your thoughts down on paper can have a soothing, therapeutic effect. It can be a friend when you're alone or provide structure for your day. If you have some artistic skill, spend a little more and get paper that will soak up your watercolors or hold ink better.

For those who are prepared to share all their innermost thoughts with the world, perhaps a travel blog, Twitter or Facebook provides a better option.

Thinking of setting up a travel blog? Here are your best options

The following three template-based blogging tools are among the most popular and easy to use and will let you customize the site and add the widgets you want (maps, calendars etc). And they're free.

- **Wordpress** (⊛wordpress.org). Most plug-ins, huge range of templates.
- **Blogger** (⊛blogger.com). Best for multiple bloggers, easiest to get started.
- **Tumblr** (⊛tumblr.com). Best for images and simplicity; has most artistic feel.
- **TravelPod** (⊛travelpod.com). One of the originals, now owned by TripAdvisor. You can upload via your mobile and even turn your trip into a printed book. Ads inserted into your content, which some may not appreciate, can be removed for an annual subscription.

Have a look around. There is plenty of competition here, with new sites you may like better popping up.

The easiest way to take good travel photographs

Bringing along a camera is pretty obvious. Which kind – and how to use it – isn't. The temptation for many is to get a "good camera" – that is, one above their level of expertise. Or to not bring one because they like the one on the smartphone… also a mistake (many stop taking pictures when the battery gets low or memory fills up). If you're a professional or exceptional amateur, bring what you need. Just be aware of the security risk of carrying valuable gear. Remove the brand names from the bags, try to select a case that doesn't look like a camera case, and minimize your lenses and accessories.

If you're not a pro, go for a relatively inexpensive digital pocket camera. Keep size in mind. The smaller it is, the easier it may be to get to it quickly or even keep in your hand a while. And that's going to help you catch those

WHEN NOT TO TAKE PHOTOS

There's a reason it's called **taking a picture**: rarely is permission requested. It may be your camera, but it's their image or holy site and either of those trumps whatever you've got in your hand, even if you're holding a Nikon with a Swiss lens. The path to pictorial enlightenment involves respecting local bans on photography and asking all subjects for the right to snap their photo. Everything else – including the zoom-lens sniper approach – is nicking pictures. That sounds a bit dramatic, but for many, photography is their only interaction with locals, and it's a relationship largely based on selfishness and insensitivity (the author has been guilty of this as well at times). For some cultures, our swinging lenses can feel as intrusive as if someone walked up and took your picture while you were lying on the beach half-naked or stuffing your face at a restaurant. To get those great portraits you see on guidebook covers and in magazines, simply ask permission. Or go one better and try to initiate conversation. Make a few friends or even a small connection and it will add another dimension to the picture. Then, if you can, get an address and send them a copy. Giving photos has a much nicer ring than taking them.

17

gone-in-a-heartbeat moments. Besides, if it's easy to carry and access, you'll probably use it more often and – here's one of the oldest photography tricks in the book – the more photos you take, the better your chances of getting something amazing.

If you're buying a new camera, consider skipping on the **zoom**. On pocket cameras, it jacks up the price, runs down the battery, brings down the quality and is not very powerful. If you take one to three steps forward, you'll get the same effect for free. Plus, if the moving zoom parts get so much as a grain of sand in them, kiss the camera goodbye for a month or two while it gets sent back to the manufacturer.

If you're using your phone as a backup camera, you might consider getting a lens attachment set for it. There are now several, like the "Dot iPhone Panorama Lens" or iPhone Telephoto Lens (8x zoom); ⓦphotojojo.com sells specialty photo accessories for iPhone.

Five essential photography tips for pocket camera/ smartphone users

1. Don't worry so much about the postcard shots. Just buy the postcard. Those photographers used the best equipment, found the best vantage point and waited until the lighting was perfect. Nothing will put your friends and family back home asleep quicker than endless landscape shots.

2. Photograph things that show your life on the road. It takes some effort to remember to photograph them (doorways, weird meals, freaky buses, scary toilets, charismatic taxi drivers and so on). Also, resist the urge to photograph your travel companions posing. Catch them off guard and you'll get a more honest, interesting photo.

3. With scenery, and often even with people, try to compose the photo so there's something very close, something midrange and something in the distance. If you want to photograph someone standing in front of a waterfall, for example, try positioning yourself just behind a texture-rich tree branch and allow it to appear in a third of the picture.

4. Think your picture as a grid of three by three, like tic-tac-toe. It often works well to position the center of your subject on one of those four crossings, instead of just placing the subject in the center. When the subject is moving, you want to position them on the side so they appear to be moving towards the center of the photo, not off the frame.

5. Shoot when cloudy or try using a flash in daylight. Despite the fact that things seem brighter, midday sunlight actually flattens images and provides unappealing photos. For people, animals and objects, you want overcast skies or indirect light. A cloudy day is the perfect time to get great pictures. If you must shoot people in the middle of a sunny day, use the flash to eliminate unattractive shadows or (this may sound counterintuitive) have your subjects step into a shaded area. You can get some great silhouette shots by having the sun behind your subject, but unless you're intentionally trying to do this for visual effect, you'll do well not to shoot into a light source.

Recording sound

If the sounds of a place conjure stronger memories for you than photos, or if you'd prefer to dictate your journal, you can easily save them on your smartphone or bring along a small digital recorder (there are microphone attachments for iPhone that will help you collect ambient sounds better and others that will improve the sound of interviews). This can be a nice addition to any blog posting and help encourage your reader to close their eyes and try to imagine the scene.

Basic tips for shooting video

Like photography, video has spawned stacks of books on method and technique. If you're going to shoot, here are two simple tips. The first is to hold the camera very **steady**, even if it's equipped with an electronic stabilizer. That may mean leaning against a tree or lamppost. If you're serious about getting good footage, however, bring a tripod. Nothing induces headaches like watching shaky footage. There are some new, compact, handheld, battery-operated products for phones and GoPros that utilize a "three-axis gimbal" to keep things steady while you move around. They cost about $200–350. Search for "3-axis gimbal" and the make of your phone or camera online and buy one with strong reviews.

The second tip is to resist letting the camera follow your natural head or eye movement all the time. For example, allow someone to walk across the field of vision – entering on one side and disappearing on the other. This will make editing much easier once you return home.

Though the quality won't be great and it'll eat up memory even more than photos, filming videos on your phone is quick, simple and requires no specialist equipment. Make sure you shoot in landscape rather than portrait orientation, though, as that works better on most screens.

CARRYING YOUR GEAR

The biggest challenge with carrying camera equipment in any situation is to be constantly aware without being suspicious. The gear is valuable, but you have to remember that it's just gear and it's replaceable. For example, I'm often in remote places and find myself in the middle of a group of kids who want to see my camera – look through the lens, take a few pictures. Some photographers freak about that. My feeling is that some kid has never seen a camera, really wants to, and I'm not going to deprive them of that. I'll keep a hand on the strap, but let them play with it.

That doesn't mean I make it easy for professional thieves whose full-time job is trying to figure out what people have and how to get it. Camera bags attract too much attention. I currently use a regular bike-messenger bag. I wear dark clothes and my camera is dark, so that works as camouflage while it's half tucked under my arm. Then I think about the picture before I take it. I don't compose my shots through the viewfinder, so I'm not keeping my camera visible for long.

This doesn't always work, though. I was in the Central African Republic going through a crowded market. I was carrying my gear in this utility belt around my waist. I call it my Batman belt. It's so close to the body, I can feel if anyone touches it. And it's not easy to cut through or open. Plus my shirt flops over it so it's not easy to see. Anyway, I thought I felt something. So I turned around and there was this guy holding my light meter. The reporter with me said that it looked like there was some kind of silent agreement between us. I just fixed his gaze. Then calmly removed the light meter from his hand.

Chris Anderson
Photojournalist, *New York Times Magazine, Magnum Photos*

17

> **MEMENTOS OF YOUR TRIP**
>
> Most of the best are free and easy to carry. You might collect small, flat items that catch your eye and evoke a memory: concert and train tickets, a beer label, fortune-cookie prediction, even a sample of the abrasive toilet paper that once gave you some trouble. Scan them or cram them into your journal for safe transport.

Drawing and painting

Watercolors, color pencils and sketching charcoal are relatively cheap and extremely easy to transport. Even if you don't have much artistic skill, or much that you're aware of, this is an ideal time to give it a shot. It's a nice alternative to reading or writing when you're stuck somewhere for a long time. Which, invariably, you will be at some point. Pick up a "how-to" paint/draw book and learn as you go.

What to do with souvenirs you buy

Send them home! Few travelers need any help selecting souvenirs, but most seem to need some help carrying them. No matter how small, lightweight and space-saving the items may seem individually, the best thing you can do – unless you're at the tail end of your trip – is a big round of shopping when you get to a market you like, then **ship everything home the same day** (see p.150). Your glass turtle earrings, Dutch windmill decanter and Mona Lisa bottle opener will have a much better chance of getting broken, stolen or lost under your care than that of a postal service. Naturally, there are several levels of security available (as well as private couriers) at a range of prices. Consider the reliability of the postal service (are you in Denmark or Turkey?), the weight of the package and the value of what you're sending, before you ship. There's no magic formula, but it's not uncommon to pay more for postage than for the actual item enclosed. Keep that in mind when you're about to buy that set of terracotta roof tiles in Spain.

Watch out for illegal souvenirs

Another thing to consider is the legality of exporting **antiques**. Just because a vendor in a market is willing to part with it doesn't mean you're allowed to bring it out of the country, so the authentic fifteenth-century porcelain spittoon you bargained for may not be getting off the plane with you when you land back home. Nor is it likely to arrive in the mail. If it looks old and valuable, consult your guidebook. You may need to get a certificate of authenticity from a museum. Shopping caution also applies to plants, seeds and items made from wild animals, which may be removed by customs officials. You won't be reimbursed for any of this, but you may get fined.

18

Returning home

Nothing seems stranger during your trip-planning process than taking a moment to consider your return details. But this information may affect your planning, so best that it's addressed, at least briefly, now. Let's assume you've conquered Europe and all you have left is to return home. With a comfortable bed and a fresh set of clothes in sight, it's tempting to lower your guard. Instead, you're going to need to brace yourself for a potentially rough re-entry.

Even if Europe is similar in many ways to your own culture, many people coming home from a long trip still experience a shock – often bigger on their return than when they first went abroad, and at a time when they're least prepared for it. It's a lifestyle shift as much as a cultural one. On the bright side, there are a few simple things you can do to turn the experience into a smooth landing, and the most important of these is learning what to expect.

Stages of re-entry

The stages of re-entry mirror those of culture shock: honeymoon, crisis, recovery and readjustment.

The **honeymoon** is the initial exhilaration of returning home, and precisely what most are expecting: a warm welcome, familiar bed, inquisitive friends who are dying to hear your stories.

The surprise left-hook (or "**crisis**") is the reverse culture shock, which lasts until you acclimatize to your home surroundings and eventually return to your old self (with a bit more wisdom and experience).

The degree of the reverse culture shock you experience largely depends upon how integrated you became into foreign cultures during your journey, and how different they are from your own. Upon returning, you may miss the regular and close social interaction you had with your foreign community and other travelers. You may find yourself revolted by the aggressive marketing campaigns you had previously learned to ignore. More likely, you may feel a distance has come between you and your friends and family because they can no longer relate to your "new" well-traveled persona – one that has grown and been shaped by your range of different experiences. Instead, they're treating you the same way and don't have the patience to hear the thirty hours of stories required to bring them up to speed. And if you're returning to a job, you may notice reduced responsibilities and little acknowledgment for your overseas accomplishments.

This is compounded by The Questions. If you've ever broken your leg and had to explain what happened to everyone you met for a month, you already have a good understanding of what it's like to be a human recording. But when you're trying to sum up a few months or a few years of life-changing experiences in one or two cute lines, it's even more frustrating. The Questions tend to be the same worldwide. They'll start with "How was the trip?", go on to "What was your favourite?" and quickly get to "So what are you going to do now?"

Eventually you'll **recover** and **adjust** as you ease back into routines, accept your difference and apply your newfound approaches to various situations.

Making a re-entry game plan

Scuba diving and cultural immersion are similar in at least this one respect: a little decompression is a good idea. Before you return home, try to build in a little stop for **mental refueling**. It needn't be a month of silence at a monastery: a beach will do fine. You just need a place with minimal stimulus. It can take a while to process the lifetime of experiences that you've just crammed into a ridiculously short period. And more important still, you need to begin to engage with the concept of returning home. You're going to have enough to worry about when you get back, so try to work out a game plan in advance: where you're going to stay, who you plan to visit and so on. So, if you do plan to stay at a beach, make sure it's a beach with wi-fi.

Brace others for your arrival

The best single thing you can do in this respect is to keep your friends and family up to speed during your trip with regular dispatches from the road… tweets, Facebook updates, email, travel blog. Your friends and family will have far more patience to read about your experiences in bite-sized chunks as you go than to listen to them all in one sitting when you get home.

Write a helpful last dispatch from the road

When you're just about to head home, take some time to sum up your trip in your last dispatch. Answer the questions they're likely to ask. List your favorite places, favorite experiences, craziest misadventure… things you expect you can spare yourself from having to answer a hundred times in person. Tell them what your plans are. Those around you will want to get that extra dose of info when they see you in person. Help them out. Give them something they can ask about. You might say, "I'll be carrying around a very small selection of photos I wasn't prepared to put online. For a beer, I'll be happy to show them to you."

Stay in touch with people you met

Stay in touch with the friends you made on your trip. It improves the chance you'll see them again and have a free place to stay (and a cultural guide) when you head abroad next time, and gives you a free support network. Facebook makes this ridiculously easy.

18

Keep involved with the places

Join an organization that supports a place or cause you found on the road. Study that language you were dying to speak at the time but couldn't. Read fiction or nonfiction books on the subject. If you do eventually head back to any of these places, you'll be able to appreciate them on another level.

Seek out travelers in your area

There's probably a hostel in your area filled with Europeans (and Aussies and Kiwis and Americans and Canadians, if that's whom you miss). Spending time with travelers, visiting students or an immigrant crowd can be just enough of a dose to remind you that you're sane after all.

Find patience

It's common to feel superior to those around you who haven't had such international experiences. Suddenly, their views may seem pedestrian and insular and you feel the continued need to "set them straight." Just remember: your own views may not be that popular, either. Time outside your own country tends to highlight its faults, and you may come off sounding like a born-again critic. Take heart. You will have enlightened perspectives, but don't expect others to come around easily.

Get busy

If you have the possibility to arrange your work/study schedule before returning, keep this in mind: a little downtime at home is wonderful, but too much can be self-defeating. Finding that right balance is up to you, but in general the less the better. One or two weeks is usually sufficient.

Revive the memories

If you need a quick fix, you might try escaping back into your travels for a brief tour. This is where a good scrapbook/Pinterest board and well-kept journal come in handy (see p.180). Using your notes and images, it can often be helpful to write about your experiences more fully. Who knows? This may be the chance to release that budding travel writer within.

Treat your home city like a destination

Chances are you never fully embraced your town like those you visited during your travels. Hit those museums you never bothered to visit, try some new pubs, even stay in traveler accommodation for a night. Apply your spirit of exploration to your home turf and chances are you'll see it in a new light.

Start traveling again

If all else fails (except your finances), hit the road again. It doesn't have to be a long trip, or even an international one. Just taking some trains and buses, packing up your rucksack, sleeping in a few ratty hotels and meeting some other travelers can be enough.

First-Time Europe

Where to go

OTTOMAN HOUSES, MANGALEMI DISTRICT, BERAT

Albania

Capital Tirana
Population 3,029,000
Language Albanian
Currency Lek (L)
Minimum daily budget €20

When to go May–September for the best weather; the place is never crowded with tourists

When not to go Wet, rainy weather sees many hotels and guesthouses close November–March

Albania

Tell your friends or family that you're off to Albania, and you'll likely receive a stock response: "Isn't it dangerous?", "Isn't there a war going on there?", and "Is that even *in* Europe?" are some of the most common. Speak instead to those who have been, and the associations with the country's name become infinitely more positive – you'll hear of rippling mountains, Ottoman architecture, pristine beaches and endlessly hospitable locals. Following decades of isolationist rule, this rugged land still doesn't seem to fit into the grand continental jigsaw, with distinctly exotic notes emanating from its language, customs and cuisine. Pay a visit to this beguiling corner of Europe now, before it garners the popularity it deserves.

Main attractions

❶ Tirana Sip espresso in Albania's colorful capital, a buzzing city with a mishmash of garishly painted buildings, traditional restaurants and trendy bars. Tirana is better for strolling than sightseeing, but there's plenty to keep you occupied in the southbound stretch from Skanderbeg Square to the Grand Park, which narrowly bypasses the trendy Blloku district on the way.

❷ Kruja This gorgeous hilltop town was the focal point of national hero Skanderbeg's resistance to the Ottoman invasions of the fifteenth century, and you'll see his likeness all over the place.

❸ Berat Ottoman houses climb the hillsides of this beguiling town, their dark, rectangular windows staring from whitewashed walls like a thousand eyes. Steep, cobblestone paths lead up to the hilltop Kalasa, a fourteenth-century citadel whose wonderfully eerie interior is up there with the finest old towns in the Balkans.

❹ Gjirokastra Sitting proudly above a sparsely inhabited valley, this is one of Albania's most attractive towns, and home to some of its friendliest people. Its days as an Ottoman trading hub have bequeathed it a wealth of sparkling Ottoman houses, which line a maze of steep cobbled streets. The Old Town's centerpiece is its imposing citadel, which is clearly visible from any point in town. ⓦ gjirokastra.org

Also recommended

● **Bunkers** The country is covered with around 750,000 concrete bunkers from its period of national paranoia. They're next to useless now – though young, privacy-seeking couples occasionally put them to interesting use – but great for selfies.

● **Ionian coast** Find yourself a deserted beach on one of the Mediterranean's most remote and least developed stretches –

AVERAGE DAILY TEMPERATURES AND MONTHLY RAINFALL

	Jan	Feb	Mar	Apr	May	June	July	Aug	Sept	Oct	Nov	Dec
Tirana												
max °C	12	13	15	18	24	28	31	31	27	23	16	13
min °C	2	3	5	8	11	16	17	17	15	10	8	5
rainfall mm	131	158	129	117	117	89	34	35	61	106	207	174

staring straight at the Greek island of Corfu, Saranda makes an appealing base.

- **Take a cable car up Mount Dajti** This dark, looming mountain is easily visible from Tirana. The mountain's network of paths feels surprisingly remote even though you're only 25km from the capital.

- **Hunt down the Blue Eye** On the way between Gjirokastra and Saranda, an underwater spring forms a pool of deepest blue. Its setting in a cool, remote grove is quite spectacular – the water is delicious, and you can swim in it until you get the chills (which won't take long, even in summer).

Food and drink

Albania's largely meat-based cuisine brings together elements of Slavic, Turkish and Italian fare, but for all this choice modern Albanian youth – and many a tourist – subsists almost entirely on snack food, particularly *burek* (a pastry filled with cheese, meat or spinach) and *sufllaqë* (sliced kebab meat and French fries stuffed in a roll of flatbread). The alcoholic drink of choice is rakia, though local wine is excellent value at around €4 per bottle from a shop.

Transport

Getting from A to B is a little tricky in Albania – you're advised to be flexible, exercise patience, and to treat travel information as a guideline rather than gospel.

Most travel is conducted by bus, though there are no actual stations – this becomes nightmarish in Tirana. Buses are supplemented by minibuses known as *furgons*, which are more numerous but run to no fixed schedule.

Albania also boasts a limited, ageing train network; neither Eurail nor InterRail passes are valid, and would be pretty pointless in any case.

Events

- **Tirana International Film Festival** By far the biggest film festival in Albania

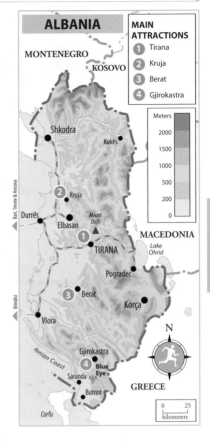

– okay, that's not much of a sell, but you'd have to hunt clean across the continent to find something more cinematically offbeat than the Albanian silver screen. Plenty of international films are shown here too. Dec; ⓦ tiranafilmfest.com

- **BunkerFest** Launched in 2011, this event makes use of some of the hundreds of thousands of concrete bunkers strewn across Albania. It's a bit of an ad-hoc affair, usually revolving around DJ sets and graffiti art, and some years it doesn't take place at all – ask at Tirana's hostels for details. Usually May.

Albania online

Albania info ⓦ albania.al

STRAUSS MONUMENT, STADTPARK, VIENNA

Austria

Capital Vienna

Population 8,608,000

Language German

Currency Euro (€)

Minimum daily budget €45

When to go Mid-December to March for skiing, July and August for hiking, or June, when the Alps are in full bloom, crowds are manageable and prices have yet to hit their peak

When not to go Many theaters and performance centers close during July and August

Austria

As the homeland of personalities as diverse as Mozart, Hitler, Schwarzenegger and Freud, you could say Austria brings out the best and worst in people. It's one of the world's richest and most stable democracies, and has plenty of the Alps thrown in for those who enjoy risking life and limb. Fantastic skiing and hiking in the west of the country draw the outdoor adrenaline nuts, while there is enough grand imperial art and architecture in Vienna to leave the culture vultures gasping for air. What the kleptomaniac Habsburgs couldn't steal from their vassal states, they commissioned themselves, leaving the Kunsthistorisches Museum with one of the largest art collections in the world. There's a lot of Egyptian, Greek and Roman antiquities, but also enough of Ye Olde Masters to fill entire rooms.

For those whose taste leans towards the less dusty side of culture, Austria has a bubbling electronic music scene, too. It might not be the zaniest of countries, but it's making strides in that direction. Traditionally pork-loving Austrians are even warming to such unheard-of concepts as vegetarian dining. What will they embrace next?

Main attractions

❶ **The Austrian Alps** Hundreds of 3000m-plus peaks will take care of your climbing needs. If you prefer the assistance of a ski lift to get you up the mountain, every self-respecting village has at least a dozen.

❷ **Eisriesenwelt caves** A walk-in refrigerator of gigantic proportions, with over 40km of frozen waterfalls and weird-looking ice sculptures. They're easily accessible from the town of Werfen, south of Salzburg, and are open between May and October. Even in the summertime, the temperature hovers around freezing point, so bring a fleece. ⓦ eisriesenwelt.at

❸ **The KunstHausWien, Vienna** The modern exhibitions are upstaged by the building they're housed in. Once inside the museum, the walls twist, floors undulate and trees grow out of third-story windows. The architect, Friedensreich Hundertwasser (1928–2000), ranks as one of the most original architects of the twentieth century. ⓦ kunsthauswien.com

❹ **Mozart's Salzburg** This famous border town is not only worth a visit to pay homage to the man, but also has churches so cute you'll want to pinch them, plus plenty of art, city squares and chocolate galore. ⓦ salzburg.info

❺ **MuseumsQuartier, Vienna** A total floor area of 60,000 square meters makes this one of the most impressive mega-museums in the world. The Viennese complex houses,

AVERAGE DAILY TEMPERATURES AND MONTHLY RAINFALL

	Jan	Feb	Mar	Apr	May	June	July	Aug	Sept	Oct	Nov	Dec
Vienna												
max °C	2	4	9	14	19	22	25	25	21	14	7	4
min °C	-3	-2	2	5	9	13	15	15	12	6	2	-1
rainfall mm	38	42	41	51	61	74	63	58	45	41	50	43

AUSTRIA

0   50
kilometers

Nuremberg ▲   Prague ▲   ▲ Prague   ▲ Brno
CZECH   REPUBLIC
SLOVAKIA
Stuttgart
Augsburg
GERMANY   Munich
Linz   **3 5 6**
Krems
Danube
Bodensee   Melk   **VIENNA**
Bregenz   **4**   Salzburg
Bad Ischl   Hallstatt   Hochschwab   Budapest
Kitzbühel   **2**
Innsbruck   **1**   T A U E R N   Graz
LIECHTENSTEIN   Grossglockner   M O U N T A I N S
**SWITZER-   Silvretta High   HUNGARY
LAND**   Alpine Road   Villach
I T A L Y   Klagenfurt
Verona   Venice   Maribor
Ljubljana   **SLOVENIA**
CROATIA

Meters
2000
1500
1000
0

MAIN ATTRACTIONS

1 The Austrian Alps
2 Eisriesenwelt caves
3 The KunstHausWien, Vienna
4 Mozart's Salzburg
5 MuseumsQuartier, Vienna
6 Schönbrunn, Vienna

among other things, the Leopold Museum (Austrian art), the Kunsthalle Wien, the ZOOM Children's Museum and the Tanzquartier Wien (the Center for Contemporary Dance). Ⓦ mqw.at

6 Schönbrunn, Vienna If you find the Habsburg Palace in downtown Vienna confusing and gridlocked, this 1685 "summer cottage" commissioned by Emperor Leopold I gives you a much better idea of how Viennese royalty spent the taxpayers' money. When crowds arrive, head outside – the park out the back is bigger than Monaco. Ⓦ schoenbrunn.at

Also recommended

● **Cruise the Austrian Alps on a motorbike** Long and winding Alpine roads offer unparalleled two-wheel riding. Classic tours include the Grossglockner mountain, the Silvretta High Alpine Road, the Tauern mountains and the tour around the Hochschwab.

● **Ski the Hahnenkammrennen, Kitzbühel** Let's face it – your chances of competing in the actual race are about as slim as Kate Moss. But you can always do a

couple of practice runs to test your mettle. The start is at 1665m, the finish at 802m, and the total course spans 3.3km. You might want to ratchet up your insurance first, though. Ⓦ hahnenkamm.com

● **Bring the hills alive on a Sound of Music tour** Plenty of tours follow in the dance steps of the von Trapp family, but Panorama Tours (Ⓦ panoramatours.com) had the backing of Fräulein Maria herself. Trips center on the city of Salzburg but also include the palaces of Frohnburg and Leopoldskron. The whole wonderfully (or painfully) kitsch experience is typically tackled with a bus tour that can be arranged anywhere in town.

● **Take a yodeling course** When in the Alps, strike a blow for nonverbal throat noises and make lots of alternative friends at the same time. Just don't use your newfound vocal skills in downtown Vienna. To get a little warm-up, try Ⓦ jodelkurs.com.

Food and drink

When Austrian xenophobes ask what immigrants have ever done for Austria, the rest of the country answers, "Cheap food!" All the usual suspects can be found, especially in student areas in the larger cities. You can tank up your gut for around €5. For a hearty Austrian sit-down meal, figure on €18–20. Coffee is particularly expensive, so make every cup last.

Transport

Austria is as well equipped as any other environment-conscious Western democracy when it comes to public transport. The rail network is not the fastest in Europe, but it is punctual and clean and the views are often incredible. Where rail services terminate, the Postbus system will take you farther. The former is run by the ÖBB (who operate the trains as well) and hence they leave from train stations, while the Postbus service departs from post offices. Both are usually cheaper but slower than the train. Their prime functions are delivering mail and shuttling kids to school, though there are a few late-night services that can bring you home after a night on the town.

In Vienna, the Vienna Card (Ⓦwienkarte .at) is worth looking into. It gives you 48 or 72 hours of unlimited free travel by underground, bus and tram, and discounts to nearly all museums, concerts and restaurants. You can pick up the card in almost any hotel or department store around the city.

By train
- **Eurail Austria Pass** Any three, four, five or eight days of travel in thirty days in first or second class.
- **Eurail Austria-Switzerland Pass** Any four, five, six, eight or ten days of travel in two months.
- **European East Pass** (also valid in the Czech Republic, Slovakia and Hungary) Any five days of travel in one month. Five additional travel days can be added.
- **InterRail Austria Pass** Ranges from any three, four, six or eight days of travel in one month. You can take as many trains as you want during each travel day.

For tips and tricks on maximizing your rail pass, see "Costs and savings" (p.63).

By bus
Busabout (see p.44) allows some travel in Austria. For internal bus info, see Ⓦpostbus .at/en. For buses to other countries, see Ⓦeurolines.at.

Events

- **Silvesterball, Vienna** The Silvesterball (formerly the Kaiserball – Imperial Ball) at the Hofburg on New Year's Eve kicks off the traditional ballroom season in Vienna, and it's not as hard a party to get into as you might think – just expensive. Even if you miss it, there are plenty of other opportunities later in the year to waltz until the end. Dec 31; Ⓦhofburgsilvesterball.com
- **ImPulsTanz, Vienna** Dancing, or something that looks vaguely like it, is nonstop during this month-long celebration of rhythmic movement in Vienna. World-famous choreographers and dance companies perform all over the city, and there are courses and workshops for those who want to get in on the action themselves. Mid-July to mid-Aug; Ⓦimpulstanz.com
- **Lederhosen Festival** See Austrians clad in traditional Austrian attire at the annual Lederhosen Festival in Windischgarsten. Mostly it's an excuse to drink good beer. July; Ⓦlederhosentreffen.at
- **Floating Opera** Featuring a floating stage on Lake Constance, the Bregenzer Festspiele (Bregenz Festival) is a performing arts festival held every July and August; Ⓦbregenzerfestspiele.com/en

Austria online

Austria info Ⓦaustria-tourism.at
Rail Ⓦoebb.at
Bus Ⓦpostbus.at/en
Vienna info Ⓦaboutvienna.org

TOWN HALL SQUARE, TALLINN

The Baltic States

ESTONIA
Capital Tallinn
Population 1,315,000
Languages Estonian
Currency Euro (€)
Minimum daily budget €30

LATVIA
Capital Rīga
Population 1,979,000
Language Latvian, Russian
Currency Euro (€)
Minimum daily budget €30

LITHUANIA
Capital Vilnius
Population 2,906,000
Language Lithuanian
Currency Euro (€)
Minimum daily budget €28

When to go May–August for the weather and outdoor café scene

When not to go December–March can be severe, with icy-cold temperatures and few daylight hours

The Baltic States

Estonia, Latvia and Lithuania have clearly gone to great lengths to maintain their independence and defined borders after breaking away from the Soviet empire 25 years ago, yet the three of them are still often grouped under a heading that sounds like a 1970s heavy metal band. There are several nations bordering the Baltic Sea that could have also landed this rather unfortunate moniker, but for these three it stuck.

You may not be familiar with the Baltic States, and let's face it – they're not on most peoples' must-see lists. So why go? Long since emerged from behind the Iron Curtain, these former Soviet nations are now thriving cultural and outdoor destinations, and typically far cheaper than other more popular European cities. Tallinn's Hanseatic Old Town is one of Europe's best-preserved medieval cities (and a UNESCO World Heritage Site). And Rīga isn't far behind with its charming old-town architecture. There are even some great beaches along the coast, including the popular sandy stretches on Estonia's Saaremaa island and Latvia's summer party spot: Liepāja.

Main attractions

❶ **Pärnu, Estonia** You won't find too many foreigners taking a beach vacation in Estonia, but this resort is a big draw locally. The white sandy beaches attract thousands, and those who want to get away from the crowds head for the nearby dunes and mud baths. Ⓦ parnu.ee

❷ **Orthodox Maritime Cathedral of St Nicholas, Karosta** If you're into Russian Orthodox-style turnip cupolas, this 1901 cathedral in Latvia won't disappoint. The gilded domes and other interior features were restored in the 1990s after years of disrepair, during which time the cathedral served as a cinema and sports center. Ⓦ karosta.lv

❸ **Tallinn's old town** Often compared

AVERAGE DAILY TEMPERATURES AND MONTHLY RAINFALL

	Jan	Feb	Mar	Apr	May	June	July	Aug	Sept	Oct	Nov	Dec
Tallinn (Estonia)												
max °C	-2	-3	2	7	14	18	20	19	13	8	3	-1
min °C	-6	-7	-4	1	6	10	13	12	8	3	-1	-4
rainfall mm	33	23	25	30	38	51	66	71	71	58	53	43
Rīga (Latvia)												
max °C	-2	-2	3	9	16	19	21	20	15	10	4	0
min °C	-6	-6	-2	2	7	11	13	13	9	5	1	-4
rainfall mm	33	23	25	36	43	58	71	69	66	53	51	38
Vilnius (Lithuania)												
max °C	-3	-2	2	10	18	21	22	21	16	10	3	-1
min °C	-8	-8	-4	1	7	10	12	11	8	3	-1	-5
rainfall mm	43	33	38	48	51	76	84	69	66	56	51	53

to Prague, Estonia's capital has been a destination for budget travelers for a while, and has an exuberant nightlife to match. Soviet rule was a sort of backward blessing for this old city (except the part when the Soviets bombed the old quarter one day in 1944 and flattened ten percent of it). The economic stagnation kept development to a minimum, so the old city has remained largely intact. Check out the area round Toompea Hill, where the aristocracy and clergy once lived. Ⓦvisittallinn.ee

❹ **Toomkirik, Tallinn** The Cathedral of St Mary the Virgin, Estonia's oldest church, was built in 1223 and remains the burial site of German and Swedish noblemen. It houses the largest organ in the country. Ⓦtoomkirik.ee

Also recommended

● **Explore Lahemaa Park, Estonia**
Estonia's largest national park, Lahemaa combines dense forest, coastal bluffs, lakes, waterfalls and eighteenth-century manor houses. Situated in the north of the country, the park encompasses the Koljaku–Oandu

THE BALTIC STATES

FINLAND

Gulf of Finland

TALLINN ❸❹ LAHEMAA NATIONAL PARK Narva

0   50 kilometers

N

Kopu Peninsula Kärdla Vormsi
Hiiumaa Käina Haapsalu
Kassari Muhu Virtsu
Saaremaa Kuivastu SOOMAA NATIONAL PARK
Kuressaare PARK ❶ Pärnu
Abruka

ESTONIA

Lake Peipsi

RUSSIA

Lake Võrtsjärv Tartu

BALTIC SEA

Gulf of Riga

GAUJA NATIONAL PARK Valmiera
Cēsis

Ventspils

Kuldiga Jūrmala RĪGA Sigulda Ērgli

LATVIA

❷ Liepāja Jelgava Rundāle Bauska Rēzekne

Palanga Hill of Crosses Šiauliai Panevėžys Daugavpils

Klaipėda Nida Curonian Spit

LITHUANIA

BELARUS

Kaliningrad KALININGRAD (RUSSIA) Kaunas VILNIUS
Trakai

Meters
200
100
0

POLAND

MAIN ATTRACTIONS
❶ Pärnu, Estonia
❷ Orthodox Maritime Cathedral of St Nicholas, Karosta
❸ Tallinn's old town
❹ Toomkirik, Tallinn

and Laukasoo reserves, a wet sea forest and – brace yourself – 7000-year-old bog respectively. Ⓦkeskkonnaamet.ee

● **Visit Hiiumaa (aka Dagö), Estonia** If you're looking for ecotourism, consider this sparsely populated Estonian island 22km west of the mainland. The island's lovely, 1000-square-kilometer stretch of coast is protected from overdevelopment, and there's no shortage of wildlife: elk red deer, wild boars, foxes, lynxes, black storks, golden eagles and cranes. Ⓦhiiumaa.ee

● **Climb the Hill of Crosses, Lithuania** Ten kilometers north of the Lithuanian town of Šiauliai, this is one of the world's most spectacular cemeteries. Thousands of crosses dot the hillside like wildflowers. Some are memorials, others are devotional, but the wooden and metal crosses make for a moving (if slightly creepy) hike. Ⓦlcn.lt/en/bl/sventoves/kryziuk

● **Canoe Gauja National Park, Latvia** The Gauja, Salaca and Abava rivers in this Latvian lake region provide some of the best paddling around, and there's plenty of flora and fauna to keep you and your camera occupied. Ⓦgnp.lv/en

● **Haunted Karosta Prison, Latvia** In operation as recently as 1997, Karosta has been used by the Soviets, the Nazis and most recently the Latvians as a military prison. Ⓦkarostascietums.lv

● **"Sahara of Lithuania" sand dunes** Massive deforestation in the sixteenth century got the sands shifting and the waves and winds did the rest. At a pace of 20m a year, the sands enveloped fourteen villages over three hundred years. The dunes can be found in Curonian Spit National Park, crisscrossed with well-marked cycling trails. Ⓦnerija.lt/en

Food and drink

It's not difficult to find a nice meal for €25, but dining is where you're likely to save the most. A simple meal, for example, can be had for under €8, even in Latvia and Estonia. Pep yourself up for pork and potatoes, soup and sausage, and smoked fish. In summer, you can skip the blood pancakes if you please, but don't miss the fresh berries. If you want to drink something extra special (and extra revolting) in Latvia, try the Riga Black Balsam, a brake-fluid-like 45 percent ABV concoction. Equally strong, the syrupy sweet Vana Tallinn liqueur is also a palate challenger, whether you add it to coffee or champagne.

Transport

Getting around the Baltic States is still quite cheap (and slow). No rail passes cover the area, but there is a local rail service, running two types of train: "passenger" and "fast." Both are slow, but inexpensive. Busabout doesn't operate in the region either, but Eurolines does (Ⓦeurolines.lt).

In the capital cities, there's a comprehensive network of trams, trolleys and buses, but these can get very crowded. Save money by buying a ticket before boarding, or better, buy a ten-ticket pack.

Events

● **Jazzkaar, Tallinn** It can't be easy getting the big names to make a trip to the Baltics, but that's exactly what the Jazzkaar festival has managed to do over the years. Acts have become increasingly international, with artists gathered from France, Portugal, Cuba, Brazil, Japan, the US and the UK performing across the city. April; Ⓦjazzkaar.ee

● **Mārtiņi Festival** Not to be confused with 007's favorite cocktail, this is an ancient festival that marks the start of winter in Latvia. (There are, however, Mārtiņi balls – nonalcoholic wads of beans, peas, potatoes and hemp.) It also marks the start of the masquerade season. Nov 10.

● **Midsummer** People flee to the countryside when the summer solstice arrives.

Special foods (cheeses and pies) are made for the occasion, while flower-and-grass wreaths are strung up. Usually around June 20.

● **Õllesummer, Tallinn** The largest summer festival in Estonia, Õllesummer attracts almost a hundred performers across seven stages, luring nearly 60,000 visitors. Early July; Ⓦ ollesummer.ee

● **Vilnius Jazz Festival** Jazz junkies turn up en masse for this East–West music fusion, while Lithuania's Russian Drama Theater comes alive for the days the acts come to town. Mid-Oct; Ⓦ vilniusjazz.lt

The Baltic States online

Estonia info Ⓦ visitestonia.com
Rail Ⓦ elron.ee
Tallinn info Ⓦ visittallinn.ee/eng
Latvia info Ⓦ latvia.travel/en
Rail Ⓦ ldz.lv
Rīga info Ⓦ virtualriga.com
Lithuania info Ⓦ visitlithuania.net
Bus Ⓦ eurolines.lt
Vilnius info Ⓦ vilnius.lt

Belgium and Luxembourg

BELGIUM

Capital Brussels

Population 11,259,000

Languages Flemish, French and German

Currency Euro (€)

LUXEMBOURG

Capital Luxembourg City

Population 570,000

Languages Luxembourgish (national language), French and German (administrative languages)

Currency Euro (€)

When to go May–September, when the weather's at its warmest. Fortunately, the crowds aren't much of an issue, outside of Bruges

When not to go Overcast skies, raincoats and umbrellas can be prevalent year-round, but November–March provides the strongest dose of misery from above

Minimum daily budget €42

Belgium and Luxembourg

Belgium's cultural diversity belies its reputation among travelers as merely a great country to pass through. The EU's central administrative offices here may have added to its diversity, but the notorious bureaucracy that comes with the influx of Eurocrats has been a difficult image issue to overcome. Belgium has three official languages. The French-speaking Walloons in the south make up about forty percent, the Flemish speakers up north account for nearly sixty percent, and there are small pockets of German speakers on the eastern border who barely show up on the lingual radar screen. The effect is a divided country (and incredible gourmet beer and rectangular waffles).

Luxembourg, though just barely large enough to be found on a hand-held map of Europe, is a fairy tale of villages and woodlands that, unlike Belgium, clings fiercely to its identity. In the north of the country, there's skiing, hiking and rock climbing, waterfalls and fast-flowing rivers, and towering castles. The south has a history of winemaking, and you can reach just about any spot in the country from the capital within an hour.

Main attractions

❶ **The Bock casemates, Luxembourg City** In 963 AD, Sigefroi, Count of Ardennes, laid the cornerstone of Luxembourg City on a rocky outcrop now called "the Bock." The most impressive remains of this high fortress are the labyrinthine casemates – built in 1644 – which sheltered 35,000 people when the city was bombed during World War II. There are 17km of this damp maze of subterranean passageways open to the public.

❷ **Bruges** The most popular tourist attraction in Belgium is this entire town, the best-preserved medieval city in Europe. On some streets you feel as if you're wandering through a museum's thirteenth-century installation. ⓦbezoekers.brugge.be

❸ **Grand Place, Brussels** Unfolding like a personal discovery as you enter from one

AVERAGE DAILY TEMPERATURES AND MONTHLY RAINFALL

	Jan	Feb	Mar	Apr	May	June	July	Aug	Sept	Oct	Nov	Dec
Brussels												
max °C	14	14	16	18	22	27	30	30	27	23	18	15
min °C	6	6	8	9	13	17	19	19	17	14	9	7
rainfall mm	53	53	46	36	25	10	3	10	30	58	56	53
Luxembourg City												
max °C	3	4	10	14	18	21	23	22	19	13	7	4
min °C	-1	-1	1	4	8	11	13	12	10	6	3	0
rainfall mm	61	65	42	47	64	64	60	84	72	53	67	51

MAIN ATTRACTIONS

1. The Bock casemates, Luxembourg City
2. Bruges
3. Grand Place, Brussels
4. Waterloo, Belgium
5. Manneken Pis, Brussels

BELGIUM & LUXEMBOURG

---

of the many narrow side-streets, the Belgian capital's twelfth-century central square is a popular place to sip coffee or eat an intimate meal while gazing at some of the finest Baroque guildhalls in the country. The Hôtel de Ville is the only building that survived King Louis XIV's bombing in 1695 and is open for tours.

4 Waterloo, Belgium In 1815, the Duke of Wellington drafted a message in this town announcing the defeat of Napoleon. The Battle of Waterloo (which was mostly fought in nearby Braine-l'Alleud) is commemorated with the Butte du Lion (Lion's Mound) monument and a platinum-selling song by Abba.

5 Manneken Pis, Brussels This tiny statue of a urinating boy, sculpted in bronze by Jerôme Duquesnoy in 1619, has an undefined history (some say he extinguished a fire with his you-know-what), yet the city has embraced this rather unorthodox landmark, sometimes dressing up the boy in one of his many hundreds of costumes

(which allow for simulated urination). And, thanks to the tourist industry, you can take home a "urinating boy" key chain or bottle opener to help rekindle the feeling you had when you first laid eyes on him.

Also recommended

● **Play some chess** Head to *Le Greenwich*, rue Royale 316, an "Old World" café in Brussels known for its top-notch chess matches, and test your skills against one of the local masters. Ⓦ greenwich-cafe.be

● **Try the local brew** Belgian beer must, possibly by law, only be served in the glass that was specifically made for it, such is the level of sophistication (and marketing) in this country. Some of the beers have a higher alcohol content than wine and, if you sink a few of those cute little bottles, you may have a difficult time finding your way back to your hostel. But if you only taste one a day, it'll take about a year to try them all.

- **Visit Spa** Not just any old spa, *the* spa. Since Roman times, the Belgian town of Spa in the Ardennes has been known for its curative baths. The rich and famous of the sixteenth century came here, and Victor Hugo was a regular. There are still several spas in this town you can visit: Pouhon Pierre-le-Grand Spa, the town's main mineral spring, and Les Thermes de Spa (Ⓦthermesdespa .com), a smart baths complex, are the places to head for.
- **Hang in the Grote Markt, Antwerp** Home to a burgeoning fashion industry and the country's best nightlife, Antwerp centers on this pedestrianized, triangular market square with Renaissance-style city hall. There's a gilded statue of St George astride a rearing horse as he spears a dragon, and a Baroque Brabo fountain by Jef Lambeaux.

Food and drink

You can find sandwiches for under €6, and there's the usual assortment of kebabs and pizzas, but in general you'll have to choose between your wallet and your palate – one is likely to suffer. A decent meal can be found for under €20. The food in the French part of the country is on a par with the best French cuisine. In the Flemish part, it's much like the food in the Netherlands.

Transport

As compact countries, Belgium and Luxembourg are easy to get around, and the short distances make the fares relatively cheap. There are no domestic flights and even the official tourist website recommends the trains over the intercity buses. In the major cities, trams and buses are available – the only subway is in Brussels, for which a ten-journey or three-day ticket is good value if you're in town for more than a day. Check out the multi-mode travel cards for longer visits.

Luxembourg has one main rail route with a few lesser lines that branch off

(Ⓦmobiliteit.lu). Buses supplement the other areas. Ask at the train station for special one-day travel cards.

By train
- **Eurail Benelux Pass** (valid in Belgium, Luxembourg and the Netherlands) Three, four, five or eight days of travel in one month. Several more rail deals are available through the Belgian rail website (Ⓦbelgianrail.be).
- **Eurail Benelux-Germany Pass** (also valid in Germany) Choose between four, five, six, eight and ten days of travel in two months.
- **Eurail Benelux-France Pass** (also valid in France) Choose between four, five, six, eight and ten days of travel in two months.
- **InterRail Benelux Pass** Three, four, six or eight days of travel in one month.
- **Weekend Ticket** You get fifty percent off rail fares if you leave after 7pm on Friday and return by the Sunday of the same weekend. It's also possible to leave and return the same day. The catch is that tickets are only transferable, changeable or refundable if you buy them over the counter.

For tips and tricks on maximizing your rail pass, see "Costs and savings" (p.63).

By bus
A Busabout pass (see p.44) allows some travel in Belgium. Because so much of Belgium is accessible by train, buses are only used for short distances and parts of the Ardennes with few rail lines. For internal bus prices, see Ⓦwww.delijn.be. In Luxembourg, domestic buses can be found at Ⓦmobiliteit.lu. For buses from Belgium to other countries, see Ⓦeurolines.be.

Events

- **Binche carnival, Belgium** Binche hosts the famed orange-throwing parade (don't throw them back; they're good luck) when dozens of Gilles – men born and raised in Binche – march with what appears to be

John Lennon masks and giant ostrich-feather hats. This multi-day carnival fest is one of the oldest in Europe. Feb (Shrove Tues); Ⓦcarnavaldebinche.be

● **Dancing Procession of St Willibrord, Echternach** There are probably several ways to purge your sins, but since the death of St Willibrord in 739, pilgrims in Echternach have been shaking a leg while shaking loose the evil spirits. People come from across Europe to dance to the sound of the sixteenth-century bell in the town's abbey. May (Whit Tues); Ⓦwillibrord.lu

● **National Day, Luxembourg** National Day is June 23, but for more action than the traditional cathedral *Te Deum* and military parade, show up the evening before for a torchlight parade, fireworks and a huge party. Several other towns around the country have celebrations, complete with pyrotechnics. June 22–23.

● **Ommegang pageant** Brussels' Grand Place gets invaded by 3000 spectators (including the royal family) for the Ommegang, a procession of nobles in period costume as well as craftsmen and soldiers. To view the pageant, book in advance with the tourist office. Try the town of Mechelen if the one in Brussels is sold out. First Tues & Thurs of July; Ⓦommegang.be

Belgium and Luxembourg online

Belgium info Ⓦvisitbelgium.com
Rail Ⓦbelgianrail.be
Bus Ⓦwww.delijn.be
Brussels info Ⓦvisitbrussels.be
Luxembourg info Ⓦont.lu
Rail and bus Ⓦmobiliteit.lu

Bosnia-Herzegovina

Capital Sarajevo

Population 3,867,000

Language Bosnian, Croatian, Serbian

Currency Convertible Mark (KM)

Minimum daily budget €25

When to go Summer can be stinking hot in Mostar, but in Sarajevo it's usually balmy

When not to go You'll find very few travel buddies in the hostels from November–March, while April and May can be damp

Bosnia-Herzegovina

A land where turquoise rivers run swift and sheep huddle on steep hillsides, Bosnia-Herzegovina is one of Europe's most visually stunning corners. With muezzins calling the faithful to prayer under a backdrop of church bells, it also provides a delightful fusion of East and West in the heart of the Balkans. Appropriately, the country is now marketing itself as the "heart-shaped land," unintentionally revealing more perhaps than just the shape of its borders: this remains a country cleaved into two distinct entities, the result of a bloody war in the mid-1990s. However, while Bosnia-Herzegovina was not too long ago making headlines for all the wrong reasons, it's now busily, and deservedly, re-etching itself on the world travel map as a bona fide backpacker magnet of some repute.

Main attractions

❶ Sarajevo With its spiky minarets, grilled kebabs and the all-pervasive aroma of ground coffee, many travelers see in this city a Slavic mini-İstanbul. It's one of the friendliest capitals in Europe, having shrugged off its painful recent history – the fun-loving, easy-going Sarajevans do a great job of painting over the scars of those tumultuous years. Ⓦ sarajevo-tourism.com

❷ Mostar A delightful city focused on its famous Old Bridge which, meticulously rebuilt after destruction during the war, must be the most photographed object in the Balkans – and rightly so, especially when local lads are making terrifying dives into the crystal-clear water way down below. Ⓦ turizam.mostar.ba

❸ Jajce This small Bosnian town is simply adorable – its Old Town is ringed with walls and topped with an impressive citadel, while a little further afield you'll find a splendid 21m-high waterfall. Ⓦ visitjajce.com

❹ Trebinje Herzegovina's most appealing town, most famed for the sixteenth-century Arslanagić Bridge – a longer version of the one in Mostar. In what must have been quite a feat, it was moved here, stone by stone, from the village of Arslanagić some 5km away, in 1972. Ⓦ trebinjeturizam.com

Also recommended

● Rafting around Bihać Herzegovina has no shortage of great rafting locales, but this Bosnian town beats them all. The crystal-clear River Una rushes through it, though you'll find the best rafting a little further upstream; the river is highest in the spring and autumn. Ⓦ discoverbihac.ba

AVERAGE DAILY TEMPERATURES AND MONTHLY RAINFALL

	Jan	Feb	Mar	Apr	May	June	July	Aug	Sept	Oct	Nov	Dec
Sarajevo												
max °C	4	6	11	16	21	25	27	28	22	17	10	4
min °C	-3	-3	1	5	9	12	14	14	10	6	2	-2
rainfall mm	66	63	70	76	72	89	72	66	91	85	85	86

MAIN
ATTRACTIONS
1 Sarajevo
2 Mostar
3 Jajce
4 Trebinje

- **See where World War I started**
Though modest in appearance, Sarajevo's
Latin Bridge has some weighty history
behind it – this was the scene of the
assassination of Archduke Franz Ferdinand
and thus the spark of World War I; a plaque
on the wall indicates the exact spot where
Ferdinand met his fate.

- **Siege-time, Sarajevo** Of huge
importance during the siege of Sarajevo was
a tunnel burrowed under the airport – 800m
long and, for most locals, the only way into
or out of the city. Part of it is now open as a
museum, accessible on daily tours.

- **Tea in Blagaj** A grand little side-trip
from Mostar, this village is home to an
astonishingly powerful waterfall, which

comes bursting out of a cliff at a rate of
43,000 liters per second. Some of this is
skimmed off to make tea and coffee, which
you can order at the adjacent terrace for just
€0.80, including a chunk of *lokum* (Turkish
delight).

Transport

Bosnia-Herzegovina isn't the easiest
country to get around, since much of its
transport infrastructure – particularly the
rail network – was damaged during the
war. Things are improving, however, and
decent bus services will almost always be
able to get you where you want to go; it'll
just take a little longer than you might

expect (see Ⓦbhtourism.ba; oddly, they're in the "Getting here" section). Also note that connections between the two separate entities of country – the Federation of Bosnia and Herzegovina and the Republika Srpska – aren't regular.

There are also a few railway lines across the country, though severe underfunding means that most trains are too slow or irregular to be worth considering; the one exception is the twice-daily route linking Sarajevo and Mostar, which is fabulously scenic.

By train

- **Balkans Flexi Pass** (also valid in Bulgaria, Greece, Romania, Serbia, Montenegro, Macedonia and Turkey). Any five, ten or fifteen days in one month.

Food and drink

Centuries of Ottoman rule have left Turkish fingerprints on the nation's cuisine. You'll find *čevapčići* joints everywhere, selling grilled meat rissoles (€2–4) that are usually served up with *somun* (spongy bread) and chopped onion. Similarly hard to avoid are stands selling *burek*, greasy pastries filled with meat, spinach, cheese and sometimes pumpkin or potato. Sweeties also have a Turkish ring to them, with syrupy *baklava* pastries available everywhere. The consumption of coffee here has been elevated to something approaching an art form (€0.50–1), while alcohol-wise

there are a few good domestic beers, a lot of wine, and also *rakia*, a potent spirit as popular by night as coffee is by day.

Events

- **Baščaršija Nights** It's hard to sum up Sarajevo's pride-and-joy festival, which takes place across one full month, though it traditionally kicks off with a performance by the local philharmonic orchestra. There are usually 40–50 separate events covering the full artistic rainbow, including ballet, theater, music and art exhibitions. July; Ⓦbascarsijskenoci.ba
- **Jazz Fest Sarajevo** Excellent jazz festival, with some stellar international names often popping by during the week-long proceedings – past performers have included Miles Davis protégé Al Foster, hippy-era free-jazz gal Carla Bley and Cuban violinist Omar Puente. Usually November; Ⓦjazzfest.ba
- **Sarajevo Film Festival** This is now one of the most prestigious film festivals in Europe, and by far the biggest such deal in the Balkans. There's one good reason for this – it remains largely focused on the region's own output, which is increasing in importance with each passing year. August; Ⓦsff.ba

Bosnia-Herzegovina online

Bosnia-Herzegovina info Ⓦbhtourism.ba
Sarajevo info Ⓦsarajevo-tourism.com

Bulgaria

Capital Sofia

Population 7,185,000

Language Bulgarian

Currency Lev (Lv)

Minimum daily budget €24

When to go Mid-April to mid-September, when the weather is warm. If snowfall is plentiful, you can ski from just before Christmas until April

When not to go October–February, when there's little relief for non-skiers

Bulgaria

Tucked away in the southeastern corner of Europe, Bulgaria calls itself the "Jewel of the Balkans," but that may be overstating things just a tad. It has come a long way since it threw off the choke-hold of the Ottoman Empire in 1870. Bulgaria's image has altered dramatically in recent years, thanks largely to the modernization of the country's tourist infrastructure coupled with soaring foreign interest in inexpensive rural and coastal properties. Independent travel is common: costs are relatively low, and for the committed there is much to take in. The traditional towns, romantic architecture and mountain scenery provide enough to sculpt an interesting itinerary.

There's a strong Russian influence here (Cyrillic alphabet included), partly out of gratitude to the 200,000 Russian casualties suffered while liberating Bulgaria from the Turks in 1878. Today, only 85 percent of the country's inhabitants are Bulgarian. Besides almost a million Turks, there are smaller minorities of Macedonians and Roma (Gypsy).

Finding Bulgaria on the map isn't the only thing that trips up some travelers; nodding up and down means "no" and shaking your head from side to side means "yes."

rightfully fill up during the summer holidays. The best ones can be found northeast of Varna. If you need a day in the shade, the cliff-caves which form Aladzha Monastery are 7km southwest of Golden Sands.

❸ **Nesebâr** This former Byzantine trading hub is at least 2500 years old, and you can't swing a cat in it without hitting a medieval church. It's all about adorable little squares, cobbled streets and a crumbling city wall – impressively jammed together on a tiny peninsula shooting out into the Black Sea.

Main attractions

❶ **Valley of the Roses** Roses have been grown in the fertile valley east of Sofia since the Phoenicians were the hottest act in town. You won't find a more all-encompassing celebration of their beauty anywhere in the world.

❷ **The Black Sea Riviera** Arguably Bulgaria's greatest asset, the beaches of the Black Sea

Also recommended

● **Ski on the cheap** There's good skiing to be had in Bulgaria, and facilities have improved a lot in recent years. Aim for Borovets, Bansko or the Rhodope mountains. ⓦbulgariaski.com

● **Sip some water** Mineral water, that is. The Bulgarian stuff has been world famous in the Balkans since the pre-tap-water days.

AVERAGE DAILY TEMPERATURES AND MONTHLY RAINFALL											
	Jan	Feb	Mar	Apr	May	June	July	Aug	Sept	Oct	Nov	Dec
Sofia												
max °C	2	4	9	14	19	23	26	26	22	16	8	3
min °C	-4	-3	1	5	9	12	14	14	11	6	1	-2
rainfall mm	33	36	38	53	69	79	56	43	41	36	51	43

There are 1600 wells to choose from, but if you only have time to fill your water bottle in one or two spots, try Hissar in the middle of the country, and Pomorie outside Burgas. If you've previously been abusing your liver, get the stuff with sulfate in it, said to get that organ back into shape.

● **Check out the birds** Bulgaria has some quality birdwatching that can be done on a one-day trip from Sofia. In Vitosha Nature Park and Dragoman Marsh, you might spot ferruginous ducks, sedge warblers and black woodpeckers. There are longer tours for serious birders who may spot a Squacco heron or Imperial eagle.

Food and drink

Bulgarians keep full with meals of meat, potatoes, beans and salads. These, plus the precarious liquors (*rakia* and *mastika*) used to toss it back, are going to be your cheapest feed. Breakfast is a nice bread-based snack on the run picked up at most hole-in-the-wall kiosks and washed down with *boza*, a gluggy millet drink loved by those who've managed to acquire a taste for it. Lunch is the main meal of the day and offers the best value. A late dinner – which you should be able to find for less than €10 – signals the switch from aperitifs to serious drinking.

Transport

Due to the Balkan mountain range, traveling east–west is going to be faster and easier than any north–south routes. You can get across the country by train in first class for under €25 (worth it, if you have long legs). The buses are slow, but the trains are even slower.

Sofia has a well-organized public transport system of buses, trams and trolleybuses.

And the roughly €0.55 fare is extremely reasonable. The trick is getting good information, as the signs (sometimes just a rusted pole) leave a lot to the imagination. Don't forget to buy an extra ticket for your rucksack and punch both tickets when you get on – or face a stiff (€10) fine.

By train
● **Eurail Bulgaria Pass** Any three, four, five or eight days of travel in one month.
● **Balkans Flexi Pass** (also valid in Bosnia-Herzegovina, Greece, Romania, Serbia, Montenegro, Macedonia and Turkey). Any five, ten or fifteen days in one month.

For tips and tricks on maximizing your rail pass, see "Costs and savings" (p.63).

By bus
Busabout doesn't operate in Bulgaria. For internal bus prices, see Ⓦetapgroup.com. For buses to other countries, see Ⓦeurolines.bg.

Events

● **Trifon Zarezan** This wine festival takes place on "Vinegrowers' Day" and is a blessing of the grape harvest. Its roots (no pun intended) go all the way back to the Thracians, an illiterate group of ancients who nevertheless enjoyed the odd cup of *tinto*. Feb 1 or 14.
● **Ladouvane** The name means "Singing to Rings," but this festival is all about unmarried women looking for husbands. Confusingly enough, it's celebrated on opposite ends of the year in different parts of the country – either New Year's Eve or Midsummer's Day – so if you're a lovelorn man, make sure you're in the right place at the right time.
● **Festival of Roses, Kazanlûk** With over seventy percent of the world's production, Bulgaria has long cornered the market on rose oil. Not as lucrative as petroleum, alas, but still a matter of some national pride. In early summer, homage is paid to this symbol of youth and beauty. First Sun in June.

Bulgaria online

Bulgaria info Ⓦbulgariatravel.org
Rail Ⓦbdz.bg
Bus Ⓦetapgroup.com

DUBROVNIK

Croatia

Capital Zagreb

Population 4,230,000

Language Croatian

Currency Kuna (Kn)

Minimum daily budget €38

When to go May–June and September are good for beating crowds on the Adriatic

When not to go July and August are hot, expensive and jam-packed with tourists. Best avoided unless you're going for the Dubrovnik Summer Festival, in which case you have no choice

Croatia

The Croatian coastline is one of the most spectacular in Europe, and though the country's tourist industry is now fully fledged, the accompanying development has been fairly unobtrusive and there are plenty of secluded rocky beaches and pristine old towns to explore. As well as a stunning array of architecture, the country has a rich cultural heritage and a rapidly expanding festival scene. Already a hit destination among those in the know, Croatia's recently acquired EU membership means it's set to grow in popularity.

Many rock climbers come to Croatia, and there are even a few inland ski resorts – though the Croatians themselves go to neighboring Slovenia or Austria to ski. The far south is also a good jumping-off point into less explored Montenegro (see p.266).

Main attractions

❶ **Dubrovnik** Lapped by the glittering Adriatic Sea, this 1300-year-old architectural city gem is the country's irresistibly beautiful star attraction.

❷ **Diocletian's Palace, Split** You'd think that Italy would have all the best Roman ruins in the world, but these rock piles in the southern city of Split must make it into the Top 10 at least. The ruins are what are left of the retirement home of the Roman Emperor Diocletian.

❸ **Lotrščak Tower, Zagreb** The medieval center of Croatia's capital is a treat for the eyes, and no place will give you a better view than this old watchtower at the southern gate of the inner city. Among the sights is the Cathedral of the Assumption of the Blessed Virgin Mary.

❹ **Korčula** This Dalmatian island south of Split claims to be the birthplace of Marco Polo. Whether or not it's true, it's captivating enough to merit a visit. If you can, try and catch the Moreška (performances held weekly May–Sept), a twelfth-century sword dance. Ⓦ visitkorcula.eu

Also recommended

● **Skinny-dip in the Adriatic Sea** Croatia has a claim to fame as the first European country to open its arms to nude bathers – or naturists, to use the rather eco-sounding euphemism. Rab Island is where the bare-bum tradition started back in the 1930s, but the sites to head for today include Valalta outside Rovinj, Koversada near Vrsar, and Poreč on the Istrian peninsula. Note: single men aren't welcome without a member card from the International Naturist Federation (Ⓦ inffni.org). Not to worry – there are plenty of non-official nudie beaches, too. Just to be

AVERAGE DAILY TEMPERATURES AND MONTHLY RAINFALL												
	Jan	Feb	Mar	Apr	May	June	July	Aug	Sept	Oct	Nov	Dec
Zagreb												
max ˚C	3	5	11	16	21	24	27	26	22	16	8	4
min ˚C	-4	-3	1	5	9	13	14	14	11	6	2	-1
rainfall mm	52	48	56	68	83	95	79	79	79	93	86	66

MAIN ATTRACTIONS

1 Dubrovnik

2 Diocletian's Palace, Split

3 Lotrščak Tower, Zagreb

4 Korčula

on the safe side, make sure you're not the first naked person on the beach.

- **Dive off Mljet island** Even though the cool Adriatic offers less exotic diving than tropical waters, French scuba-gear inventor Jacques Cousteau called the waters around Mljet (near Dubrovnik) "one of the most beautiful diving locations in the world." Ⓦ mljet.hr

- **Climb Anića kuk** The innards of Croatia are as rocky as the coast is flat, making it great for climbing. Good routes are accessible from big cities such as Zagreb and Split, but for the truly hair-raising stuff, head for Paklenica (between Rijeka and Split), and take on the 350m-high face of Anića kuk. Ⓦ climb-croatia.com

- **Visit Dubrovnik's Franciscan monastery** Dubrovnik's Franciscan monastery is also a museum and is open to the public. It may look old, but much of the original church from 1498 was in fact destroyed in a 1667 earthquake.

Food and drink

Croatia has a varied and distinctive range of cuisine, largely because it straddles two culinary cultures: the fish- and seafood-dominated cuisine of the Mediterranean and the hearty meat-oriented fare of central Europe. You can save money by grabbing at least one meal a day from a street vendor. Inexpensive cheese-stuffed pastries (*burek*) will keep you going for a few hours. Supermarkets can set you up with the basics, but if you aim for a market instead, like the Dolac market in Zagreb, you'll get a cultural experience thrown in for free.

Transport

Trains are a good deal, with a greater network found in the north and the east, though there is no coastal service. Eurail passes are available both in single-country and regional variants, and InterRail also covers the country. The buses are more common transport along the coast (and thus should be booked in advance in the summer). Busabout doesn't cover Croatia in its bus network, but it does run hop-on hop-off sailing cruises along the Croatian coast. And Eurolines (Ⓦautotrans.hr) operates in the country. Plus, if you're coast-hopping and not in a hurry, ferries offer a nice alternative.

By train

● **Eurail Croatia Pass** Any three, four, five or eight days of travel in one month.
● **Eurail Croatia-Slovenia-Hungary Pass** Any four, five, six, eight or ten days of travel in two months.
● **Eurail Austria-Croatia-Slovenia Pass** Any four, five, six, eight or ten days of travel in two months.
● **InterRail Croatia Pass** Any three, four, six or eight days of travel in one month.

For tips and tricks on maximizing your rail pass, see "Costs and savings" (p.63).

Events

● **Rijeka Carnival** The advent of spring (well, at least the thought of it getting nearer) has been turning things upside down here for over a hundred years. Costumed inhabitants parade through the streets, scare off evil spirits, celebrate their escape from Turkish invasion and generally have a blast. Feb; Ⓦri-karneval.com.hr
● **Split Summer Festival** The Croatian National Theater has been putting on a big show since 1954, and every summer season sees a variety of concerts, dance shows, operas and exhibitions from both Croatian and international performers. Mid-July to mid-Aug; Ⓦsplitsko-ljeto.hr
● **International Puppet Festival, Zagreb** Either you love 'em or they freak you out. Puppets are all the rage in Zagreb as summer winds down. When you're not taking in a show, you can check out a puppet exhibition or learn how to make your own puppet. All performances are judged by two juries – one made up of experts and one of kids. Aug/Sept; Ⓦpif.hr/en

Croatia online

Croatia info Ⓦcroatia.hr
Rail Ⓦhzpp.hr
Bus Ⓦautotrans.hr
Ferries Ⓦjadrolinija.hr
Zagreb info Ⓦzagreb.hr
Dubrovnik info Ⓦexperience.dubrovnik.hr

The Czech Republic

Capital Prague

Population 10,535,000

Language Czech

Currency Czech koruna (Kč)

Minimum daily budget €22

When to go May and September–October, when the sightseeing is at its best (good climate, fewer visitors). May–October for hiking

When not to go July and August (for Prague), when it can be hard to see the cobblestones for all the tourists standing on them. Outside of Prague, many castles and museums close down October–April

The Czech Republic

The Czech Republic has emerged as one of the star economic engines and tourist attractions of former Communist Europe and keeps raising the bar for its neighbors. Nowadays this small country feels very much where it belongs: right at the heart of Europe.

The most famous Czechs fall into two categories: in one, there's Franz Kafka, Milan Kundera and playwright-turned-dissident-turned-president Václav Havel; and on the other side of the ring, Jaromír Jágr and Martina Navratilova). But when you arrive, the literary and ice-hockey powers are overshadowed by the country's wealth of architects. The Czech Republic has been a natural trading center for centuries, a geographic advantage that has worked against it as well, since more powerful nations have been anxious to march in and take the country for themselves when the opportunity presented itself. Miraculously, Matička Praha ("little mother Prague") emerged largely unscathed from World War II.

The modern travel hippies making jewelry and playing *Stairway to Heaven* may be limited to the streets of Prague, but the knock-your-socks-off architecture isn't. Several towns, such as Cheb, Kutná Hora and Loket, can boast striking Renaissance and Baroque facades. With hiking, spas and mountain biking, there's also plenty to do once your neck tires of staring at all the soaring spires.

Main attractions

❶ **Staroměstské náměstí (Old Town Square), Prague** You can probably count on one hand the number of people who've visited Prague and never seen the Old Town Square. This 17,000-square-meter centerpiece is the heart of the city, and has been since the tenth century. Today, cafés, buskers and Segway touts compete for your attention, but this commercial circus still can't hide the beauty of the square. If you follow the flow of human traffic, you'll make the short, cobblestoned stroll to the 600-year-old Charles Bridge, lined with Baroque statues.

❷ **Prague Castle** Across the river from the Old Town Square, the 1000-year-old walled-in castle peers down on the city from its lofty perch. There's plenty of room in the compound for visitors (it's the most popular attraction in Prague) to view the seat of the Czech government since Prince Bořivoj. ⓦ hrad.cz

❸ **Josefov (Jewish Quarter), Prague** Prague's Jewish cemetery, plus a half-dozen old synagogues and a ceremonial hall, were disturbingly saved by Nazi leaders as an "Exotic Museum of an Extinct Race." Instead, this former Jewish ghetto has survived as a

AVERAGE DAILY TEMPERATURES AND MONTHLY RAINFALL

	Jan	Feb	Mar	Apr	May	June	July	Aug	Sept	Oct	Nov	Dec
Prague												
max ˚C	1	2	8	12	18	21	22	23	18	12	5	3
min ˚C	-4	-4	0	2	7	11	12	12	9	4	0	-2
rainfall mm	20	18	25	36	58	69	66	64	41	30	28	23

memorial to hundreds of years of oppression. ⓦjewishmuseum.cz

Also recommended

● **Cleanse your soul at Karlovy Vary**
World famous (in certain circles, anyway) for its regenerative waters, Karlovy Vary, southwest of Prague, is the oldest of the Bohemian spas. The Victorian atmosphere and elegant colonnades may aid the healing process; if not, the surrounding parks with wooded hills should. ⓦkarlovyvary.cz

● **Enjoy "Prague" without the crowds**
Český Krumlov is one of Bohemia's most striking towns, and is deservingly on UNESCO's World Heritage list. The charming city center is car-free and the city's castle (the second largest in the country) rests, almost picture-postcard-like, on a hill overlooking a bend in the Vltava (Moldau) River. It's best to stay overnight to avoid the hordes of day-trippers from the capital.

● **Go canyoning and caving around the Moravský kras** The heavily wooded and hilly region of the Moravský kras (Moravian Karst) is home to caves and canyons, several with evidence of prehistoric human inhabitants. You can boat on the underground river or abseil through waterfalls in Rudice. ⓦcavemk.cz

● **Take a beer tour** You can pick up a guide, rent a car and visit the breweries or take a more lazy approach and go on a pub crawl. Prague has one of Europe's largest organized pub crawls (ⓦpubcrawl.cz) if you'd rather not do it alone.

Food and drink

Normally you can't count beer as a meal, but in this part of the world some travelers seem to be doing just that. And with beer this good (and cheap), it's hard to fault them. The great mystery of Czech food is where the summer menu went. Pork, game, dumplings and cabbage are perfect in the icy Eastern winters but depressing on a hot day – at least it's cheap; you can find a nice meal for under €12. Check out some of the "wine cellars" outside of Prague for a bit more style.

Transport

The region has a comprehensive rail network that's reasonably cheap, clean and mostly dependable. There are some internal flights, but the short distances don't allow you to shave many minutes off the journey. Bus connections for longer routes are often more frequent than the trains (even if a bit slower), and can be especially useful for visiting more remote locations.

By train
● **Eurail Czech Republic Pass** Three, four, five or eight days of travel in one month.
● **Eurail Austria-Czech Republic Pass** Four, five, six, eight or ten days of travel in two months.
● **Eurail Germany-Czech Republic Pass** Four, five, six, eight or ten days of travel in two months.
● **InterRail Czech Republic Pass** Three or eight days of travel in one month.
● **European East Pass** (also valid in Austria, Slovakia and Hungary) Any five days of travel in one month. Five additional travel days can be added.

For tips and tricks on maximizing your rail pass, see "Costs and savings" (p.63).

By bus
A Busabout pass (see p.44) allows some travel in the Czech Republic. For internal bus prices, see Ⓦvlak-bus.cz. For buses to other countries, see Ⓦelines.cz/en.

Events

● **Burning of the Witches, Prague** This pre-Christian festival for warding off evil has been politically corrected with the burning of bonfires in Prague, mostly at all-night parties. April 30.
● **Khamoro World Gypsy Festival** The itinerant Roma (Gypsies) steer their show on the road into Prague for a gathering to showcase their classical music, jazz, film, theater, dance, painting and photography. May; Ⓦkhamoro.cz
● **Prague Spring International Music Festival** Early summer brings great musicians from around the world to Prague, the international stars complemented by impressive home-grown soloists and orchestras. Venues include Smetana Hall and the Rudolfinum, as well as Prague Cathedral. Mid-May to beginning of June; Ⓦfestival.cz

Czech Republic online

Czech Republic info Ⓦczechtourism.com
Rail Ⓦcd.cz
Bus Ⓦvlak-bus.cz
Prague info Ⓦpraguewelcome.cz/en

Denmark

Capital Copenhagen

Population 5,673,000

Languages Danish

Currency Danish krone (kr)

Minimum daily budget €43

When to go May–August, when the days are long enough to enjoy the frequent spurts of good weather that come your way

When not to go Mid-October to March the gloom is filled with far more freezing drizzle than snow

Denmark

Denmark is full of surprises: an unaccomplished singer and ballet dancer who goes on to become one of the world's great storytellers (Hans Christian Andersen), for example; or the north of the country being home to Europe's largest desert. Denmark may be the smallest Scandinavian nation, but it's no easier to pin down than a Greco-Roman wrestler. It shares social policies with Sweden and Norway and alcohol prices and perceptions with the rest of Europe. And, as such, neatly bridges the gap between its northern neighbors and the center of the EU.

The three landmasses that comprise the bulk of the country (Zealand, Funen and Jutland, the peninsula that's connected to Germany) each have their own sensibilities. Zealand is perhaps the most distinct, with green hills and undulating heathlands. The northwest part of the peninsula has incredible beaches, some of which are wide and compact enough to drive and bike on.

Copenhagen, Scandinavia's largest and most affordable capital, is (like the rest of the country) best conquered by bike. The only thing more stunning than the architecture is the people. As Bill Bryson wrote in *Neither Here Nor There*, "Everyone, without exception, is youthful, fresh-scrubbed, healthy, blond and immensely good-looking. You could cast a Pepsi commercial in Copenhagen in fifteen seconds."

Main attractions

❶ **Legoland** The little plastic snap-together blocks have got a good deal more sophisticated than they once were, but their simplicity is still their strength, and a visit to their Danish birthplace should cap off any lingering childhood fantasies about an entire Lilliputian Lego city. ⓦ legoland.dk

❷ **Ribe** You don't need to be a history buff to be charmed by the oldest town in Scandinavia. Dating back to the early 700s, the market town almost looks its age, partially because it was spared from modernization due to economic decline. If Ribe itself doesn't feel enough like a museum, try its VikingeCenter (Viking Center) just south of town. ⓦ ribevikingecenter.dk

❸ **Kronborg Castle, Helsingør** This castle was made famous by Shakespeare when he penned *Hamlet* and set his play in Elsinore (Helsingør in Danish). Never mind that the real Hamlet was the son of a Zealand pirate and lived on the island of Mors; the story makes for better tourism. And the castle, situated on a promontory jutting into the sea, is impressive enough. ⓦ kronborg.dk

AVERAGE DAILY TEMPERATURES AND MONTHLY RAINFALL

	Jan	Feb	Mar	Apr	May	June	July	Aug	Sept	Oct	Nov	Dec
Copenhagen												
max °C	3	2	5	9	16	19	21	21	16	12	7	4
min °C	-1	-2	0	2	7	11	13	12	10	7	3	0
rainfall mm	43	25	36	41	43	53	66	74	51	53	53	52

DENMARK

0 _____ 50
kilometers

N

MAIN ATTRACTIONS
1 Legoland
2 Ribe
3 Kronborg Castle, Helsingør
4 The Little Mermaid, Copenhagen

Skagerrak

Skagen
Hirtshals
Råbjerg Mile
Frederikshavn
Hjørring
Hanstholm
Thisted
Aalborg
Kattegat
Læsø
Varberg
SWEDEN
Anholt

Lemvig
Viborg
Randers
Grenå
Silkeborg
Herning
Århus
Ebeltoft
Skjern
Jutland
Skanderborg
Helsingør
Helsingborg
Hillerød 3

1 **Legoland**
Vejle
COPENHAGEN 4
Esbjerg
Lunderskov
Fredericia
Kalundborg
Roskilde
Malmö
2
Ribe
Odense
Kerteminde
Zealand
Ringsted
Funen
Næstved
Tønder
Fåborg
Svendborg
Sønderborg
Flensburg
Gelting
Bagenkop
Rødby
Nykøbing
GERMANY
Gedser

Meters
100
0
below
sea level

4 The Little Mermaid, Copenhagen

Perhaps the most petite of Denmark's attractions, the statue sitting atop a small rock a few meters from shore at the entrance to Copenhagen's harbor attracts an astounding number of visitors (and graces possibly even more postcards). The mermaid was made famous as Hans Christian Andersen's heroine, but the statue, despite losing its head on a number of occasions, has taken on a following of her own.

Also recommended

● **Dip your feet in the "Marriage of the Waters"** Rent a bike in the artists' community of Skagen, in the northernmost part of Denmark, and pedal 4km north to the Grenen lighthouse. Here you can stand on the very tip of the country, with one foot in the Kattegat Sea and the other in the Skagerrak Sea, and peer out at a faintly visible line where the two seas meet.

● **Take a bike tour around Funen** Stay in farmhouses and castles and, after a long day in the saddle (and if your budget allows), sample one or more of the famous gourmet restaurants in the area. ⓦvisitfyn.com

● **Walk Denmark's desert** Few realize that Denmark has Europe's largest desert, known locally as the Råbjerg Mile. Okay, it's not all that big, but its dunes did mostly bury a church. It's on the coast, right near the northern tip of the country, and offers a playful contrast to the other scenery in the area.

Food and drink

Traditional Danish food is often characterized by rather stodgy meat or fish and veg combos, although the quality of ingredients is invariably excellent, especially these days with many chefs espousing the farm-to-plate or organic cooking ethos. You'll find most places you stay will set you up with a filling breakfast, included with the accommodation. If not, it's probably available for a relative bargain. Lunch deals for under €12 can be found; the traditional lunch (*frokost*) is *smørrebrød* – filling slices of rye bread heaped with meat, fish or cheese, and assorted trimmings. For dinner, your hostel may provide the best option, even if that's just a kitchen where you can make it yourself. A decent meal in a restaurant isn't going to cost less than €25.

Transport

Denmark is covered by trains, and the few parts that aren't have good bus services. In Copenhagen, you can rent a bike for a small fee at your hostel. If you're going to use public transport a lot, a Copenhagen Card (Ⓦcopenhagencard.dk) for one, two, three or five days will save you money, and also gets you into 74 museums and attractions for free.

By train
- **Eurail Denmark Pass** Any three, four, five or eight days of travel.

- **Eurail Scandinavia Pass** (also valid in Finland, Norway and Sweden) Any two, five, six, eight or ten days of travel in two months.

For tips and tricks on maximizing your rail pass, see "Costs and savings" (p.63).

By bus
Busabout doesn't operate in Denmark. For internal buses, see Ⓦrejseplanen.dk. For buses to other countries, see Ⓦeurolines.dk.

Events

- **Roskilde festival** Every year, Denmark's (and northern Europe's) biggest music gig (30min by train from Copenhagen) ignites a pilgrimage stretching to all corners of the continent. The week-long festival kicks off with a bang and doesn't stop no matter how much it rains. Late June or early July; Ⓦroskilde-festival.dk
- **Copenhagen Jazz Festival** For ten days every summer, many of the world's greatest jazz musicians congregate in the nation's capital and turn it on its head. Early July; Ⓦfestival.jazz.dk
- **Århus festival** Jesters, jugglers, archers, thespians, jousters and thousands of visitors invade Århus for nine days of cheer and tomfoolery. Late Aug/early Sept; Ⓦaarhusfestuge.dk

Denmark online

Denmark info Ⓦvisitdenmark.com
Rail Ⓦdsb.dk
Bus Ⓦrejseplanen.dk
Copenhagen info Ⓦvisitcopenhagen.dk

KIASMA, HELSINKI

Finland

Capital Helsinki

Population 5,475,000

Languages Finnish (also Swedish along the southwestern coast)

Currency Euro (€)

Minimum daily budget €40

When to go June–August for the warmest weather and midnight sun; late January–May for world-class cross-country skiing

When not to go November–March, unless you love skiing or plunging into a hole in the ice after a sauna

Finland

Once the Finns were able to get the occupying Swedes and Russians out of their hair (independence was gained in 1917), they could get back to their national pastime: sitting in a sauna and coaxing the vodka out of their systems with a birch branch. Skiing and hiking in Europe's largest preserved wilderness are also popular. This unique combination may explain why Finns believe that 75°C in a sauna is chilly, but 25°C outside is hot.

For those who'd rather take a more cosmopolitan approach to this Nordic climate, Helsinki offers art and architecture in abundance. The former capital, Turku, is the country's oldest city.

Many travelers use Finland as a gateway to Russia – it's just a short train or ferry ride from Helsinki to St Petersburg – but be careful you don't zip by too quickly. The country is worthy of a trip all on its own.

Main attractions

❶ **Kiasma, Helsinki** The capital's museum of contemporary art is so striking (with its gleaming steel exoskeleton) it will surely lure you inside. The high-tech interior alone may be worth the price of admission, even if the experiential installations sometimes aren't. ⓦkiasma.fi

❷ **The North Pole** Rovaniemi may be a few thousand kilometers from the North Pole, but don't tell Santa, who has set up shop in the North Pole Shopping Centre (where else!) and has a team of elves who take photos and answer children's

letters. With European flights dropping off passengers all winter for an intimate chat with the multilingual Santa, this is as close as you'll get to the real thing. See ⓦsantaclauslive.com to find out about getting some face time with St Nick.

❸ **Stockmann Department Store, Helsinki** You can't miss it. It's one of Europe's largest department stores, selling everything you need and even more that you don't. ⓦstockmann.com

❹ **Helsinki Train Station** This 1914 industrial-looking terminal is believed to be architect Eliel Saarinen's finest work.

❺ **Uspenski Cathedral, Helsinki** The green turnip domes of this Russian Orthodox cathedral create the most striking of sights when approaching Helsinki from the water. Inside, there's a cornucopia of icons and incense-burners, and Slavonic choirs set the mood.

Also recommended

● **Try an ice dive** If you like to dive, you might like this: cutting a hole in the ice and

AVERAGE DAILY TEMPERATURES AND MONTHLY RAINFALL											
	Jan	Feb	Mar	Apr	May	June	July	Aug	Sept	Oct	Nov	Dec
Helsinki												
max °C	-3	-3	1	2	7	15	21	19	13	8	2	1
min °C	-9	-9	-5	-1	5	9	12	11	6	2	2	7
rainfall mm	46	36	36	38	43	46	61	74	66	69	66	56

FINLAND

MAIN ATTRACTIONS

1. Kiasma, Helsinki
2. The North Pole
3. Stockmann Department Store, Helsinki
4. Helsinki Train Station
5. Uspenski Cathedral, Helsinki

0 — 200 kilometers

NORWAY
Utsjoki
Inari
LEMMENJOKI NATIONAL PARK
Kiruna
Muonio
Lapland
Kemijärvi
Arctic Circle
Rovaniemi
Kuusamo
Tornio
Kainuu
Oulu
Kuhmo
SWEDEN
OSTROBOTHNIA
Kokkola
Sonkajärvi
Kajaani
Umeå
Joensuu
Gulf of Bothnia
Vaasa
Kuopio
Jyväskylä
Savonlinna
Pori
Tampere
Viipuri
Nådendal
Lahti
HELSINKI
Åland Islands
Turku
St Petersburg
Eckerö
Mariehamn

RUSSIA

Meters
400
200
0

---

slipping below the bluish surface into the freezing water (with excellent visibility). When it's really cold (by Finnish standards, that's around minus 20°C), you need to have a sauna nearby. Not so much to warm up, but to get your scuba gear off in. It will literally freeze to your body.

● **Take a walk in Lemmenjoki National Park** This Finnish national park deserves more than a day's stroll. Some of the best trekking in Lapland – rivers, Arctic landscapes, waterfalls – awaits, though getting there may take more effort than the walking. A postbus leaving from Inari will suffice, or grab a river taxi from Kultala.

● **Watch a reindeer race** Fearless Finns don't actually drive reindeer to the North Pole, but they do race them chariot style. Standing on downhill skis just behind the reindeer with short reins, they shout and whip them into a sprint and compete side by side in an Arctic *Ben-Hur*. In winter, races are held all over Finland, often through the closed-off streets of small towns.

● **Take a snowshoe or snowmobile safari through Lapland** If you're heading to Finland in wintertime, you might as well embrace it. Strap some high-tech tennis rackets to your feet, or hold on tight as you speed over frozen rivers and through snow-covered woods on a snowmobile. For more information on tours go to ⓦarcticincentives .fi or ⓦlaplandsafaris.fi.

Food and drink

You'll need to figure on €8–10 for fast food, €15–25 for a decent meal and over €45 for fine dining. As in the rest of Scandinavia, sticking to falafels, pizza, hot dogs and supermarket food is a matter of budget survival.

Transport

Regular train travel is quite reasonable and covers the country particularly well on north–south routes. And if you can find two or more other travelers heading to the same place, you can book a group ticket at the train station and get about twenty percent off. Buses take care of east–west travel and connect well with the trains.

Helsinki transport (Ⓦhsl.fi/en) isn't exactly a bargain, so consider getting a Travel Card (*matkakortti*), a reloadable smartcard sold at R-Kiosks (similar to London's Oyster Card), which gives a 25 percent discount on fares. Or go for a Helsinki Card (Ⓦhelsinkicard.fi), which allows unlimited travel on all public transportation as well as free entry to several museums and some discounted theater tickets. You even get a free sightseeing tour thrown in. It's cheaper if you buy it online.

By train

● **Eurail Finland Pass** Any three, four, five or eight days in one month.
● **Eurail Scandinavia Pass** (also valid in Denmark, Norway and Sweden) Any two, five, six, eight or ten days of travel in two months.

For tips and tricks on maximizing your rail pass, see "Costs and savings" (p.63).

By bus

Busabout doesn't operate in Finland. For buses to other countries, see Ⓦexpressbus.fi (Finnish only).

Events

● **Midsummer Day** The biggest event of the year is a private one, and to truly experience it you need to meet a Finn and get invited along. Most flee the cities for summer cottages, welcoming the longest day with bonfires and overzealous alcohol consumption. Mid-June.
● **Savonlinna Opera Festival** Finland's most famous festival is held at the ambience-rich medieval Olavinlinna Castle. The operatic blowout lasts a month. Early July; Ⓦoperafestival.fi
● **Wife-Carrying Championships, Sonkajärvi** The country's most media-savvy event is the annual wife-carrying championships. Strapping Finns carry their wives over a 253.5m obstacle course, competing for the fastest time. The winner receives his wife's weight in beer. Early July; Ⓦeukonkanto.fi
● **Air Guitar World Championships** Yes, this is a real event (they also have mosquito-swatting championships). It's held in Oulu, and it's quite serious. You have to be good to get in, and that makes for a great spectacle. Ⓦairguitarworldchampionships.com

Finland online

Finland info Ⓦvisitfinland.com
Rail Ⓦvr.fi
Helsinki info Ⓦhel.fi

France

Capital Paris

Population 66,121,000

Languages French (also Alsatian, Basque, Breton, Catalan, Corsican, Flemish and Provençal)

Currency Euro (€)

Minimum daily budget €44

When to go March–May and September–October, when the weather is great and the tourists are fewer; June–August for the Mediterranean (but also its busiest time); November–March, when it's ski season in the Alps and Pyrenees

When not to go Mid-July to August, when most of the French take their holidays – everything closes and the transport system feels the strain

France

France still carries a certain mystique, preserved in part by the wickedly decadent pastries served up in *boulangeries*, the tiny shops that regularly stock no fewer than twenty types of goat's cheese, doctors who still prescribe red wine for common ailments, small doggies with couture outfits that leave even smaller landmines on the pavement for you to navigate, and zippy cars that take on roundabouts at Mach 3.

In other words, France is still French enough to fulfill the high expectations of most travelers. But brace yourself also for *McDonald's* and 7-Elevens and neighborhoods with far more North African cuisine than baguettes and foie gras. As long as you don't expect an artisan crêpe-maker with a beret juggling Grand Marnier on every street corner, France will not disappoint. The country that brought the world the Yellow Leader's jersey, the croissant, Debussy and champagne still has much to offer. In Paris, you'll have a hard time walking ten minutes without bumping into a building you've seen on a postcard. In Chamonix, you'll pull a neck muscle taking in all the vistas. In Lyon, you can find enough Michelin-starred chefs to fill a rugby team, with plenty left over to cheer. There's a good reason France is the world's most popular tourist destination.

Main attractions

❶ **The Louvre, Paris** This museum could eat most sports stadiums for breakfast and still have space left over to confuse the most directionally gifted art connoisseur. It first opened in 1793 and was immediately stuffed full of stolen goods pillaged by Napoleon's armies. Courtesy of architect I.M. Pei, it now sports a snazzy glass-pyramid entryway with a reflective pool that helps calm the impatiently waiting crowds. The world record for seeing the *Mona Lisa*, *Winged Victory* and *Venus de Milo* and getting back out of the front door is something like two hours. Ⓦlouvre.fr

❷ **Palace of Versailles** Louis Quatorze certainly knew how to live. Or so it would seem. There's the grand entrance, room enough to properly house an entire class of illegitimate children, endless gardens that require an army of trimmers and pruners,

AVERAGE DAILY TEMPERATURES AND MONTHLY RAINFALL

	Jan	Feb	Mar	Apr	May	June	July	Aug	Sept	Oct	Nov	Dec
Paris												
max °C	7.5	7	10	16	17	23	25	26	21	17	12	8
min °C	1	1	3	6	9	12	14	14	11	8	4	2
rainfall mm	54	46	54	46	63	58	54	52	54	56	56	56
Marseille												
max °C	11	12	14	17	21	26	29	28	25	20	14	12
min °C	3	3	6	8	12	16	19	18	16	11	7	3
rainfall mm	48	41	46	46	46	25	15	25	64	94	76	58

MAIN ATTRACTIONS

1 The Louvre, Paris
2 Palace of Versailles
3 Eiffel Tower, Paris
4 Mont St-Michel
5 The French Alps
6 Notre-Dame, Paris

and a hall with more mirrors than a Las Vegas magic act. It's good to be king. **W** en.chateauversailles.fr

3 Eiffel Tower, Paris Built for the International Exhibition of Paris in 1889, this giant phallic radio antenna has become not just the urban icon for Paris but for all Europe. It didn't win over the French right away: many petitioned to have it torn down. You can still ride the elevator or you could make the world's most famous stair-climb and earn the spectacular view. **W** toureiffel.paris

4 Mont St-Michel This outcropping town on the north coast of France with its eighth-century abbey and jumble of Gothic buildings looks like a sandcastle come to

life. The tidal water that cut Mont St-Michel off from the mainland for half the day began to stop short in the early 2000s but in 2015 a €150-million hydraulic dam was completed that brought back the water and made it a mystical island once again. **W** ot-montsaintmichel.com

5 The French Alps In the winter, the Alps are a skiers', snowboarders' and ice-climbers' paradise. In the summer, the hikers, mountain bikers and rock climbers take over. Either way, you can't lose. The soaring jagged peaks seem fresh off the pages of a fairy tale.

6 Notre-Dame, Paris The lady with the stone flying buttresses sits on the Île de la Cité in the middle of Paris. In fact, stand out in front of the main entrance and you'll find a spot in the cobblestones that marks the very center of the city.

Also recommended

- **Skate through Paris** At 10pm every Friday, at the base of the Montparnasse tower, up to 30,000 in-line skaters congregate to commence their three-hour (30km) tour of Paris, an established event that now consumes the city. It runs all year long, unless it's raining or the streets are wet. Ⓦ pari-roller.com
- **Taste wine in Bordeaux** Even if you fancy yourself as a beerophile, a tasting tour of the greatest vineyards on the planet is a remarkable experience. The hardest part may be spitting the wine out (on a long day of tasting, the idea is to keep yourself from slipping under the table).
- **Cycle in Corsica** Corsica lives up to its billing as the *île de beauté* (the island of beauty); roads wind by cliffs and beaches as they circle this unlikely piece of French property off the southeastern coast. The capital, Ajaccio, is as well known for its cuisine as it is for being the birthplace of its most famous son, Napoleon.
- **Shop at the Clignancourt Market, Paris** It doesn't really matter what you're looking for, or even if you buy anything, the market will keep your eyes and nostrils on full alert. There are elaborate antiques – and mass-produced fakes that will fool people back home for a fraction of the price – and every street-food vendor worth his salt (and cayenne pepper) seems to have a stall.
- **Barge through Bordeaux** Thomas Jefferson wrote of barging, "Of all the methods of traveling I have ever tried, this is the pleasantest," and you can actually float all the way from the Atlantic coast to the Mediterranean. Just head up the Garonne to the Dordogne – which will bring you to Toulouse – then take the Canal Lateral to the Canal du Midi. Travelers tend to pony up for

week-long rides on lavishly renovated models with full catering and scheduled pit stops at wineries.
- **Sample cheese in the Savoie** Each region of France is famous for its own particular type of cheese, and you'd fare well following your own taste buds. However, if you're not sure which of the 350-plus kinds to try, head to the Savoie, the region that packs in the most cheese diversity.
- **Watch the Tour de France go by** Join the fifteen million people who line the roads each year to watch the 220 or so riders and 1800 support vehicles zip by in a few eye-blinks. In some of the more popular spots along the big climbs in the Alps and Pyrenees, you may have to camp out to get a good view; in other places, five minutes ahead of time will suffice. The route changes each year. Ⓦ letour.fr
- **Learn to bake croissants and baguettes** It's not a complete secret. There are baking courses offered in major cities and Paris has them in English. See Ⓦ cordonbleu .edu/lcb-paris/en.
- **Browse for perfume in Grasse** Centuries of gardening and perfume mixing in Grasse have seen it blossom into the olfactory epicenter of Europe. Master sniffers (called *nez*, or "noses") train for years to recognize thousands of scents. If you're not interested in a tour of the perfumeries, a garden stroll will still delight the senses.

Food and drink

Eating out in France isn't particularly cheap, but the quality of the food is often excellent and, even in the big cities, you'll be able to find restaurants offering a basic three-course meal for €18, and it won't cost you more than €2 to pick up a warm baguette. Wine is cheap (even more so if you buy it at a store). If you're whipping up your own meal, any wine vendor can recommend the vintage that best accompanies your food – and it shouldn't cost more than €8.

Transport

France currently has the world's fastest inter-city train (tied with Japan and Germany) in operation, and perhaps the best high-speed rail network on the planet. The bus system isn't quite so comprehensive. The cheapest way of getting round Paris is to buy a Paris Visite Ticket, which is valid on the métro, bus, RER and the Montmartre funicular. For information on Paris transport go to Ⓦ ratp.fr.

By train
● **France Rail Pass** Any three days of travel in one month. Additional days can be added up to nine days.
● **Eurail Benelux-France Pass** (also valid in Belgium, Luxembourg and the Netherlands) Choose between four, five, six, eight and ten days of travel in two months.
● **Eurail France-Italy Pass** Any four, five, six, eight or ten days of travel in two months.
● **Eurail France-Spain Pass** Any four, five, six, eight or ten days of travel in two months.
● **Eurail France-Switzerland Pass** Any four, five, six, eight or ten days of travel in two months.

For tips and tricks on maximizing your rail pass, see "Costs and savings" (p.63).

By bus
A Busabout pass (see p.44) allows you to travel throughout France. For buses to other countries, see Ⓦ eurolines.fr.

Events

● **Nice Carnival** A million spectators take in the parade, music and fireworks, while papier mâché figures are danced down the street on giant floats. "Fat Tuesday" following Lent; Ⓦ nicecarnaval.com
● **Monaco Grand Prix** The glam stop on the Formula One circuit, with cars racing through the pretzelled roads that comprise James Bond's stomping ground. May; Ⓦ visitmonaco.com
● **Paris Grand Steeplechase** The most prominent horseracing event on the French calendar. Watch fantastic leaps over the Hippodrome d'Auteuil's carefully clipped hedges and precariously placed ditches. Mid-to late May; Ⓦ france-galop.com
● **Biarritz Surf Festival** Dude, it's not just one of Europe's biggest surfing events: as world-class riders rip up the waves, Biarritz gets inundated with surfing enthusiasts who jump-start the beach party. July.
● **French Open Tennis Championships, Paris** The world's elite players duke it out on the famously unforgiving red-clay courts of Stade Roland-Garros. Last week in May to first week in June; Ⓦ rolandgarros.com
● **Avignon Festival** The great city of the popes is the only place to be during the three-week festival, when over 100 venues show multiple plays every day, alongside opera, classical music and film. The accompanying Le Festival Off is the world's biggest fringe festival. July; Ⓦ festival-avignon.com
● **International Kite Festival, Dieppe** The world's best gather to show their piloting skills at Europe's biggest kite festival. Early Sept; Ⓦ dieppe-cerf-volant.org

France online

France info Ⓦ rendezvousenfrance.com
Rail Ⓦ sncf.fr
Paris info Ⓦ parisinfo.com

COLOGNE CATHEDRAL

Germany

Capital Berlin

Population 81,276,000

Language German

Currency Euro (€)

Minimum daily budget €43

When to go The weather's at its finest March–September, while March–May and September–October provide the best combination: nice climate, few tourists

When not to go The Dark Rainy Miserable Season (possibly the actual name) is November–February. If you're heading to popular attractions, July and August are packed with people trying to do exactly the same thing

Germany

You can leave your stereotypes (that Germany is a robotic industrial powerhouse that favors rules over creativity and hockey haircuts over fashion) behind with your 2000-watt hairdryer. OK, maybe there's a dash of truth in there, but Germany today is a modern, multicultural patchwork of regional and international identities that are as diverse as its open fields, thick forests and mountain terrain. Its large cities are throbbing with haute couture shops, and its beer gardens continue to serve up some of the world's best brew.

The shadow of World War II still lingers for many who visit, but new generations of Germans have moved beyond carrying this heavy inherited burden with them 24/7. No German city celebrates innovation and creativity quite like Berlin, which bursts with youth, art and energy. It's one of Europe's brightest stars, with a pulsing nightlife and outstanding array of cool cafés and bars.

For the traveler, western Europe's largest and most populous nation is extremely accessible. Smaller festivals can be found almost year-round and getting to them with public transport couldn't be easier.

Main attractions

❶ **Heidelberg** A picturesque town featuring picturesque Heidelberg Castle and picturesque postcards. It couldn't be more… well, scenic. Visitors rarely miss a stroll along the Hauptstrasse through the old town. ⓦheidelberg.de

❷ **Reichstag, Berlin** Germany's past and future are represented in a unique building.

Construction started in 1884, and a decade later it was the parliament for Bismarck's German Empire. After the collapse of the Berlin Wall in 1989, British architect Sir Norman Foster's glass dome capped off the Hitler-tainted building's rebirth as a symbol of united democracy. Visitors can walk right up to the dome (be sure to book in advance) and even have a meal there. ⓦbundestag.de

❸ **Cologne Cathedral** The *dom* is a positively enormous thirteenth-century Gothic cathedral in the center of the city (a few steps from the central train station) that makes a trip to Cologne worthwhile on its own. ⓦkoelner-dom.de

❹ **The Marienplatz glockenspiel, Munich** This hyperactive cuckoo clock in central Munich forms part of the town hall's Gothic facade. Time your visit for 11am, noon or 5pm and you'll get to see the re-enactment of Duke William V's wedding to Renata von Lothringen.

❺ **Neuschwanstein Castle** If you're one of those picky travelers who'd rather see the

AVERAGE DAILY TEMPERATURES AND MONTHLY RAINFALL

	Jan	Feb	Mar	Apr	May	June	July	Aug	Sept	Oct	Nov	Dec
Berlin												
max °C	2	4	8	12	18	21	23	23	19	13	7	3
min °C	-3	-3	1	3	7	12	13	13	10	6	2	-1
rainfall mm	43	37	38	42	55	71	53	65	46	36	50	55

MAIN ATTRACTIONS

1. Heidelberg
2. Reichstag, Berlin
3. Cologne Cathedral
4. The Marienplatz glockenspiel, Munich
5. Neuschwanstein Castle
6. Dachau concentration camp

Meters
1000
500
200
0

DENMARK

Sassnitz
Kiel
Travemünde
Rostock
Lübeck
Hamburg
POLAND

Bremen
BERLIN
Potsdam
Hannover
NETHERLANDS
Goslar
Leipzig
Meissen
Naumburg
Dresden
Rhine
Düsseldorf
Erfurt
Cologne
Weimar
Bonn
Marburg
Aachen
CZECH REPUBLIC
Koblenz
Frankfurt
Bamberg
BELGIUM
Rhine
Mainz
Würzburg
N
LUXEM-BOURG
Worms
Nuremberg
Trier
Heidelberg Rothburg
Regensburg
Baden-Baden
Stuttgart
Dachau concentration camp
FRANCE
Strasbourg
Tübingen
Augsburg
Munich
Neuschwanstein Castle
Freiburg im Breisgau
Lake Constance
Füssen
Oberammergau
Berchtesgaden
0   100
kilometers
Konstanz
Garmisch-Partenkirchen
Mittenwald
BLACK FOREST
Innsbruck
GERMANY
SWITZERLAND
Rhine
AUSTRIA

original than be satisfied with the Disney replication, you'll need to brave the crowds and make a pilgrimage to this famous "Sleeping Beauty" castle. (Extra kitsch bonus: there's also the Musical Theater Neuschwanstein, a nightly performance based on King Ludwig II's tragic life.)
Ⓦ neuschwanstein.de

❻ Dachau concentration camp No matter what you've read or how many movies you've seen on the subject, it's hard to appreciate what happened under Hitler's regime without a trip to a concentration camp memorial. Dachau wasn't the largest such death machine but it was the first to be built, and a few hours of wandering the grounds will leave a powerful imprint on your soul.
Ⓦ kz-gedenkstaette-dachau.de

Also recommended

- **Have a soak in Baden-Baden**
Germany's most famous spa lies in the heart of the Black Forest. Its famed curative mineral waters bubble up from thermal springs at temperatures over 68°C. The Caracalla Therme is popular with families, but for a more upscale (and less clothed) experience, try the Roman-Irish bath at Friedrichsbad.
Ⓦcarasana.de

- **Cycle along the Danube** The cycle path that runs along the Danube River passes monasteries, castles, meadows and forests on a route that is littered with UNESCO World Heritage Sites. If you get hooked, you can continue all the way down to Vienna and Bratislava.

- **Windsurf Lake Constance** Near the Swiss border, the winds of Lake Constance lure German windsurfers by the dozen. Rent a board at Strandbad Eichwald. If your arms get tired, you can also fish the lake (with a permit) for pike, perch and eel. Or head to Lindau, rent a bike, and circle the water on two wheels. Alternatively, just take a dip; the surrounding mountains provide a magical backdrop for a swim.

- **Mountain bike the Black Forest** The Black Forest Bike Park has the largest network of mountain-bike trails in the world – about 1400km worth, and with routes for all levels. There are several places to access the trails: the Elz and Simonswälder valleys, Triberg, Schonach, Schönwald, Furtwangen, St Georgen, Hardt, Lauterbach, Schramberg and Tennenbronn.

Food and drink

German cuisine doesn't get the sort of fanfare that welcomes Italian and French culinary arts, and for good reason. It is, however, nice and filling in a meat-and-potatoes and deep-fried-anything sort of way. The bread is excellent and you'll find plenty of puffy pastries, but these German street snacks aren't especially cheap. For the very tightly budgeted, supermarket shopping and Turkish food (Germany has a large Turkish population) is the key. The beer isn't ridiculously priced for the amount you get. The problem, budget wise, is that this delicious swill comes in sizes you could use to put out a fire. Figure on €15 for a meal.

Transport

German transport is clean, fast, comfortable and reliable, but not particularly cheap. The buses are mostly owned by Deutsche Bahn and run in conjunction with the trains, which makes for convenient connections, but monopolizes pricing. Within the larger cities, you'll most likely want a strip card (multiple use) or day-card if you plan to hop on the city transit subways (U-Bahn and S-Bahn) for more than three rides.

By train

- **German Pass** Any three, four, five, seven or ten days of travel in one month. Or continuous passes running five, ten or fifteen days.

- **InterRail Germany Pass** Any three, four, six or eight days of travel in one month.

- **Eurail Benelux-Germany Pass** (also valid in Belgium, Luxembourg and the Netherlands). Choose between four, five, six, eight and ten days of travel in two months.

- **Eurail Germany-Poland Pass** Any four, five, six, eight or ten days in two months.

- **Eurail Germany-Switzerland Pass** Four, five, six, eight or ten days of travel in two months.

- **BahnCard** This comes in three flavours. The BahnCard 25 gives a 25 percent discount, the BahnCard 50 gives a 50 percent discount, and the BahnCard 100, which is wickedly expensive and not useful for budget-minded folk. Students under 27 can buy the BahnCard 50 for half the price. If you plan to spend more than €200 (roughly the cost of a return ticket from Frankfurt to Munich), this is a good way to save.

For tips and tricks on maximizing your rail pass, see "Costs and savings" (p.63).

By bus

Busabout barely operates in Germany, merely serving Berlin, Dresden, Munich and Stuttgart. For internal bus prices, see ⓦberlinlinienbus.de. For buses to other countries, see ⓦeurolines.de.

Events

- **Cologne Carnival** Germany's biggest pre-Ash Wednesday blowout bash is in Cologne, which is celebrated with as much ritual and dedication to frivolity as it is in Rio. The second day of the three-day event is Rose Monday, and if you're there, it's hard to miss the giant parade through town, with political-themed floats and a bizarre collection of costumes. If you want to dress up, the only guideline is "brighter is better." Late Feb/early March; ⓦkoelnerkarneval.de
- **Rhine in Flames** On five selected dates between spring and autumn, pyrotechnics from decorated barges cruising the Rhine River fill the night sky with color, while blue flares (known as "Bengal fires") light up the

castles and palaces. May, July, Aug & Sept; ⓦfirework.rhine-river.com
- **Munich's Oktoberfest** Germany's largest event and the world's biggest beer party. They never seem to run out of the magical beverage, served in liter-sized mugs. Don't be fooled by the name, it starts in September. ⓦoktoberfest.de
- **New Year's Day ski jumping in Garmisch-Partenkirchen** Of all the good arguments for not getting into ski jumping, the best one is that you have to stay sober every New Year's Eve. Why? Because the sadistic competition organizers at Garmisch-Partenkirchen insist on hosting the world's most prestigious competition on January 1. Pick a favorite and get in on the cheering, or choose a spot to nurse your hangover. When nearby Zugspitze (Germany's highest mountain at 2962m) comes into focus again, you'll know you're sober.

Germany online

Germany info ⓦgermany-tourism.de
Rail ⓦbahn.de
Bus ⓦberlinlinienbus.de
Berlin info ⓦberlin.de
Munich info ⓦmuenchen.de

PALACE OF WESTMINSTER, LONDON

Great Britain

Capitals London (England), Edinburgh (Scotland) and Cardiff (Wales)

Population 61,370,000

Languages English (also Welsh, Scots and Scottish Gaelic)

Currency Pound sterling (£)

Minimum daily budget €48

When to go May–September, when the weather should be lovely (if it's not raining and there's no heat wave), but with so much to do inside (museums, pubs, getting lost on the Underground), you can get by just fine if the weather turns miserable

When not to go July and August are crowded at the best budget accommodations, while October–March can be seriously cold and rainy, making seeing London by foot rather unpleasant

Great Britain

A famous headline that ran in the British press read: "Fog in the Channel, Continent Cut Off." In the Channel Tunnel there may be an underground umbilical cord of sorts, but in the minds of the Brits there's little question who the parent in the relationship is. That is to say, there's a strong sense of cultural independence. The Brits are profoundly British and only European by default. Moreover, the nation has developed the sort of pride one can only acquire as the power center of a colonial empire. Never mind the state of the empire today; the rich history and leftover architecture seems to be enough. Yet, with common immigration issues, and integrated trading markets, Britain is closer to mainland Europe than it sometimes likes to admit.

The nations of Wales and – at least for now – Scotland, each with proud cultures and rich histories of their own, are politically connected to England via the central government in London, though recent years have brought increasing devolution. The names get a bit confusing from here on. The official name of the country is the United Kingdom of Great Britain and Northern Ireland. When people speak about the UK, they're referring to this: the political grouping of England, Scotland, Wales and Northern Ireland. When they say "Great Britain" or "Britain," they're excluding Northern Ireland

(but sometimes they don't mean to). That's the confusing part for most visitors. England, Scotland and Wales (and Northern Ireland) each try to qualify a team for the football World Cup and European Championships, but only the United Kingdom sends a team to the Olympics (under the banner of "Great Britain and Northern Ireland"). Go figure.

There are far more famous sights than your wallet and schedule will allow, but the cheap international air tickets and language combine to make London an excellent starting point for many travelers, so you won't be the only one trying to get your footing on

AVERAGE DAILY TEMPERATURES AND MONTHLY RAINFALL

	Jan	Feb	Mar	Apr	May	June	July	Aug	Sept	Oct	Nov	Dec
London												
max °C	7	7	9	12	16	19	22	22	18	14	10	7
min °C	3	3	4	5	7	10	12	12	10	8	5	4
rainfall mm	64	51	51	48	56	56	66	76	64	74	69	69
Edinburgh												
max °C	6	7	8	11	14	17	19	18	16	12	9	7
min °C	1	1	2	3	6	9	11	11	8	5	3	2
rainfall mm	56	41	48	38	51	51	64	69	64	61	64	63
Cardiff												
max °C	8	8	11	13	17	19	22	21	18	15	11	9
min °C	2	2	4	5	8	10	12	12	10	7	4	3
rainfall mm	119	91	89	65	65	66	61	90	104	117	117	128

the travel trail. Make sure you make it out of the capital though: the hamlets and towns in the countryside resemble scenes out of Frodo's Shire, while the regional cities are a maze of thriving, bustling commerce and fashion (and near misses, as tourists forget to look right as they cross the street).

Main attractions

❶ Hampton Court Palace, Greater London For nearly 200 years, Hampton Court was the center of England's royal and political history. The State Apartments of Henry VIII,

whose Great Hall features a double hammer-beam ceiling, are among the most popular attractions, though some time should be saved for exploring the extensive gardens, plus one of the most vexing hedge mazes you'll encounter. It's 35 minutes from London by train from Waterloo station. Ⓦ hrp.org.uk
❷ Houses of Parliament, London The original building can be traced back to the eleventh century and is today home of the House of Commons (elected) and House of Lords (if you own more than ten polo ponies or a Gulfstream jet). It's mostly known for Big Ben, which is not the clock, but the

MAIN ATTRACTIONS

1. Hampton Court Palace, Greater London
2. Houses of Parliament, London
3. Westminster Abbey, London
4. British Museum, London
5. Tower of London
6. Bath
7. Edinburgh Castle
8. London Eye

GREAT BRITAIN

0 — 150 kilometers

Orkney Islands

NORTH SEA

Skye
Portree
Kyle of Lochalsh
Loch Ness
Inverness
CAIRNGORMS NATIONAL PARK
Aberdeen
Mallaig
Fort William
Mull
SCOTLAND
Oban
Stirling
St Andrews
Glasgow
Rosyth
EDINBURGH
Melrose

ATLANTIC OCEAN

Cairnryan
Larne
Stranraer
Newcastle
NORTHERN IRELAND
Belfast
Carlisle
Durham
Windermere

IRISH SEA
York
Hull
DUBLIN
Leeds
Liverpool
Manchester
REPUBLIC OF IRELAND
Holyhead
Chester
Pwllheli
ENGLAND

Rosslare
Aberystwyth
Birmingham
Norwich
Cork
Fishguard
Stratford
Cambridge
WALES
Swansea
CARDIFF
Oxford
Harwich
Bristol
Bath
Windsor
LONDON
Canterbury
Glastonbury
Stonehenge
Dover
Salisbury
Winchester
Exeter
Portsmouth
Brighton
Calais
St Ives
Weymouth
Boulogne
Penzance
Plymouth

FRANCE

N

Meters
600
450
150
0

13.8-ton bell inside (the clocktower itself is now officially called the Elizabeth Tower). For reasonably good entertainment, queue up for access to the public galleries to watch proceedings in the House of Commons. See Ⓦ parliament.uk for parliamentary session times.

❸ **Westminster Abbey, London** Every Coronation since 1066 has taken place in this architectural masterpiece. There are also over 3000 people buried here, including Geoffrey Chaucer, Charles Dickens, Charles Darwin, Isaac Newton, Laurence Olivier and Ben Jonson, an Elizabethan poet who was buried standing up. Ⓦ westminster-abbey.org

❹ **British Museum, London** When a colonial superpower decides to bring home souvenirs, it doesn't mess about. Many of the world's treasures can be found under this one (impressive) roof, and admission is free. Ⓦ britishmuseum.org

❺ **Tower of London** The Tower of London isn't much of a tower, but it is the best-preserved medieval castle in any European capital. It's been the royal living quarters, a prison for notorious traitors and, once, even housed lions and bears. Today, it's best known as the only place you can get nearly as close to the royal jewels as Camilla. Ⓦ hrp.org.uk/TowerOfLondon

❻ **Bath** Here you'll find the Royal Crescent, a majestic half-ring of buildings designed by John Wood in 1767. There's also Bath Abbey, with arching stained-glass windows and ornate spires. But the big pulls (with prices to match) are the Roman Baths (Ⓦ romanbaths.co.uk), built approximately 2000 years ago over a hot spring, and the state-of-the-art Thermae Bath Spa complex (Ⓦ thermaebathspa.com), with two open-air hot pools.

❼ **Edinburgh Castle** This castle looks like it's dropped straight out of *The Lord of the Rings*. Occupying the top half of a rocky hill in the center of the city, this ancient fortress and current UNESCO treasure gets over 1.4 million visitors a year and seems to sell as many postcards. Ⓦ edinburghcastle.gov.uk

❽ **London Eye** If you tire of things designed and built by dead people, take a spin in what was once the world's largest Ferris wheel (138m). At the moment it's number four in the world, and takes 3.75 million visitors per year. Pre-book tickets online to avoid the lines. Ⓦ londoneye.com

Also recommended

● **Join in the summer solstice at Stonehenge, England** The most interesting time to visit this ancient enigma is during the longest day of the year, when about 35,000 people show up. What's the big deal about this pile of rocks? Stonehenge is believed to have been built by the Druids, but how they moved these four-ton stones from 400km away (in the Preseli mountains in Wales) in 2000 BC, a time when hydraulic fork-lift operators were hard to find, is something of an engineering marvel.

● **See a play at Shakespeare's Globe** A reconstruction of the original open-air playhouse, the Globe Theatre in London is Shakespeare's backyard. The season runs from Aptil to October. Ⓦ shakespearesglobe.com

● **Hike or ski Cairngorms National Park, Scotland** The Cairngorms' 3800 square kilometers contain the UK's largest arctic mountain landscape (including four out of five of Scotland's highest mountains), plus a quarter of Britain's threatened birds, mammals and plants. Loaded with forests, lochs and glens, there's enough variety to suit any avid hiker or skier. Ⓦ cairngorms.co.uk

● **Play golf at St Andrews, Scotland** The Royal and Ancient Golf Club of St Andrews is unlikely to accept you as a member, but that doesn't mean you can't play a round on the 600-year-old Old Course, the world's first golf course – as long as you can provide an official handicap card. The bunkers are the size of squash courts, the wind is typically hovering just around gale force and the thick gorse bushes can eat golf balls by the twelve-pack, if the €110–235 green fee doesn't eat your wallet first. Ⓦstandrews.org.uk.

● **Loch Ness Monster Tour** You won't likely see Nessie, unless you include the ones in the gift shop, but the bus and boat ride do provide a nice historical tour of the area. It may just be the most kitsch thing you do on your entire trip. And they might even throw in some whisky tasting.

Food and drink

There are loads of fantastic inexpensive treats, especially the Indian offerings at the local curry house and a selection of trendy sandwich delis and hip gastropubs. Still, a portion of hot chips (French fries) with salt and vinegar is hard to beat (about €2). Much of the traditional pub food doesn't seem all that fresh or appetizing, especially since they seem to think it's a selling point to announce that there's blood in some of the items. Black pudding (made with pig's blood and eaten at breakfast), for example, sounds more like something you'd expect to find in Transylvania. Restaurants can be budget killers, but even higher-end establishments often offer reasonably priced lunchtime and early evening deals, and there's plenty of non-*McDonald's* fast food if funds are really tight.

Transport

Britain has the unique distinction of being home to Europe's most expensive rail service, and without getting any prizes for efficiency, speed or comfort. No Eurail passes cover Britain, though InterRail and numerous regional rail passes do – for all the options, see Ⓦinterrail.eu and Ⓦbritrail.com. The bus (or coach as the long-distance variety is usually called) is a very popular option in Britain, especially for single trips. It takes a bit longer, but unless you book your train tickets in advance, there are significant savings to be had.

As much fun as London is to traverse by foot, it's somewhat easier and much faster by Underground (aka "the Tube"). For more than a short trip, a one-day or seven-day Travelcard (also valid on buses, trams, Docklands Light Railway and National Rail trains within London) is the way to go. For more flexibility, you can get an Oyster card, which you can fill up with funds; it debits your account as you pass through the entry, which translates into a decent saving over buying tickets as you go (see Ⓦtfl.gov.uk).

Car drivers shouldn't forget the €11.50 congestion charge to drive into London (€14 if you pay the next day); see Ⓦcclondon.com.

London River Services runs public transport on the Thames from Embankment to Woolwich. Many operators offer a third off boat tickets if you have a Travelcard or Oyster card.

By train

● **Interrail Great Britain Pass** Choose between three, four, six or eight days of travel within one month in Wales, Scotland and England.

● **BritRail Consecutive Pass** Ranges from two, three, four, eight, fifteen or twenty-two days to a month of travel in Wales, Scotland and England.

● **BritRail Flexi Pass** Any two, three, four, eight or fifteen days of travel in one month. Note: This one needs to be booked from home six months in advance. Can be combined with a Eurail pass if you're between 16 and 25, which shrinks the price by fifty percent.

● **Britrail Freedom of Scotland Pass** Any four days of travel in eight days, or eight days of travel in fifteen days.

For tips and tricks on maximizing your rail pass, see "Costs and savings" (p.63).

By bus

A Busabout pass (see p.44) connects London with Paris and mainland Europe. For internal bus prices, see Ⓦnationalexpress.com. For buses to other countries, see Ⓦeurolines .co.uk.

Events

- **Grand National, Aintree** You might call it "the Ironman Triathlon for horses." Four and a half miles long with thirty wicked fences – many riders are happy if they can just hold on until the finish. There's a statue on hand at the Aintree racecourse in Liverpool so you can pay homage to Red Rum, the Grand National's greatest champion. April; Ⓦaintree .co.uk

- **Chelsea Flower Show, London** Even if you don't have the greenest of fingers, or know a fern from a Ficus, the Chelsea Flower Show is likely to impress. At the end of spring, the eleven-acre site at the Royal Hospital becomes a blooming wonderland of color with more fragrances than an airport duty-free shop. May; Ⓦrhs.org.uk/chelsea

- **Glastonbury Festival, Somerset** The open-air music festival of all open-air music festivals (much of it spent under a tent). The perimeter of the Worthy Farm venue stretches for more than 10km, and you'll find more diversity here than Darwin found in the Galapagos Islands, not to mention some of the world's top music acts. Tickets go on sale nine months in advance and sell out in minutes. June; Ⓦglastonburyfestivals.co.uk

- **Wimbledon Championships, London** The world's greatest tennis tournament is played on a surface that most people associate more with golf. Tennis aficionados, celebrities and long lines of fans turn out to see who will hold the jug trophy (men) and the oversized hors d'oeuvre plate (women) over their head at the end of the two-week contest. June/July; Ⓦwimbledon.org

- **Edinburgh Fringe Festival** August in Edinburgh means one thing: the Festival, of which the Fringe forms the largest part. From near and far, high and low, come the world's jugglers, fire eaters, comedians, singers, dancers, prancers… Nearly two million tickets get sold for this three-week, eclectic performing-arts bash. Aug; Ⓦedfringe.com

- **Notting Hill Carnival, London** Each summer, the streets of Notting Hill in west London fill with technicolor floats, costumed dancers and a million spectators (Europe's largest street fest) as the spleen-shaking sound systems fill the air. Last weekend in Aug; Ⓦthenottinghillcarnival.com

- **Bonfire Night** (Guy Fawkes' Night) On November 5, 1605, the Gunpowder Plot, a conspiracy to blow up the English Parliament and King James I, was under way. Someone leaked the plot to Lord Monteagle, word spread and it failed. The anniversary of the foiling of this rebellious deed has become a national event, celebrated nationwide with fireworks and bonfires, during which effigies of the conspirator, Guy Fawkes, are burned.

Great Britain online

Britain info Ⓦvisitbritain.com
Rail Ⓦnationalrail.co.uk
Coach Ⓦnationalexpress.co.uk
London info Ⓦvisitlondon.com
Edinburgh info Ⓦedinburgh.org
Cardiff info Ⓦvisitcardiff.com

MELISSÁNI CAVE, KEFALLONIÁ

Greece

Capital Athens

Population 11,769,000

Language Greek

Currency Euro (€)

Minimum daily budget €35

When to go Mid-April to mid-June and September to mid-October, when the attractions are less crowded, the temperature is pleasant, and accommodation easy to find

When not to go In the heart of summer (mid-June to August), when the heat is searing, and the winter months (November–February), when the tourist infrastructure goes into lockdown mode

Greece

For the backpacker, Greece has traditionally been about island hopping, ouzo drinking and plate smashing. But this country has far more to offer than some ever realize. The land that gave the world the Olympics, Socrates, drama, democracy, an enormous chunk of our vocabulary and the inspiration for toga parties deserves more than a cursory glance. From the vastly improved Athens, with its Acropolis views, to the cliffs and black-sand beaches of Santorini, the Greek gods seem to have blessed the country with ample sights and activities – let's just hope they tend to the shattered Greek economy as well one of these days.

Before heading out to explore the country's 2000-island archipelago, where you can easily lose yourself for years, you might head up the mainland or down to the Peloponnesian peninsula, where many of the most outstanding archeological sites and monuments can be found.

Main attractions

❶ **Acropolis, Athens** You may not get above the *nefos* (smog), but the views are still stunning from this ancient site, often called the "Sacred Rock" of Athens. Four masterpieces are assembled on this rocky hill: the Parthenon, the Propylaia, the Erechtheion and the Temple of Athena Nike. ⓦ acropolisofathens.gr

❷ **Medieval city of Rhodes** Perched at the northern tip of the island of the same name, this is one of the most festive UNESCO World Heritage Sites you'll come across. Bustling bars and restaurants now occupy this walled city that was previously run by the Order of St John of Jerusalem (1309–1523), Turks and Italians. You can sit on the beach just outside the walls and look out to the Turkish coast.

❸ **Delphi** One of Greece's greatest cultural treasures, Delphi lies just 150km northwest of Athens, harboring the Temple of Apollo, Castalian Spring and Corycian Cave in its hillside complex. It's not just another collection of ruins, though; according to mythology, Delphi was the "navel of the Earth" (center of the world).

❹ **Olympia** The site of the first Olympic Games (776 BC), Olympia still houses some of Greece's most important monuments: the Temple of Zeus, the Temple of Hera, the Stadium, the Bouleuterion, the Gymnasium and the Prytaneion (site of the eternal flame).

❺ **Knossós' Royal Palace, Crete** According to legend, King Minos's wife gave birth to the half-bull, half-man Minotaur at Knossós on the island of Crete. The labyrinth-like West Court is where the Minotaur caught his victims, and where Daedalus and his son,

AVERAGE DAILY TEMPERATURES AND MONTHLY RAINFALL

	Jan	Feb	Mar	Apr	May	June	July	Aug	Sept	Oct	Nov	Dec
Athens												
max °C	13	13	16	19	23	28	32	31	28	23	18	14
min °C	7	7	8	11	15	19	23	22	19	15	12	8
rainfall mm	48	41	41	23	18	8	5	8	10	53	56	63

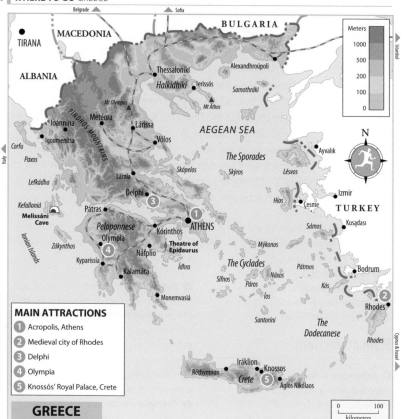

Icarus, were imprisoned and created wings of wax for their ill-fated escape.

Also recommended

● **Row into the Melissáni Cave** "Cave" may be a loose definition for this geological wonder on the island of Kefalloniá, since part of the roof collapsed thousands of years ago, leaving most of the football-pitch-sized submersed area in daylight. What you won't be able to see from a rowboat is that a series of subterranean passages connects the cave to the other side of the island, 28km away.

● **Climb the cliff-top monasteries of Metéora** James Bond climbed the walls to one of these monasteries using only his shoelaces in *For Your Eyes Only*, but it was a favorite spot among travelers long before that. The agile ninth-century hermits who first settled in the caves and rock fissures would descend every Sunday for Mass.

● **Visit the gods of Mount Olympus** Mount Olympus, Greece's highest peak, served as a sort of Melrose Place for the Greek gods. Today, it's Greece's oldest and most carefully protected national park. Staying at refuges along the way, visitors can trek among the peaks, stopping at the Plateau of the Muses to summit Stefani (the throne of Zeus), and look down on the world like the gods once did.

● **Kayak around the Ionian Islands** The waters between Greece and Italy are a calm and clear passageway, sheltered from the prevailing northeastern winds, where you can kayak between famous islands and uninhabited little jewels. Sightings of loggerhead turtles, monk seals and dolphins are common.

● **Attend a show at Epidaurus**
Throughout the summer (on Fridays and Saturdays), the well-preserved Ancient Theater of Epidaurus takes a step back in time to put on classical Greek dramas. The acoustics are excellent but the tickets are hard to get. Ⓦgreekfestival.gr

Food and drink

A nice restaurant meal costs about €15, but you can snack your way to a full meal for less than that. Small kebabs and cheese pies are delicious and cheap. You can find oven-baked *moussaka* and *tzatzíki* (yogurt, garlic and cucumber dip) everywhere.

Transport

Mainland Greece is an easy place to travel around by a combination of buses and trains. The rail lines are cheap but somewhat limited, while the buses reach even the smallest villages. Eleven ferry companies serve the islands domestically, but are not terribly punctual, and erratic services to some islands make scheduling difficult. High-speed ferries go twice as fast for twice the price. For three times the price, you can fly. One of the most charming ways to island hop is by tagging a lift on a private yacht or by taking one of the colorful wooden skiffs, called *kaïkia* (caïques). On the islands, bikes and scooters are popular to rent, but be warned: Greece has the second-highest traffic fatality rate (after Portugal) in Europe.

By train
● **Eurail Greek Pass** Any three, four, five or eight days of travel in one month.
● **Balkans Flexi Pass** (also valid in Bosnia-Herzegovina, Bulgaria, Macedonia, Montenegro, Romania, Serbia and Turkey). Any five, ten or fifteen days in one month.

For tips and tricks on maximizing your rail pass, see "Costs and savings" (p.63).

By bus
Busabout (see p.44) operates in Greece, with a four-island Flexi-Hopper pass covering Mykonos, Paros, Ios and Santorini. For internal bus prices, see Ⓦktelbus.com.

By ferry
Greece is often best navigated by boat. To check times and book tickets, visit Ⓦhellasferries.gr or Ⓦminoan.gr.

Events

● **Easter** Easter is the biggest holiday in Greece, with celebrations across the country. In central Macedonia, villagers walk barefoot across hot coals. In Ierissós, there's line dancing. In Áyios Nikólaos, you'll see the Burning of Judas; in Corfu, jar smashing. Greek Orthodox Easter, however, does not always fall on the same Sunday as the Catholic and Protestant Easter, since it's calculated with a different calendar.
● **Rockwave, Athens** The capital's premier rock festival brings in headliners such as Ozzy Osbourne, Metallica, The Black Keys and Robbie Williams to keep the 50,000-plus visitors entertained for four days of live music. June–July; Ⓦrockwavefestival.gr
● **Hellenic Festival** Athens' Herodes Atticus Theater is taken over in June by a range of cultural performances: modern and ancient theater, ballet, opera, jazz and symphonic. Ⓦgreekfestival.gr

Greece online

Greece info Ⓦvisitgreece.gr
Rail Ⓦtrainose.gr
Bus Ⓦktelbus.com
Ferry Ⓦgtp.gr
Athens info Ⓦcityofathens.gr

CHESS PLAYERS, SZÉCHENYI BATHS, BUDAPEST

Hungary

Capital Budapest

Population 9,835,000

Language Hungarian

Currency Forint (Ft)

Minimum daily budget €30

When to go March–May is ideal, but be prepared for spring showers; June–August is warm and sunny, but can be crowded in parts around July and August; September and October are also pleasant

When not to go November means cold rain, and after that it's just cold; August is called "the cucumber-growing season" because there's not much else happening with so many Hungarians on holiday

Hungary

When most travelers head to Hungary, they bring few of the preconceptions that typically get carted along with them to France, Italy or England. And, for many, Hungary feels like one of those surprise foreign movies that you never realized you'd enjoy so much. Make no mistake, Budapest doesn't pack the architectural punch of Paris, but there's plenty of Magyar magic in this town, and without any of that Parisian pretence. The country's history reads like a James Clavell novel, so don't miss out on your guidebook's brief summary. Little bonus trivia: the ballpoint pen, match, Rubik's Cube and helicopter were all invented by Hungarians.

If you want the charm, luxury and tree-lined walkways of western Europe and the prices of eastern Europe, Hungary offers a nice compromise. The language may be an enigma, but there's no mystery about the rich wines and elegant thermal spas. The lakes are lined with resorts and there's a lively – though not frenetic – café scene. Budapest straddles the River Danube with Buda to the west, rising dramatically from the banks, and Pest sitting on the edge of the eastern Great Plain.

Main attractions

❶ **Castle Hill, Budapest** Castle Hill beckons to travelers when they arrive. It's the "What's that?!" up on the hill that holds Budapest's most important museums and monuments. Make the trip over the river and up and you'll find both the Old Town and Royal Palace within this walled area. Plus, some of the best views in town. The Royal Palace itself now houses the Hungarian

National Gallery, the National Széchényi Library and the Budapest History Museum; allow plenty of time.

❷ **Lake Balaton** Just 100km outside Budapest, this lake is one of Europe's largest. The south shore has most of the glitz and hotels (specifically the town of Siófok), while the north shore has the hiking trails and historical sights. Balatonfüred, once a writers' colony and political retreat, seems to bridge the gap. ⓦ balaton.gotohungary.com

❸ **Gellért Hill, Budapest** When your legs have recharged after Castle Hill, the next panoramic climb is to the Citadella, a fortress atop Gellért Hill that also serves as Budapest's unofficial symbol. On the way down, stop at the *Gellért Hotel*, an old-world lodging with a remarkable spa that feels as if you're swimming in a half-submerged church. ⓦ gellertbath.hu

❹ **Eger and the Valley of the Beautiful Woman** The gorgeous town of Eger, set among the rolling Bükk hills, boasts a fabled

AVERAGE DAILY TEMPERATURES AND MONTHLY RAINFALL

	Jan	Feb	Mar	Apr	May	June	July	Aug	Sept	Oct	Nov	Dec
Budapest												
max °C	2	4	11	16	21	24	26	26	22	15	7	3
min °C	-4	-3	2	5	11	13	15	15	11	1	1	-2
rainfall mm	41	38	34	41	61	68	45	55	39	34	59	48

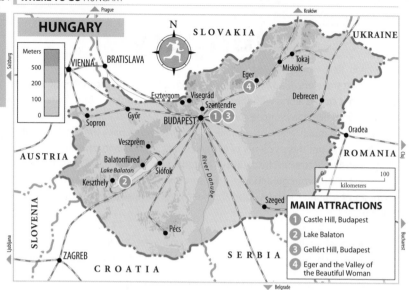

MAIN ATTRACTIONS

1 Castle Hill, Budapest

2 Lake Balaton

3 Gellért Hill, Budapest

4 Eger and the Valley of the Beautiful Woman

fortress which famously repulsed Ottoman attack in 1552. A short walk southeast is the "Valley of the Beautiful Woman", crammed with boutique wine cellars.

Also recommended

● **Take a bath** Taking a dip in the warm thermal and cool mineral springs that bubble under Budapest is the perfect antidote to the tired legs and traveler grime you get from sightseeing, though some of the baths are architectural wonders themselves. Two baths (Palatinus and Hajós) are located on Margaret Island, just between Buda and Pest. The Király baths – sitting just on the Buda side, with four pools and a sixteenth-century sky-lit dome – are flanked by the Lukács baths to the north and the Rác, Rudas and Gellért baths to the south. Best of all though are the Széchenyi Baths in Pest. The hottest in the capital, they boast large outdoor pools where old men play chess on floating boards, and fun features like water rapids and underwater bubble jets.

● **Row down the Danube** Rowing and kayaking are possible on the Danube. In Budapest, you can rent boats, kayaks or canoes on Margaret Island or along the Roman Riverbank.

● **Head underground** The Mátyás Caves can be found right under Budapest, formed by thermal waters gushing through thousands of years ago. The tiny passageways don't make for a leisurely stroll; you may spend more time on your belly than your feet. Helmets, overalls and headlamps are the way to go. Trips can be arranged through several of the hostels in town.

● **Take a day-trip to Veszprém** A few hours by bus or train out of Budapest is one of Hungary's most impressive sights: the walled-in castle district of Veszprém, resting atop a plateau. Formerly a royal residence, it now serves as a museum of Baroque art and architecture.

● **Visit the House of Terror** This shocking museum is housed in what was once the headquarters of the dreaded ÁVH secret police. It was here that political activists (any kind) were taken for interrogation and torture. The museum is meant both to honor the victims and to act as a reminder so that such atrocities never happen again. ⓦterrorhaza.hu

Food and drink

There are slim pickings for vegetarians in this farmhouse-style meat-and-potatoes-based cuisine. Goulash soup doesn't get everyone excited, but it's worth a try while you're here. A traditional three-course meal can be had for less than €18, and a simple, filling meal for less than €8. A beer in a nice bar starts under €3. Which all means it's a fine place to treat yourself.

Transport

You won't break any speed records on Hungarian public transport, but it'll get you around. The toughest part might just be getting information without access to the web at every train and bus stop. The trains are dependable, although also dependably late. You'll probably have better luck buying tickets at a MÁV office (Ⓦ mavcsoport.hu) than the train station. (A reservation is cheap and avoids standing for hours on the train.) Eurail and InterRail passes cover Hungary, but buses can be quicker between many of the destinations.

In Budapest, a Budapest Card (available for 24hr, 48hr or 72hr; Ⓦ budapest-card.com/en) gets you into museums, gives you discounts on restaurants and spas, and entitles you to free transport. Don't forget to punch each metro ticket you use in the machines provided on every bus, tram, trolleybus and at each metro station entrance, however.

By train
- **Eurail Hungary Pass** Any three, four, five or eight days of travel in one month.
- **Eurail Hungary-Romania Pass** Any four, five, six, eight or ten days in two months.
- **European East Pass** (also valid in Austria, Czech Republic and Slovakia) Any five days of travel in one month. Five additional travel days can be added.

For tips and tricks on maximizing your rail pass, see "Costs and savings" (p.63).

By bus
For domestic bus prices, see Ⓦ volanbusz.hu. For buses to other countries, see Ⓦ eurolines .hu.

Events

- **Budapest Spring Festival** The onset of spring signals the start of Hungary's biggest annual cultural event. There are chamber concerts, opera, jazz, dance, film screenings and more scattered at venues throughout Budapest. You'll see the best Hungarian performers, in addition to international artists. March/April; Ⓦ fesztivalvaros.hu
- **International Guitar Festival, Balatonfüred** During a week in late June/ early July, you can listen free to the plucking and strumming of top-end guitar music on the shore of Lake Balaton. There are even master classes on offer for skilled student players. Ⓦ balatongitar.hu
- **Sziget Festival** A stamina-sapping eight days long, Sziget is now firmly established as one of Europe's biggest rock and pop festivals. Staged on an island north of the center, it features a stellar line-up of rock, pop and world music acts, alongside dance, theater, films and children's events. Mid-Aug; Ⓦ sziget.hu

Hungary online

Hungary info Ⓦ visit-hungary.com
Rail Ⓦ mavcsoport.hu
Bus Ⓦ volanbusz.hu
Budapest info Ⓦ budapestinfo.hu

GUINNESS AS USUAL

GUINNESS
IS GOOD FOR YOU

Ireland

REPUBLIC OF IRELAND
Capital Dublin
Population 4,630,000
Languages English (also Irish, spoken mainly on the western seaboard)
Currency Euro (€)
Minimum daily budget €36

NORTHERN IRELAND
Capital Belfast
Population 1,848,000
Language English
Currency Pound sterling (£)
Minimum daily budget €42

When to go April, May and September are ideal. June–August is (with a bit of Irish luck) lovely, even if crowded

When not to go Prices go up in the summer, and the miserable winter weather chases so many away that many small hotels and restaurants outside the main cities shut from October to the end of March

Ireland

The Irish landscape has an enchanting and mystical nature that's nearly as disarming as the Irish themselves. Despite the hyper-saturated weather conditions ("horizontal rain" is common in some parts) and lack of leprechauns, few leave without being touched by the country's green charm.

For all the years of strife between the Republic and Northern Ireland – thankfully now largely a thing of the past – we've thrust them together for the sake of the traveler, who is not confined by boundaries or history. Both countries share the same landmass, and even many of the same bus and rail connections. They also share green, rolling hills; wild, rugged coastlines; and people with an uncanny ability to strike up conversation. As the expression goes in Ireland, "It never rains inside a pub." And they're not just a shelter from the elements; the pub is a social engine that powers the country, whether you're tasting traditional Irish stew, listening to folk tunes on the fiddle, or getting a long, almost-coherent Guinness-fueled tale from a pub regular. In *Ulysses*, Joyce noted: "A good puzzle would be to cross Dublin without passing a pub."

Ireland's economic woes may still make headlines, but the ebb of Irish seeking fortune abroad has turned into a flow of tourists, and the country has become one of the top destinations in Europe. Things may seem a bit gray at times, the urban architecture less impressive than in other European cities, but if it's the personal connections that make the strongest memories, you'll be hard-pressed to find more welcoming citizens over on the continent.

Main attractions

❶ **Guinness Storehouse, Dublin**
Guinness may look like discarded brake fluid, but this thick stout with a scientifically measured head of foam is worshipped like a minor deity. And the Guinness Storehouse in Dublin is the high altar. Naturally, you have to suffer a marketing blitz to get to the liquid lunch at the end of the tour.
Ⓦguinness-storehouse.com

❷ **Dublin Castle** One of the best parts of Dublin Castle, built in the thirteenth century by order of King John, is the bit beneath it. Excavations of the Undercroft have revealed part of the city's old Viking ramparts and steps leading down to a moat.
Ⓦdublincastle.ie

AVERAGE DAILY TEMPERATURES AND MONTHLY RAINFALL

	Jan	Feb	Mar	Apr	May	June	July	Aug	Sept	Oct	Nov	Dec
Belfast												
max °C	7	7	9	11	14	16	17	17	15	11	8	7
min °C	4	5	6	7	9	12	13	13	11	8	6	6
rainfall mm	86	58	67	53	60	63	64	80	85	88	78	78
Dublin												
max °C	8	8	9	11	14	17	19	18	16	13	10	6
min °C	3	3	4	5	7	10	12	12	10	8	5	4
rainfall mm	15	10	10	8	15	36	48	46	25	20	18	20

3 Blarney Stone Blarney Castle in southwest Ireland holds the famous Blarney Stone – given to Cormac McCarthy by Robert the Bruce in 1314, a time when stones were appropriate gifts – high up in its battlements. To kiss it (and give yourself the gift of the gab – that is, an eternity of yapping) you have to lie down, tilt your head back, get lowered in upside down by a helper and plant your pucker on the stone. Ⓦ blarneycastle.ie

4 Giant's Causeway The only World Heritage Site in Northern Ireland is a geological phenomenon on the North Antrim coast. Caused by a volcanic eruption sixty million years ago, the rock formations look something like a ceramic plate warehouse, or perhaps the world's largest collection of petrified tortoise shells. Ⓦ nationaltrust.org .uk/giants-causeway/

5 Ireland by horseback Go riding along the Celtic trails of western Ireland in such locales as Burren National Park. Ride along the coast or on remote forest lanes. Many outfitters offer such equestrian holidays. Ⓦ burrennationalpark.ie

MAIN ATTRACTIONS
1 Guinness Storehouse, Dublin
2 Dublin Castle
3 Blarney Stone
4 Giant's Causeway
5 Ireland by hoseback

Rathlin Island
Portrush
Coleraine
Giant's Causeway
Derry
Larne
Glencolmcille
Bangor
Donegal
NORTHERN IRELAND
BELFAST
Sligo
Enniskillen
Ballina
Newry
Dundalk
Knock
Drogheda
Westport
Newgrange
Clifden
Mullingar
Athlone
Galway
DUBLIN
REPUBLIC OF IRELAND
Curragh Racecourse
Dún Laoghaire
Galway Bay
Aran Islands
Doolin
THE BURREN
Wicklow
IRISH SEA
ATLANTIC OCEAN
Ennis
Shannon
Kilkenny
Limerick
Limerick Junction
Cashel
Tralee
Wexford
Rosslare
Dingle
Mallow
Waterford
Valentia
Ring of Kerry
Killarney
Blarney Castle
Cobh Junction
Hook Head
KERRY WAY
Cork
Cobh
BEARA WAY
Dunmanus Bay

Meters
1000
500
100
0

0   50
kilometers

IRELAND

Also recommended

- **Watch Gaelic games** Croke Park in Dublin plays host to the All-Ireland Hurling finals; something between lacrosse and field hockey, this uniquely Irish sport is not for the timid. While you're there, you might check out the Gaelic football finals. It's just like regular football, except there's none of that offside nonsense. And you can use your hands, provided you alternate using your feet as well. And if the ball sails over the goal, you still get a point (if it goes in, you get three). Other than that, just like football. Ⓦ gaa.ie

- **Go fishing** Ireland is famous for its fishing, and it's not uncommon for people to show up at the airport with a rod and reel. Permits are mandatory, as is a state national license, if you're going after salmon or sea trout. There's over 5000km of coastline to cast in for the big one. Ⓦ fishinginireland.info

- **Take a walk in the country** Believe it or not, walking is one of Ireland's biggest draws. There are several designated walking trails, such as the Wicklow, Kerry and Beara ways, to help you reach some of the most beautiful sections of the country. Or you can head to The Burren, a starkly desolate limestone plateau with a primeval allure.

- **Dive the Irish Sea** Ireland is unlikely to be the first place that comes to mind when you want to go scuba diving, but it has some of Europe's best conditions. At Dunmanus Bay near Cork, Bantry Bay around Hook Head and Galway Bay near Wexford, you'll find plenty of dive sites. For a wreck dive, there's the HMS *Drake* off Rathlin Island on the northeast coast.

Food and drink

There are more hearty, inexpensive dishes in this country than you can shake a shamrock at. Most can be bought in a pub and few are fit for vegetarians. A typical meal is unlikely to break your budget – €15 is standard for a small feast. For a real treat, try the oysters, one of Ireland's most celebrated catches.

Transport

Rail fares aren't cheap, so many travelers without a rail pass go by bus, bike or thumb.

By train

- **Irish Explorer** Any five days in fifteen consecutive days; valid in Ireland only. Can only be purchased at ticket offices.
- **Eurail Ireland Pass** Any three, four, five or eight days in one month.
- **Translink yLink Card** In Northern Ireland those aged 18–23 can buy a discount card (around £7) that gives up to fifteen percent discounts on buses and up to 33 percent discounts on rail travel in Northern Ireland and fifty percent on cross-border services to the Republic. You should be able to make up the cost of the card with just a few trips. See Ⓦ translink.co.uk.

For tips and tricks on maximizing your rail pass, see "Costs and savings" (p.63). For internal rail prices, see Ⓦ irishrail.ie (Republic) and Ⓦ translink.co.uk (Northern Ireland).

By bus

Open-Road Pass Any three to fifteen days of travel, within time frames of six to thirty days. Bus only; valid in Ireland and Northern Ireland except Dublin, and not on cross-border routes. See Ⓦ buseireann.ie.

Busabout doesn't operate in Ireland or Northern Ireland. For buses to the UK (from Ireland only), see Ⓦ buseireann.ie.

Events

- **St Patrick's Day** Ah, finally, your chance to dress up like a leprechaun and drink yourself silly. There's far more than a parade for this multi-day event (see box, pp.28–29). Ⓦ stpatricksday.ie
- **Irish Derby** This annual equestrian event takes place at the Curragh, one of Europe's oldest sporting venues. Most of the country tunes in to watch the top horses speed around the racecourse. June; Ⓦ curragh.ie

- **Bloomsday, Dublin** Every June, the work of author James Joyce is celebrated on the day his masterpiece, *Ulysses*, is set, and the literati retrace the steps of the book's famous character, Leopold Bloom. June 16; Ⓦbloomsdayfestival.ie

- **Banks of the Foyle Halloween Carnival, Derry** Ireland's best Halloween carnival gets cranked up in Derry as over 35,000 witches, ghouls and a mix of Harry Potter-types take to the streets. Fireworks, ghost tours and the like can be found in this spooktacular fest. Oct 31; Ⓦderrycity.gov.uk/halloween

Ireland online

Ireland info Ⓦdiscoverireland.ie
Ireland rail Ⓦirishrail.ie
Ireland (and Northern Ireland) bus info
Ⓦbuseireann.ie
Dublin info Ⓦvisitdublin.com
Northern Ireland info
Ⓦdiscovernorthernireland.com
Northern Ireland rail Ⓦtranslink.co.uk
Belfast info Ⓦgotobelfast.com

Italy

Capital Rome

Population 60,963,000

Language Italian

Currency Euro (€)

Minimum daily budget €42

When to go April–May and October–November, when the landscape colors are at their best, the temperatures are more moderate and it's relatively less crowded

When not to go August. Italians take their vacations then, so many shops and businesses are shut, and the tourists are the only ones walking the searing streets

Italy

From frescoes to Ferraris, Venice to Versace and the Pope to pasta, there's something in this boot-shaped, football-obsessed nation for every sort of traveler. You can take a warm dip in the Med at one end of the country or go skiing at the other. There's fashion on the streets of Milan and fish in the markets of the little villages dotted around Sicily. The rich textile town of Treviso, just north of Venice, couldn't be more different to the rougher areas of Naples. At times, the country seems so diverse, the only thing holding it together is the national football team. In other words, a short visit to Venice, Florence or Rome will provide little more than a snapshot of this culturally overflowing land.

Main attractions

❶ The Vatican, Rome OK, technically this is a city-state, not an attraction within Italy, but guidebooks have been guilty of pairing them for decades with less justification than this. Let your jaw drop when you enter St Peter's Basilica, considered Christianity's most magnificent Renaissance church. And get ready to queue for Michelangelo's Sistine Chapel (or book ahead), though many find the maps and frescoes on the way to the chapel even more compelling than the main draw.

❷ Assisi Perched halfway up Mount Subasio, overlooking the town of Perugia, this walled city with a fourteenth-century fortress (Rocca Maggiore) is the birthplace of St Francis (1182). Work began on his basilica

in 1228, two years after his death, and if you can get past all the religious pilgrims, it's one of the most enchanting towns in the country.

❸ The Colosseum, Rome Rome's most awe-inspiring ancient monument, the Colosseum (completed in 80 AD) was the ultimate arena for public games: the Romans would flock here for gladiatorial contests and cruel spectacles, and even the occasional mock sea battle.

❹ Venice It's sinking (possibly under the weight of all the tourists), and there's a chance the water may be knee-deep in St Mark's Square by the time you visit, but to stroll Venice without crowds (off season, or at sunrise) may top your European visual highlights. There's a reason so many use it for comparison (Amsterdam, Stockholm

AVERAGE DAILY TEMPERATURES AND MONTHLY RAINFALL

	Jan	Feb	Mar	Apr	May	June	July	Aug	Sept	Oct	Nov	Dec
Rome												
max °C	13	13	15	17	22	25	28	28	26	22	17	14
min °C	4	4	6	8	12	16	19	19	17	13	8	6
rainfall mm	81	71	69	66	51	33	15	25	69	114	112	97
Venice												
max °C	6	8	12	16	21	24	27	27	23	18	11	7
min °C	-1	1	4	8	13	16	18	18	15	10	4	0
rainfall mm	56	53	61	74	69	79	69	79	66	76	89	62

MAIN ATTRACTIONS

1. The Vatican, Rome
2. Assisi
3. The Colosseum, Rome
4. Venice
5. Florence

and St Petersburg all describe themselves as the "Venice of the North"). There's little need for an overpriced gondola ride – a cheap city bus-boat will do just fine. Do yourself a favor while visiting and get lost; put away your map and wander the narrow back-alleys until you need to ask a local for directions.

5 Florence This city offers more art history per square meter than any other place outside the Louvre. You could spend a year here and not see it all. In fact, several guidebooks far thicker than this book are devoted entirely to Florence. This Renaissance wonderland boasts the Uffizi Gallery, Ponte Vecchio, the Duomo, Michelangelo's *David*, and the Basilica di San Lorenzo, to name but a few.

Also recommended

● **Walk the Cinque Terre** The five postcard-perfect fishing villages of the Cinque Terre (Riomaggiore, Manarola, Monterosso, Vernazza and Corniglia) along the northwest coast are connected by a cliff-side hiking trail that can be completed in one long day or divided up into a few days with hotel stays and good meals.

● **Climb the vie ferrate in the Dolomites** The *vie ferrate* (iron ways) are a magnificent system of steel ladders and fixed cables, originally built during World War I to help Alpini troops move through the mountains. With only modest modifications, they now allow beginner climbers to clip in and safely ascend to incredible heights.

● **Take a wine tour** Brunello di Montalcino is the Rolls-Royce of Italian wines. You can tour Montalcino, Chianti, or try the Cabernet Sauvignon of the Tuscan coast. The choice is limitless – you can taste some of the world's top wines almost everywhere you go.

● **Learn to make pasta** Italy isn't just famous for its food, but increasingly so for its culinary courses. More luxurious ones will house you at an upscale Tuscan villa for a week while you learn to make local dishes. Others have a more down-to-earth farmstay-like atmosphere. One thing is certain: you won't go hungry.

● **Watch a volcano blow** Check your insurance coverage (see p.99), then take a ferry from Naples or the north of Sicily to the island of Stromboli, hike a few hours with a guide up to the top of its volcano (you can't miss it), watch the sunset and then stick to see Mother Nature's fireworks at night as small eruptions send orange molten lava 50–100m up into the air. You may need to book in advance to get a tour and it may feel a bit too dangerous for some, who may prefer viewing the eruptions from a boat tour. ⓦmagmatrek.it/en

● **Take in a football match** The bigger clubs like AC Milan, Juventus and Roma are among the best in the world, but you might find it more culturally enlightening to watch a game at a smaller stadium. Just make sure you're wearing the right colors. Rather, make sure you're not wearing the wrong colors.

Food and drink

Italy may be famous for its cuisine, but if you want to *mangiare* on the cheap, especially in the tourist areas, you'll likely be underwhelmed by what you get. Pasta may be difficult to mess up, but it's not always easy to find the truly divine dishes. Pizzas taste better than average (occasionally amazing), and are relatively cheap, but make sure you also try the distinctive regional cuisines – don't be afraid to ask what the *piatti tipici* (local dishes) are. Prices vary around Italy, but generally it's more expensive up north with better deals down south. There's a reason you'll see so many people standing at cafés and bars – prices are higher if you grab a seat.

Transport

Major train and bus lines are quick and reliable (when not on strike); even the small village buses are surprisingly timely. And, aside from the high-speed rail, it's quite cheap. Always check the local prices before you use your rail or bus pass; it's better value to pay €15–20 for a short ride than waste a day of your pass.

The Rome public transport system sells a daily transport pass ticket, a three-day pass and a seven-day pass. Tickets can be bought at newsstands, hotels and vending machines. For more information, see ⓦatac.roma.it.

By train
● **Eurail Italy Pass** Any three, four, five or eight days within one month.
● **Eurail France-Italy Pass** Any four, five, six, eight or ten days of travel in two months.

For tips and tricks on maximizing your rail pass, see "Costs and savings" (p.63).

By bus
A Busabout pass (see p.44) allows you to travel throughout Italy. For buses to other countries, see ⓦeurolines.it.

Events

- **Alba Truffle Festival** You can call them fungi if you like, or *tuber magnatum pico*, if you want to impress. But in Alba, the home of the delicacy found in the ground by trained dogs, they're known as *tartufo bianco* – white truffles. More prized than France's black truffles, top chefs shell out over €1500 per kilo for these "white diamonds," most popular on omelets, fresh pasta and risotto. Some truffle oils even fall within the price range of normal people. Mid-Oct to mid-Nov; Ⓦ fieradeltartufo.org

- **The Italian Job** If you like the movie you might want to catch this movie-inspired sponsored rally. A train of Mini Coopers speeds across the Alps, picks up a load of local wine and then heads back to the UK to auction it off for charity. Late Oct–Nov; Ⓦ italianjob.com

- **Carnevale, Venice** Perhaps the only thing better than seeing St Mark's Square without tourists is seeing it during Carnevale, which comes alive with theatrical, dance and acrobatic performances. The most famous and traditional aspect of the festival is the traditional masked balls, which feature elaborate eighteenth-century costumes. See "European festivals and events" (box, pp.28–29) for more. Feb–March; Ⓦ carnevale.venezia.it

- **Verona Opera Festival** Even if you don't like opera, seeing grand performances in Verona's exquisite Roman amphitheater will stir your emotions. All classes of society come together for this highlight of Italy's summer calendar. June–Aug; Ⓦ arena.it/arena/en

- **Il Palio, Siena** This madcap medieval horse-race in Siena's town square is surrounded by days of rituals and pageantry – nearly all of it just as much fun for visitors as the race itself. See "European festivals and events" (box, pp.28–29) for more. Ⓦ thepalio .com

- **Regata Storica, Venice** A trial of strength and skill for the city's gondoliers, this floating parade of antique boats and rowers in period dress couldn't be any more photo-friendly if it had been invented by a team from Nikon. Spectators are expected to support the contestants and may even get issued with the appropriate colors. First Sunday in September. Ⓦ regatastoricavenezia.it

Italy online

Italy info Ⓦ italia.it
Rail Ⓦ trenitalia.com
Rome info Ⓦ rome.info
Florence info Ⓦ firenzeturismo.it
Venice info Ⓦ en.turismovenezia.it

Montenegro

Capital Podgorica

Population 620,000

Language Montenegrin (although more than sixty percent prefer Serbian)

Currency Euro (€)

Minimum daily budget €30

When to go May–September, when the mountains are perfect for hiking and the 117 beaches are nice and toasty

When not to go November–February, when the entire country is treated to some of the most insistent rain in Europe

Montenegro

With 294km of unspoiled coastline along the glittering Adriatic, Montenegro is an emerging travel hotspot. In addition to the beaches, the country's mountainous interior is ideal for adventure-travel junkies with developed trails for hiking and biking as well as rafting and canyoning. Montenegro's most precious jewel – phenomenally photogenic Kotor – sits just a little inland at the end of a fjord-like bay. The beach town of Budva is the other real highlight, while the capital, Podgorica, gets few visitors but certainly has its charms.

Main attractions

❶ **Kotor** Named a UNESCO World Heritage Site in 1979, Kotor is Montenegro's biggest tourist spot, with tiled roofs and a clear Venetian tilt to its architecture. Not a sunbathing destination, but there's plenty to keep you busy.

❷ **Durmitor National Park** A land of jagged, pine-cloaked mountains and alpine pastureland, Durmitor is the most scenic place in inland Montenegro. Centered around the town of Žabljak, the park encompasses Tara River Canyon, a 1000m-deep rip in the Earth bisected by a crashing river.

Also recommended

● **Budva** Of Montenegro's seemingly never-ending chain of picturesque coastal towns, Budva is by far the most popular. Filled to the brim with bars, restaurants and limestone houses, its Old Town is almost as pretty as the one in nearby Kotor.

● **Ride the train** The Belgrade–Bar railway connects the capital of Serbia with the Montenegrin coastal city of Bar, and notches up 254 tunnels and 435 bridges. Most of it runs through Serbia, but the prettiest parts are in hilly Montenegro. Look out for the 200m-high Mala Rijeka viaduct outside Podgorica. ⓦzeleznicesrbije.com

Food and drink

The close proximity of Italy is evident in the Montenegrin diet, with plenty of pizza, pasta, cheese and wine. Homegrown meals include the artery-clogging national dish, *karađorđeva šnicla*, a breaded veal-cutlet roll stuffed with cheese. Great seafood is, unsurprisingly, found near the coast.

Locals are proud of their *rakija* grape brandy, and the beer to drink is a Nikšićko, which will cost anywhere between €2 and €4.

AVERAGE DAILY TEMPERATURES AND MONTHLY RAINFALL

	Jan	Feb	Mar	Apr	May	June	July	Aug	Sept	Oct	Nov	Dec
Bar												
max °C	8	9	13	17	22	25	29	29	25	20	14	10
min °C	0	2	4	7	11	14	17	17	14	10	6	2
rainfall mm	172	148	133	122	87	64	43	59	104	146	199	182

Transport

For a country with such a small population, the frequency of intercity buses is quite remarkable. In addition, many of the main travel arteries have been upgraded, and travel times are accordingly short.

By train

The only train line is the one from Bar on the coast inland to Podgorica and on to the border with Serbia (with a sideline to the northern town of Nikšić), but it's the cheapest way to get around.

By bus

Buses will take you anywhere in the country for no more than €30. See Ⓦblueline-mne .com/bluetraveleng.html for info on routes.

Events

● **Boka Night** Night-time procession of pimped-out boats along Kotor's harbor. *Boka* means "bay," but the party spills out all across the city. After the winning boat has been chosen, the festivities end in fireworks. Late Aug; Ⓦtokotor.me/en

● **Petrovac Jazz Festival** So you might not have heard of many of the musicians on stage, but the setting of this festival alone merits a visit. Some good jazz in a Roman city on the Adriatic coast, with a 600m downtown beach – what's not to enjoy?

Note: Not to be confused with a host of other Petrovacs in Serbia and Bosnia. Late Aug; Ⓦpetrovacjazzfestival.webnode.com

Montenegro online

Montenegro info Ⓦvisit-montenegro.com
Rail Ⓦzcg-prevoz.me
Bus Ⓦblueline-mne.com/bluetraveleng.html

Morocco

Capital Rabat

Population 32,634,100

Language Arabic

Currency Dirham

Minimum daily budget €23

When to go September–April along the coast, when the weather is still good but the crowds have gone; December–February for skiing

When not to go Mid-June and August are crowded on the coast, and winters up north can be wet

Morocco

Just an hour's ferry ride from Spain, Morocco seems worlds away from Europe. It has a deeply traditional Islamic culture and, despite its 44 years of French and Spanish colonial rule, a more distant past constantly makes its presence felt. A visit here is a challenging, intense and rewarding experience.

Berbers, the indigenous peoples, make up over half of Morocco's population; only around ten percent of Moroccans claim to be "pure" Arabs. More obvious is the legacy of the colonial period: until independence in 1956, the country was divided into Spanish and French zones, the latter building *villes nouvelles* (new towns) alongside the long-standing Medinas (old towns) in all the country's main cities.

Many people come to Morocco on cheap flights, mainly to Marrakesh, but coming by boat from Europe, your most likely introduction to the country is Tangier in the north, still shaped by its heyday of "international" port status in the 1950s. To its south, in the Rif Mountains, the town of Chefchaouen is a small-scale and enjoyably laidback place, while inland lies the enthralling city of Fez, the greatest of the four imperial capitals (the others are Meknes, Rabat and Marrakesh). Further south, Marrakesh is an enduring fantasy that won't disappoint. The country's loveliest resort, Essaouira, a charming walled seaside town, lies within easy reach.

Main attractions

❶ **Fez** Not just the place that gave its name to the funny party hat, but also one of the world's oldest medieval cities. Its Medina (fortified city), Fès el Bali, is the largest car-free urban zone in the world.

❷ **Marrakesh** The third-largest city in Morocco after Casablanca and Rabat, but probably the most pleasant thanks to its mild climate. Don't miss the hectic Jemaa el Fna or the country's largest souk.

❸ **The Sahara** The mighty sandbox is just around the corner. Even if you're an adventurous type, visit as part of a tour group or bring someone who knows what they're doing. Venturing out on your own is not a good idea.

Also recommended

● **Ski the Atlas** Morocco's ski resort, Oukaïmeden, is an unexpected find some 70km south of Marrakesh.

AVERAGE DAILY TEMPERATURES AND MONTHLY RAINFALL

	Jan	Feb	Mar	Apr	May	June	July	Aug	Sept	Oct	Nov	Dec
Tangier												
max °C	16	16	18	19	22	26	28	28	26	23	18	16
min °C	7	7	9	11	12	12	18	18	17	14	11	8
rainfall (mm)	103	98	71	62	37	16	2	2	14	65	134	129
Marrakesh												
max °C	18	20	23	26	29	33	38	38	33	28	23	19
min °C	4	6	9	11	14	17	19	20	17	14	9	6
rainfall (mm)	25	28	33	31	15	8	3	3	10	23	31	31

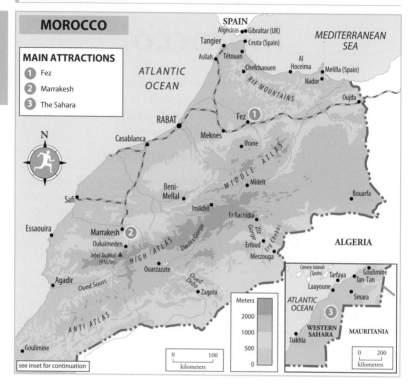

MOROCCO

MAIN ATTRACTIONS
1. Fez
2. Marrakesh
3. The Sahara

SPAIN
Algeciras
Gibraltar (UK)
Tangier
Ceuta (Spain)
MEDITERRANEAN SEA
Asilah
Tétouan
Al Hoceima
Melilla (Spain)
ATLANTIC OCEAN
Chefchaouen
Nador
RIF MOUNTAINS
Oujda
RABAT
Fez ①
Casablanca
Meknes
Ifrane
MIDDLE ATLAS
Midelt
Bouarfa
Beni-Mellal
Safi
Imilchil
Er Rachidia
Essaouira
Marrakesh ②
Ziz Gorge
Erg Chebbi
ALGERIA
Oukaïmeden
HIGH ATLAS
Dadès Gorge
Erfoud
Merzouga
Jebel Toubkal (4167m)
Ouarzazate
Oued Drâa
Agadir
Oued Souss
Zagora
Canary Islands (Spain)
Tarfaya
Goulimine
Tan-Tan
Laayoune
Smara
ATLANTIC OCEAN
ANTI ATLAS
Meters
2000
1000
500
0
WESTERN SAHARA ③
Dakhla
MAURITANIA
Goulimine
see inset for continuation
0 100 kilometers
0 200 kilometers

- **Walk through the Blue Streets of Chefchaouen** This town's charming Medina can feel more like a Smurf village; the streets and most of the buildings are painted sky blue. Sip mint tea and gaze at the buildings blending in with the sky and mountains.

Food and drink

The main dish is usually a *tajine* (casserole); classic *tajines* include chicken with lemon and olives, and lamb with prunes and almonds. The most famous Moroccan dish is couscous, a huge bowl of steamed semolina piled with vegetables, mutton, chicken or fish. A budget meal won't cost more than €8–15, and a bed for the night can be found for €18–25. Restaurants outside of tourist areas close for lunch during Ramadan.

Transport

Most budget travelers either enter the north by ferry and take a train south (from the new railway station in Tangier) or fly a budget carrier directly to Marrakesh. InterRail passes valid in Spain will get you discounts on ferry crossings to Morocco. Buses are often overcrowded and not nearly as popular among travelers as trains. For shorter distances travelers often use *grands taxis* (shared) or private taxis, typically an air-conditioned 4WD vehicle, instead.

By train

The trains in Morocco are among the best in Africa, but beside the new high-speed line between Tangier and Casablanca, that's not saying much. There are about seven departures per day from Tangier to Marrakesh (9hr) and five to Fez (5hr).

Events

● **Erfoud Date Festival** No, it's not a matchmaking event. It's a celebration of the harvest of everybody's favorite sticky fruit – a staple of North African agriculture since biblical times. Even if you're not a diehard fan, the stark beauty of this desert town and its surroundings will floor you. Three days sometime between late Sept and early Nov.

● **Aïd el Fitr** The breaking of the Ramadan fast means up to four days of eating, drinking, thanksgiving and rejoicing for Muslims and is celebrated all across Morocco. For the full experience, take part in the month-long fast first. Just keep in mind that this is fundamentally a religious festival, so keep your merriment respectful. Held any time between July and October.

● **Festival des Musiques Sacrées du Monde, Fez** Since launching in 1994, the World Festival of Sacred Music has drawn big acts from around the world to the city of Fez – it now lays a strong claim to be the country's most interesting and inspiring cultural festival. Late May; ⓦfesfestival.com

Morocco online

Morocco info ⓦvisitmorocco.com
Rail ⓦoncf.ma
Bus ⓦctm.ma

The Netherlands

Capital Amsterdam

Population 16,933,000

Languages Dutch (also Frisian)

Currency Euro (€)

Minimum daily budget €40

When to go Mid-March to mid-May, when the tulips and daffodils are in bloom and when you'll get the best views of the country, while missing the crowds

When not to go Late October and November, when there's freezing rain, and December–February, unless you're happy to ice-skate your way around the country

The Netherlands

The preconceived images of windmills, wooden clogs and tulips have given way in recent decades to sex, drugs and tulips. Sure, you can buy small amounts of marijuana in coffee shops. And yes, prostitution is legal. But it's a shame to visit and leave without learning more about the Netherlands than this.

The country is one of Europe's most developed and densely populated, yet the Dutch maintain a charming balance between the fun-loving attitude found along the Mediterranean and the more reserved and regulated philosophy of the Scandinavian countries. Among the many misconceptions is the country's name. It's often called Holland – even by the tourist board, who believe this is an easier name for foreign visitors to remember – but this is technically incorrect. Holland is one of the most populated regions, and the one where many of this once-great colonial power's sailors came from, but "the Netherlands" is the official name.

Nearly half of this nation is below sea level, and much of it has been physically reclaimed from the sea. The part that does rise above the watermark looks, at least on a topographical profile map, like the chart of a patient who just flatlined. Which is why the country is so popularly navigated by bike. Or by canal, on the barges in the summer or by ice skates in the winter (it's no accident the Dutch bring home Olympic speed-skating medals by the crate). The capital, Amsterdam, is centrally located and rarely missed by those trying to conquer Europe in a summer. You may be lured in by the famous vices and a reputation for budget travel, but you'll often find this visually stunning city serves only as a gateway to a very accessible country largely overlooked by most travelers.

Main attractions

❶ Van Gogh Museum, Amsterdam
The drawings, notebooks and letters of this one-eared Dutch Master come with a chronologically displayed collection of his paintings. Famous works such as *The Potato Eaters* and the *Sunflowers* series and the tortured *Wheatfield with Crows* can all be found here. ⓦvangoghmuseum.nl

❷ Anne Frank House, Amsterdam In July 1942, Otto and Edith Frank and their daughters, Margo and Anne, went into hiding in this building on Prinsengracht in Amsterdam. Along with a few others, they hid for two years before they were betrayed and deported to Auschwitz. Both sisters died just weeks before their concentration camp was liberated, but Anne's diary survived, and has since been published in more than sixty languages. The house is now a popular museum (1.2 million visitors per year by recent count – make sure you book online in advance to avoid the lengthy queues). ⓦannefrank.nl

AVERAGE DAILY TEMPERATURES AND MONTHLY RAINFALL

	Jan	Feb	Mar	Apr	May	June	July	Aug	Sept	Oct	Nov	Dec
Amsterdam												
max °C	8	6	8	12	17	19	21	21	18	14	9	7
min °C	5	0	3	4	8	12	13	13	11	8	4	3
rainfall mm	78	45	94	37	51	62	73	61	81	106	76	69

❸ **Tulips, Keukenhof Gardens** It will take some time to tiptoe through them all, but you can rent a bicycle and pedal through fields of them extending to the horizon. Or you can pay to enter the tourist-friendly Keukenhof Gardens, where they've been impressively arranged in every conceivable manner. The tulips are in bloom from mid-March to mid-May. ⓦ keukenhof.nl

❹ **Amsterdam's Red Light District** Started as a place to "comfort" the returning sailors after long voyages, the district is now mostly a strange sight: bored women in ornate lingerie beckoning passers-by (often tourist families with grandmothers in tow) to come a little closer to their door-sized windows. Innocently snap a picture and you'll likely find your camera tossed in the canal by a human tank in a leather jacket. For all its famed erotica, this area is one of the least arousing places you'll stumble across.

Also recommended

● **Sample some cheese** Cheese is no laughing matter in the Netherlands, where

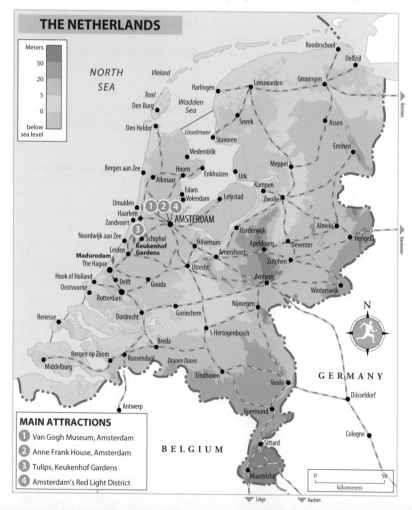

THE NETHERLANDS

Meters
50
20
5
0
below sea level

NORTH SEA

Vlieland
Texel
Den Burg
Den Helder
Wadden Sea
IJsselmeer
Harlingen
Leeuwarden
Groningen
Roodeschool
Delfzijl
Sneek
Assen
Emmen
Medemblik
Meppel
Bergen aan Zee
Hoorn
Enkhuizen
Urk
Kampen
Alkmaar
Edam
Volendam
Lelystad
Zwolle
IJmuiden
Haarlem
Zandvoort
AMSTERDAM
Harderwijk
Almelo
Noordwijk aan Zee
Schiphol
Keukenhof Gardens
Hilversum
Apeldoorn
Deventer
Hengelo
Leiden
Madurodam
The Hague
Amersfoort
Zutphen
Hook of Holland
Oostvoorne
Delft
Gouda
Utrecht
Arnhem
Winterswijk
Rotterdam
Renesse
Dordrecht
Gorinchem
Nijmegen
Breda
's Hertogenbosch
Bergen op Zoom
Roosendaal
Drunen Dunes
Middelburg
Eindhoven
Venlo
Antwerp
Roermond
Düsseldorf
Cologne
Sittard
BELGIUM
GERMANY
Maastricht
Bremen
Hannover

N

0   50
kilometers

MAIN ATTRACTIONS
❶ Van Gogh Museum, Amsterdam
❷ Anne Frank House, Amsterdam
❸ Tulips, Keukenhof Gardens
❹ Amsterdam's Red Light District

Liège   Aachen

it's been made for over 1600 years and can still be found in round chunks the size of wagon wheels; Gouda, Edam and Leiden are the best-known varieties. At a traditional cheese market, like the one in Alkmaar (April–Sept Fri 10am–12.30pm), which has been held here since the 1300s, you can see porters in white uniforms carrying sleds of heavy cheese. Ⓦ kaasmarkt.nl

● **Go kite-skating** With exceptional winds and long stretches of firm beach, kite-skating (racing along the beach on a special skateboard with a powerful kite) is perfect for this environment. In IJmuiden, Renesse, Oostvoorne and the Drunen Dunes area, you'll find the best conditions to try this unique sport.

● **In-line skate along the coast** The Netherlands is considered one of the best in-line skating countries in the world. Strap on a daypack and go. Routes have been mapped out to take you along the most beautiful spots on the coast, past dunes, dikes and even along sections of the famed "Eleven-City Skating Tour."

● **Tour the Heineken brewery** The old Heineken brewery, just a stone's throw from the Van Gogh Museum in Amsterdam, may not be churning out beer any more but it's still serving it, at least to the hordes of tourists who come to see the old vats and stables. Three beers are included on this walk-through infomercial, as well as a souvenir glass. See Ⓦ heinekenexperience.com.

● **Walk the mud flats** The Wadden Sea is the largest continuous nature reserve in Europe and, when the tide is low, it's possible to walk the uncovered mud flats. These are actually sandbanks crisscrossed by channels, leaving a soft footing that makes for a low-impact but strenuous hike.

● **Cycle across the Netherlands** You can easily rent a bike and find your way around Amsterdam, but there's really no reason to stop there. Dedicated signed trails lead you from town to town. You don't need a dual-suspension mountain bike, either. A simple

three-speeder should do the trick.

● **See the tiny version of The Netherlands** Madurodam is a miniature Dutch city (scaled at 1:25) located just outside The Hague. Most of the buildings are between waist and head height. As a child, the former queen, Beatrix, was appointed mayor of the tiny uninhabited town, but that duty now belongs to a local youth council.

Food and drink

The Dutch aren't famous for their food and, even though you can certainly find excellent top-tier restaurants, this may not be the best place for a big splurge. Fast-food street snacks, especially around the Red Light District in Amsterdam and other nightspots, offer filling cheap eats. There's plenty of Indonesian culinary influence (a former colony), and the noodle dishes are excellent and a good way to keep your batteries charged. If you eat at hostels, you can find a good meal for €10–15, but you should be able to do better than that out on the town or at a supermarket.

Transport

There aren't many places in this country you can't reach by rail, whether it's on the quiet city trams that catch wandering tourists off guard or the high-speed rail links to Brussels and Paris. Dutch Railway has reasonable fares and frequent and modern trains that welcome Eurail and other pass-holders.

For inner-city trams, buses and metro, get yourself an OV-chipkaart (Ⓦ ov-chipkaart.nl) and preload it with cash. Get the reloadable kind if you're staying more than a day and the disposable kind for single use or short stays. There is also a 24-hour ticket. The other way to go is the I Amsterdam City Card (Ⓦ iamsterdam.com/en/i-am/i-amsterdam-city-card), which gives you unlimited transport and free entry to the top museums. It can be bought at tourist offices and comes in three flavors: 24 hours, 48 hours and 72 hours. For information on transport around Amsterdam, go to ⓦgvb.nl.

By train
● **Eurail Benelux Pass** (also valid in Luxembourg and Belgium). Three, four, five or eight days of travel in one month.
● **Eurail Benelux-Germany Pass** (also valid in Germany). Choose between four, five, six, eight and ten days of travel in two months.
● **Eurail Benelux-France Pass** (also valid in France). Choose between four, five, six, eight and ten days of travel in two months.
● **InterRail Benelux Pass** Three, four, six or eight days of travel in one month.

For tips and tricks on maximizing your rail pass, see "Costs and savings" (p.63).

By bus
Busabout (see p.44) only serves Amsterdam, connecting it with Bruges in Belgium and Berlin in Germany. For internal bus prices, call the contact at ⓦconnexxion .nl (the website is Dutch-only). For buses to other countries, see ⓦeurolines.nl.

Events

● **King's Day, Amsterdam** Much-loved Queen Beatrix may have abdicated in 2013 after 64 years on the throne but up to a million people still descend on Amsterdam for this annual street party, now held in honor of her son, Willem-Alexander. On this day, all street trade is unregulated so there's a citywide (and nationwide) rummage sale to the delight of secondhand shoppers. Many are out for more laughs than profit. At night the party continues in the clubs. April 27.
● **International Nijmegen Four-Day Marches** The four-day, 50km-a-day walking marathon (running is not allowed) is centered on the city of Nijmegen (pronounced nigh-may-gen) and is one of the most grueling physical challenges in Europe. (There are still Dutch octogenarians who do it every year in wooden clogs. And they will pass you!) Or just stay downtown and party as seemingly half of the country descends on the city to cheer the walkers on. Third Tuesday of July; ⓦ4daagse.nl
● **Amsterdam Pride Parade** The Amsterdam Pride Parade isn't just one of the biggest gay carnivals in the world, it's also the only one with floats that actually float. The spectacular show moves down Amsterdam's main canals with costumed dancers and probably a few things you (or the other 300,000 visitors) never thought you'd see. Find a spot on a bridge for the best views. Aug; ⓦamsterdamgaypride.nl

The Netherlands online

Netherlands info ⓦholland.com
Rail ⓦns.nl
Bus ⓦconnexxion.nl
Amsterdam info ⓦiamsterdam.com

HIKER IN THE LOFOTEN ISLANDS

Norway

Capital Oslo

Population 5,194,000

Languages Norwegian

Currency Norwegian krone (kr)

Minimum daily budget €68

When to go January–April for some of the world's best cross-country skiing; June–September for hiking, biking and sightseeing

When not to go November and December, when it's dark and freezing cold. January and February aren't much better, but at least winter activities are under way by then

Norway

Norway offers the most spectacular landscape in Europe and is a country best enjoyed outdoors. The weather isn't always that accommodating, but that doesn't stop the Norwegians. "There's no such thing as bad weather, only bad clothing," goes the popular saying. And if you don't let the occasional rain shower (or freezing rain shower, or blizzard) get in your way, Norway is like a giant playground for the outdoor enthusiast.

Norway's oil reserves have made it one of the richest countries in Europe. The oil has also made Norwegians less worried about trade, which is one of the reasons they have stayed out of the EU. Besides, as Sweden voted to enter the EU, they had a slight obligation to do the opposite.

The Norwegians have been explorers since the Viking ages. Thor Heyerdahl was the twentieth-century hero of the high seas, conquering them on a boat that looked to the untrained eye like a big bale of hay. Many of today's heroes, however, are cross-country skiers and biathlon competitors – if you see a crowd of burly men hovering around a bar TV in the winter, chances are they're watching one of these two events.

For the traveler, Norway is one of the most expensive countries in Europe and, with the exception of seafood, has one of the least appealing cuisines. A few days in the fjords, however, and this is easily forgotten – in part because of the natural beauty and in part because, if you're camping, you're actually spending less than you would staying in hostels in Spain.

Main attractions

❶ **Kon-Tiki Museum, Oslo** In 1947, Thor Heyerdahl crossed the Pacific on a balsa-wood raft to prove that the first Polynesian settlers could have sailed from pre-Inca Peru. This adventure – and the rest of his research – are celebrated in this excellent museum. Ⓦkon-tiki.no

❷ **National Gallery, Oslo** Norway's largest public collection of art is most notably the home of Edvard Munch's masterpiece, *The Scream* (which gained additional attention when it was stolen in 1994, then recovered), but also hosts paintings by Cézanne and Manet. Ⓦnasjonalmuseet.no

❸ **"Norway in a Nutshell" tour** This tour of Sognefjord by train, boat and bus is an extremely popular (and expensive) day-trip using either Oslo or Bergen as a starting/finishing point. As one Norwegian called it, "Fjords for people who can't be bothered to do them." Ⓦfjordtours.com

❹ **Coastal steamer** In 1893, the Vesteraalens Dampskibsselskab steamship company opened an express route between

AVERAGE DAILY TEMPERATURES AND MONTHLY RAINFALL

	Jan	Feb	Mar	Apr	May	June	July	Aug	Sept	Oct	Nov	Dec
Oslo												
max °C	-1	-2	4	9	17	20	22	21	16	9	4	0
min °C	-7	-7	-3	1	7	11	13	12	7	3	-2	-6
rainfall mm	49	36	47	41	53	65	81	89	90	84	73	55

NORWAY

MAIN ATTRACTIONS

1 Kon-Tiki Museum, Oslo
2 National Gallery, Oslo
3 "Norway in a Nutshell" tour
4 Coastal steamer

·········· The Hurtigruten route

Nordkapp
Hammerfest Honningsvåg
Kirkenes
Alta
Tromsø
RUSSIA
Lofoten Narvik
Islands
Svolvær
Å
Bodø
Arctic Circle Fauske
Mo-i-Rana Luleå
NORWEGIAN FINLAND
SEA
SWEDEN
Gulf of Bothnia
Kiruna
Östersund
Meters
2000
1000
400
0
Trondheim
Ålesund Åndalsnes
Dombås
Stryn
Balestrand Mundal
Sognefjord Trysilelva
Voss Flåm Lillehammer River
Bergen Finse
OSLO
Sandefjord STOCKHOLM
Stavanger Larvik BALTIC ESTONIA
Kristiansand SEA
Gothenberg

0   250
kilometers

Trondheim and Hammerfest along the same rocky and treacherous route that was rejected by the larger shipping companies. Today, they carry passengers as well, and the Hurtigruten "rapid route" ferry is now called – at least in all of the tourist propaganda – "the world's most beautiful voyage." Ⓦ hurtigruten.com

Also recommended

● **See the northern lights** You don't need to head up to Hammerfest as Bill Bryson did in his book *Neither Here Nor There*; this celestial show can be viewed across the country (Feb, March and Oct are ideal, the rest of winter is also good). There's no magic winter date to see the psychedelic display, but if you leave the big cities and find some large stretch of flat terrain

for a wide-open view (or take a quick drive out of town on a clear night), and give yourself at least a few days, chances are you won't miss it.

● **Hut-to-hut hiking through the fjords** Norwegians don't quite understand all of the tourists who want to see the fjords from the deck of a cruise ship. To them, the fjords are for hiking, and those who live near mountains are typically walking in them daily. To take advantage of this active approach, check out Norway's extensive hut-to-hut trail system. The cabins have beds, food, blankets and pillows – you just bring sheets and some good waterproof hiking gear. Ⓦ dnt.no

● **Kayak the fjords** A great way to view the fjords is from a sea kayak. The waters are calm, it's hard to get lost, there are small towns along the way with guest rooms and food, and the kayaks can be rented all across Norway.

- **Raft the mountain rivers** In addition to the spectacular scenery, Norway boasts excellent rafting. This can be done in several spots, including the Trysilelva River in Hedmark, and Dagali River in Voss.

- **Fish for salmon in a fjord** You can go fishing just about everywhere, but the best spots require a guide (or a good tip) and, more importantly, a license, which you can pick up around the country. Many local deep-sea angling associations and tourist information offices organize fishing trips. Typically, the best time for salmon fishing is from mid-July to mid-August, but this can vary a lot from region to region. Ⓦ inatur.no

Food and drink

Norwegian food can be excellent: fish is plentiful, while reindeer steak and elk can be sampled in the north. However, eating well on a tight budget can be difficult. Alcohol is prohibitively expensive and, if you're trying to save money, this is a decent place to cut back on consumption. Even *McDonald's* and the average gas-station hot dog are shockingly pricey, so it's a case of bulk cooking with items at the supermarket if you want to squeak by on a budget. A decent meal isn't going to cost less than €18.

Transport

Norway has relatively few train lines compared to the rest of Europe. A number of them – Oslo to Bergen, Oslo to the airport and Oslo to Lillehammer – are modern and quick. The rest can be painfully slow. This can also be said for the roads – often single lanes with minimal passing opportunities and low speed limits – and the buses that travel along them. The railways have some excellent scenic routes, but the bus network is more extensive and there are plenty of picturesque passages to be viewed from the road. All transport is extremely pricey, so this is the place to use a rail or bus pass.

By train

- **Eurail Norway Pass** Any three, four, five or eight days in one month.

- **Eurail Scandinavia Pass** (also valid in Denmark, Finland and Sweden). Any two, five, six, eight or ten days of travel in two months.

For tips on maximizing your rail pass, see "Costs and savings" (p.63).

By bus

Busabout doesn't operate in Norway. For buses to other countries, see Ⓦ eurolines.no.

Events

- **Constitution Day** On May 17, 1814, Norway declared independence from Denmark and established its own constitutional government. To celebrate this day, many Norwegians dress up in traditional costume of colorful handmade *bunad* (decorated according to their region) to march down the street of their local town. Some of the more sports-oriented take to the high-elevation glacial tracks on skis. May 17.

- **Pagan bonfires** On the longest day of the year, the sun doesn't set in many parts of the country. Even in the south, it barely dips below the horizon. To celebrate the summer solstice – though named for Sankt Hans (the feast day of St John the Baptist), really it's ancient pagan ritual – huge bonfires are lit all over Norway. 23 June.

- **The Bislett Games, Oslo** One of the biggest track and field meets of the year takes place in this classic old stadium in the center of Oslo. The track is notoriously fast, so many top athletes time their peak condition with this event to go after world records. June or July; Ⓦ oslo.diamondleague.com

Norway online

Norway info Ⓦ visitnorway.com
Rail Ⓦ nsb.no
Bus Ⓦ nor-way.no
Oslo info Ⓦ visitoslo.com

Poland

Capital Warsaw

Population 38,494,000

Language Polish

Currency Złoty (zł)

Minimum daily budget €28

When to go Mid-May to June and September to mid-October, when the weather's decent and you'll miss the (relative) crowds

When not to go July and August, when the walking trails, lakes and beaches get swamped with people, and November–February, when it's cold and dark, and many hostels are closed

Poland

Poland is a nation steeped in tradition and history, although the past twenty years have witnessed such dizzying economic development that the country is starting to feel more and more like western Europe. Still, beneath the gleaming surface lies a culture firmly rooted in eastern European hospitality and community values, and fascinating reminders of the turbulent past are everywhere.

Poland offers a slightly more rugged experience than countries in western Europe, but it's far easier on the wallet. You can find the luxury living, but there's also all the sports and outdoor pursuits you're likely to ever want, from horseback riding to sailing or scuba diving; the challenge is just carving out enough time to do them. There are beaches on the Baltic, craggy mountains in the south, and lakes and green rolling hills; there's also a long tradition of Slavic hospitality, with feast-like meals for even casual visitors. As the Polish saying goes: "A guest in the house is God in the house." The trick, of course, is getting invited through the front door.

Main attractions

1 Kraków This southern city emerged from World War II relatively unscathed, a treasure-trove that ranks with Prague and Vienna as one of the architectural gems of central Europe. The church spires and old, cobbled square provide the ideal backdrop for lounging in cafés and people-watching; it may look like a history lesson, but the city is very much alive and buzzing. Ⓦ krakow.pl

2 Oświęcim (Auschwitz) Most know this industrial town 60km west of Kraków by its German name: Auschwitz. The largest of the concentration camps, much of it was destroyed as the Nazis retreated in 1945, but there's still plenty to get a sense of the magnitude of this death factory. It's estimated that around 1.3 million people were killed here (and at the nearby linked camp Birkenau) during the Holocaust. It's hard to forget a trip to this haunting memorial. Ⓦ auschwitz.org

3 Royal Castle, Warsaw Like much of Warsaw, the Royal Castle was rebuilt (1971–77), having lain in ruins since the war. The Baroque lines seen at a distance give way to Gothic traits once inside – many of the original tapestries, paintings, even the furniture have been crafted into place in each room. Ⓦ zamek-krolewski.pl

Also recommended

● **Pay homage to Copernicus** Nicolaus Copernicus, the famous astronomer who "stopped the sun and moved the earth," was born in Toruń. The town itself, with soaring Gothic buildings, is worth a visit anyway, but Toruń's planetarium packs extra meaning to

AVERAGE DAILY TEMPERATURES AND MONTHLY RAINFALL

	Jan	Feb	Mar	Apr	May	June	July	Aug	Sept	Oct	Nov	Dec
Warsaw												
max °C	1	1	7	12	18	21	23	23	18	12	6	2
min °C	-4	-4	0	3	8	11	13	12	8	4	1	-6
rainfall mm	28	25	30	38	51	66	76	71	46	41	38	30

MAIN ATTRACTIONS
1 Kraków
2 Oświęcim (Auschwitz)
3 Royal Castle, Warsaw

POLAND

the journey. Ⓦ visittorun.pl

● **Hike the Tatras** Poland's outdoor life is often overlooked by visitors, but head into the Tatra mountains and you'll get a taste of the Poland the locals enjoy. The Pieniny, Bieszczady and Karkonosze mountains will all do as well.

● **Sail across the Mazurian lakes** Few would put "Poland" and "sailing" in the same sentence, but the Mazurian lakes are packed with hundreds of boats in summer. In winter, the sailing continues on ice, with championships held in the Mazurian region.

● **Head underground** Caving is common near Kraków and in the Tatra mountains. There are literally thousands of caverns to choose from, but just a handful are ready for commercial visitors without experience. The

most famous are the Bear's Cave near Kłodzko and the Paradise Cave near Kielce.

● **Salt of the earth** Fifteen kilometers outside of Kraków are the salt mines at Wieliczka. Since medieval times, creative miners with time on their hands have carved incredibly elaborate (mostly religious) sculptures from the salt. There's even a seventeenth-century chapel with decorations made out of the stuff. It's been listed by UNESCO World Heritage since 1978. See Ⓦ kopalnia.pl.

● **Former Jewish ghetto** Before World War II, Warsaw had one of Europe's most thriving Jewish communities. Most lived in the areas of Mirów and Muranów, which the Nazis turned into the Warsaw Ghetto in 1940. It was flattened after the 1943 Ghetto Uprising, but there are a few remnants of the Ghetto to visit, most of them clustered together in one area.

Food and drink

The best place to fill up is a "milk bar," which is open from early morning until 6/7pm and offers traditional Polish meals for prices well under the syllable count on the items you're ordering. Soups, particularly *barszcz* (beetroot broth) and *żurek* (a sour soup of fermented rye), are an integral part of the meal, or even a meal unto themselves. The main dishes often don't look *haute cuisine* (there's only so much you can do with stewed cabbage), but you'll find several that agree with your palate and even more that are at least wallet-friendly. A decent restaurant meal will cost about €8, and a good one can be had for €12.

Transport

Trains are moderately efficient (provided you're not stuck on a "normal service" train that stops at every third mound of dirt) and well priced. See Ⓦpolrail.com for info on passes. In rural areas, the bus is often faster than the train. The national bus carrier, PKS, specializes in cramped and slow service. Polski Bus (Ⓦpolskibus.com), a private company, is better, but most useful out of Warsaw.

In Warsaw, the 24-hour transport ticket allows unlimited travel on buses and metro. Just remember to validate it when you make your first trip (Ⓦztm.waw.pl). The Warsaw Card (Ⓦwarsawcard.com) covers transport for 24, 48 or 72 hours and also gets you into all the big museums and a bunch of the small ones, either free or at a discount. Kraków is very accessible on foot, but if you're hitting loads of museums and want to save energy on travelling between them, try the two- or three-day Kraków Tourist Card (Ⓦkrakowcard .com), which entitles the holder to free travel on city buses and trams, and free entry to more than forty museums and attractions. It

even includes airport transport on a local bus, and transport to the Wieliczka salt mine.

By train
- **Eurail Poland Pass** Any three, four, five or eight days in one month.
- **Eurail Germany-Poland Pass** Any four, five, six, eight or ten days in two months.
- **InterRail Poland Pass** Any three, four, six or eight days in one month.

For tips and tricks on maximizing your rail pass, see "Costs and savings" (p.63).

By bus
Busabout doesn't operate in Poland. For internal bus prices, see Ⓦpks.poznan.pl (Polish only). For buses to other countries, see Ⓦeurolines.pl.

Events

- **Music in Old Kraków Festival**
Established by the early-music ensemble Capella Cracoviensis in the 1970s, this annual event continues to grow. It's now a seventeen-day happening with concerts filling venues across the city. Aug; Ⓦkrakow.pl
- **Wratislavia Cantans, Wrocław** Every year, 2000 performers and 25,000 spectators flood into the thousand-year-old city of Wrocław for a cultural jamboree: classical concerts, ballet performances, films and art exhibitions. Sept; Ⓦwratislavia.art.pl
- **Warsaw Autumn Festival** Organizers pack twenty concerts into nine days in this premier event, which was started in 1956. The audience can expect to hear Schönberg and Webern, as well as avant-garde, experimental performances. Sept; Ⓦwarszawska-jesien.art.pl

Poland online

Poland info Ⓦpoland.travel
Rail Ⓦrozklad-pkp.pl
Bus Ⓦpks.poznan.pl
Warsaw info Ⓦwarsawtour.pl
Kraków info Ⓦkrakow.pl

Portugal

Capital Lisbon

Population 10,311,000

Languages Portuguese

Currency Euro (€)

Minimum daily budget €30

When to go March–October for the south,
May–September for Lisbon and the north

When not to go November– February, when
the weather's chilly, even in the Algarve.
June–August is best avoided if you're not partial
to crowds

Portugal

Neatly tucked away on the "other" side of Spain, this centuries-long gateway to Africa and the Americas is often missed by travelers who, heading south into the Iberian peninsula, tend to get caught up in Spain's attractions and run out of time. Those who do make it typically make a pit stop in Lisbon before beelining it to the Algarve for a glimpse of the poster-pin-up beaches, leaving the many small-town and countryside gems largely undiscovered.

The Portuguese take life slowly (unless behind the wheel of a car) and savor the little things: folk festivals, fish, fruit, flowers and food drenched in olive oil. The ethos of the nation is very much tied to the sea: Vasco da Gama is more than a historical seafarer in Portugal; he embodies the spirit of the country.

The nation is cut tidily in half by the River Tagus. To the south, where the Moors and Romans once had strongholds, you'll find darker-skinned people and a more Mediterranean lifestyle. To the north, you'll find a more Celtic and Germanic sort.

Main attractions

❶ **Lagos** The spectacular combination of cliffs and white beaches in Lagos sells plenty of postcards and even more beer; the beach scene in this Algarve town is a party stop on the travel circuit, though it's steadily pricing itself out of most people's range. Renting a bike, moped or even a horse will make beach exploration easier.

❷ **Évora** This walled town has seemingly been dropped into a field of vineyards, olive trees and flowers. The cathedral and Roman temple provide popular focal points, but the ossuary chapel, made from thousands of human skulls and bones, is too bizarre to miss.

❸ **The Rossio, Lisbon** The actual name of this plaza is Praça D. Pedro IV, but if you want to sound like a local (or just want to be able to pronounce it), go with "Rossio." Busy at almost all hours of the day and night and housing some old-style cafés and a grand theater, the square still acts as the heart of Lisbon.

❹ **The ruins of St George's Castle, Lisbon** Used to defeat the Moorish invaders, St George's offers the classic panoramic overlook of Lisbon, with a great view of Santuario do Cristo Rei, the 34m replica of Rio de Janeiro's *Christ the Redeemer* statue, and the remains of a cathedral destroyed in the 1755 earthquake.

Also recommended

● **Hike Madeira** The volcanic island of Madeira, a 90-minute flight from Lisbon,

AVERAGE DAILY TEMPERATURES AND MONTHLY RAINFALL												
	Jan	Feb	Mar	Apr	May	June	July	Aug	Sept	Oct	Nov	Dec
Lisbon												
max °C	14	15	17	18	21	25	28	28	27	21	17	14
min °C	7	8	9	11	12	15	17	18	17	14	11	9
rainfall mm	110	111	69	64	39	21	5	6	26	80	114	108

PORTUGAL

MAIN ATTRACTIONS

1 Lagos

2 Évora

3 The Rossio, Lisbon

4 The ruins of St George's Castle, Lisbon

0 _____ 100
kilometers

ATLANTIC OCEAN

Tuy & Vigo

Viana do Castelo
Braga
Barcelos
Guimarães
Amarante
Vila Real
Mirandela
Bragança
Porto
Tua
Pocinho
Salamanca
Aveiro
Viseu
Guarda
Figueira da Foz
Coimbra
Marinha Grande
Pombal
Leiria
Fátima
São Pedro de Muel
Batalha
Tomar
Peniche
Alcobaça
Óbidos
Marvão-Beira
Castelo de Vide
Marvão
Mafra
Vila Franca de Xira
Sintra
LISBON
Barreiro
Setúbal
Alcácer do Sal
Casa Branca
Évora
Praia de Melides
Santiago do Cacem
Sines
Porto Côvo
Vila Nova de Milfontes
Odemira
Zambujeira do Mar
Portimão
Lagos
Tunes
Tavira
Sagres
Silves
Faro
Olhão
Vila Real de Santo António
Huelva
Sevilla

SPAIN

Madrid

Meters
1000
500
200
0

MADEIRA

ATLANTIC OCEAN

Porto Moniz
Ilhéu Mole
Ponta Delgada
Calheta
Pico Ruivo (1862m)
Ribeira Frio
Santa Cruz
Ilhéu da Cevada
Ponta do Sol
FUNCHAL

ATLANTIC OCEAN

0 ___ 10
kilometers

- - - - - - Bus link

Madeira (see inset)

is a little over 50km wide, but it has been providing shelter to transatlantic travelers since 1420. Mountain trails make for azure panoramas, while wildflowers and lush landscape take care of the rest.

- **Test some port** With its low lighting, squidgy sofas and soft music, the Institute of Port Wine in Lisbon (a short tram ride uphill from Praça dos Restauradores) is a great place to while away the hours with friends. A glass of the national snifter costs anywhere between €1 and €25 and goes best with Serra da Estrela – a viscous cheese scooped up with crackers. Better yet, tour the wineries

and get a shot for free at the end of the historic walkabout. Ⓦivdp.pt

- **Eat a meal to the sound of Fado** Fado is the traditional music of Portugal, and in a Fado-themed restaurant, classic Portuguese food is served while guitar players and singers perform their lament. For a list of Fado restaurants in Lisbon, see Ⓦvisitlisboa.com.

- **Surf the Atlantic coast** Portugal's waves aren't in the same league as Hawaii's, but there are enough breakers around the country to keep most beginner and intermediate surfers happy. Peniche, just outside of Lisbon, is one of the top spots.

Surfing's also popular in Lagos and Sagres on the Algarve, and Sines, just between Lisbon and the Algarve.

● **See fish get tanked** When Lisbon hosted the World Expo in 1998, the Oceanário de Lisboa served as a centerpiece. Located, appropriately enough, right next to the harbor, this modern aquarium offers environmental soundscapes and interactive media, in addition to a vibrant array of sea life. Ⓦ oceanario.pt

● **Wander in Alfama** Alfama is the oldest district in Lisbon – one that survived the 1775 earthquake. The streets are as confusing as they are historic, so it's ideal for getting lost and then wandering into one of the quaint bars in the area.

Food and drink

Portuguese food is cheap and served in plentiful portions. You'll find some of Europe's best seafood here, and it's decently priced. Add to this some *vinho verde* (green wine – so-called because it should be consumed before the wine has aged) and you've got one of the best meals you'll find on your trip for under €20.

Transport

Trains are reasonably priced, so any journey less than two hours is not going to be worth using a day of your Eurail pass. Buses cover many of the same routes as trains, in less time, and for competitive prices. Since many also leave from cities' central train stations, it's easy to compare if you're buying tickets individually. If you're thinking of renting a car or scooter, be warned: Portugal has the highest traffic fatality rates in western Europe.

Look into a Lisboa Card (Ⓦ askmelisboa .com) if you're just in the capital for a day or two and are trying to hit every attraction. They come in 24-hour, 48-hour and 72-hour versions and includes free transport (bus, metro, tram, cable car and rail to the beautiful hilltop town of Sintra) and up to fifty percent off entry to museums and monuments.

By train

● **Portugal Pass** Any three, four, five or eight days of travel in one month.

● **Eurail Portugal-Spain Pass** Four, five, six, eight or ten days of travel in two months.

For tips and tricks on maximizing your rail pass, see "Costs and savings" (p.63).

By bus

Busabout doesn't operate in Portugal. For internal bus prices, see Ⓦ rede-expressos.pt and Ⓦ eva-bus.com.

Events

● **Funchal Carnival** Consider heading to the island of Madeira to celebrate this pre-Lenten event. The capital, Funchal, is overrun with party-goers, as a parade of floats takes to the streets, and comes alive to the sound of samba troupes. Late Feb.

● **Festa do Colete Encarnado, Vila Franca de Xira** Portugal's answer to the running of the bulls, where the macho and the mad dodge bulls let loose on the streets. During the daily Portuguese-style bullfights, the bull is wrestled, but not killed, which is more impressive and less gruesome than the Spanish version. First Fri of July.

● **A Festa das Cruzes, Barcelos** This flower fight in the northern city of Barcelos has been a recurring event since 1504. It's ostensibly a Catholic celebration of the Miracle of the Cross, but townsfolk and visitors alike take the opportunity to dress up, drink and be merry. Early May.

Portugal online

Portugal info Ⓦ visitportugal.pt
Rail Ⓦ cp.pt
Bus Ⓦ rede-expressos.pt
Lisbon info Ⓦ visitlisboa.com

DETAIL FROM *THE LAST JUDGEMENT*, VORONEȚ MONASTERY

Romania

Capital Bucharest

Population 19,822,000

Languages Romanian

Currency Leu (L)

Minimum daily budget €25

When to go May–June, when the weather's best (crowds aren't much of an issue). September and October have decent weather as well

When not to go July and August, when it's crowded along the Black Sea and at the painted monasteries of southern Bucovina. November–February is normally too cold for sightseeing

Romania

Nowhere in eastern Europe defies preconceptions quite like Romania. It still suffers from a poor image abroad, but don't be put off – this intriguing country, dotted with picturesque towns and rural communities following traditions little changed since the Middle Ages, is easily accessible and a pleasure to explore.

It's no secret that the new money is leaving many in Romania behind on the journey towards development but other nations in the region share a similar path. One of the old-style customs that's still found in abundance, though, is hospitality. Romanians welcome you into their unassuming homes and feed you to bursting capacity. Medieval towns, stately castles and excellent hiking trails await, and for about half the price (and a fraction of the tourists) of western Europe's flagship cities.

Main attractions

❶ **Bran Castle** Also known as "Dracula's Castle," the popular castle actually has no ties to Vlad Tepeş, the medieval prince associated with the vampire extraordinaire. It doesn't look so ominous either, but what did they expect with white walls and Disney-style towers? None of this seems to prevent the tourists from coming, though. Ⓦbran-castle.com

❷ **Sighişoara** This atmospheric medieval town in Transylvania is another destination on the Dracula trail. Vlad Tepeş was born within the citadel's walls, in the "Dracula House," which is now – surprise, surprise! – a bar and restaurant.

❸ **Palace of Parliament, Bucharest** It's the second-largest building in the world (after the Pentagon), but Ceauşescu ploughed over 7000 homes and 26 churches to build it in the 1980s, so there's understandably less pride in this engineering achievement than there otherwise might be. Guided tours need to be booked a day in advance. Ⓦcdep.ro

❹ **Painted monasteries of southern Bucovina** These frescoed monasteries near Suceava in Romania's northeast corner are UNESCO treasures – the Voroneţ church is known as the "Sistine Chapel of the East." Despite their remote location, the sites do get crowded in high season.

Also recommended

● **Go twitching in the Danube Delta** From late spring to mid-autumn, the Danube Delta is home to hundreds of species of bird. Binoculars are a good idea, but you don't need any other equipment. If you'd rather not bird-watch on your own, tour operators will happily guide you to the best spots. With a bit of luck, you might even see a black pelican colony.

● **Go skiing** Romania may not be the first place that comes to mind when you plan a ski trip, but don't rule out this bargain

AVERAGE DAILY TEMPERATURES AND MONTHLY RAINFALL

	Jan	Feb	Mar	Apr	May	June	July	Aug	Sept	Oct	Nov	Dec
Bucharest												
max °C	2	4	10	17	22	26	28	28	24	17	8	3
min °C	-5	-4	1	6	11	14	16	15	11	6	1	-3
rainfall mm	43	38	36	46	66	86	56	56	36	28	46	43

A map of Romania showing main attractions and surrounding countries.

ROMANIA

MAIN ATTRACTIONS
1. Bran Castle
2. Sighişoara
3. Palace of Parliament, Bucharest
4. Painted monasteries of southern Bucovina

vacation. Cross-country skiing, snowboarding and tubing are also possible, with peaks around 3000m. The major ski resorts are Poiana Braşov, Sinaia and Predeal.

● **Track wolves in the Carpathian mountains** The forested slopes of Romania's Carpathian mountains help shelter the gray wolf, and Zărneşti, at the southern tip, makes the best base for setting out on their trail. See ⓦ cntours.ro for details of guided trips.

● **Drive the Transfăgărăşan** BBC's former *Top Gear* presenters called it "The best road in the world." There are 90km of twists and turns through the Carpathian mountains, reaching an altitude of 2034m, with views of Bâlea Lake and Bâlea Waterfall.

Food and drink

Because most Romanians can't afford to eat out, many restaurants cater to

wealthy foreign visitors and up their prices accordingly. Finding a local hangout with local rates may take some looking, especially around Bucharest and the more touristy areas. Outside of these places, you can easily dine for less than €8 and pick up a bottle of Romanian wine for under €3 to wash it down with. However, this is beer country, and it's as cheap as any you'll find in Europe.

Transport

Romania has an impressive railway infrastructure that covers the entire country. Trains are the best way to get around; they're cheap and tend to arrive on time. Local trains are a bargain but stop at every other telephone pole. The Express trains only sound fast, but are inexpensive. The fastest intercity trains cost a bit more. There are several bus companies offering connections between

Romania's main cities, but they typically aren't as cheap or quick as the trains. Several bus companies provide daily services to İstanbul (700km) for under €30.

Prices for Bucharest's trolleybuses and trams are low by any standard, but the city's "express buses" are roughly double the standard fare.

By train

● **Balkans Flexi Pass** (also valid in Bosnia-Herzegovina, Bulgaria, Greece, Macedonia, Montenegro, Serbia and Turkey). Any five, ten or fifteen days in one month.
● **Eurail Romania Pass** Any three, four, five or eight days of travel in one month.
● **Eurail Romania-Hungary Pass** Any four, five, six, eight or ten days in two months.

Because of the low train fares, Eurail and InterRail passes aren't nearly as essential here as they are in other European countries. For tips and tricks on maximizing your rail pass, see "Costs and savings" (p.63).

By bus

Busabout doesn't operate in Romania. For buses to other countries, see Ⓦeurolines.ro.

Events

● **Whit Sunday Székely pilgrimage**
A Franciscan monastery 2km northeast of Miercurea Ciuc, in the eastern Székely Land, hosts the year's biggest traditional folk and religious festival, which dates back to the fifteenth century and is held in thanks for the Székely victory at Marasszentimre. Black-clad pilgrims still assemble in the yard and church to sing hymns and touch the wooden Madonna in the sanctuary. March/April.
● **Medieval Days** For three days in late July, Sighişoara hosts this festival of arts, crafts and music. People dress in traditional costume and stage music and theatrical performances. July; Ⓦsighisoaramedievala.ro
● **Halloween in Transylvania**
What better place to be for Halloween? Celebrations, shows and tours follow in the footsteps of Bram Stoker's infamous character. Oct 31.
● **Pageant of the Juni, Braşov** To commemorate the only day of the year when Romanians could freely enter this Saxon city, the town's youth dress up in costumes – some over 150 years old – and ride through the old quarter on horseback. First Sunday after Orthodox Easter (April/May).
● **Sâmbra Oilor** This festival in Bran celebrates the sheep herds' annual return from the high mountains (hurray!). Sept.

Romania online

Romania info Ⓦromaniatourism.com
Rail Ⓦcfr.ro
Bus Ⓦautogari.ro
Bucharest info Ⓦromaniatourism.com/bucharest.html

Russia

Capital Moscow

Population 144,031,000

Language Russian

Currency Ruble (R)

Minimum daily budget €37

When to go May–June and September–October, when you'll avoid the rain and tourist crowds

When not to go April is slushy, July and August wet (yet popular with tourists), and November–February bitterly cold

Russia

Perhaps one of the strangest things about Russia is its very presence in a European guidebook. How can a land that stretches all the way from the North Korean border up to the Bering Strait be part of Europe? Look closer at a map and you'll see Europe's eastern borders are shaped, in part, by the Ural mountains. Both St Petersburg and Moscow lie on the European side.

Formerly a powerful tsarist empire and a Communist superpower, Russia continues to be a source of fascination for travelers. While access is still made relatively difficult by lingering Soviet-style bureaucracy – visas are obligatory and accommodation usually has to be booked in advance (see box, pp.96–97) – visitors are doubly rewarded by the cultural riches of the country and the sense of accomplishment of having jumped through all the right hoops to get in.

Churchill's famous 1939 description of the Soviet Union still applies to Russia. It is "a riddle wrapped in a mystery inside an enigma." Few on the outside can begin to understand or decipher its cultural complexities. As a traveler, though, you'll get a chance to chip away at Russia's mystifying facade, even if you're just hitting the sights, getting lost in the subway system or trying to buy some chocolate biscuits from a street vendor. The national character reveals itself with enough time and interaction.

Main attractions

❶ **The Kremlin, Moscow** Still the seat of power for Russia, much of this walled-in triangular city of churches, armories and palaces on Borovitsky Hill is open to the public. You can pace the grounds where Khrushchev engaged in the Cold War, Stalin unleashed his raids of terror, and Lenin orchestrated his radical vision of government. Ⓦ kreml.ru

❷ **Hermitage Museum, St Petersburg** The only museum in the world that you might put in the ring against the Louvre, this colossal structure houses particularly impressive collections of Italian Renaissance and French Impressionist paintings, as well as works by Rembrandt, Picasso and Matisse. What started as the private art collection of Peter the Great (and was expanded by Catherine the Great) finally opened its doors to the public in 1917. It would take years to see it all. Ⓦ hermitagemuseum.org

AVERAGE DAILY TEMPERATURES AND MONTHLY RAINFALL

	Jan	Feb	Mar	Apr	May	June	July	Aug	Sept	Oct	Nov	Dec
Moscow												
max °C	-6	-1	1	9	17	21	22	20	14	7	0	-4
min °C	-12	-11	-6	1	7	11	13	11	6	1	-4	-9
rainfall mm	36	28	33	38	51	66	81	71	58	51	43	43
St Petersburg												
max °C	-4	-4	1	8	16	19	21	19	13	7	2	-2
min °C	-9	-9	-4	1	7	11	13	12	7	3	-2	-7
rainfall mm	28	25	25	30	43	56	66	76	61	51	41	36

RUSSIA

Meters
200
100
0

N

MAIN ATTRACTIONS

1 The Kremlin, Moscow

2 Hermitage Museum, St Petersburg

3 Red Square, Moscow

4 Moscow metro

5 The Peter and Paul Fortress, St Petersburg

6 The Church of Our Savior on Spilled Blood, St Petersburg

White Sea

Murmansk

Arkhangel'sk

FINLAND

HELSINKI

Gulf of Finland

Lake Ladoga

St Petersburg 2 5 6

TALLINN

ESTONIA

Novogrod

Yaroslavl'

River Volga

RĪGA

LATVIA

Tver'

LITHUANIA

VILNIUS

BELARUS

MINSK

Smolensk

MOSCOW 1 3 4

Yekaterinburg, Omsk & Vladivostok

Note: This map shows only the western parts of Russia, corresponding to the area covered by this country profile.

0   200
kilometers

Brest   Kiev & Kharkov   Rostov & the Caucasus Mountains   Samara

3 Red Square, Moscow Perhaps the world's most spectacular city center, this enormous cobbled square is big enough to land a Cessna in (which 19-year-old German-born Mathias Rust did in 1987, just before taxiing to a Soviet labor camp for 432 days while his plane doubled in value and got sold to a Japanese collector). It plays host to enormous military parades every Victory Day (May 9), is framed by the GUM department store (which during the Soviet era sold consumer goods at a time when they weren't easily found), St Basil's Cathedral (the one with the multicolored turnip spires that adorn almost every postcard) and the Kremlin. You'll also find the entrance to Lenin's Mausoleum, where the waxy, embalmed body of the former leader rests Snow White-style inside a glass box.

4 Moscow metro Head underground for a real architectural and engineering wonder. After a long ride down the escalator, it's hard to tell if you've entered a museum or a five-star hotel lobby. The last thing it feels like is a subway station. The marble, sculptures and exquisite lighting make it hard to believe – in the case of Moscow, anyway – that it's the busiest system in the world, carrying eight million passengers a day.

5 The Peter and Paul Fortress, St Petersburg Or, if you care to try your hand at Russian, Petropavlovskaya Krepost. This military fortress is as strategic as it is stunning. It was built under Peter the Great in the first half of the eighteenth century and subsequently turned into a bestselling postcard for the Russian tourist bureau. The traditional burial place for Romanov tsars, practically all of them (including Peter the Great and the last one – Nicholas II) and their families are buried here. Outside, the main spire sticks up like a lance ready to do battle with the clouds, and the "irregular hexagon" shape of the fort looks more like a symmetrical snowflake when viewed from above.

❻ **The Church of Our Savior on Spilled Blood, St Petersburg** Emperor Alexander II was assassinated in 1881 in St Petersburg. Without conspiracy theorists or Oliver Stone around, the only thing left to do was build a church to honor his memory. This dazzling onion-domed edifice, completed in 1907, now sits on the very spot and contains – hold on to your paintbrush – 7000 square meters of mosaics. Ⓦeng.cathedral.ru/spasa_na_krovi

Also recommended

● **Skate a Russian river** To make the most of Russia's arctic winter, buy a cheap pair of skates and join the locals for some free frozen fun on the lakes and rivers.

● **Ski the Caucasus** Done the Alps and want something new? Limited skiing can be found in Dombay, in the western Caucasus mountains, and Cheget, close to Mount Elbrus. Heli-skiing is possible, but make sure you don't pay up until the helicopter comes – they're notorious for skipping out with your advance payment.

● **Experience space** If you arrive in Russia loaded with cash and don't mind spending it in a hurry, swing by the Yuri Gagarin Cosmonaut Training Center at Star City, northeast of Moscow, and take a low-orbit flight in a MIG-29 aircraft at twice the speed of sound or go weightless on a space-training flight. Ⓦgctc.su

● **Take an icy dip** Join the St Petersburg Walrus Club for a plunge in the Neva River. Of course, you'll have to cut a hole in the ice first. This extraordinary winter custom occurs by the Peter and Paul Fortress, near the Lenin Stadium and at several other locations.

Food and drink

Moscow and St Petersburg are bursting at the seams with cafés and restaurants covering everything from budget blowouts to *elitni* (elite) extravagance. The good news is that you don't have to tip. The bad news is that a tip has already been added, and the bill isn't as cheap as you might hope. Traditional fare is notoriously bland, but modern Russia is making improvements in this area and you'll find plenty of great dishes if you do a little research. And if you look in the places that have familiar food, you won't find the sort of prices you're hoping for. Fortunately, the vodka is cheap. And it almost counts as a meal.

Transport

Russia's train network is extensive, and up to twenty trains a day connect Moscow and St Petersburg (5–8hr). Neither Eurail or InterRail passes cover Russia. Otherwise, the slow trains are cheap and there are plenty of travel agencies around to help you avoid waiting in lines at the station. Train prices seem to vary like the weather. Don't be surprised if two ticket agents at the same train station quote different prices for the same train. Local buses are also cheap and can be an excellent option. The catch is you need to figure them out; there are long, confusing lines and few English-speakers. If you're heading there from eastern Europe, you can get some great deals.

Busabout doesn't operate in Russia, so you will have to try your luck at the bus station counter. Buses are old and rickety, but tickets are ridiculously low (Ⓦwaytorussia.net/Transport/Domestic/Bus.html). Buses are the cheapest and most unreliable way to get around. The best way is to show up at the major stations and look for a "kassa" (ticket window). For modern buses to and from Moscow and St Petersburg, try Ⓦluxexpress.eu.

In both Moscow and St Petersburg, you'll find a range of metros (over 150 stations in Moscow alone), buses, trams and trolleybuses. Tickets are subsidized and cheap. Less than €1 will get you where you want to go around the city.

Events

- **Stars of the White Nights Festival** St Petersburg's renowned Mariinsky Theater (aka The Kirov) jump-starts summer with this taxing schedule of performances, launched by Valery Gergiev, the indefatigable conductor of the Mariinsky Opera's orchestra. May–June; Ⓦmariinsky.ru
- **Easter in Moscow** The holy day of

the Russian Orthodox Church is most notably observed in Moscow's spectacular Kolomenskoe Church, with its flower-like domes soaring 70m into the air.

- **Russian Winter Festival** This twelve-days-of-Christmas-timed festival is celebrated in cities across Russia. Singers and musicians from around the world perform in the largest cities, including in Moscow's Izmaylovo Park. If you get the chance, try some Russian pancakes (blini) with caviar.

Russia online

Russia info Ⓦrussia-travel.com, Ⓦvisitrussia.org.uk
Rail Ⓦrussiantrains.com
Moscow info Ⓦmoscow.info
St Petersburg info Ⓦvisit-petersburg.ru

EXIT FESTIVAL, NOVI SAD

Serbia

Capital Belgrade
Population 7,176,000
Language Serbian
Currency Dinar (din)
Minimum daily budget €25

When to go Spring and autumn are best

When not to go November–March can be bitterly cold, and June surprisingly rainy

Serbia

Serbia is a buzzy and boisterous country, compact enough for visitors to sample both Belgrade's urban hedonism and the gentler pace of the smaller towns or national parks within a few days – and it's one of Europe's most affordable destinations to boot. Serbia's young, European-minded population brings a bubbling energy to its bars, cafés and clubs, producing an adrenaline-charged nightlife unmatched anywhere else in the Balkans. The general determination to have a good time confounds the expectations of many a traveler, arriving with memories of the 1990s, when Serbia's name was not often off war reporters' lips. Today, it's just as likely to attract headlines for its crop of world-class tennis players or the annual EXIT festival in Novi Sad.

Main attractions

❶ Belgrade Explore the nightlife and café culture of Serbia's hectic, hedonistic capital city – at its best in spring and summer, when all ages throng the streets at all hours. With a seemingly endless supply of bars and clubs, the city's pulsing nightlife is one of the unexpected high points on any European itinerary. Ⓦ tob.co.rs

❷ Novi Sad This city has long charmed visitors with its comely buildings – remnants of Austro-Hungarian rule. Today it's an emphatically young town – especially in the summer, when thousands of international revelers swarm to Petrovaradin Fortress for the four-day EXIT festival. Ⓦ novisad.rs/eng/tourism

❸ Subotica A wonderful counterpoint to the capital, with its Secessionist buildings, green spaces, wide pavements and burghers riding around on old-fashioned bicycles all contributing to its unspoilt, wholesome air. Ⓦ visitsubotica.rs

❹ Studenica Monastery The finest of Serbia's fresco-laden medieval monastic churches, established in 1190. Its superb frescoes were the work of an innovative but still anonymous Greek painter.

Also recommended

● **The Konak of Princess Ljubica** No, it's not a Serbian Disney film, but an 1831 Belgrade building which underlines the Balkans' position as a cultural crossroads: a Napoleon III-themed room sits alongside a Turkish-style one with a Koran stand. It seems nineteenth-century Belgraders loved socializing too: there's a big semicircular sofa for chatting guests in nearly every room. Ⓦ mgb.org.rs

AVERAGE DAILY TEMPERATURES AND MONTHLY RAINFALL

	Jan	Feb	Mar	Apr	May	June	July	Aug	Sept	Oct	Nov	Dec
Belgrade												
max °C	5	7	12	18	24	26	29	29	24	18	11	6
min °C	-1	0	3	8	13	16	17	18	14	9	4	0
rainfall mm	44	40	48	56	59	98	62	58	55	50	55	57

● **Learn about the Serbian Da Vinci**
Belgrade's engaging Nikola Tesla Museum celebrates the eponymous nineteenth-century inventor and engineer. Credited with inventing the AC current, he also helped to develop wireless communications and remote-control technologies.
Ⓦ tesla-museum.org

● **Dark tourism, Niš** Also known as "The Skull-Tower," Ćele Kula makes for gruesome sightseeing. It dates from a battle in 1809, when the victorious Turkish Pasha ordered that the heads of the Serbian soldiers killed be stuffed and mounted on the tower; 952 went into creating this macabre totem pole, though today only 58 remain.

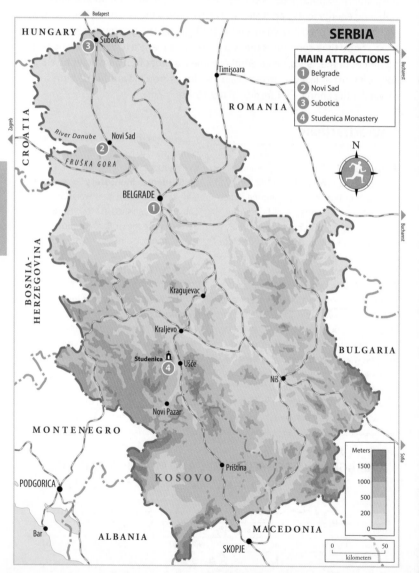

SERBIA

MAIN ATTRACTIONS
1 Belgrade
2 Novi Sad
3 Subotica
4 Studenica Monastery

Food and drink

Serbian cuisine is overwhelmingly dominated by meat, and many dishes manifest Turkish or Austro-Hungarian influences. Breakfast typically comprises a coffee, roll and cheese or salami; also popular are *burek*, a greasy, flaky pastry filled with cheese or meat, and the ubiquitous *ćevapčići*, rissoles of spiced minced meat served with onion. With the reliance on meat, it's a tough call for vegetarians, though there are some tasty local salads. You won't want for coffee, beer or wine, and everyone should at least sample *slijvovica* (plum *rakija*); pace yourself to avoid waking up with a shocked head and raw throat.

Transport

Serbia's bus network is on the whole efficient and reliable. Most internal services run regularly throughout the day, and there are excellent links to neighbouring countries. Timetables (often in Cyrillic) can be confusing, so it's well worth asking your hostel to check bus times for you.

Keep hold of the coin handed back with your ticket – you'll use it to pass through to the platform – and note that you should hang onto your outbound ticket if taking a return journey.

Serbia's unreliable rail network is likely to be of limited use; that said, fares are around half the price of the buses.

By train

- **Balkans Flexi Pass** (also valid in Bosnia-Herzegovina, Bulgaria, Greece, Macedonia, Montenegro, Romania and Turkey). Any five, ten or fifteen days in one month.

Events

- **EXIT Festival** The Petrovaradin Fortress in Novi Sad hosts what has slowly morphed into one of Europe's premier music events, attracting some of the very biggest names in pop, techno and hip-hop. Four days at the beginning of July; ⓦ exitfest.org
- **Belgrade Beer Fest** Summer's a grand time to be in fun-loving Belgrade, and here's an additional excuse to drink way too much booze. The fare on offer is largely big-label lager from Serbia and other European countries, but nobody gets sniffy about the lack of highbrow ale – just grab a nice, cold Jelen, and make a bunch of local friends. August; ⓦ belgradebeerfest.com

Serbia online

Serbia info ⓦ serbia.travel
Rail ⓦ zeleznicesrbije.com
Bus ⓦ bas.rs
Belgrade info ⓦ tob.co.rs

SKIING AT JASNÁ

Slovakia

Capital Bratislava

Population 5,426,000

Languages Slovak

Currency Euro (€)

Minimum daily budget €24

When to go May–June and September–October, when the sightseeing is at its best (good climate, fewer visitors). May–October for hiking

When not to go Since it's not one of Europe's marquee destinations, it doesn't get painfully crowded in the summer. May and September are still going to be ideal

Slovakia

Slovakia may not be blessed with anything matching the architectural wonders of Prague, but since splitting from the Czech Republic in 1993 it retained the best alpine skiing and hiking. There are also plenty of castles to keep culture buffs busy.

Main attractions

❶ **Bratislava** Old City torture chambers, a museum of wine, and the Primate's Palace can all be found in the Old Town center. The castle hovering above the River Danube was part of the Roman Empire for 400 years and offers great views of the city plus a folk museum. Ⓦ visit.bratislava.sk

❷ **Skiing Jasná** There aren't many places in Europe where you can find a six-day ski pass for under €100. Ⓦ jasna.sk

❸ **Bojnice Castle** In a land dotted with amazing castles, this one stands out as one of the finest. It was originally a wooden castle, but was built with stone by the Poznań family in the thirteenth century. Ⓦ bojnicecastle.sk

Also recommended

● **Hike the Vysoké Tatry** The narrow peaks of the Vysoké Tatry (High Tatras) tower over glacial valleys with dizzying cliff faces, and, down at lower elevations, thick forests cover the hillsides. With a hundred glacial lakes and gurgling streams neatly packed into a small area with trails, it couldn't be better suited for hiking. The end of August is a good time to go, and Starý Smokovec is perhaps the best starting point. Ⓦ vt.sk

● **Visit Devín Castle** It sits right on the confluence of the Morava and Danube rivers and provides views across the river to Austria and Hungary. The first walled structure there was erected by Romans and there still stands a turret known as the Virgin Tower where, according to legend, a noble lady leapt to her death when her uncle wouldn't allow her to be with the lord of the castle.

Food and drink

Slovak cuisine is an edifice resting on three mighty columns: the potato, the pig and the cabbage. Because of Slovakia's many neighbors, you'll find hints of Polish, Hungarian and Ukrainian delights as well. Expect lots of soups, pork and beef, with the occasional goose or wild boar. A nice meal can be found for under €15.

Transport

The region has a comprehensive rail network that's reasonably cheap, clean and mostly dependable. The two main airports are in

AVERAGE DAILY TEMPERATURES AND MONTHLY RAINFALL											
	Jan	Feb	Mar	Apr	May	June	July	Aug	Sept	Oct	Nov	Dec
Bratislava												
max °C	2	4	11	16	21	24	26	26	22	15	7	3
min °C	-3	-2	2	4	9	13	14	14	11	6	1	-1
rainfall mm	36	41	38	36	56	71	63	61	38	41	53	-1

Košice and Bratislava. There are some internal flights, but you'll get a far better deal going by bus for such short distances.

- **InterRail Slovakia Pass** Ranges from three to eight days of travel in one month.
- **Eurail Slovakia Pass** Any three, four, five or eight days of travel in one month.
- **Eurail Slovakia-Czech Republic Pass** Any four, five, six, eight or ten days in two months.
- **European East Pass** (also valid in Austria, the Czech Republic and Hungary) Any five days of travel in one month. Five additional travel days can be added.

For tips and tricks on maximizing your rail pass, see "Costs and savings" (p.63).

For internal bus prices, see Ⓦ cp.atlas.sk. For buses to other countries, see Ⓦ eurolines.sk.

Events

- **Bratislava Jazz Days** The first international star appeared here in 1982. Since then, the likes of Bill Evans, Herbie Hancock, Bobby McFerrin and Wynton Marsalis have played this festival. Sept/Oct; Ⓦ www.bjd.sk

Slovakia online

Slovakia info Ⓦ slovakia.travel
Rail Ⓦ zsr.sk
Bus Ⓦ cp.atlas.sk
Bratislava info Ⓦ bratislava.sk

LAKE BLED

Slovenia

Capital Ljubljana

Population 2,065,000

Languages Slovene

Currency Euro (€)

Minimum daily budget €38

When to go September, when the weather's ideal for outdoor pursuits, or December–March for skiing

When not to go July–August, when the coast gets crowded, and November–February, when it's too chilly for sightseeing

Slovenia

Sandwiched between Italy, Croatia, Austria and Hungary, Slovenia will likely be on the route of many travelers. The ones who stop for a look around will find a charming and comfortable place to travel, with Habsburg and Venetian architecture and a ubiquitous assortment of impressive European churches, castles, monasteries, medieval cities and mansions from the Renaissance. Located on the southwestern side (the tourist bureau prefers "the sunny side") of the Alps, Slovenia offers incredible mountain vistas and perhaps the most affordable (and undiscovered) skiing in Europe. Think Switzerland at seventy percent off.

Slovenia managed to avoid much of the strife that plagued other nations during the messy disintegration of the Yugoslav Republic, and integrated quickly with western Europe, joining the Eurozone in 2007. Administered by German-speaking Habsburg overlords until 1918, Slovenes absorbed the culture of their rulers while managing to retain a strong sense of ethnic identity through their Slavic language.

Main attractions

❶ **Ljubljana** Narrow streets snake through the Old Town while cafés buzz with 63,000 university students. This charming, once-Roman town may not have the architectural magnificence of Prague, but it doesn't have the gaggles of tourists either. ⓦvisitljubljana .com

❷ **The Adriatic coast** Every country cherishes its coastline, and Slovenia is no exception. The small stretch along the

Adriatic (just 100km across the water from Venice) is home to Piran, with its Venetian Gothic architecture and narrow streets, and nearby Fiesa, edged by a clean sandy beach and tranquil boat-restricted waters.

❸ **Bled** This town has three draws: a medieval castle that served as a summer residence to the Yugoslav royal family and South Tyrolian bishops; a fifteenth-century belfry with a "bell of wishes" (anyone who rings it will get what they wish for); and the Alps hanging like curtains in the background, which any Slovenian will gladly sell you if you believe the thing about the bell.

Also recommended

● **Climb Mount Triglav** Action junkies and outdoor enthusiasts in Slovenia head for the triple-crested Mount Triglav (2864m), the country's highest peak. Slavs once believed the mountain to be the lair of a three-headed deity who ruled the sky, the earth and the

AVERAGE DAILY TEMPERATURES AND MONTHLY RAINFALL

	Jan	Feb	Mar	Apr	May	June	July	Aug	Sept	Oct	Nov	Dec
Ljubljana												
max °C	2	4	9	14	19	23	26	26	22	16	8	3
min °C	-4	-3	1	5	9	12	14	14	11	6	1	-2
rainfall mm	33	36	38	53	69	79	56	43	41	36	51	43

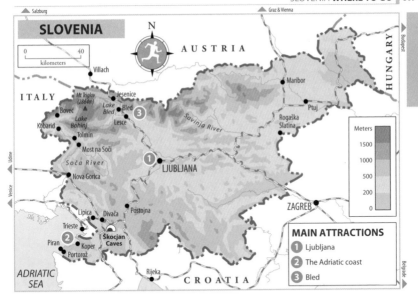

underworld. Today, the pilgrimage up Triglav has become a confirmation of Slovenian identity. The best routes start near Bled, at Savica waterfall and Stara Fužina.

- **Visit the Škocjan Caves** When the area was covered by the sea millions of years ago, limestone deposits were left on the bottom. A tunnel now passes through them and into an underground canyon that stretches 500m, a jungle of stalactites and stalagmites that's home to 250 types of plant and five types of bat. Ⓦpark-skocjanske-jame.si

- **Go wine tasting** Slovenia has supposedly been making wine since before the time of the Romans, so it's not surprising that they figured out how to do it well over the years. There are fourteen distinct wine-growing regions to explore, but if you want to concentrate your palate on a specific area that doesn't require driving, make base camp in Ptuj and sample the Haloze hills and the Jeruzalem-Ljutomer districts. A bike will get you from one tasting to the next if you can't find someone willing to drive.

- **Soak in a spa** Rogaška Slatina is not just an objectionable Scrabble word, it's also Slovenia's oldest and largest spa town,

with a mind-boggling assortment of cures. Everything from the rather uncomfortable-sounding "lymph drainage pressotherapy" to the scary "elecktro-acupuncture" and the mysterious "surprise bath" (Surprise! Here's your bath!). See Ⓦterme-olimia.com for more treatment information.

- **Ride the rapids** Take your pick of kayaks, canoes, rafts or hydrospeed boards for the white water of the Soča and Savinja rivers.

Food and drink

Fresh fruit and vegetables at outdoor markets are a bargain, as are breakfast pastries and street snacks. Liver and brains (fried or grilled to your disliking) are common dishes, but the strudel desserts with apple and rhubarb or home-made cheesecake are delicious, and the Italian influence means plenty of inexpensive pasta as well. A full meal, even without brains, can be found for under €10.

Transport

- **Eurail Austria-Slovenia-Croatia Pass** Four, five, six, eight or ten days of travel in two months.

● **Eurail Hungary-Slovenia-Croatia Pass** Four, five, six, eight or ten days of travel in two months.

Busabout doesn't operate in Slovenia and nor is there a Slovenian Eurolines website, but you can find the transport info you need for the bus at Ⓦ ap-ljubljana.si, or train at Ⓦ slo-zeleznice.si. The trains are smooth and efficient, and local bus companies fill up on popular routes in the summer, so book ahead if you're heading to the coast.

Ljubljana is easily explored on foot, or by bike, but public transport is affordable. There's a 24-, 48- or 72-hour "Ljubljana Card" that allows unlimited bus travel, 16-plus free museums, a guided city tour and day's internet access. See Ⓦ visitljubljana.com for more details.

Events

● **Kurentovanje, Ptuj** The biggest Mardi Gras celebration in Slovenia; for ten days leading up to Shrove Tuesday there are masked balls, oodles of free-flowing wine and street performances. Mid-Feb; Ⓦ kurentovanje.net

● **Festival Ljubljana** The premier cultural event in Ljubljana sees dance, theater and international music performances in the capital for more than two months of the summer. Past performers include José Carreras, Wynton Marsalis and Slide Hampton, and attendance for the combined events tops 50,000. July–Sept; Ⓦ ljubljanafestival.si

● **The Cows' Ball** It's not a bovine dance ritual; just an excuse for drinking and merrymaking when the cows return to the valleys around Lake Bohinj from their high-altitude pastures. Mid-Sept.

Slovenia online

Slovenia info Ⓦ slovenia-tourism.si
Rail info Ⓦ slo-zeleznice.si
Bus info Ⓦ ap-ljubljana.si
Ljubljana info Ⓦ visitljubljana.com

ALHAMBRA GATE, GRANADA

Spain

Capital Madrid

Population 46,335,000

Languages Castilian (also Catalan, Galician and Basque)

Currency Euro (€)

Minimum daily budget €30

When to go One of the reasons Spain is so popular is that it's good for travel all year round. The south is ideal April–June and September–October, and quite mild November–February. The north is best May–June and September

When not to go July and August can mean tortilla-frying heat and a crush of tourists. In the north, November–February can be chilly

Spain

To move beyond the hackneyed images of bullfights, crowded beaches and pitchers of sangria, you need simply set foot in Spain. There's more to the country than most ever anticipate, and every little town seems to maintain its own architectural treasures, from the mind-blowing works of Gaudí in Barcelona to the ornate *Hostal Dos Reis Católicos*, the world's oldest hotel, in Santiago de Compostela. The wealth of variety alone is perplexing. The far south still has Moroccan remnants of Moorish invaders, while the rolling green hills and Celtic music in the northern provinces of Galicia and Asturias (regional instrument: the bagpipe) seem to have more in common with Ireland and Scotland. Roman aqueducts and Gothic cathedrals come together, with a few medieval castles thrown in to boot.

You can retrace the painting grounds of the famous artists (the museums are stuffed with Picasso, Velázquez, Dalí and El Greco) or watch flamenco dancers clatter the cobblestones with the hope of collecting your loose change. And if an icy gazpacho fails to cool you on a hot Andalucian day, your only choice is to make for the ocean, which is rarely far off.

With all this, plus a kind sky that rarely rains for more than a day or two at a time, it's not surprising that Spain is the world's second most popular destination (after France). With comparatively cheaper prices, it's an even bigger draw for the budget-minded crowd, many of whom make the short hop over the Strait of Gibraltar from Algeciras to Tangier in Morocco – a taste of Africa within a ferry ride of Europe.

Main attractions

❶ La Sagrada Família, Barcelona

This Gaudí masterpiece has been under construction since 1882. You read right. And it's not expected to be completed until 2026. So, even if you're with someone who has seen it before, remind them that things will have changed. You can bring your camera, but picking your favorite angle might take a few hours and nearly all two million of last year's visitors will tell you that pictures just don't do this towering structure justice. ⓦ sagradafamilia.org

❷ Plaza Mayor, Madrid
This old-town-enclosed square in Madrid is the perfect place to buy (and pay too much for) a good coffee while you soak up the ambience.

AVERAGE DAILY TEMPERATURES AND MONTHLY RAINFALL

	Jan	Feb	Mar	Apr	May	June	July	Aug	Sept	Oct	Nov	Dec
Madrid												
max °C	11	12	16	17	22	28	32	32	28	20	14	11
min °C	0	2	3	6	9	13	16	16	13	8	4	2
rainfall mm	46	43	38	46	41	25	10	10	30	64	64	48
Seville												
max °C	16	17	21	22	26	31	35	35	32	26	21	17
min °C	6	7	8	10	13	17	19	19	18	13	9	7
rainfall mm	84	72	55	60	30	20	2	7	21	62	102	92

MAIN ATTRACTIONS

① La Sagrada Família, Barcelona

③ Beaches

⑤ Alhambra, Granada

② Plaza Mayor, Madrid

④ Prado Museum, Madrid

Kings have been crowned here; trials of the Inquisition held; bulls fought. Not only is it the most important historical landmark in the city, it has been beautifully preserved.

③ **Beaches** The Canary Islands (a few chunks of Spain located off the coast of Morocco), Balearic Islands (southeast of Barcelona, in the Med) and the entire Costa del Sol pull in the majority of Spain's tourists who aren't looking for much more culture than a beach towel and some sun block. The sun gods willingly oblige with a blanket of warm, clear weather.

④ **Prado Museum, Madrid** Even at the time it opened in 1819, the Prado was one of the most important art collections in Europe. There's far too much to see without a few weeks of museum-dedicated time, so most confine their browsing to the famous Spaniards – and even then it's a daunting pursuit. Ⓦ museodelprado.es

⑤ **Alhambra, Granada** Resting majestically atop an enormous citadel in the center of Granada, the Alhambra is a visual overload. The Alcazaba, Generalife gardens and Palacios Nazaríes take nearly a day to explore. Started by Ibn al-Ahmar, the structure's Moorish columns and domes and light-reflecting water basins inspire even the weariest traveler. Ⓦ alhambra -patronato.es

Also recommended

● **Walk the Camino de Santiago** Completing the entire journey to the city of

Santiago de Compostela on foot takes most people 35–45 days, though no one says you have to do the entire thing. Some attempt this pilgrimage route across northern Spain on bike. ⓦcaminosantiago.com

● **Watch Real Madrid or Barcelona** Perhaps never before have so many football stars been collected on two teams. Or so much money spent on them. Messi, Ronaldo, Neymar, Suárez, James Rodríguez – see them at the Santiago Bernabéu Stadium or Camp Nou, and there's a good chance you'll be watching them stroll to victory. See ⓦrealmadrid.com and ⓦfcbarcelona.com.

● **Go canyoning in the Pyrenees** Slip into a wetsuit, strap on a helmet and drop into the Barranco de Lapazosa. Near the Ordesa y Monte Perdido National Park, this is one of the world's most spectacular spots to splash, jump and rappel downstream in a ravine.

● **See the Guggenheim, Bilbao** Frank Gehry's gleaming metallic creation isn't on the main tourist route; if you want to catch a glimpse of this modern architectural treat, it'll take around five hours by train. ⓦguggenheim-bilbao.es

● **Visit Dalí's House** Salvador Dalí's surreal melting clocks and bent views can be found in many places, but if you want to step into his universe, try the Dalí House museum in Portlligat, just outside Barcelona. ⓦsalvador-dali.org

● **Ski the Sierra Nevada mountains** In late spring, you can ski all morning on 1300 vertical meters of slopes, then hop in a car or bus and head to the beach for a lazy afternoon of sunbathing: it's just 150km from Europe's southernmost ski resort to the Costa del Sol. ⓦsierranevada.es

● **Learn to surf** Spain has some excellent conditions for learning to surf. While Biarritz may be known as the European birthplace of surfing, San Sebastián has the highest density of bars in Europe, just in case you'd like to take a break.

Food and drink

Tapas in hip bars (€3–6) may be tasty, but they're far from the best way to fill up. A *tortilla española* (potato and onion omelet) will get you much further for your money. Don't miss out on the local wines (ask for the regional specialty), and buy them in a shop, not a restaurant, when you do your taste-testing. Also, be wary of low-priced seafood anywhere where you can't actually see the open ocean from the place you're ordering.

Transport

Spain is fairly well covered by a simple network of rail lines, with a complicated pricing system. The luxury high-speed (and expensive) AVE trains work well, with an increasing number of them departing from Madrid; budget travelers may need to hop between regional trains to get around cheaply. All this switching can be tricky and may involve an alternative route. If the local ticket-sellers are reluctant to work this out, consult the useful English-language version of RENFE's website (ⓦrenfe.com).

Bus services are comfortable and dependable and often faster than the slower trains. In Madrid, you can pick up a Madrid Card lasting 24, 48, 72 or 120 hours (that's five days), which gets you admission to more than fifty museums (ⓦmadridcard.com). Add on a Madrid Tourist Ticket and you get public transport, too.

By train

● **Eurail Spain Pass** Any three, four, five or eight days of travel in one month.

● **Eurail Spain-Portugal Pass** Four, five, six, eight or ten days of travel in two months.

● **Eurail France-Spain Pass** Four, five, six, eight or ten days of travel in two months.

For tips and tricks on maximizing your rail pass, see "Costs and savings" (p.63).

By bus

A Busabout pass (see p.44) allows you to travel throughout Spain. For internal bus prices, see Ⓦalsa.es. For buses to other countries, see Ⓦeurolines.es.

Events

- **Carnaval, Sitges** For a wild dose of Carnaval (which can be celebrated virtually anywhere in Spain), try Sitges, near Barcelona. Expect little sleep, ample beer, and a pulsing mass of outrageous costumes. Mid-Feb; Ⓦsitges.cat/carnaval
- **Las Fallas, Valencia** Spectacular floats (*ninots*) of wood, wax and papier-mâché are marched through the town during this six-day fiesta. Only one *ninot*, by popular vote, is saved, while the others are burned in the final night of celebrations. March 12–19; Ⓦfallasfromvalencia.com
- **Feria de Abril, Seville** This end-of-April festival in Seville is a week-long party, with flamenco dancing, a horse fair and (you'll never guess) bullfights, and has become the place for Spain's socialites to mingle. Mid-April; Ⓦvisitasevilla.es
- **The Running of the Bulls, Pamplona** The town may look like it's been invaded by pizza delivery men, but the white outfits with red scarves are the traditional dress for running alongside a stampeding herd of bulls through a series of narrow passageways. The 1km-long, early morning *encierro* (bull run) has almost become secondary to the night-long fiesta preceding each day's run and bullfight (see box, pp.28–29). July 6–14; Ⓦsanfermin.com
- **La Tomatina, Buñol** If you've never been trapped inside a pasta sauce factory during an explosion, here's your chance to get the next best thing: a free-for-all tomato fight in the square of this tiny Spanish town. Participants travel from around the globe to freely fling ripe tomatoes at strangers (see box, pp.30–31). Last Wed in Aug; Ⓦlatomatina.info

Spain online

Spain info Ⓦspain.info
Rail Ⓦrenfe.com
Bus Ⓦwww.alsa.es
Madrid info Ⓦesmadrid.com
Barcelona info Ⓦbarcelona.cat
Seville info Ⓦvisitasevilla.es

GAMLA STAN, STOCKHOLM

Sweden

Capital Stockholm

Population 9,794,000

Language Swedish

Currency Swedish kronor (kr)

Minimum daily budget €46

When to go June–August, when days are generally mild, lovely and long. May and September require a bit more luck for good weather

When not to go November and December. There are nice Christmas markets in December, but it's hard to count on a white Christmas. You may just get the dark, freezing, rainy part. January and February aren't much better, but at least winter activities are under way

Sweden

If this Nordic land conjures up images of Abba's disco outfits, IKEA's stylish discount furniture, boxy Volvos or Björn Borg's tennis headband, there's little of Sweden that will disappoint. Robyn, Tove Lo and Lykke Li may be more contemporary, but Abba's music is still more popular than the national anthem; the Swedish countryside produces more giant blue IKEA boxes than berries; Volvo is softening the corners on their boxes, but still subscribes to a basic design the shape of a sauna; and Björn Borg, in addition to the headband, now has a popular underwear line.

For those slightly more tuned in to Swedish culture, there's idyllic archipelago living, the trendy glass-blowers of the Småland region, herring in the summer, and *glögg* (a spicy warm wine) around Christmas.

There are also 96,000 lakes, some of the best beaches in Europe and, up north, an inexhaustible supply of pristine hiking trails where there's a good chance you won't encounter another soul. Stockholm is the big urban attraction, and deservedly so, but the bicycle-friendly university towns of Lund and Uppsala clamor for a visit. And don't forget to try the meatballs.

Main attractions

❶ Vasa Museum, Stockholm Sweden's most popular museum has just one exhibit, a mighty wooden warship that was launched from that very spot in 1628. Moments after it touched the water on its inaugural journey, the flawed, top-heavy ship tipped over and sank, where it was preserved in the mud of Stockholm's harbor. In an ironic twist, this failure has earned more money for Sweden than if the ship had been built correctly in the first place. Ⓦ vasamuseet.se

❷ Glass Kingdom Hidden within the thickly forested region of Småland, several boutique glass factories can be found churning out trendy transparent glasses, bowls and sculptures. You can see the glass-blowers in action, pulling glowing orbs out of the white-hot furnaces, before buying some of their creations in the attached shop. Orrefors and Kosta Boda are the most popular brands, and many of the glass artists are as well known as pop stars around Sweden. Ⓦ visitsmaland.se

❸ Gamla Stan, Stockholm Stockholm's Old Town rests on just one of the capital's fourteen islands. From above, it looks like a maze of tiny streets surrounding the Royal Palace (which resembles Buckingham Palace, yet, in a feat of architectural one-upmanship, was built with one more room). The Old Town is packed with tourists, but there are narrow enough side streets – several not much wider than your shoulders – to allow for some exploration.

AVERAGE DAILY TEMPERATURES AND MONTHLY RAINFALL

	Jan	Feb	Mar	Apr	May	June	July	Aug	Sept	Oct	Nov	Dec
Stockholm												
max °C	-1	-2	3	8	16	19	21	20	14	9	4	0
min °C	-6	-7	-3	-1	5	9	12	12	7	3	-1	-5
rainfall mm	39	27	26	30	30	45	72	66	55	50	53	46

4 **Visby** This medieval port on the island of Gotland (accessible by plane and just a few hours by ferry from east-coast cities) is perched on a hill, lined with cobblestones and ringed by a high stone wall. It's probably the most picturesque and charming town in Sweden, with more than forty towers and scores of church ruins remaining from the Hanseatic period. ⓦgotland.com

5 **Skansen, Stockholm** A vast open-air museum packed with re-created farms, windmills and 150 buildings from Sweden's past. There's a zoo with monkeys, snakes, moose and bears, plus a petting area where kids can get a little closer to goats and kittens; the kitten enclosure has become the traditional place for Stockholm's children to throw away their pacifiers (aka dummies) when they give them up for good. ⓦskansen.se

Also recommended

● **Hike Sarek National Park** The glaciers, peaks, valleys and lakes of this remote northern park cover 2000 square kilometers. The trails are demanding and best suited for advanced hikers who can pack and carry what they need (there are few huts or bridges), so those who make the effort will have a vast wilderness all to themselves. ⓦsverigesnationalparker.se

● **Kayak the archipelago** Stockholm's archipelago has 24,000 islands, and if you don't have access to a sailboat – or the ability

SWEDEN

MAIN ATTRACTIONS
1 Vasa Museum, Stockholm
2 Glass Kingdom
3 Gamla Stan, Stockholm
4 Visby
5 Skansen, Stockholm

to sail one – a kayak is the next best way to get around. Bring a tent, a good map and a cell phone (there's coverage over most of the islands), and book inexpensive cabins along the way.

- **Skate on thin ice** One of the most popular recreational sports in Sweden is long-distance ice-skating. You do need some special equipment, including 55cm-long blades, but this can be easily purchased or rented for a tour. More important is that you know where you're going and take safety precautions, just as the locals do. Ⓦ sssk.se/english/index.htm
- **Run the Stockholm Marathon** Held in late May or early June, this 42.2km race through Stockholm is one of the world's most beautiful marathons. There are other ways to get the same vistas, but few that will earn the equivalent respect from the locals. Ⓦ stockholmmarathon.se

Food and drink

Thanks in part to IKEA, Swedish meatballs (*köttbullar*) are familiar across the world. However, there is rather more to the national cuisine than this. Seafood is particularly good, with marinated salmon (*gravlax*) and herring (*strömming*) being served everywhere. Falafels and pizza are the most easily found cheap fillers, but if you plan to eat out, do so at lunchtime. Most restaurants offer lunch specials for €10 that include a salad bar, warm meal, cold drink and coffee. Order the same food in the restaurant at dinnertime and you'll pay about €40 for it. Alcohol is particularly expensive, but picking up your beer or wine from one of the government-run Systembolagets will make a significant saving.

Transport

Getting around Sweden is comfortable and often quick, but never cheap. Rail and bus passes are an especially good way to move about in these parts. And that goes for inner-city transport as well (it's possible to pay €5 for a fifteen-minute subway ride in Stockholm if you buy a single ticket). The capital's transit authority offers 24- and 72-hour travel cards, which give you unlimited travel on metro, buses and local trains. There's also a Stockholm Card for 24, 48 or 72 hours that allows unlimited public transport, admission to 75 museums and boat sightseeing. For more details, visit Ⓦ visitstockholm.com.

By train
- **Eurail Sweden Pass** Any three, four, five or eight days of travel in one month.
- **Eurail Scandinavia Pass** (also valid in Denmark, Norway and Finland) Any two, five, six, eight or ten days of travel in two months.
  For tips and tricks on maximizing your rail pass, see "Costs and savings" (p.60).

By bus
Busabout doesn't operate in Sweden. For internal bus prices, see Ⓦ swebus.se. For buses to other countries, see Ⓦ eurolines.se.

Events

- **Crayfish party** It's a national event without a national party or fixed date. The idea is to make friends with a local and get invited to a private bash. Swedes don silly hats as they sing drinking songs and wash down minuscule amounts of crayfish meat with schnapps (spiced vodka) and beer. Late July or Aug.
- **Midsummer's Day** The longest day of the year (at least, the closest Friday and Saturday to the longest day) is celebrated with the pagan rite of maypole dancing and schnapps drinking. There are decorations around towns, but it's essentially a family holiday. Mid-June.

Sweden online

Sweden info Ⓦ visitsweden.com
Rail Ⓦ sj.se
Bus Ⓦ swebus.se
Stockholm info Ⓦ visitstockholm.com

MOUNTAIN BIKING, SAANENLAND

Switzerland

Capital Bern

Population 8,265,000

Languages German, French, Italian and Romansch

Currency Swiss franc (SFr)

Minimum daily budget €48

When to go Any time. June–August is excellent for exploring nature, November–March sees the country turn into a mountain playground, and April–May and late September–October bring comfortable weather, without the crowds. Skiing in the Alps lasts from the end of November until April

When not to go November–February in the cities and around the lakes is icy cold and not an ideal time for wandering

Switzerland

The best-known art in Switzerland may very well be the panoramic postcards for sale on racks throughout the country. When you look around, it seems the only thing missing is frames around the mountains. The best way to see the peaks, of course, is to put down your camera and strap on a pair of skis or hiking boots. Switzerland is also famous for its political neutrality, milk chocolate, yodelers, timepieces that cost more than small airplanes and an army equipped with tiny folding knives.

What many don't know is that this teeny, wealthy, mountainous country is a potpourri of cultures speaking four languages: French, German (Switzerdeutsch is the dialect), Italian and the little-known and little-used Romansch. Together, this motley confederacy of cantons has picked up more Nobel prizes (per capita) than any other country. And you can bet your last cowbell that the somber gaggle of bankers is going to keep the country's finances secure.

Main attractions

❶ Zermatt A glam skiing and mountaineering resort tied to the fame of perhaps the most visually stunning Alp: the Matterhorn (4478m). The car-free town is best explored on foot, and there's a cog railway that will lift you up to the rocky ridge of Gornergrat for even more impressive vistas. ⓦzermatt.ch

❷ Château de Chillon Perched on the shore of Lake Geneva, the most visited historical building in Switzerland was started in the eleventh century and has been modified numerous times since. Dungeons, courtyards and towers make it a fairy-tale castle and 360-degree photo op. Not surprisingly, the dreamy home found its way into the writings of Lord Byron. ⓦchillon.ch

❸ Zürich Geneva may have the Red Cross, but Zürich has had an explosion of trendy cafés, bars and shops. The Old Town offers a cultural afternoon of wandering – you don't need to open a numbered bank account to visit, but it certainly helps. ⓦzuerich.com

❹ Lake Thun Welcome to *schloss* (castle) country. There's Schloss Thun, Schloss Oberhofen, and Schloss Hünegg (which mixes in Art Nouveau renovations). You can visit all three on a one-day boat trip on Lake Thun and still have time to try the nearby 100m bungee jump. ⓦthunersee.ch

Also recommended

● **Explore the Franches-Montagnes** If you're going to head up into the mountains, you may as well avoid a superhighway of

AVERAGE DAILY TEMPERATURES AND MONTHLY RAINFALL

	Jan	Feb	Mar	Apr	May	June	July	Aug	Sept	Oct	Nov	Dec
Zürich												
max °C	2	3	8	12	17	19	23	22	18	13	6	3
min °C	-2	-2	2	4	9	12	14	14	11	7	2	0
rainfall mm	61	61	69	84	102	127	127	124	99	84	71	71

MAIN ATTRACTIONS
1 Zermatt
2 Château de Chillon
3 Zürich
4 Lake Thun

tourists gasping for oxygen. This range offers fewer visitors, cross-country skiing and gentle horses. Saignelégier is a good place to start your exploring.

● **Fly a glider in the Alps** Take advantage of the updrafts with a ride (or lesson) in a glider. Soar over cliffs and ride thermals as high as they'll take you (and your pilot). Switzerland is one country that deserves a bird's-eye view. To find a local listing of flight centers, try Ⓦ landings.com.

● **Go lugeing** The most famous luge course in the world is the Cresta Run, built in St Moritz for the 1884–85 season. It's now a private club, but you can try your head at it (you go head first, skeleton-style) on the ice track. Traveling 1200m at 90kmph isn't impressive for a bullet, but it's not bad for a sledge. For five runs with some instruction, you pay a small fortune. Book ahead. Ⓦ cresta-run.com

● **Cycle around Switzerland** Nine national cycle routes (3300km in total) crisscross the country, most of them well away from traffic; route maps and information in English are available from tourist offices. Eurotrek can rent you a bike, book hotels along your route and transport your gear from hotel to hotel. See Ⓦ eurotrek.ch for tour information.

Food and drink

In the south, there's an Italian influence; in the west, French cuisine; while it's German dishes everywhere else. The food is excellent – fondues, polenta, chocolates and a collection of famous cheeses await visitors – but the question is whether you can afford it. The country with the world's most expensive *McDonald's* prices doesn't welcome budget diners with open arms. Kebabs and falafels are among the most popular survival meals for the tourist. Younger travelers can also head for a nearby university cafeteria and find something filling for under €10.

Transport

Switzerland offers some of the most scenic routes in the world on funiculars, cable cars, cog railways, trains, buses and boats. All are clean, expensive and arrive and depart with the accuracy of a Swiss watch. There are several unique rail passes. For more information, see Ⓦ swisspass.ch.

In Zürich, a 24-hour pass is good for travel on all public transport, but a better deal might be the 24- or 72-hour Zürich Card pass (Ⓦzuerich.com/en/visit/your-city-travel-pass), which also allows free admission to 34 museums and a culinary surprise at 21 restaurants.

By train

- **Swiss Travel Pass** Three, four, eight or fifteen consecutive days of travel. Includes 50 percent discount on most mountain railways, free public transport in 75 cities and towns, plus admission to 480 museums. See Ⓦswisstravelsystem.com.
- **Eurail Austria-Switzerland Pass** Any four, five, six, eight or ten days of travel in two months.
- **Eurail France-Switzerland Pass** Any four, five, six, eight or ten days of travel in two months.
- **Eurail Germany-Switzerland Pass** Four, five, six, eight or ten days of travel in two months.
- **InterRail Switzerland Pass** Three, four, six or eight days in one month.
- **Swiss Half-fare Card** Fifty percent off all trains, buses, boats and most city public transport for a month.

For tips and tricks on maximizing your rail pass, see "Costs and savings" (p.60).

By bus

A Busabout pass (see p.44) allows some travel within Switzerland. PTT PostBuses (Ⓦpostbus.ch) permit some travel with a non-Eurail Swiss pass. For buses to other countries, see Ⓦeurolines.ch and Ⓦexpressbus.ch.

Events

- **Yehudi Menuhin Festival, Gstaad**
Yehudi Menuhin founded this festival in 1956 to bring chamber music to the swanky Swiss Alps resort of Gstaad. Well, it seemed like reason enough at the time. The event has grown and the concerts are held in the churches and surrounding villages, with performances by world-renowned soloists. July–Sept; Ⓦmenuhinfestivalgstaad.com
- **Sonchaux Acro Show, Villeneuve**
Watch for falling psychopaths! The world's best paragliders and base-jumpers descend on Villeneuve for a few days as part of the Acrobatics World Cup. The pros land on a tiny floating platform in the middle of a lake, where over 30,000 spectators wait for an embarrassing face plant. Late Aug; Ⓦacroshow.ch
- **Santa Claus World Championship, Samnaun** St Nick gets to show his competitive edge in this odd but colorful contest in the ski resort of Samnaun. There's no milk and cookie eating, but previous years have seen reindeer rodeo, sledging and skiing on primitive skis. Late Nov; Ⓦclauwau.com
- **St Moritz Christmas Market** If you haven't finished your Christmas shopping come the beginning of December, this is the place to go. Tree decorations, woodcraft, dolls and snacks – nothing you actually need – are hyperinflated and put on display for purchase. Dec 3; Ⓦstmoritz.ch
- **Montreux Jazz Festival** Europe's most famous jazzfest is like a tractor beam for the world's top musicians. Performers from B.B. King to Prince to Leonard Cohen – and nearly anyone you can think of in between – have played this event in Montreux, a town delightfully sandwiched between the edge of Lake Geneva and the Alps. Ⓦmontreuxjazz.com

Switzerland online

Switzerland info Ⓦmyswitzerland.com
Rail Ⓦsbb.ch
Bus Ⓦpostbus.ch
Bern info Ⓦberne.ch
Zürich info Ⓦzuerich.com
Geneva info Ⓦgeneve-tourisme.ch

Turkey

Capital Ankara

Population 78,214,000

Language Turkish

Currency Turkish lira (₺)

Minimum daily budget €28

When to go May and October are ideal – great weather, few tourists. June and September have the best weather, but also the crowds

When not to go December–March is rainy and cold (though February–March are fine on the southeast coast). July and August are hot and crowded, the southeast especially so

Turkey

No other country provides as spectacular a bridge between East and West as Turkey, and nowhere more tangible as in the cultural epicenter, İstanbul. On one side of İstanbul is Europe: on the other, Asia. This quickly modernizing city has retained its magical frenetic energy, mixing minarets and churches with luxury hotels, clubs and smooth-talking carpet salesmen who speak eight languages and can guess which town you're from by your dialect.

With the range of poverty and wealth, European and Asian influences, Ottoman and Byzantine styles, religious and secular peoples, it seems like the country has an identity crisis. And it just may. But this fusion, combined with an outpouring of hospitality and food to die for, makes it an enormously rewarding place for the traveler.

Outside of İstanbul, there are spectacular ruins, several of the finest beaches on the Aegean Sea (with cheaper food and accommodation than Greece's) and some of the wildest geological formations on the planet, from Pamukkale to Cappadocia.

Main attractions

❶ **Covered Bazaar, İstanbul** İstanbul is worth visiting for the shopping alone. And the old city's Kapalı Çarşı, or "Covered Bazaar," is the logical place to start. This labyrinth of streets and passages houses more than 5000 shops, with names that recall the days when each trade had its own quarter: "Goldsmiths' Street," "Carpet Sellers' Street," "Skullcap Makers' Street." Sit down for tea with some of the sellers and let them charm you into buying a few souvenirs you never realized you wanted. ⓦ kapalicarsi.com.tr

❷ **Pamukkale** Chances are you'll catch your first glimpse of Pamukkale (translated as "Cotton Castle") on a postcard. Calcium-oxide-rich waters paint the Çal Dağı hillside white, creating a series of Gaudí-like dripping terraces. Try to view this stunning geological formation early without thousands of people crawling all over it and turning the white surface dark with foot scum. There are several ways in which you can experience the balmy waters for yourself, including a trip to the Pamukkale Thermal Baths, home to a sacred pool where the water bubbles up at a constant 35°C.

❸ **Topkapī Palace, İstanbul** One of İstanbul's big draws, this expansive fifteenth-century estate served as the center of the Ottoman Empire for four centuries and is difficult for most travelers to miss. Among the maze of rooms, you'll find inner courtyards, a throne room, a circumcision room and a harem. ⓦ topkapisarayi.gov.tr

❹ **Dolmabahçe Palace, İstanbul** When the Ottomans moved on from Topkapī Palace

AVERAGE DAILY TEMPERATURES AND MONTHLY RAINFALL

	Jan	Feb	Mar	Apr	May	June	July	Aug	Sept	Oct	Nov	Dec
İstanbul												
max °C	6	7	11	14	18	21	24	24	21	15	9	7
min °C	1	1	3	6	9	12	14	14	11	8	4	2
rainfall mm	54	46	54	46	63	58	54	52	54	56	56	56

MAIN ATTRACTIONS

1. Covered Bazaar, İstanbul
2. Pamukkale
3. Topkapi Palace, İstanbul
4. Dolmabahçe Palace, İstanbul
5. Blue Mosque, İstanbul
6. Ephesus

in 1853, they decided to build on the Asian side of the Bosphorus. The Dolmabahçe Palace doesn't look as magnificent from the outside, but the opulence within will put even the most overdecorated Las Vegas lobby to shame. It's also where Kemal Atatürk (Turkey's first president) died on November 10, 1938 – if you want to know when, just look at the clocks, which have been set to his exact time of death (9.05am).
Ⓦ millisaraylar.gov.tr

⑤ Blue Mosque, İstanbul If you're looking for a Smurf-colored mosque, forget it – it's the blue tilework on the insides that gives this mosque its name. If you want to walk barefoot across countless handwoven rugs while marveling at the serenity and architecture, you won't be disappointed

by this seventeenth-century Mehmet Aga creation, known locally as the "Sultanahmet Camii." Ⓦ sultanahmetcami.org

⑥ Ephesus Walking around the dry stacks of cut stone of Ephesus, it's hard to imagine that it once sat on the Aegean coast, now 8km away. And even harder to imagine the Temple of Artemis in full glory, when it was once a Wonder of the World. The site as a whole, however, has been impressively preserved.

Also recommended

● **Take a Turkish bath** Nothing scrapes off the travel grime quite like a trip to a hammam. These enormous marble steam-rooms, often fitted with hot baths, showers and cooling-down chambers, can be found all over Turkey. Let a masseur scrub you with an abrasive mitt and you'll see chewing-gum-sized wads of dead skin tumbling off your body. Then he or she will pound your muscles to a pulp, crack your joints, and you'll emerge feeling like a boneless chicken. In a good way, of course.

- **Explore İstanbul's sewer** Literally translated, Yerebatan Sarnıcı is the "Sunken Palace." It's İstanbul's largest underground cistern, naturally air-conditioned and renovated for public access. This one-time plumber's nightmare has been atmospherically spruced up – the water dripping from the ceiling is now accompanied by pulsing lights and creepy music. Ⓦyerebatan.com/homepage
- **Sleep in a cave** Head into the Swiss-cheese-like region of Cappadocia and you'll find a mind-boggling assortment of caves. Some of these Hittite dwellings (often called "Fairy Chimneys") have been converted into damp youth hostels that offer a nice respite from the heat. You'll also find underground cities and rock churches.
- **Pick out an "Evil Eye"** Nazar Boncuğu, or "Evil Eye" charms as they're commonly known, are cheap and come in many shapes and sizes: earrings, necklaces, hatpins and so on. The little blue eye is an old superstition to ward off misfortune. Wear one and you'll likely get a smile from the locals. It's a nice way to let them know you're interested in more than snapping pictures of old ladies making carpets. Something they'll enjoy pointing out while they sell you a tea set, anyway.

Food and drink

In no other country listed in this book can you eat so well for so little. The street snacks and "fast food" around Turkey are to die for: Turkish pizzas, baklava, salted cucumber on a stick, Turkish delight, pistachio nuts, yogurt – you won't go hungry or break your budget.

Leave a bit of pocket change for a tip (five percent) and that will be fine. Offer it again if they decline the first time.

Transport

Most people travel by bus in Turkey. How much you spend depends on what type of bus you take, from the slightly run-down to the incredibly modern (complete with snacks and a liberal sprinkling of the ubiquitous lemon cologne). There are some express train services, but these are mostly between İstanbul and Ankara (and most are still slower than the bus). The exception is the high-speed train that jets from Ankara to the city of Eskişehir in an hour and a quarter, and on to Kadıköy in İstanbul in three hours thirty minutes. In 2013 the Bosphorus tunnel was finally opened to the public, providing an undersea rail link between European and Asian İstanbul.

By train
- **Balkans Flexi Pass** (also valid in Bosnia-Herzegovina, Bulgaria, Greece, Macedonia, Montenegro, Romania and Serbia). Any five, ten or fifteen days in one month.
- **InterRail Turkey Pass** Three, four, six or eight days in one month.

Note that Eurail doesn't cover Turkey. For tips and tricks on maximizing your rail pass, see "Costs and savings" (p.60).

By bus
Busabout doesn't operate in Turkey. For internal bus prices, see Ⓦvaran.com.tr.

Events

- **Kırkpınar Oil Wrestling Festival, Edirne** Every summer, the large stadium near Edirne on the Greek–Turkish border erupts into wrestlemania. The week-long "sudden-death" format narrows the 1000-plus field of olive-oil-covered competitors down to a few slick champions. July.

● **Mevlâna Whirling Dervishes Festival, Konya** Spin your way over to Konya (with over a million others) for this religious spectacle in the ancient Selçuk capital. The Dervishes (Sufi members of the Mevlevî Order) whirl to achieve mystical union with God. Dec; Ⓦ mevlana.net

● **İstanbul Music Festival** In early summer, such atmospheric İstanbul venues as the church of Haghia Eirene welcome an international cast of performers playing traditional Turkish music, classical numbers and everything in between, from *West Side Story* to Venetian masters of Baroque. June; Ⓦ muzik.iksv.org

Turkey online

Turkey info Ⓦ goturkey.com
Rail Ⓦ tcdd.gov.tr (see Ⓦ turkeytravel planner.com to make sense of the timetable)
Bus Ⓦ varan.com.tr

First-Time Europe

Directory

Apps

Listings apps

Eventful It taps into your GPS and finds nearby events, concerts, shows, wherever you may be and can be set up to send email alerts for events based on your interests

LocalEats Searches fifty international cities (as well as the top US ones) for local eateries by category, price, rank, neighborhood etc

Localeur Casual and entertaining website and app built on the idea of insightful recommendations from locals

WhereTraveler Provides insider tips on dining, shopping, entertainment and sightseeing. It even helps you convert currencies, calculate tips and translate languages. Still mostly for cities in the US, but is spreading internationally. More than 100 destinations in total

Map apps

Google Maps Lets you download map areas for offline use

OffMaps2 Also cheap and iPhone friendly. Lets you download the maps you want using OpenStreetMap and view offline

Money apps

Trail Wallet Let's you keep track of how much money you're spending, and you don't have to be an accountant to use it. Switch between local currencies and synch with Dropbox to save your data in the cloud

XE Currency Converter Converts currencies and calculates prices

Photo and video apps

Camera+ Add controls to help turn your phone camera into an almost fully functional compact digital camera

Hipstamatic Retro filter for your photos to give them that "I was there in the 60s" look

Hyperlapse App from Instagram (see below) that lets you shoot professional time-lapse videos with your phone. The app helps smooth out shakes and bumps, so you don't need a tripod

Instagram A photo filter and photo-sharing app that has achieved almost cult status

Pano Turns up to sixteen photos into a stunning panoramic shot

Panorama 360 Camera As the name implies, it turns your photos into a single 360-degree panorama pic

Snapseed A surprisingly powerful photo editing app

TripColor A simple and easy-to-use photo-blog system that lets you – while offline – take pics, mark the location on a map, add text and then have it upload automatically when you finally find a wi-fi connection

Other useful apps

InstaWeather Superimposes local weather data on top of your photos, to let everybody know just how comfortable (or badass) you are

iTriage Diagnose that weird illness with the free offline symptom checker

NinthDecimal Formerly known as JiWire, this free wi-fi finder is the best way to avoid roaming charges. This app can track down the source closest to where you are

Peaks Point your phone towards a mountain and this app will tell you its name, elevation and how far away it is

Photo Translator Can't read a sign in a foreign language? No problem. Point your phone's camera at it and this app will instantly translate

Quizlet Digital flashcards that combine time-killing with learning. Remember to put together your own sets of cards before venturing off the wi-fi grid

TripIt Consolidates all your travel bookings (flights, hotels, car rentals) into one easy-to-use app. Often works best to upload everything via computer first, then just access as needed via the app

Whatsapp Online messaging app. You can send text or voice messages and media to your contacts (individually or in a group), and also call them – all completely free if you're using wi-fi

Accommodation

Collaborative travel

Ⓦ **couchsurfing.com** With well over ten million members and continuing to climb, this is still the main game in town

Ⓦ **tripping.com** A more modern interface and some other nice bells and whistles, but same basic concept as Couchsurfing

Home exchanges

Ⓦ **homeexchange.com** Largest exchange company with over 65,000 listings in 150 countries worldwide

Ⓦ **homeexchangeguru.com** A good starting point before you jump in

Ⓦ **homeforexchange.com** The third largest such agency

Ⓦ **homelink.org** Second largest in terms of listings, and the most expensive service. They have the most listings of any agency in Germany and Ireland, and are strong in UK, US, Belgium, the Netherlands, Switzerland and Norway

Ⓦ **Intervac.com** Fourth largest, with the most listings of any agency in Sweden and Finland

Hostels and B&Bs

Ⓦ **bedandbreakfast.com** An international bed-and-breakfast directory

Ⓦ **hihostels.com** Hostelling International's main site

Ⓦ **hostels.com** Global hostel finder and booking engine

Ⓦ **hostelz.com** Hostel booking engine with reviews

Peer-to-peer rentals

Ⓦ **airbnb.com** This is the one that put this sort of rental system on the map. Covers 34,000 cities and towns in 190 countries, which practically means every country on Earth

Ⓦ **campinmygarden.com** Private gardens as micro-campgrounds. Like Couchsurfing, but with tents

Ⓦ **flipkey.com** TripAdvisor's horse in this race, boasting 300,000 places to stay in 11,000 cities

Ⓦ **homeaway.com** One of Airbnb's global competitors, grouping together twelve online sites for a massive selection

Ⓦ **roomorama.com** Probably the most stylish site of the pack

Ⓦ **tripping.com** In addition to providing a Couchsurfing-like service, they have also aggregated the peer-to-peer rentals in one easy search

Communications

Cell phones

Ⓦ **ipipi.com** SMS messaging worldwide including text to email service

Ⓦ **onesimcard.com** Prepaid mobile service that greatly reduces the costs of calls when traveling

Ⓦ **telestial.com** Looking for a SIM card you can roam with? Compare rates between your local providers

Ⓦ **which.co.uk/technology/phones/ guides/using-mobile-phones-abroad** UK consumer magazine's guide to using cell phones abroad

Country calling codes

Ⓦ **countrycallingcodes.com** Get the dialling codes for every country, plus the ones you need to dial out of the country you're in

Free email

Ⓦ **mail.google.com** Free storage up to 15 GB

Ⓦ **outlook.com** Unlimited storage

Ⓦ **yahoo.com** Unlimited storage

Online calling

Ⓦ **apple.com/mac/facetime** Apple's version of Skype for those with Macs, iPhones and iPads

Ⓦ **messenger.yahoo.com** Yahoo's version of free video- and voice-chatting. Convenient if you're mostly in touch with Yahoo users

ⓦ **onavo.com** Onavo Extend compresses your data and helps minimize the amount you are sending

ⓦ **plus.google.com/hangouts** Call or chat through Gmail, Google+ or the Hangouts app. Can only do one-on-one calling to people without Google accounts, but there are extra features such as group Hangouts for Google users

ⓦ **skype.com** Call for free to other online devices and for a small fee to landlines and cellphones anywhere in the world. Now integrated in Facebook so you can chat with friends online

Satellite devices

ⓦ **delorme.com** Backcountry satellite device that sends emergency beacons, lets people follow you on a map and pairs with your smartphone to text and update social media

ⓦ **findmespot.com** Backcountry satellite device that can send an emergency beacon and can update a list of friends/family with an "I'm okay" message. Also connects to your smartphone via an app for various media updating

Satellite phones

ⓦ **globalstar.com** Extensive, but not quite global

ⓦ **iridium.com** Provides the most complete global coverage

Eating

ⓦ **eatwith.com** Shared dining in homes in seventeen European countries. May not be cheaper than McD, but miles more authentic, connecting and enjoyable.

ⓦ **vizeat.com** Brunch, lunch, dinner or drinks in locals' homes in over fifty countries

Health

ⓦ **cdc.gov** The US Centers for Disease Control has the latest updated information on vaccinations and outbreaks

ⓦ **ecdc.europa.eu** The European Centre for Disease Prevention and Control

ⓦ **who.int/countries/en/** The World Health Organization site has country-by-country health profiles

Insurance

ⓦ **insuremytrip.com** A good starting point for policy searches

ⓦ **roughguides.com/travel-insurance** Rough Guides recommends World Nomads insurance packages which should cover most needs

ⓦ **travelguard.com** A place to peek at popular policies

ⓦ **worldtravelcenter.com** An excellent spot for comparing different options

Money

ATMs worldwide

ⓦ **amextravelresources.com/#/specialist-by-destination** A list of AmEx offices worldwide, where you can also get cash advances against your card

ⓦ **mastercard.us/cardholder-services/atm-locator.html** For MasterCard holders

ⓦ **visa.via.infonow.net/locator/global** For Visa card holders

Currency exchange

ⓦ **oanda.com** Quick conversions in 180 currencies

ⓦ **weswap.com** Travelers crossing currency boundaries swap money directly and for minimal cost, via their WeSwap MasterCards.

Discount cards

ⓦ **hihostels.com** Hostelling International cards

ⓦ **isic.org** International student identity cards, teacher cards and youth cards

ⓦ **vipbackpackers.com** Discounts for select private hostels

Money transfer

Ⓦ**moneygram.com** Money transfers and bill payments at Thomas Cook, AmEx and various banks and post offices

Ⓦ**westernunion.com** Another money transfer option

Reading resources

Adventure travel

Ⓦ**afar.com** Travel magazine (and more) aimed at the curious traveler who wants to get under the skin of their chosen destinations

Ⓦ**wanderlust-magazine.co.uk** *Wanderlust* magazine covers the classic travel destinations, plus reviews and interviews

Budget travel

Ⓦ**budgettravel.com** Arthur Frommer's *Budget Travel* magazine is mostly focused on cheap holidays, but has good information for longer trips as well

Ⓦ**outpostmagazine.com** Shoestring globetrotting with a pleasing layout

Ⓦ**tntmagazine.com** *TNT* magazine, with UK and Aus/NZ editions for work and flat-finding

Ⓦ**transitionsabroad.com** Great information on working, studying and living overseas

Guidebook sites

Ⓦ**fodors.com** A very user-friendly site aimed at travelers with more pocket change than the average

Ⓦ**letsgo.com** Let's Go is an American classic for the college stomp in Europe, but its core audience are now expanding their horizons

Ⓦ**lonelyplanet.com** This site covers every country on the planet and has a much-subscribed travel discussion site called The Thorn Tree

Ⓦ**roughguides.com** Set up for independent travelers of all budgets, with in-depth country information, dedicated features, an online community and travel tips

Ⓦ**travelerstales.com** Pushing the experiential side of guiding, Travelers' Tales

offers books full of true stories from people just like you

Major newspaper web travel pages

Ⓦ**onlinenewspapers.com** Has links to newspapers all over the world
The pick of the international bunch are:

Ⓦ**guardian.co.uk/travel** *The Guardian*

Ⓦ**independent.co.uk/travel** *The Independent*

Ⓦ**latimes.com/travel** *The Los Angeles Times*

Ⓦ**nytimes.com/travel** *The New York Times*

Ⓦ**nzherald.co.nz/travel** *The New Zealand Herald*

Ⓦ**telegraph.co.uk/travel** *The Telegraph*

Ⓦ**theglobeandmail.com/life/travel** *The Globe and Mail*

Ⓦ**thestar.ca/life/travel** *The Toronto Star*

Map specialists

Ⓦ**mapworld.co.nz** New Zealand

Ⓦ**randmcnally.com** US

Ⓦ**stanfords.co.uk** UK

Ⓦ**worldofmaps.com** Canada

Online-only travel publications

Ⓦ**bootsnall.com** A great travel resource with anecdotes that explain how to avoid some of the potholes on the road less traveled

Ⓦ**connectedtraveler.com** Offers a refreshing perspective on cultural travel

Ⓦ**gadling.com** Travel news and happenings around the world

Ⓦ**jaunted.com** News and pop culture travel info

Ⓦ**journeywoman.com** Highlights the female perspective and offers tips and tales

Ⓦ**literarytraveler.com** Tracing steps of famous authors and learning about their inspirations are just part of the literary journey

Ⓦ**matadornetwork.com** A site for travelers who are in touch with their feelings

Ⓦ**responsibletravel.org** Points out the impact of tourism and how to minimize yours while you're on the road

Ⓦ**traveller.com.au** Australian travel resource

Ⓦ**worldhum.com** A travel version of Arts & Letters Daily with original articles, interviews and reviews

Upmarket travel

Ⓦ**concierge.com** Conde Nast's foray into the online travel world – reviews of "six-star" hotels and plenty of "must-see" items for those with ample money to spare

Ⓦ**islands.com** More cultural depth than you might expect, although you can practically get a tan flipping through the pages

Ⓦ**travelandleisure.com** Ranks everything from hotels to airlines and finds some room for interesting (albeit comfortable) travel in between

Ⓦ**traveler.nationalgeographic.com** A well-crafted travel magazine that's not afraid to show the effects of tourism – or the benefits of a comfortable room

Sights

Ⓦ**tickitaly.com** Special site for purchasing tickets to Italian museums, from the Uffizi to the Vatican

Ⓦ**vayable.com** Can hook you up with a local tour guide for a more genuine themed experience than you would find booking via the tourist office. Available in ten European destinations from Paris and London to Athens and İstanbul

Ⓦ**viator.com** Skip the lines and buy museum tickets in advance worldwide. Click under "Beat the Crowds in Europe"

Ⓦ**whc.unesco.org** World Heritage Sites

Transport

Flight booking engines

Ⓦ**cheapflights.co.uk** Search engine for other discount brokers and consolidators, though not comprehensive

Ⓦ**edreams.com** Multi-language portal with cheap trains and hotels as well as flights

Ⓦ**expedia.com** Microsoft's online travel agency

Ⓦ**kayak.com** Finds you the best deal, then points you to the site where you make the actual booking

Ⓜ**momondo.com** Award-winning flight, hotel and travel deal search engine

Ⓜ**opodo.com** Booking engine for flights, hotels, car rentals and package holidays, with versions in English, German, French, Italian, Spanish, Portuguese and the Nordic languages

Ⓦ**orbitz.com** The airlines' web project – a group booking engine with fares from 450 airlines

Ⓦ**skyscanner.net** This simple-to-use site searches all carriers and finds the best prices

Ⓦ**travelocity.com** One of the early pioneers and still a leading booking site

Airlines and airports

Ⓦ**airlineandairportlinks.com** Links to all airports

Ⓦ**sleepinginairports.net** A budget traveler's guide to sleeping in airports

Budget airline travel in Europe

Ⓦ**airberlin.com** Germany's second largest international carrier

Ⓦ**easyjet.com** One of the most popular budget carriers in Europe, with main airports at Luton, Bristol, Gatwick and Stansted in the UK

Ⓦ**flybe.com** Short for "Fly British European," it has bargain flights from mainly regional British airports to more than fifty destinations around the continent

Ⓦ**flythomascook.com** Cheap flights from twenty UK airports to fifty destinations in the Med, the US and the Caribbean

Ⓦ**fr.xl.com** French carrier with charter flights to southern Europe, the US and to the Caribbean

Ⓜ**germanwings.com** Airline serving 86 airports in total, including nineteen in Germany and ten in the UK

Ⓦ**jet2.com** Budget airline based in the northern UK (Leeds, Manchester, Belfast, Edinburgh, Glasgow, Newcastle and East

Midlands) plus Alicante that flies to major hubs in mostly sunny spots

ⓦ**norwegian.no** It's not easy to get around Norway on the cheap, but this site will help ease the travel expenses; also a great source of cheap transatlantic flights

ⓦ**ryanair.com** Europe's largest budget carrier, Ryanair is the Irish company that came up with the whole low-fare, anti-perk concept, and offers flights between thirty European countries plus Morocco

ⓦ**www.thomsonflights.com** Operating from airports around the UK, and offering some of the best rates to European hotspots going – especially with last-minute deals

ⓦ**transavia.com** This service runs out of the Netherlands; its main hubs are Amsterdam, Rotterdam/Hague, Eindhoven, Groningen and Paris

ⓦ**tuifly.com** Cheap flights within Europe and to North Africa, with main hubs in Cologne and Hanover

ⓦ**wizzair.com** This eastern European carrier operates budget flights on over a hundred routes from Bosnia-Herzegovina, Bulgaria, Hungary, Latvia, Lithuania, Macedonia, Poland, Romania, Serbia, Slovakia and Ukraine

ⓦ**wowair.com** If you want to fly to Keflavik, this is your airline. It gets you close to Reykjavik for a shamefully good deal, and almost makes the country seem affordable

Trains

ⓦ**eurail.com** Go direct for the daddy of all European rail passes

ⓦ**interrail.com** Europe rail passes for Europeans

ⓦ**raileurope.com** Europe rail passes for North Americans

ⓦ**railplus.co.nz** Europe rail passes for Kiwis

ⓦ**railplus.com.au** Europe rail passes for Australians

ⓦ**railserve.com/Passenger/Europe** Links to rail services across Europe

ⓦ**seat61.com** Excellent worldwide guide to travel by train

Buses

ⓦ**busabout.com** Takes travelers around Europe at their own pace. It's not quite a tour bus, but not independent travel either. Offers a range of passes that allow extended travel on the network

ⓦ**eurolines.com** Europe's major intercity bus network. Tickets are typically bought per journey, but there are several passes, which makes Eurolines the cheapest way to see Europe on public transportation

ⓦ**megabus.co.uk** Low-cost bus service between cities available only in the UK. Tickets are bought online point-to-point

Cars and motorcycles

ⓦ**aaa.com** America's Automobile Association

ⓦ**caa.ca** Canadian Automobile Association

ⓦ**driverabroad.com** Advice for self-driving travelers abroad

ⓦ**europebycar.com** Buys in bulk and offers discount deals with European rental companies on short-term rentals and tax-free leases for longer rentals

ⓦ**horizonsunlimited.com** Tips and tales on motorcycling around Europe

ⓦ**kemwel.com** Another rental consolidator. Also offers motor homes

ⓦ**rac.co.uk** UK association, offering similar services to the AA

ⓦ**theaa.com** The UK's Automobile Association for all things automotive

ⓦ**viamichelin.com** Driving directions throughout Europe

ⓦ**wickedcampers.co.uk** Cheap (and controversial) campervan hire from most European cities

Ferries and freighters

ⓦ**brittanyferries.com** UK carrier plying waters to France and Spain

ⓦ**dfdsseaways.se** Services run between England and both France and the Netherlands, plus Denmark–Norway, Germany–Lithuania and Sweden–Estonia

ⓦ**fjordline.no** Norwegian carrier, servicing Norway and Denmark

Ⓦ **freightercruises.com** UK-based freighter bookers

Ⓦ **hellasferries.gr** Ferry carrier with routes between Italy, Greece and Albania

Ⓦ **minoan.gr** Greek ferry operator offering routes between Italy and Greece

Ⓦ **polferries.se** Polish ferry operator with routes between Poland and Scandinavia

Ⓦ **routesinternational.com/ships.htm** Links to ferry services across Europe

Ⓦ **silja.com** Baltic operator with routes between Scandinavia, Estonia and Latvia

Ⓦ **vikingline.se** Operates between Sweden, Finland and Estonia

Transport sharing

Ⓦ **blablacar.co.uk** With a twenty-million-strong community, this is the largest of dozens of sharing companies that have sprung up to make better use of people's idle cars. Serves the UK and eighteen other countries in Europe. You type in a request and receive an email alert if someone is driving your way on your chosen date

Ⓦ **getmyboat.com** Rents out 30,000 boats in 135 countries. Choices range from canoes to mega-yachts depending on your needs – fishing, watersports or just cruising

Ⓦ **justpark.com** A clever app for travelers in the UK that connects drivers with 20,000 Britons (mostly Londoners) who have a parking spot that they're not using

Ⓦ **mitfahrgelegenheit.de** Germany-based car-sharing site operating in France, Poland, Austria, England, Spain, Switzerland, Germany and Greece

Ⓦ **uber.com** Matches customers who need a ride with Uber-approved drivers of private cars who are nearby. Taxi companies worldwide are not happy, but the concept has spread to more than 300 cities in 58 countries

Travel advisory

Customs

Ⓦ **cbp.gov** How to figure out what you can bring back into the US

Embassies and consulates

Ⓦ **embassy.goabroad.com** Find an embassy anywhere in the world and get updated visa information

Safety

Ⓦ **fco.gov.uk** The UK's Foreign Office is a good starting point, if in certain cases excessively cautious

Ⓦ **smarttraveller.gov.au** The Australian government's advisory and consular assistance service doesn't pull any punches. Tips include what to do if you get arrested or sexually assaulted overseas

Ⓦ **travel.state.gov** The US State Department warnings can be a little imprecise – if one spot is potentially dangerous, they put the whole country on the list

Ⓦ **voyage.gc.ca** Canada's warning page offers all the basic plan-ahead info

Tourist offices

Ⓦ **worldtourismdirectory.com** Find a tourist bureau worldwide

Travel tools

Conversions

Ⓦ **digitaldutch.com/unitconverter** This speedy site converts weights, measurements, distances and so on

Ⓦ **toomanyadapters.com** Under the banner "Technology for Travelers," this site gathers all possible tech info for the road, from how to get a SIM card in Portugal to tips on portable wi-fi range extenders

Events

Ⓦ **eventful.com** 22 million registered users rely on this site for info on sporting events, concerts, movies, exhibits, nightclubs, family stuff and lots more

Global adaptors

Ⓦ **voltagevalet.com** The lowdown on how to plug in any electrical appliances you may be lugging with you

Language

Ⓦ **translate.google.com** The only translate tool you'll need. For phrases to websites it'll even detect the language and provide the translations accordingly.

Online maps

Ⓦ **earth.google.com** The Big Kahuna of online maps, with tons of stuff you never dreamed was possible

Ⓦ **maps.google.com** Does all the things Google Earth doesn't

Travel gear

Ⓦ **altrec.com** An online-only retailer with gear from all brands

Ⓦ **ems.com** Loads of gear with many web deals

Ⓦ **gogogear.com.au** A site for getting gear down under – they even have all the cheap stuff (ear plugs, sink plug, etc) for one-stop shopping

Ⓦ **rei.com** The megastore US retailer has regular online specials

Ⓦ **spinlister.com** Rent bikes, skis, snowboards, stand-up paddleboards, etc direct from the owners in 55 countries

Ⓦ **zilok.com** Lets you rent just about anything (a sewing machine, PlayStation or Hummer) from both companies and individuals

Weather

Ⓦ **intellicast.com/global** Global ten-day forecasts

Ⓦ **worldclimate.com** Average temperature and rainfall for a huge number of destinations

World facts

Ⓦ **cia.gov/library/publications/the-world-factbook** No cloak-and-dagger stuff, just one of the best sources of information around

Ⓦ **countryreports.org** From flags to maps to national anthems, here's a good starting point for learning a little about the countries you're heading to

Ⓦ **nationalgeographic.com** The National Geographic Society offers a top-end presentation of the planet

Working and volunteering

Working

Ⓦ **anyworkanywhere.com** Find work in dozens of countries and get help with visa information

Ⓦ **iagora.com** An online community featuring entry-level jobs and internships around Europe

Ⓦ **jobmonkey.com** Search by job type, from skiing to teaching

Ⓦ **jobsabroad.com** This site allows searching by country or job type, and has links to study and volunteer programs

Ⓦ **liveworkplay.com.au** An Oz-based site with useful working-holiday information, including visa permits

Ⓦ **michaelpage.com** Professional work-placement agency

Ⓦ **monster.com** Jobs for skilled workers all over the world

Ⓦ **overseasjobcentre.co.uk** Guide to working and living abroad, working holidays and gap years

Ⓦ **taskrabbit.com** Can be a good place to earn some short-term money if you're a whizz at gardening, putting together IKEA furniture, etc. Signing up involves a screening. Outside the UK currently only available in London

Ⓦ **wwoof.org** Directory of World Wide Opportunities on Organic Farms

Teaching English

Ⓦ **cambridgeesol.org** Home of Cambridge ESOL programs; allows you to find nearest location

Ⓦ **eslcafe.com** Dave's ESL Café is a TEFL forum with general job-searching and classroom-teaching tips and lessons

Ⓦ **teflinternational.com** For getting a cheaper TEFL certificate; countries include France, Greece, Italy and Spain

Volunteering

Ⓦ **globeaware.org** Caters to those who want to volunteer on their vacation and are willing to pay handsomely for the short-term, well-planned experience

Ⓦ **goabroad.com/volunteer-abroad** Huge directory of international volunteer programs, which you can search by location

Ⓦ **idealist.org** Idealist works to connect people, organizations and resources with the aim of free and dignified lives for all

Ⓦ **metowe.com** Upper-end volunteer trips, but typically well put together. Can help place families as well

Ⓦ **takingitglobal.org** Online global community that helps point people towards opportunities to take action

Ⓦ **vfp.org** Volunteers for Peace is a US-based organization with inexpensive international programs

Ⓦ **volunteerinternational.org** A regularly updated list of volunteer opportunities and internship exchanges provided by an alliance of nonprofit organizations based in the US

Small print and index

A ROUGH GUIDE TO ROUGH GUIDES

Published in 1982, the first Rough Guide – to Greece – was a student scheme that became a publishing phenomenon. Mark Ellingham, a recent graduate in English from Bristol University, had been travelling in Greece the previous summer and couldn't find the right guidebook. With a small group of friends he wrote his own guide, combining a highly contemporary, journalistic style with a thoroughly practical approach to travellers' needs.

The immediate success of the book spawned a series that rapidly covered dozens of destinations. And, in addition to impecunious backpackers, Rough Guides soon acquired a much broader readership that relished the guides' wit and inquisitiveness as much as their enthusiastic, critical approach and value-for-money ethos.

These days, Rough Guides include recommendations from budget to luxury and cover more than 120 destinations around the globe, as well as producing an ever-growing range of ebooks.

Visit **roughguides.com** to find all our latest books, read articles, get inspired and share travel tips with the Rough Guides community.

Rough Guide credits

Editor: Edward Aves
Layout: Pradeep Thapliyal
Cartography: Rajesh Mishra and Ashutosh Bharti
Picture editor: Phoebe Lowndes
Proofreader: Diane Margolis
Managing editor: Andy Turner
Assistant editor: Payal Sharotri
Production: Jimmy Lao

Cover design: Nicole Newman
Editorial assistant: Freya Godfrey
Senior pre-press designer: Dan May
Programme manager: Gareth Lowe
Publisher: Keith Drew
Publishing director: Georgina Dee

Publishing information

This tenth edition published February 2016 by
Rough Guides Ltd,
80 Strand, London WC2R 0RL
11, Community Centre, Panchsheel Park,
New Delhi 110017, India
Distributed by Penguin Random House
Penguin Books Ltd, 80 Strand, London WC2R 0RL
Penguin Group (USA), 345 Hudson Street, NY 10014, USA
Penguin Group (Australia), 250 Camberwell Road,
Camberwell, Victoria 3124, Australia
Penguin Group (NZ), 67 Apollo Drive, Mairangi Bay,
Auckland 1310, New Zealand
Penguin Group (South Africa), Block D, Rosebank Office
Park, 181 Jan Smuts Avenue, Parktown North, Gauteng,
South Africa 2193
Rough Guides is represented in Canada by DK Canada, 320
Front Street West, Suite 1400,Toronto, Ontario M5V 3B6
Printed in Singapore
© Doug Lansky, 2016
Maps © Rough Guides

344pp includes index
A catalogue record for this book is available from the
British Library
ISBN: 978-0-24120-416-0
The publishers and authors have done their best to
ensure the accuracy and currency of all the information
in **The Rough Guide to First-Time Europe**, however,
they can accept no responsibility for any loss, injury, or
inconvenience sustained by any traveller as a result of
information or advice contained in the guide.
1 3 5 7 9 8 6 4 2

FSC™ C018179 — MIX — Paper from responsible sources — www.fsc.org

Help us update

We've gone to a lot of effort to ensure that the tenth
edition of **The Rough Guide to First-Time Europe** is
accurate and up-to-date. However, things change – places
get "discovered", opening hours are notoriously fickle,
restaurants and rooms raise prices or lower standards. If
you feel we've got it wrong or left something out, we'd like
to know, and if you can remember the address, the price,
the hours, the phone number, so much the better.

Please send your comments with the subject line
"Rough Guide First-Time Europe Update" to mail@
uk.roughguides.com. We'll credit all contributions and
send a copy of the next edition (or any other Rough Guide
if you prefer) for the very best emails.
Find more travel information, connect with fellow
travellers and plan your trip on ⓦroughguides.com.

Acknowledgements

Doug Lansky: I'd like to thank Henrik Harr for his research as well as all the readers who've sent in tips to help keep the
book fresh, relevant and more useful than ever.

Photo credits

All photos © Rough Guides except the following:
(Key: t-top; c-centre; b-bottom; l-left; r-right)

p.1 Alamy Images/Jim Zuckerman
p.2 4Corners/Maurizio Rellini/SIME
p.5 Getty Images/AFP Photo Koca Sulejmanovic
p.9 SuperStock/Siegfried Kuttig (tl); Alamy Images/Aflo Co. Ltd (b)
p.11 Alamy Images/Hemis
p.13 Alamy Images/Images & Stories (t); Getty Images/Cultura/Zero Creatives (c); SuperStock/imageBROKER (br)
p.14 Alamy Images/Gary Woods (tl); Corbis/Peter Adams (b)
p.15 Alamy Images/RIEGER Bertrand/hemis.fr (t); Alamy/Hemis (c)
p.16 Alamy Images/David Lyons (t); Dreamstime.com/Danielal (c); SuperStock/Jose Antonio Moreno
p.191 Alamy Images/Peter Eastland
p.194 Alamy Images/Michelle Chaplow
p.198 Dreamstime.com/Tatiana Savvateeva
p.203 AWL Images/Tom Martin
p.208 Dreamstime.com/Nightman1965
p.212 4Corners/Reinhard Schmid
p.216 Dreamstime.com/Nikolai Sorokin
p.220 Dreamstime.com/Vitaly Titov & Maria Sidelnikova
p.224 Dreamstime.com/David Beaulieu
p.228 AWL Images/Peter Adams
p.232 AWL Images/Matteo Colombo
p.237 AWL Images/Walter Bibikow
p.248 Alamy Images/Mick Rock

p.252 AWL Images/Peter Adams
p.256 Robert Harding Picture Library/Gavin Hellier
p.261 AWL Images/Francesco Iacobelli
p.266 Dreamstime.com/Sorin Colac
p.270 Dreamstime.com/Simon Hack
p.274 Alamy Images/Marc Hill
p.279 Alamy Images/DuncanImages
p.283 Alamy Images/Jan Włodarczyk
p.287 Alamy Images/Robert Harding World Imagery
p.291 Alamy Images/Dennis Cox
p.295 Dreamstime.com/Javarman
p.300 Courtesy of Exit Festival
p.304 123RF.com/lofik
p.307 Dreamstime.com/Europhotos
p.311 Dreamstime.com/William Perry
p.316 Dreamstime.com/Mapics
p.320 AWL Images/Norbert Eisele-Hein
p.324 Dreamstime.com/Softdreams

Front cover & spine Train station information board, Belgium © Alamy Images/imageBROKER
Back cover Vatoúmi Bay, Andípaxi, Greece © AWL Images/Nick Ledger (t); The Colosseum, Rome, Italy © AWL Images/Francesco Lacobelli (bl); Babushka dolls, Riga, Latvia © Alamy Images/ Robert Harding World Imagery/Yadid Levy (br

Map symbols

The symbols below are used on maps throughout the book

─ ─ ‐ ‐	International boundary	ʌ|ʌ	Springs	⛴	Ferry
═══	Railway	♦	Point of interest	⛪	Monastery
───	Coastline	✈	Plane	♜	Castle
▲	Mountain peak	🚌	Bus	∴	Ruins
⌂	Cave	🚋	Train	🎿	Ski resort

Index

Maps are marked in grey